New Testament Interpretation and Methods

The Biblical Seminar
45

NEW TESTAMENT INTERPRETATION AND METHODS
A Sheffield Reader

edited by

Stanley E. Porter &
Craig A. Evans

Sheffield
Academic Press

Copyright © 1997 Sheffield Academic Press

Published by Sheffield Academic Press Ltd
Mansion House
19 Kingfield Road
Sheffield S11 9AS
England

Printed on acid-free paper in Great Britain
by The Cromwell Press Ltd
Melksham, Wiltshire

British Library Cataloguing in Publication Data

A catalogue record for this book is available
from the British Library

1-85075-794-1

CONTENTS

PREFACE TO THE SERIES

This Series, of which *New Testament Interpretation and Methods* is one, collects what the Series editors believe to be the best articles on the topic published in the first 50 issues (1978–1993) of *Journal for the Study of the New Testament*. Founded in 1978, with one issue in its inaugural year, *JSNT* was produced from 1979 to 1990 in three issues a year, and then, from 1991 to the present, in four issues a year. The continuing success of the journal can be seen in several ways: by its increasing circulation, by its increased publication schedule, by its fostering of a significant supplement series, which has now reached its 130th volume (*JSNT* Supplement Series), by its public exposure and influence within the scholarly community, and, most of all, by the quality of the essays it publishes. This volume contains a representative group of such articles on a specific area of New Testament studies.

Once it was decided that such a Series of volumes should be issued, the question became that of how the numerous important articles were going to be selected and presented. The problem was not filling the volumes but making the many difficult choices that would inevitably exclude worthy articles. In the end, the editors have used various criteria for determining which articles should be reprinted here. They have gathered together articles that, they believe, make significant contributions in several different ways. Some of the articles are truly ground-breaking, pushing their respective enquiry into new paths and introducing new critical questions into the debate. Others are assessments of the critical terrain of a particular topic, providing useful and insightful analyses that others can and have built upon. Others still are included because they are major contributions to an on-going discussion.

Even though back issues of *JSNT* are still in print and these essays are available in individual issues of the journal, it is thought that this kind of compilation could serve several purposes. One is to assist scholars who wish to keep up on developments outside their areas of specialist research or who have been away from a topic for a period of time and wish to re-enter the discussion. These volumes are designed to be representatively selective, so that scholars can gain if not a thorough grasp of all of the developments in an area at least significant insights into major topics of debate in a field of interest. Another use of these volumes is as textbooks for undergraduates, seminarians and even graduate students. For undergraduates, these volumes could serve as useful readers, possibly as supplementary texts to a critical introduction, to provide a first exposure to and a sample of critical debate. For seminary students, the same purpose as for undergraduates could apply, especially when the seminarian is beginning critical study of the New Testament. There is the added use, however, that such material could provide guidance through the argumentation and footnotes for significant research into a New Testament author or topic. For graduate students, these volumes could not only provide necessary background to a topic, allowing a student to achieve a basic level of knowledge before exploration of a particular area of interest, but also serve as good guides to the detailed critical work being done in an area. There is the further advantage that many of the articles in these volumes are models of how to make and defend a critical argument, thereby providing useful examples for those entering the lists of critical scholarly debate. While some of the contributors may have altered their positions, or at least have moved further along in their opinions—it is often dangerous to accept any scholarly opinion as definitive—we believe that there is still much of merit in the variety of positions represented in this volume.

Many more articles could and probably should be reprinted in further volumes, but this one and those published along with it must for now serve as an introduction to these topics, at least as they were discussed in *JSNT*.

The editors would like to thank Ted Goshulak, Reference Librarian for Trinity Western University's Marion Alloway Library, and Wendy Porter for assistance in tracking down many obscure bibliographical references.

Craig A. Evans   Stanley E. Porter
Trinity Western University   Roehampton Institute London
Langley, B.C. Canada   England

ABBREVIATIONS

AB	Anchor Bible
AGJU	Arbeiten zur Geschichte des antiken Judentums und des Urchristentums
ANRW	*Aufstieg und Niedergang der römischen Welt*
ATR	*Anglican Theological Review*
BAGD	W. Bauer, W.F. Arndt, F.W. Gingrich and F.W. Danker, *Greek–English Lexicon of the New Testament*
BBB	Bonner biblische Beiträge
BETL	Bibliotheca ephemeridum theologicarum lovaniensium
Bib	*Biblica*
BNTC	Black's New Testament Commentaries
BR	*Biblical Research*
CBQ	*Catholic Biblical Quarterly*
EKKNT	Evangelisch-Katholischer Kommentar zum Neuen Testament
EvQ	*Evangelical Quarterly*
EvT	*Evangelische Theologie*
ExpTim	*Expository Times*
FRLANT	Forschungen zur Religion und Literatur des Alten und Neuen Testaments
HDR	Harvard Dissertations in Religion
HTKNT	Herders theologischer Kommentar zum Neuen Testament
HTR	*Harvard Theological Review*
IDB	G.A. Buttrick (ed.), *Interpreter's Dictionary of the Bible*
IDBSup	*IDB*, Supplementary Volume
Int	*Interpretation*
JAAR	*Journal of the American Academy of Religion*
JBL	*Journal of Biblical Literature*
JETS	*Journal of the Evangelical Theological Society*
JR	*Journal of Religion*
JSNT	*Journal for the Study of the New Testament*
JSNTSup	*Journal for the Study of the New Testament*, Supplement Series
JSOT	*Journal for the Study of the Old Testament*
JSP	*Journal for the Study of the Pseudepigrapha*
JSPSup	*Journal for the Study of the Pseudepigrapha*, Supplement Series
JTS	*Journal of Theological Studies*
LCL	Loeb Classical Library
LQ	*Lutheran Quarterly*
NCB	New Century Bible

NICNT	New International Commentary on the New Testament
NovT	*Novum Testamentum*
NTAbh	Neutestamentliche Abhandlungen
NTD	Das Neue Testament Deutsch
NTL	New Testament Library
NTS	*New Testament Studies*
OCD	*Oxford Classical Dictionary*
PL	J. Migne (ed.), *Patrologia latina*
R B	*Revue biblique*
R E	*Realencyklopädie für protestantische Theologie und Kirche*
RelSRev	*Religious Studies Review*
ResQ	*Restoration Quarterly*
RHE	*Revue d'histoire ecclésiastique*
RhMus	*Rheinisches Museum*
SBL	Society of Biblical Literature
SBLASP	SBL Abstracts and Seminar Papers
SBLDS	SBL Dissertation Series
SBLSP	SBL Seminar Papers
SBT	Studies in Biblical Theology
SE	*Studia Evangelica I, II, III*
SecCent	*Second Century*
SJLA	Studies in Judaism in Late Antiquity
SJT	*Scottish Journal of Theology*
SNTS	Society for New Testament Studies
SNTSMS	Society for New Testament Studies Monograph Series
SR	*Studies in Religion/Sciences religieuses*
TAPA	*Transactions of the American Philological Association*
TDNT	G. Kittel and G. Friedrich (eds.), *Theological Dictionary of the New Testament*
Theol.Jahrb.	*Jahrbücher für deutsche Theologie*
TLZ	*Theologische Literaturzeitung*
TS	*Theological Studies*
TSK	*Theologische Studien und Kritiken*
TTod	*Theology Today*
TU	Texte und Untersuchungen
TZ	*Theologische Zeitschrift*
VTSup	*Vetus Testamentum*, Supplements
WUNT	Wissenschaftliche Untersuchungen zum Neuen Testament
ZWT	*Zeitschrift für wissenschaftliche Theologie*

LIST OF CONTRIBUTORS

John M.G. Barclay, University of Glasgow, Scotland

Clifton C. Black, Perkins School of Theology, Southern Methodist University, Dallas, Texas

Larry Chouinard, Kentucky Christian College, Grayson, Kentucky

F. Gerald Downing, St Simon and St Jude, Bolton, England

Robert M. Grant, University of Chicago, Illinois

J.D. [Hester] Amador, Santa Rosa Junior College, Santa Rosa, California

David Horrell, University of Exeter, England

Paul E. Koptak, North Park Theological Seminary, Chicago, Illinois

Jacob Neusner, University of South Florida, Tampa, Florida, and Bard College, Annandale-on-Hudson, New York

Richard L. Rohrbaugh, Lewis and Clark College, Portland, Oregon

Welton O. Seal, Jr, St John's Baptist Church, Charlotte, North Carolina

Christopher M. Tuckett, University of Oxford, England

Frances M. Young, University of Birmingham, England

PRINCIPLES

JSNT 3 (1979), pp. 29-60

THE GRIESBACH HYPOTHESIS IN THE NINETEENTH CENTURY

Christopher M. Tuckett

There is a growing awareness among New Testament scholars that the theory of Markan priority is not as securely established as it was once thought to be. Although there have always been isolated voices raised against the consensus of opinion, such questionings received a major impetus with the publication of W.R. Farmer's book, *The Synoptic Problem* (New York: Macmillan; London: Collier–Macmillan) in 1964. Farmer proposed that the Griesbach hypothesis, the theory dominant in the late eighteenth and early nineteenth centuries, was the best solution to the Synoptic Problem. However, before setting out the positive side of his theory, Farmer devoted the major part of his book to a history of the study of the Synoptic Problem since the rise of biblical criticism, and one of the results of his survey was the claim that extra-scientific factors had been at work in the establishment of the two-document hypothesis.[1] The Griesbach hypothesis had been adopted by Strauss, Baur and others in the so-called 'Tübingen school', and had been used by them to develop their theories which had resulted in radical scepticism about the historical reliability of the Gospels. Farmer claims that when the Tübingen school fell, the Griesbach hypothesis fell with it. 'The real enemy was the Tübingen school and only incidentally the Griesbach hypothesis, which Baur had accepted. But there can be no doubt that the Griesbach hypothesis lost "popular" support with the collapse of the Tübingen school.'[2]

1.   In his article, 'A Response to Robert Morgenthaler's *Statistische Synopse*', *Bib* 54 (1973) pp. 417-33 (429), Farmer corrects the possible misinterpretation of his book (e.g. as made by W. Schmithals in his review of Farmer's book, in *TLZ* 92 [1967], col. 425) by which readers might conclude that only unscientific factors were at work.

2.   *Synoptic Problem,* p. 58; in an earlier article, 'A Skeleton in the Closet of

On the other hand, the two-document hypothesis was established mainly by the influence of Holtzmann in Germany, and in England by Sanday, who brought over many of the results of German criticism. Farmer claims that both scholars sought to build on a consensus of opinion which was often very artificial, and which sometimes ignored the Griesbach hypothesis in an unwarranted way.[3] However, in displacing the Griesbach hypothesis, the theory of Markan priority satisfied a theological need: it established a firm basis for the historicity of at least the Markan narrative in the face of the overall scepticism of the Tübingen school and of the generally accepted view that Matthew's Gospel was not written by an eye-witness. Furthermore, Holtzmann's success in 1863, in establishing a form of the two-document hypothesis with one of its basic sources very similar to Mark, was not due to any new evidence discovered since Weisse's work 23 years earlier. Nor was it due to any scientifically established facts. Rather, what attracted people to Holtzmann's theories was the portrayal of the life of Jesus which he drew out of the Markan narrative; this then served as a firm basis for

Gospel Research', *BR* 6 (1961), pp. 18-42, Farmer said that the collapse of the Tübingen school was 'a decisive key for unlocking the mystery of what happened in Germany' (p. 18), referring to the demise of the Griesbach hypothesis and the rise of the theory of Markan priority.

3.   For Holtzmann, see *Synoptic Problem,* chapter 2, esp. pp. 38, 43; for Sanday, see *Synoptic Problem,* pp. 51ff. It should be noted that the main part of Farmer's criticisms of Sanday refer to the latter's article in Smith's *Dictionary of the Bible,* 'Gospels', where Sanday started his survey in 1863, 'clearly referring', says Farmer (p. 53) to the date of publication of Holtzmann's work. Thereafter, it is claimed, Sanday ignored earlier proponents of the Griesbach hypothesis (such as De Wette and Bleek), and dismissed the hypothesis as the 'Tübingen theory' because of the way it had been adopted by Baur. In fact, this may have been due to Sanday's terms of reference for this essay. Sanday was not writing the full article for the *Dictionary,* he was only writing a supplement for the second edition to follow the article (by Archbishop W. Thomson) which had appeared in the first edition, and which was reprinted unchanged in the later edition. 1863 referred primarily to the date of the first edition of the *Dictionary,* which happened to coincide with the publication of Holtzmann's book. Sanday's brief was then to describe the developments which had taken place since the first edition—thus the fact that the work of men like De Wette and Bleek was ignored was due simply to the fact that their work had appeared before 1863. Those who did support the Griesbach hypothesis, and whose work appeared after 1863 (e.g. Keim and Davidson), were duly noted by Sanday. The Griesbach hypothesis was largely ignored simply because it had gained hardly any new adherents in the period under consideration.

liberal Protestant theology. 'The decisive factor in the triumph of the Markan (or 2-document) hypothesis was not any particular scientific argument or series of arguments, however important some of these may have been. The decisive factor in this triumph according to Schweitzer was theological.'[4]

The inference that Farmer draws is that the Griesbach hypothesis has never received a fair hearing. He says that any proponent of a source theory must show 'why this solution was first proposed favourably, and why critical opinion in favour of this solution did not develop into a lasting consensus... Arguments against the view that Matthew is the earliest gospel, Luke second and Mark third are unconvincing... This view was abandoned in favour of another that was less satisfactory, for reasons which scholars would now deny.'[5]

Farmer's general thesis, that the success of the theory of Markan priority was due to theological reasons, so that a viable alternative could be found to replace the radical scepticism of Baur and others in his school, has received support from another angle in the recent book by H.H. Stoldt, *Geschichte und Kritik der Markushypothese.*[6] Farmer's main concern was with the period following Holtzmann's work in 1863, and with the way in which his theory was all too easily accepted, especially in England. Stoldt's concern is rather with the earlier period, and he gives a detailed study of the work of some of the initial advocates of the theory of Markan priority in Germany in the mid-nineteenth century.

---

4. *Synoptic Problem,* p. 57. Farmer refers explicitly to A. Schweitzer, *The Quest of the Historical Jesus* (trans. W. Montgomery; London: A. & C. Black, 1950) pp. 203ff.

5. *Synoptic Problem,* pp. 200-201. However, in his historical survey, Farmer deals almost exclusively with the criticisms of the Griesbach hypothesis in England, by Woods, Abbott and Stanton. Earlier nineteenth-century criticisms of the hypothesis in Germany are only alluded to very briefly and the details are not considered. This near silence has certainly been taken by others to imply that such criticisms did not exist. D. Dungan, 'Mark—The Abridgement of Matthew and Luke', in D.G. Miller (ed.), *Jesus and Man's Hope* (Pittsburgh: Pittsburgh Theological Seminary, 1970), I, pp. 51-97, writes: 'It [Farmer's book] gave a detailed historical proof that Griesbach's hypothesis had never really been disproved' (p. 52); similarly, B. Orchard, *Matthew, Luke and Mark* (Manchester: Koinonia, 1979), writes, on the basis of Farmer's book, that support for the Griesbach hypothesis, in both Germany and England, 'dwindled away for reasons not directly connected with its soundness as an hypothesis' (p. 8).

6. Göttingen: Vandenhoeck & Ruprecht, 1977.

Stoldt's general conclusions are that none of the arguments for Markan priority has any force; moreover, the advocates of the theory were themselves motivated to put forward their views as part of a reaction against the Tübingen school, in particular against D.F. Strauss.[7] He claims that all the arguments used in the past to prove the priority of Mark are at best inconclusive and at worst completely circular. However, the advocates of the theory wanted to respond to Strauss's work, and believed that they could do this best by attacking indirectly, that is, by trying to prove his source theory wrong. By this, the historicity of at least the Markan narrative could be rescued, establishing it as based on the eye-witness testimony of Peter. Stoldt also draws the conclusion that the Griesbach hypothesis was unfairly rejected because of its association with Strauss's work. Most of the arguments against the theory were either circular, assuming what was to be proved, or simply made the theory look ridiculous in describing Mark's alleged procedure in emotive, over-loaded terms.[8] Thus, at the end of his book, Stoldt claims that, given the fact that none of the arguments for Markan priority are convincing, one can, and should, return to the theory of Owen and Griesbach (that Mark is the latest Gospel to be written) without more ado.[9]

There is thus a body of opinion which claims that the Griesbach hypothesis has been dismissed without adequate consideration, and that those who proposed the theory of Markan priority, as well as those who accepted it, were motivated to do so for reasons which really had nothing to do with the Synoptic Problem as such. In view of the fact that it was in the middle of the nineteenth century that the change occurred—from a situation where the Griesbach hypothesis was the accepted norm to one where the two-document hypothesis held sway—it is worthwhile to re-examine the history of the debate in this period. It is the purpose of this article to investigate to what extent the Griesbach hypothesis was, or was felt to be, so closely associated with Strauss and others in the Tübingen school that the hypothesis itself was never properly considered in its own right; and also to investigate how far the desire to restore the historical reliability of the tradition was a significant factor in predisposing biblical students to accept the priority of Mark.

---

7.   See especially Part C, 'Die idealogischen Hintergründe der Markus-hypothese', pp. 206-14.

8.   Stoldt, *Geschichte und Kritik*, p. 211. By contrast he says that Griesbach's own work was characterized by 'noble Sachlichkeit und reine Objectivität'.

9.   Stoldt, *Geschichte und Kritik*, p. 234.

There is first the question of how integral the Griesbach hypothesis was to the ideas of Strauss and others in the Tübingen school, and hence of how far the rejection of one necessarily entails the rejection of the other. As far as Strauss is concerned, it is quite true that in all four editions of his *Leben Jesu*, published between 1835 and 1840, he accepted the results of the Griesbach hypothesis, at least to the extent of accepting that Mark was the latest Gospel to be written. He made brief allusions to some of the circumstantial details being signs of secondary embellishments, as well as claiming that Mark thereby showed affinities with the later apocryphal Gospels.[10] In the small section where Strauss dealt with the external evidence about the Gospels, he alluded briefly to the Synoptic Problem, saying that our second Gospel 'is evidently a compilation...from the first and third gospels'. In a footnote he said simply that this 'was clearly demonstrated by Griesbach'.[11] However it is clear that this was scarcely an integral part of his theories. In fact, Strauss evidently felt that he could assume the truth of the Griesbach hypothesis almost without question. Stoldt himself recognizes that Strauss 'had not produced his own theory of sources' since he thought the problem to be solved well enough by Griesbach.[12] Strauss felt no need to justify the theory and he offered no new arguments for it. It was only in his later work in 1864,[13] in the light of the growing belief in the priority of Mark, that Strauss felt it necessary to argue in detail the case for Mark being the last of the Synoptic Gospels to be written. In fact, the Synoptic Problem seems to have been of only passing interest to Strauss; he was really unconcerned about the differences between the accounts of the same story in the three Gospels, or the developments discernible between them. What interested him was the content, historical

10. D.F. Strauss, *The Life of Jesus Critically Examined* (ed. with an introduction by P.C. Hodgson; London: SCM Press, 1973), pp. 389-90 (with reference to Schleiermacher's similar judgment) and p. 501. (This English translation of Strauss's work is a re-publication of G. Eliot's translation of the fourth German edition. However, the differences between the editions are unimportant for the limited purposes of this study.) For the alleged affinity of Mark with the later apocryphal gospels, cf. Farmer, *Synoptic Problem,* p. 122.

11. Strauss, *Life of Jesus*, p. 71.

12. Stoldt, *Geschichte und Kritik*, p. 12; cf. too Hodgson's comment in his introduction to Strauss's work: 'At the time Strauss wrote *The Life of Jesus* the Griesbach hypothesis remained largely unquestioned' (p. 30).

13. D.F. Strauss, *Das Leben Jesu für das Deutsche Volk bearbeitet* (Leipzig: Brockhaus, 1864).

or otherwise, of the stories themselves, rather than any literary relationships between the various accounts in our present Gospels.[14] In contrast to Baur, whose *Tendenzkritik* foreshadows modern redaction criticism, Strauss's work was more the precursor of modern form-criticism, with its main interest in the *pre*-literary development of the tradition.

If then the Synoptic Problem was very largely a side-issue for Strauss, the situation is not totally dissimilar in the case of the later members of the Tübingen school. For it is clear that, although the Griesbach hypothesis was adopted by Baur and Schwegler in what were probably the most important publications of the school,[15] the subsequent history of the school showed that the same methods of *Tendenzkritik* could be used, and the same results of a very late dating of the Gospels obtained, with other source hypotheses than Griesbach's. Baur's detailed theories were already being questioned from within the school by the late 1840s. The theory that Luke was a secondary catholicizing revision of Marcion's ultra-Pauline Gospel was attacked by Volkmar, who showed that Luke's Gospel was probably prior to Marcion's.[16] In an article in 1851, Ritschl too was persuaded by Volkmar to change his mind on this question; moreover, in the same article, he argued the case for Markan priority, in opposition to Baur's view that Mark was a late, neutral document, seeking to balance Matthew and Luke.[17] Further, Hilgenfeld

14. Cf. Hodgson, introduction to Strauss, *Life of Jesus*, p. 31. It was precisely this that led Baur to criticize Strauss: see F.C. Baur, *Kritische Untersuchungen über die kanonischen Evangelien* (Tübingen: Fues, 1847), pp. 41-46, 71-76; he complained of Strauss's work 'dass es eine Kritik der evangelischen Geschichte ohne eine Kritik der Evangelien gibt' (p. 42). Cf. too the judgment of W.G. Kümmel, *The New Testament—The History of the Investigation of its Problems* (London: SCM Press, 1973), p. 121: 'Strauss lacks a clear understanding of the literary relationship of the Synoptics to one another'.

15. See F.C. Baur, *Kritische Untersuchungen*, and *idem*, *Das Markusevangelium nach seinem Ursprung und Charakter* (Tübingen: Fues, 1851); A. Schwegler, *Das nachapostolische Zeitalter in den Hauptmomenten seiner Entwicklung* (Tübingen: Fues, 1846).

16. In G. Volkmar, 'Über das Lukasevangelium nach seinem Verhältniss zu Marcion und seinem dogmatischen Charakter', *Theol.Jahrb.* (1850), pp. 110-39, 185-235.

17. A. Ritschl, 'Über den gegenwärtigen Stand der Kritik der synoptischen Evangelien', *Theol.Jahrb.* (1851), pp. 480-538. His earlier view on Luke was put forward in *Das Evangelium Marcions und das kanonische Evangelium des Lukas* (Tübingen: Osiander, 1846).

maintained throughout his life that Mark was prior to Luke, even if secondary to Matthew.[18] However, both Hilgenfeld and Ritschl used the same methods of *Tendenzkritik*. In the debate between Baur and Hilgenfeld, part at least of the argument centred on the precise nature of Mark's *Tendenz*, whether Mark was a completely neutral document (so Baur), or whether it was Petrine (so Hilgenfeld);[19] so too Ritschl used all of Baur's methodology to show that Mark was prior to Matthew, by appealing to Markan theological motifs which also appeared in Matthew.[20]

Baur's use of *Tendenzkritik* to determine the literary relationships between the Gospels was criticized in 1853 by Köstlin, who said that literary analysis must be the determinative factor.[21] Köstlin's own solution to the Synoptic Problem tried to combine various solutions into one. Thus, Matthew was the first of our Gospels to be written, but was dependent on an earlier Petrine version of Mark, which was the Gospel referred to by Papias. (This then explained the Petrine parts of Matthew, as well as the fact that Matthew had clearly used sources.) Luke came second, using Matthew and various other sources; finally our canonical Mark was written as a neutral, irenic Gospel, using Matthew and Luke and also the early Petrine Ur-Marcus. Thus one could explain the presence in Mark both of apparently secondary elements (e.g. the picturesque details like the cushion in 4.38, or the explanatory phrases like 7.2), and

18. See especially his article, 'Neue Untersuchung über das Markusevangelium, mit Rücksicht auf Dr. Baur's Darstellung', *Theol.Jahrb.* (1852), pp. 102-32, 259-93.

19. For further details of the debate between these two, see R.H. Fuller, 'Baur versus Hilgenfeld: A Forgotten Chapter in the Debate on the Synoptic Problem', *NTS* 24 (1978), pp. 355-70.

20. This is *Tendenz* in a weaker sense, perhaps, but the point was missed by Baur in his reply to Ritschl, 'Rückblick auf die neuesten Untersuchungen über das Markusevangelium', *Theol.Jahrb.* (1853), pp. 54-93, on pp. 85ff., where he simply said that Matthew and Mark were identical in the points alluded to by Ritschl. However, Ritschl's argument was that the points in question, concerning the commands to secrecy and the theme of the disciples' gradual recognition of Jesus, were both Markan themes recurring in Matthew. Although they fitted in well with Mark's overall presentation, they made no sense in Matthew. Thus he pointed to the command to secrecy in Mt. 8.4/Mk 1.44 which is part of Mark's plan and makes sense there, but fits badly in Matthew where Jesus is in the presence of a large crowd. So too the gradual recognition of Jesus by the disciples reaches a true climax in Mk 8.29, but in Matthew the disciples already understand (cf. Mt. 14.33) and hence the confession at Caesarea Philippi loses its point.

21. K.R. Köstlin, *Der Ursprung und die Komposition der synoptischen Evangelien* (Stuttgart: Macken, 1853).

also of other parts which could not be explained without the use of a primitive source other than Matthew or Luke (e.g. some of the details of names and times, or the note about the young man fleeing in 14.51). The former were from Mark himself, the latter from the early Petrine version of Mark. Thus Köstlin was already half way towards accepting Markan priority, or at least the priority of a source very closely related to Mark. Later still, Volkmar adopted Markan priority, interpreting Mark as a thoroughly Pauline document directed against Judaeo-Christianity as presented in the Apocalypse.[22] Mark's picture of Jesus is, he claimed, that of true Christianity, breaking the bounds of Judaism and, in the person of Paul (who represents the true Christ), striking out unfettered into the Gentile world. The subsequent development he saw as a reaction by Jewish Christians in a document called 'The Preaching of Peter' (now lost, but partly recoverable in the first half of Acts and in the Clementine Recognitions)—here Jesus is presented as Jewish, the son of Joseph and hence of David, Peter is given the pre-eminent role, and the early Jerusalem church is held up as an ideal model. This in turn provoked a reaction in Luke's writings from the side of Paulinism—Jesus' divine sonship is now traced back to birth, the Gentile mission is prefigured in the mission of the 70, Jesus' teaching prefigures the true Pauline teaching of faith, hope and love; further, the early version of Acts is supplemented to bring out the universality of the gospel, and to show that Paul was in no way inferior to Peter by adding stories about Paul parallel to those of Peter. Finally Matthew appeared as the work of a Jewish Christian sympathetic to Paulinism, accepting the Gentile mission, but stressing the motif of the fulfilment of the Old Testament in Jesus' ministry.[23]

Thus the Griesbach hypothesis was by no means integral to the Tübingen school's theories, with regard either to their use of *Tendenzkritik* or to a sceptical attitude to the historicity of the Gospels. Hilgenfeld and Volkmar showed how the general presuppositions of the school could be used with different solutions to the Synoptic Problem, even with the theory of Markan priority. The Griesbach hypothesis was of

22. G. Volkmar, *Die Religion Jesu und ihre erste Entwickelung nach dem gegenwartigen Stande der Wissenschaft* (Leipzig: Brockhaus, 1857).

23. Fuller, 'Baur versus Hilgenfeld', p. 369, comments aptly: 'This is *Tendenzkritik* run wild'. Note too his following remark about the connection between the Griesbach hypothesis and the Tübingen school: 'Not only Hilgenfeld and Ritschl, but also Volkmar and Köstlin gave up the Griesbach–Saunier position. With Schwegler's abandonment of theology after 1846, that left Baur to all intents and purposes alone.'

course integral to Baur's own working out of his theory of the way the Gospel writings developed. But the details could be changed without altering the basic presuppositions that all three Gospels were late documents, theologically motivated, and of dubious worth as history. An attack simply on the Griesbach hypothesis thus would not work as an attack on the underlying ideas of the Tübingen school. Stoldt too seems to recognize this. He writes:

> In his critical analysis of the Gospels Strauss had applied this basic principle: If the content is unacceptable, the sources must also be worthless— and among 'sources' he included the authorities adduced or quoted by the evangelists. Now his opponents turned the tables and (with a substantial alteration of the notion of 'source') established their own principle: If Strauss's source-theory is false, the content of his work—indeed, the whole of his argument—must also be false.[24]

The 'substantial alteration of the notion of "source"'shows the basic mistake in the logic here. If Stoldt is right about the underlying motives of those who first propounded the theory of Markan priority, then they could not really succeed in such an indirect way of opposing Strauss— showing his source theory to be wrong would not of itself rescue the historicity of the Gospels.

If then there was very little connection between the Griesbach hypothesis and the Tübingen school, is it nevertheless true that the connection was seen as far more integral than it in fact was by those who opposed these theories? Is there any evidence to suggest that the Griesbach hypothesis was rejected because of conscious opposition to the Tübingen school rather than as a result of being considered in its own right? In one sense, a claim that such a link was thought to exist is both unprovable and unanswerable. No one can prove conclusively what were the motivations behind the work of the nineteenth-century source critics, and it may be that unscientific factors led some scholars to make rash judgments, to pre-judge the issue, and to make some solutions more attractive than was warranted by the text. In fact, however, detailed arguments were brought forward against the Griesbach hypothesis, and very often these were quite independent of any reaction to Strauss or the Tübingen school. The seeds of the two-document hypothesis (i.e. the idea of an Ur-Gospel, and the interpretation of Papias's note on Matthew referring it to a sayings source) were already germinating well before

---

24. Stoldt, *Geschichte und Kritik*, p. 206 [editors' trans.].

the rise of the Tübingen school, and indeed prior to Strauss.[25] Indeed Markan priority itself had been advocated already in 1786 by G.C. Storr.[26] However, Storr gave few positive arguments for his view: he simply pointed to the difficulty (or impossibility as he saw it) of accounting for the omissions which Mark must have made if he had used either Matthew or Luke.

The start of an argument from order, leading to a conclusion that Mark's order was the most primitive, dates back to Lachmann's article of 1835.[27] This was the same year that Strauss first published his book, but there is no reference to the latter by Lachmann either explicitly or implicitly. He did consider briefly the Griesbach hypothesis in general terms, but rejected it on the grounds that the conflation which Mark would have had to perform would make him into a 'bungling dilettante, unsure of his way, borne hither and thither between Matthew's and Luke's gospel by boredom, desire, carelessness, folly or design'.[28] He also claimed that, in view of his results (that the order of Mark's Gospel was closest to that of his assumed Ur-Gospel), 'those who compose harmonies...should not be too contemptuous of Mark's authority', possibly with Griesbach in mind.[29] This might be regarded as a somewhat peremptory judgment on the merits of the Griesbach hypothesis, but there is no evidence of any influence at all from Strauss, and the one passing allusion to 'Mark's authority' is the only point at which Lachmann showed any concern to deal with the question of the historicity of the Gospels.[30]

Significant developments in the theory of Markan priority occurred in 1838 with the publication in that year of the books of Wilke and

25. Farmer (*Synoptic Problem*, p. 44), attributes these two ideas to Lessing and Schleiermacher respectively. However, Lessing's essay dates from 1794, Schleiermacher's from 1832. See Farmer, *Synoptic Problem*, pp. 4, 15.

26. In *Über den Zweck der evangelische Geschichte* (Tübingen, 1786), pp. 274-78, 287-95.

27. K. Lachmann, 'De ordine narrationum in euangeliis synopticis', *TSK* (1835), pp. 570-90. ET by N.H. Palmer, 'Lachmann's Argument', *NTS* 13 (1967), pp. 368-78 (page references to this edition).

28. Lachmann, 'De ordine narrationum', p. 372.

29. Lachmann, 'De ordine narrationum', p. 376; for the reference being to Griesbach, see Stoldt, *Geschichte und Kritik*, p.140.

30. Thus J. Wellhausen, *Einleitung in die drei ersten Evangelien* (Berlin: Reimer, 2nd edn, 1911), p. 35, in commenting on the work of both Lachmann and Wilke, says that they 'gehn beide von rein formellen Indizen aus, nicht von theologisch-historischen'.

Weisse.[31] Strauss's work had first been published three years earlier, so that, chronologically, it is possible that some reaction against his work kindled a desire to restore the historicity of at least Mark by the theory of Markan priority. However, Wilke's book betrays no knowledge of Strauss at all. Further, although his book was not published until 1838, it is clear that he had already formed his views at least twelve years previously, that is, well before Strauss's work appeared.[32] Rather than reacting against Strauss, his book was directed against Gieseler's theory of oral tradition as being sufficient to account for the synoptic agreements, and against some form of Ur-Gospel theory as proposed by Eichhorn. The first part of his book was devoted to showing that the verbal agreements need written sources to explain them, and hence that Gieseler's theories were inadequate. In the second part, Wilke carried out a detailed examination of the wording and phraseology, and sought to show that there was no need to look elsewhere for an Ur-Gospel: Mark was the Ur-evangelist. There is no direct evidence that Wilke was at all influenced by Strauss. Certainly he never referred to him by name. He did turn to the Griesbach hypothesis (as this was the dominant theory at the time, and also directly opposed to his own conclusions), and he offered some arguments against it. (Some of these will be considered later.) At times he struck a fairly strident tone, for example, in describing Mark as a 'Kastrator' if the Griesbach hypothesis was correct.[33] But all his criticisms concerned the purely literary claim of Griesbach that Mark had conflated Matthew and Luke.[34]

---

31. C.G. Wilke, *Der Urevangelist* (Leipzig: Gerhard Fleischer, 1838); C.H. Weisse, *Die evangelische Geschichte kritisch und philosophisch bearbeitet* (2 vols.; Leipzig: Breitkopf & Härtel, 1838).

32. See his earlier article, 'Über die Parabel von den Arbeitern im Weinberge', *ZWT* 1 (1826), pp. 71-109; on pp. 73-38, Wilke gave a number of examples where Matthew's version is longer than Mark's, but where, he claimed, Matthew's extra material disrupted the original progression of thought, which is still clearly visible in Mark's shorter version. (E.g. Mt. 19.28 interrupts the link between the disciples' question in v. 27 and Jesus' reply in v. 29; Mt. 22.1-l4 interrupts the connection between the thoughts of Jesus' opponents in 21.45-46 and their resulting action in 22.15.) 'Unzählige data seizen es überhaupt ausse Zweifel, dass der Umfang des Markusevangeliums auch die ursprüngliche Grundlage unsers Mattäus sei, wozu alles das, was der letztere Mehreres giebt, Zusatz und Nachtrag, Bereicherung und Erweiterung ist' (p. 74).

33. Wilke, *Der Urevangelist*, p. 443.

34. Cf. Wellhausen's comment, n. 30 above.

The question of historical reliability very rarely entered the discussion, and when it did, Wilke made no appeal to the authority of Peter as an eye-witness to guarantee the reliability of Mark. Rather, he said that Mark's Gospel was *not* the work of one of the immediate followers of Jesus, and that explained why the composition was determined more by general principles than by historical accuracy:

> Although its compilations are conditioned less by historical context than by preconceived general propositions, they have nevertheless assumed the appearance of a historical context. This explains precisely...that its author was no immediate companion of Jesus. A non-apostle authored the work...[35]

Thus the connection in Mk 6.30–8.21 is determined more by the desire to bring out the parallel between Jesus and Elijah than by any historical considerations;[36] the section in 3.13-35 is composed to present Jesus as parallel to Moses, and the charge of blasphemy 'is not entirely correctly supported by a specific fact from Mark, but by a generalization'.[37] Far from reacting against Strauss, Wilke's work was almost as indifferent to the question of historicity as Strauss's own—B. Weiss even accused Wilke of 'a complete indifference, which he borrowed from Strauss, to the authenticity of the contents of the Gospels'.[38] Stoldt points to many of the weaknesses in Wilke's overall presentation, for example, the ease with which Wilke arbitrarily postulated later insertions into the Markan text to avoid the difficulties of some of the minor agreements between Matthew and Luke against Mark, as well as criticizing some of Wilke's detailed explanations. Further, Wilke's treatment of the relationship between Matthew and Luke was very insubstantial and unsatisfactory. Stoldt says that Wilke, noting that Luke's Sermon on the Plain is more original than Matthew's Sermon on the Mount, incorrectly deduced that Matthew must have used Luke, and failed to allow for the possibility of a common source.[39] Some of Wilke's arguments will be considered later.

---

35. Wilke, *Der Urevangelist*, p. 684. Hence contra Stoldt, *Geschichte und Kritik*, p. 170 [editors' trans.].

36. Wilke, *Der Urevangelist*, pp. 569-70.

37. Wilke, *Der Urevangelist*, p. 574 [editors' trans.].

38. B. Weiss, 'Zur Entstehungsgeschichte der drei synoptische Evangelien', *TSK* (1861), pp. 29-100, 646-713. See too Kümmel, *New Testament*, p. 148 [editors' trans.].

39. Stoldt, *Geschichte und Kritik*, p. 40. However, he does not seem to notice that this is equally awkward for the Griesbach hypothesis which assumes direct

All that is necessary here is to notice that Wilke was not influenced by Strauss, and he did not use his theories to try to counter Strauss's scepticism—in fact he shared many of Strauss's ideas about the lack of historicity in the Gospels, even if he attacked the Griesbach hypothesis fairly virulently.

The possibility of a reaction against Strauss as influencing Weisse's work is certainly stronger. Clearly Weisse saw his work as an attempt to counter Strauss's claims. He started with a long quotation from Strauss, and, explicitly referring to the latter in his introduction, he said 'my tendency is...not negative-critical, but essentially positive' in seeking to establish a reliable picture of Jesus.[40] However, Weisse clearly recognized that the Griesbach hypothesis was held by other people besides Strauss, so that more was needed to overturn the former than simply an attack on Strauss's scepticism.[41] But it is also clear from the context that the theory of Strauss which Weisse opposed was *not* the Griesbach hypothesis but the 'tradition hypothesis', that is, the theory that there had been a long period of oral tradition which had only reached fixed written form in the mid-second century.[42] What Weisse was objecting to in Strauss's work was not the question of the precise relationship of Mark to the other two Gospels, but the general historical reliability of *all* the Gospel tradition. In considering the question of whether Mark was an eye-witness, he recognized that this was denied not only by the tradition hypothesis but also by the Griesbach hypothesis. He noted too that Strauss had adopted both, and commented wryly that the former was really meant to exclude any direct use of one Gospel by the other. But the Griesbach hypothesis was only brought into the discussion here to show that Strauss was not alone in his views on the non-eye-witness

dependence of Luke on Matthew. Stoldt's other criticism of Wilke—that he assumed his result in the way he classified and labelled the pericopes—is not so convincing. This is not part of Wilke's basic analysis which involved a detailed examination of the wording within each pericope. The actual classification does not affect the argument.

40. Weisse, *Die evangelische Geschichte*, I, p. 3 [editors' trans.].

41. Weisse, *Die evangelische Geschichte*, I, p.5.

42. Weisse, *Die evangelische Geschichte*, I, pp. 4, 10, where it is explicitly the tradition hypothesis that Weisse sees as the true basis for Strauss's mythical interpretation of the Gospels. See too B. Reicke, 'Griesbach und die synoptische Frage', *TZ* 33 (1977), pp. 341-59 (358): 'Weisse suchte vor allem eine dokumentarische Stütze gegen die nach ihm gefährliche Traditionshypothese, auf die D.F. Strauss seinen radikalen Begriff des Mythos basierte.'

character of Mark. He also noted that many recent scholars had denied that Matthew's Gospel was written by an eye-witness. However, Weisse. did not connect these two facts and then use them as an argument against, or even a comment about, the Griesbach hypothesis, that is, that it makes the earliest Gospel that of someone who had not been an eye-witness to the events.[43]

Even later in his book, Weisse never appealed to the link between Peter and Mark to establish the historicity of all the details of Mark's account. He did, it is true, seek to establish a link between Peter and Mark, and Stoldt rightly points out the weakness of Weisse's arguments here.[44] Nevertheless, Weisse never used this to try to prove the reliability of Mark's details—indeed he rejected their historical worth, seeing them as later embellishments by Mark to Peter's oral preaching. For Weisse, these were conceivable if Mark was filling out oral sources, but not if Mark was using written sources: in the latter case, they would not be worth the trouble.[45] Thus the Griesbach hypothesis, which said that these were Markan embellishments to the written texts of Matthew and Luke, did not make sense. Thus Weisse did not use the theory of Markan priority to claim that all Mark's details were historical. As Schweitzer said, Weisse 'is very far from having used Mark unreservedly as a historical source'.[46] Weisse wrote that Mark's Gospel

> is not like the work of an eyewitness, and not like the work of one who still had the immediate opportunity to fill in the gaps by a careful, searching interrogation of eyewitnesses.[47]

Thus any reaction to Strauss on the part of Weisse was only partially linked with the theory of Markan priority, and was quite independent of the problem of the Griesbach hypothesis; certainly Weisse did not think that his results implied that there is a direct eye-witness account of the Gospel events.

---

43. Weisse, *Die evangelische Geschichte*, I, pp. 4-5. Hence contra Farmer, *Synoptic Problem*, p. 22. The two were really separate issues as far as Weisse was concerned.

44. Stoldt, *Geschichte und Kritik*, pp. 171-77.

45. Weisse, *Die evangelische Geschichte*, I, pp. 64-66. Thus Weisse differed from P. Wernle, *Die synoptische Frage* (Freiburg: Mohr [Paul Siebeck], 1899), pp. 204-205, who did appeal to these details to try to prove that Mark was based on eye-witness testimony.

46. Schweitzer, *Quest of the Historical Jesus*, p. 128.

47. Weisse, *Die evangelische Geschichte*, I, p. 69 [editors' trans.].

Weisse never said very much explicitly about the Griesbach hypothesis. In a short note he endorsed Lachmann's brief criticisms and referred to the theory 'on which Lachmann to be sure pronounces severely, but by no means unjustly'.[48] Nowhere is there a detailed discussion of Griesbach or of any other proponents of the theory. This was only assumed in the final result, which was, of course, directly opposed to the Griesbach hypothesis. Weisse might thus be accused of ignoring Griesbach in an unwarranted way (though his method was more to present positively his own views than to criticize negatively the views of others), but not of allowing Strauss's adoption of the Griesbach hypothesis to influence him adversely, at least with respect to the latter.

Although many of Weisse's arguments are still used (e.g. the primitive nature of Mark's Greek, and the fact that agreements between Matthew and Luke are mostly mediated through Mark), not all of his reasons can be accepted today. Stoldt points to many of the arbitrary interpretations, by means of which Weisse tried to ascribe various pieces which were clearly narrative to his sayings source. Then, when Weisse later retracted these interpretations, he was forced to ascribe these pericopes to his other main source, thus creating an Ur-Marcus which Mark then abbreviated.[49] In part, this was based on the very rigid definition of the sayings source as accepted by Weisse. He thought (as did most in the nineteenth century) that Papias's note on Matthew was absolutely reliable and provided independent proof of the existence of such a sayings source, which could contain nothing other than sayings. He thus derived from Papias a firmly fixed idea of what the source could contain and his solution to the Synoptic Problem had to conform to that. Today most scholars would be far more hesitant about relying on Papias for proving the existence of a sayings source, and would deduce its existence (if they do so at all) from the Gospels themselves. B. Weiss did this, and Stoldt then says that there is now no proof of the existence of such a source containing more than just sayings.[50] Space does not permit a full

48. Weisse, *Die evangelische Geschichte*, I, p. 39 [editors' trans.].

49. Weisse's change of mind was in his later work, *Die Evangelienfrage in ihrem gegenwärtigen Stadium* (Leipzig: Breitkopf & Härtel, 1856), pp. 88-90, 156-165. Cf. Stoldt, *Geschichte und Kritik*, pp. 58ff.

50. Stoldt, *Geschichte und Kritik*, p. 123. Cf. too his similar criticisms of Wernle on pp. 108ff., for renaming the sayings source 'Q', and then illegitimately incorporating anything he wanted to (i.e. not just sayings) into Q, thus abolishing the distinction between the narrative source (Mark) and the sayings source (Q). However it is

consideration of this problem, but it is probably inevitable that external evidence (or lack of it) cannot be the sole criterion by which to solve the Synoptic Problem, and the existence of a second source may be demanded by internal considerations alone.

Perhaps the most devastating attack on the Griesbach hypothesis in the nineteenth century was that of B. Weiss.[51] Certainly it was very influential: Holtzmann referred to many of Weiss's arguments and thereafter not many advocated the Griesbach hypothesis.[52] Nor did those who opposed the theory feel compelled to give much space to refuting it. Holtzmann's work gained so much in popularity that the main discussion centred on the residual problems left by his two-source theory, that is, how far one could identify Mark with one of the primitive sources, and how much one could legitimately ascribe to the sayings source, etc. However, there is no evidence that either Weiss or Holtzmann was opposing only the theories of Strauss or the Tübingen school. Certainly Weiss did put forward criticisms of the arguments which claimed that Mark exhibited a neutral *Tendenz*. He pointed out that to say that Mark is completely neutral is to say effectively that no *Tendenz* at all is discernible; further, to measure a non-existent *Tendenz* by the omissions which Mark is alleged to have made is a circular argument in that it assumes the source theory under consideration. Further still, the alleged omission by Mark of all controversial issues in Matthew and Luke did not fit the facts—despite Schwegler and Baur, Mark does still include such material in the stories about the food laws (ch. 7), fasting (ch. 2) and marriage (ch. 10).[53]

Nevertheless, both Weiss and Holtzmann clearly recognized that the Griesbach hypothesis had a history of its own, and had been adopted by others for different reasons quite independently of the Tübingen school.

---

very dubious if such a rigid distinction between the different *type* of content of each source can be maintained.

51. See especially Weiss, 'Zur Entstehungsgeschichte', pp. 680-96. This important article of Weiss is not mentioned by either Farmer or Stoldt.

52. H.J. Holtzmann, *Die synoptischen Evangelien, ihr Ursprung und geschichtlicher Charakter* (Leipzig: Engelmann, 1863), pp. 113-26.

53. Weiss, 'Zur Entstehungsgeschichte', pp. 689-90; also his *Lehrbuch der Einleitung in das Neue Testament* (Berlin: Hertz, 1886), pp. 505-506. Cf. Schwegler, *Das nachapostolische Zeitalter*, pp. 474-81; Baur (*Kritische Untersuchungen*, pp. 565-67) also suggested that Mark avoided everything in Matthew and Luke involving controversial issues in the early Church, e.g. on the question of the Law, or the Gentile mission.

Weiss himself took care to separate his detailed arguments against Griesbach's theory as adopted by Fritzche, De Wette and Bleek (especially on the question of order, and Mark's apparent conflation) from those he used against the use of the theory by Baur and others in the Tübingen school.[54] So too Holtzmann recognized the difference between the two groups: he referred to the Griesbach hypothesis

> which on the one hand through De Wette and Bleek had won over many adherents to the ranks of the new theology, and on the other hand forms the foundation for all of Baur's constructions.[55]

Further, Weiss did not use the theory of Markan priority to claim that Mark's Gospel was thereby historically accurate in all its details. For he believed that Mark, though the earliest of our three Gospels, was not the earliest Gospel to be written, since it was preceded by an assumed primitive gospel. This Ur-Matthew was used by both Matthew and Mark so that Mark was, according to Weiss, secondary at many points.[56] If Weiss had wanted to secure the historical reliability of the tradition, the Griesbach hypothesis would have suited his theory just as well, since then Matthew, as the earliest Gospel, could have been dependent on the apostolic Ur-Matthew. Thus when Stoldt gives Weiss's own late summary rejection of the Griesbach hypothesis, and states: 'one senses that he is writing from a particular theological standpoint, and that though he says "Griesbach", he means David Friedrich Strauss',[57] this appears to be quite unjustified by the evidence. Weiss was well aware that the Griesbach hypothesis had other proponents, and he put forward detailed counter-arguments against them; further, his own theory of an Ur-Matthew used by both Matthew and Mark was no more conducive to securing the historicity of the tradition than the Griesbach hypothesis.

In the case of Holtzmann the situation is not very different from what has been observed before. It has already been noted that Holtzmann was well aware that the Griesbach hypothesis and the Tübingen school were partly independent of each other. The question of how far he thought that the Markan account (or at least his Ur-Marcus) was historically accurate is more difficult. He said that although there is some link

---

54. Weiss, 'Zur Entstehungsgeschichte', pp. 680-89 for the first, pp. 689-92 for the second. Similarly in his *Lehrbuch der Einleitung*, pp. 502-504, 505.

55. Holtzmann, *Die synoptischen Evangelien*, p. 113 [editors' trans.].

56. Weiss, 'Zur Entstehungsgeschichte', pp. 63-68, 665, 672.

57. Stoldt, *Geschichte und Kritik*, p. 211 [editors' trans.].

between Peter and Mark, this does not necessarily guarantee the reliability of all Mark's details, and he endorsed Weisse's remarks about the non-eye-witness character of Mark.[58] Nevertheless he does appear to have disregarded his own reservations later in his book by setting out a portrayal of the life of Jesus, drawing heavily on the small details of Mark's account.[59] How far this was important for Holtzmann is impossible to say. It is possible too that some of his difficulties about what to ascribe to his 'A' source (i.e. his Ur-Marcus) stem from more than purely literary considerations. He may have been influenced by Papias's remarks so that everything that was (a) not a saying of Jesus, and (b) preceded the call of Matthew could not belong to the Logia source, since Papias implied that the second source was a collection of sayings, and based on the testimony of the apostle Matthew. (Hence not only narratives, but also the Sermon on the Mount, were put into the 'A' source.) However, this is not Holtzmann's own way of arguing—he sought to justify his decisions on purely literary grounds, and then said that his results were remarkably confirmed by Papias.[60] Still, there is no evidence that Holtzmann was consciously opposing the theories of Strauss and the Tübingen school alone. Farmer says that Holtzmann's most weighty point against the Griesbach hypothesis 'was the scientifi-cally gratuitous but powerfully apologetic point that it was conceded by all contemporary critics that Matthew was secondary to the eye-witness period', and he refers to Holtzmann's statement: 'Nowadays we argue only *ex concesso*, if we proceed from the secondary character of the first Gospel. Likewise, the Tübingen critic has in this agreed with us.'[61] However, Farmer's judgment here is questionable. In the part of his book from which the above quotation is taken, Holtzmann is not dealing with the Griesbach hypothesis, and the remark that Matthew cannot be an apostolic writing is very much an aside. More importantly, 'sec-ondary' in the sentence quoted by Farmer does *not* mean being after the period of eye-witnesses—rather, it refers to the purely literary fact that Matthew's Gospel shows traces of having used previous sources ('Spuren der Quellenverarbeitung'). Holtzmann and the Tübingen school

---

58. Holtzmann, *Die synoptischen Evangelien*, pp. 366-73.

59. Holtzmann, *Die synoptischen Evangelien*, pp. 468-95 in the section entitled 'Lebensbild Jesu nach der Quelle A'.

60. Holtzmann, *Die synoptischen Evangelien*, p. 252.

61. Farmer, *Synoptic Problem*, p. 37, quoting Holtzmann, *Die synoptischen Evangelien*, p. 56 [editors' trans.].

were agreed not necessarily on a late absolute date of Matthew, but on the fact that Matthew must have been preceded by other sources.

This leads on to the question of how far Holtzmann set out to prove his theories, and how far he simply assumed his results. Stoldt claims that Holtzmann only argued on the basis of his hypothesis.[62] However, Holtzmann did not just assume his theories without more ado. He justified his procedure in the first part of his book, where he dealt with past attempts to solve the Synoptic Problem. His method here was to proceed negatively and certainly not to seek some artificial consensus, a kind of lowest common denominator, in an Ur-Gospel theory simply because it was a consensus.[63] Rather, he was convinced by those who had argued against the oral theory, so that written sources were required. He also accepted the view that none of the three Gospels could be the source of the other two: Luke was excluded from such a position by the evidence of his own prologue; Matthew by the fact that Mark's order was more original; and Mark mainly because of the minor agreements.[64] Thus, as a result of these negative conclusions (where Holtzmann freely used the arguments of others), the only possibility left was the existence of a written source/sources prior to our three Gospels. The task of rediscovering these sources was undertaken in the rest of the book. Nor is it true to claim that his chosen method of procedure must necessarily lead to an Ur-Marcus.[65] First, his decision to extract a common source from the parts where all three Gospels are parallel may lead to a source whose extent is that of the shortest Gospel, that is, Mark; but it will not necessarily lead to a result where the wording of the shortest Gospel is also the most original, and this Holtzmann tried to show. Secondly,

62. Stoldt, *Geschichte und Kritik*, pp. 70, 85. See too Farmer, 'A Skeleton in the Closet', p. 37, where he claims that Holtzmann's hypotheses were the 'presuppositions' of his detailed work.

63. Hence contra Farmer, *Synoptic Problem*, chapter 2. Cf. the claim that Holtzmann 'was searching for some ground of scholarly consensus' and that his work was 'based not on a firm grasp of the primary phenomena of the gospels themselves, but upon an artificial and deceptive consensus among scholars of differing traditions of gospel criticism' (p. 38).

64. Holtzmann, *Die synoptischen Evangelien*, pp. 60-61; later, in his *Einleitung in das neue Testament* (Freiburg: Mohr [Paul Siebeck], 1886), p. 357, Holtzmann suggested that Luke made a small use of Matthew—by this he explained the minor agreements, and this then allowed him to identify Mark with his original Ur-Marcus.

65. As is said by Farmer, *Synoptic Problem*, p. 41, and in 'A Skeleton in the Closet', pp. 39-40.

Holtzmann did *not* just proceed to examine the material where all three are parallel in reconstructing his 'A' source. For example, he claimed that 'A' included the Sermon on the Mount, the account of the healing of the centurion's servant, the story of the woman taken in adultery, etc. His method in fact led him to a source 'A' which was in many respects *un*like Mark (certainly it was more extensive).[66] Thus Holtzmann's study was not as circular as might appear, nor are his results pre-determined by his method.

There seems thus to be little justification for the view that the demise of the Griesbach hypothesis was closely tied up with the collapse of the Tübingen school, or with a desire to find a reliable tradition in the Gospels. This may have been the case in the minds of those who sought to establish the theory of Markan priority, but if so it never reached the stage of being a significant factor in the arguments which were adduced to oppose the Griesbach hypothesis. There was a clear awareness that the Griesbach hypothesis and the Tübingen school were not to be identified without remainder on either side, and that many people adhered to Griesbach's theory without sharing the presuppositions of the Tübingen school. What is true, and can be examined scientifically, is that specific arguments were brought against the Griesbach hypothesis considered in its own right. These arguments still have relevance today in the light of the modern revival of the Griesbach hypothesis. Three of these will be considered briefly here—the arguments concerning characteristic words, apparent conflation, and the choice and order of the material.

Wilke and Holtzmann made a lot of use of considerations of characteristic words and phrases. They claimed that Mark contained none of the characteristics of the other two.[67] If Griesbach were right, one would

66. In fact one of Stoldt's criticisms of Holtzmann is precisely that his 'A' source is so *un*like Mark that it is illegitimate to label it as an 'Ur-Marcus' (*Geschichte und Kritik*, p. 69). This is, however, not strictly relevant—the name of the source is immaterial, though Stoldt is right to point out how this now differs from Weisse's theory.

67. Wilke, *Der Urevangelist*, pp. 428ff., p. 440; Holtzmann, *Die synoptischen Evangelien*, pp. 344-45. The influence of Wilke's work on Holtzmann and others is ignored by both Farmer and Stoldt. Farmer says that Wilke's work, together with that of Gieseler, does not 'embody demonstrably significant contributions, to the ideological history of the Synoptic Problem' (*Synoptic Problem*, p. 34). Stoldt deals with Wilke separately, but thinks that it was Weisse whose contribution was the most basic for further study (*Geschichte und Kritik*, p. 28). In view of Holtzmann's explicit reference to the work of Wilke in his discussion of the Griesbach hypothesis this

expect some Mattheanisms or Lukanisms to appear in Mark. They also sought to show that in many cases, where Matthew or Luke diverges from Mark, the non-Markan version uses words or phrases characteristic of that Gospel. This would be consistent with the theory of Markan priority, entailing as it does the hypothesis that Matthew and/or Luke rewrote Mark in their own idiom. If Mark is secondary, on the other hand, one has to envisage Mark's going through his sources, carefully excising anything characteristic of that source. Zeller used a similar method to try to prove the validity of the Griesbach hypothesis. He gave a long list of words which were said to be characteristic of Matthew and/or Luke, but which also appeared less frequently in Mark, thus showing dependence of Mark on the other two.[68] Holtzmann replied to this argument (which he considered far more impressive than the use of *Tendenzkritik*) by pointing to many counter examples, such as words of 'A' (i.e. his Ur-Marcus) in Matthew and Luke. He also claimed that, since Matthew and Luke were longer than 'A', Zeller's results were not very surprising—one would expect more occurrences of a word in a longer Gospel. Also (and perhaps more questionably) he claimed that the style of 'A' had influenced Matthew and Luke, who had therefore taken over many words from 'A' and used them frequently themselves.[69]

Stoldt claims that Wilke's method of determining characteristics led him in a circular argument—for the characteristic vocabulary of Matthew and Luke is that which is *not* in Mark (and hence characteristics of Matthew and Luke could not possibly appear in Mark), whereas that of Mark is that which is common with the other two, since Mark is the original Gospel.[70] However, Wilke's argument went the other way round. The fact that Matthew's and Luke's characteristic vocabulary

shows an important omission in both historical surveys.

68. E. Zeller, 'Vergleichende Übersicht über den Wörtervorrath der sämmtlichen neutestamentlichen Schriftsteller', *Theol.Jahrb* (1843), pp. 443-543, on pp. 527-35.

69. See Holtzmann, *Die synoptischen Evangelien*, pp. 346-54. Zeller's lists are less impressive in detail. Words which appeared twice only in Matthew, and once in Mark, were counted as characteristic of Matthew and not of Mark, e.g. ἀγγαρεύειν, ἔργον, καλόν, καθέδρα, κῆνσος, κυλλός, ὀρύσσω. Even πρίν, which appears twice in Mark, and once more in Matthew, was counted. Similarly, words like κατάλυμα, κενός, λεπτόν (which appear once in Mark, twice in Luke) and ἀποδοκιμάζειν (twice in Mark, three times in Luke) were said to show that Mark was secondary to Luke. He also gave a not inconsiderable list of counter-examples.

70. Stoldt, *Geschichte und Kritik*, p. 33 (The reference to 'p. 28' of Wilke's book should read 'p. 428').

appeared in the parts of the tradition where they differed from Mark was the result of his detailed analysis, not the criterion from which he started. So too with Mark, it was the result of his analysis that Mark's Gospel preserved the original wording, not the basis from which Wilke set out to determine the latter.[71] Both Wilke and Holtzmann sought to determine what was characteristic by looking at the total number of occurrences of a word or phrase in each Gospel. Thus their argument was not circular and clearly still has relevance, although, as the debate with Zeller shows, the evidence does not all point one way.[72]

The problem of ambiguity and possible circularity recurs in the phenomenon of apparent conflation in Mark, that is, in those places where Mark has two phrases, Matthew and Luke having one each. (Mk 1.32 and 1.42 are the most famous.) The phenomenon is in itself quite ambiguous—Mark could have conflated the two phrases from his sources, or Matthew and Luke could have independently chosen different halves of Mark's expression. However, Wilke pointed out that, if such duplicate expressions as Mk 1.32 are the result of an author trying carefully to include every detail in his sources, he should have done the same at

71. The situation is slightly complicated by the fact that Wilke tended to state his results before giving the justification for them. Pp. 456-60 are very relevant for the claim made about Mark on p. 457.

72. Farmer has sought to use the observations of J.C. Hawkins, *Horae Synopticae* (Oxford: Clarendon Press, 2nd edn, 1909), pp. 169-71, on the characteristic formulae of each Gospel, pointing to the lack of Markanisms in Matthew and Luke. (See *Synoptic Problem*, pp. 157-58, and repeated in 'Modern Developments of Griesbach's Hypothesis', *NTS* 23 [1977], pp. 275-95 [276], in response to the criticism of the Griesbach hypothesis by J.A. Fitzmyer, 'The Priority of Mark and the "Q" source in Luke', in Miller (ed.), *Jesus and Man's Hope*, I, pp. 131-70 [135], who repeats the argument of Wilke and Holtzmann, at least with regard to Lukanisms.) However, Hawkins's criterion for determining such characteristic formulae is open to question: two occurrences do not necessarily make a phrase characteristic of one Gospel; further, his demand that one of the occurrences be unique to one Gospel predetermines the fact that not many Markan phrases will be included, since Mark has very little which is not paralleled in Matthew or Luke. If one extends the scope to include all words and smaller phrases (i.e. not limiting consideration to longer phrases as Hawkins did at this point) there are some Markanisms in Matthew and Luke. One could point to καὶ ἔλεγεν αὐτοῖς as in Mk 2.27/Lk. 6.5, the use of the historic present in Mk 5.35/Lk. 8.49, the use of ἀκάθαρτος in Mk 6.7/Mt. 10.1 (the word occurs twice in Matthew, 11 times in Mark), and the use of εἰσπορεύομαι in Mk 7.18/Mt. 15.17 (once in Matthew, eight times in Mark).

14.17 (where the parallels are very similar). Rather, these double expressions are probably characteristic of Mark or 'A', that is, 1.32 is very similar to 14.12 and 16.2.[73] Similarly, in 2.11, where Mark is supposed to have conflated σοὶ λέγω ἔγειρε from Luke and ἆρον...from Matthew, Weiss pointed to Mk 5.41 (σοὶ λέγω ἔγειρε) and 2.9 (ἔγειρε, ἆρον) where Mark is in both cases alone in having the relevant phrase—thus the usage in 2.11 needs no further explanation than that it is Markan.[74] Further, examples of apparent conflation can be found elsewhere in the other Gospels—for example, Lk. 8.25 speaks of the onlookers φοβηθέντες (cf. Mark) δὲ ἐθαύμασεν (cf. Matthew),[75] and indeed Weiss referred to this case and Lk. 9.5, 11, 12 to show that Luke had used both Mark and his proposed Ur-Matthew.[76]

Although the phenomenon is in itself totally ambiguous in any one case, Wilke's comments are still relevant in that they point to the difficulty which the Griesbach hypothesis faces in accounting for the choice of material by Mark, in that at times Mark takes great care to conflate all the details from his sources, and yet at other times he appears to be content to make large-scale omissions.[77] One of the answers to this general problem of Mark's choice of the material given in the past by advocates of the Griesbach hypothesis is also connected with the explanation of Mark's order. Griesbach himself thought that he had an explanation for both the content and the order of Mark. He went through the whole text of Mark showing how Mark could have derived his material by following each of his sources alternately. However, Griesbach felt it important to go further and give

73. Wilke, *Der Urevangelist*, p. 446; Holtzmann, *Die synoptischen Evangelien*, p. 114.

74. Weiss, 'Zur Entstehungsgeschichte', p. 683.

75. Wilke (*Der Urevangelist*, p. 513), commented wryly: 'Stünde diese Formel im Markus, sie würde sogleich einen Beweis abgeben müssen dass Markus die beiden Nebentexte zusammengemischt habe'.

76. Weiss, 'Zur Entstehungsgeschichte', p. 86. For the ambiguity of the phenomenon in any one case, see Farmer, *Synoptic Problem*, p. 156.

77. Cf. the criticisms of the Griesbach hypothesis on the question of Mark's omissions by C. Weizsäcker, *Untersuchungen über die evangelische Geschichte* (Stuttgart: Gotha, 1864), pp. 19-21; F.H. Woods, 'The Origin and Mutual Relation of the Synoptic Gospels', in *Studia Biblica et Ecclesiastica* (Oxford: Clarendon Press, 1885–1896), II, pp. 59-104 (67); in the modern debate, see Fitzmyer, 'Priority of Mark', p. 135.

the probable reason...why at a given time he (Mark) deserted Matthew...
and attached himself to Luke, and why putting away Luke, he once more
attached himself to Matthew; and further it can be understood why precisely in *this* passage of Matthew, and not in another, he again connects
up the thread which he had previously broken by passing over to Luke.[78]

Most of Griesbach's reasons are based on the general claim that Mark
wants to avoid the long teaching discourses—hence he switches between
sources to avoid the Sermon on the Mount in Matthew, the Sermon on
the Plain in Luke, the long diatribe against the Pharisees in Matthew 23,
and so on.[79] This thesis was heavily criticized by Weiss,[80] who pointed
out that if this was the reason, then it would not have led to the changes
which have in fact occurred. A desire simply to avoid the Sermon on
the Mount does not explain why Mark should switch to Luke after Mt.
4.22/Mk 1.20 and not go on to Mt. 4.25, nor why, having just switched,
he should immediately turn to Matthew again for Mt. 7.29/Mk 1.22; if
Mark wanted to avoid Luke's sermon, why does he desert Luke for
Matthew at Lk. 6.10 rather than at 6.19? If he wanted to avoid Matthew
23 why does he come back to it after five verses to include Luke's two-
verse parallel? Weizsäcker also pointed out the general inconsistency of
Griesbach's theory, which was meant to explain not only the order, but
also the choice, of the material in Mark. If Mark wanted to avoid long
teaching discourses why had he included two such discourses in chs. 4
and 13? Conversely, if Mark was so interested in the miracles and
exorcisms why had he omitted some that were in his alleged sources and
hence would have been grist to his mill?[81]

78. J.J. Griesbach, 'Commentatio qua Marci Evangelium totum e Matthei et
Lucae commentariis decerptum esse monstratur', in *Opuscula Academica* (ed.
J.P. Gabler; Jena: J.C.G. Goepferdt, 1825), II, pp. 358-425 (370). ET by B. Orchard
as 'A Demonstration that Mark was Written after Matthew and Luke', in B. Orchard
et al. (eds.), *J.J. Griesbach: Synoptic and Text-Critical Studies 1776–1976*
(SNTSMS, 34; Cambridge: Cambridge University Press, 1978), pp. 73-135.

79. See the notes appended to each section of Mark by Griesbach, 'Commentatio
qua Marci Evangelium', pp. 371-77.

80. Weiss, 'Zur Entstehungsgeschichte', pp. 680-81.

81. Weizsäcker, *Untersuchungen*, pp. 19-21. On the last point, see Weiss, 'Zur
Entstehungsgeschichte', p. 686. As regards the choice of material, Farmer (Modern
Developments', pp. 254-55), thinks that the shape of Peter's speeches in Acts may
have influenced Mark (e.g. Acts 1.21 starts with the 'baptism of John', as does
Mark, and has no reference to the birth stories), though it is not clear if he thinks that

Some sort of argument from order has been used by advocates of both the Griesbach and the two-document hypotheses. Griesbach himself felt that this was one of his strongest arguments, as did Baur and, today, Farmer.[82] On the other side, Woods made it his main argument, as did Abbott, Burkitt and others. Much has been made of the 'Lachmann fallacy' (not in fact made by Lachmann himself), which made the illegitimate jump from the observation that Matthew and Luke never agree in order against Mark to the conclusion that Mark must be prior to, and a source for, them. Butler, Farmer and Stoldt (among others) have rightly pointed out that the evidence only proves the priority of Mark's order on the assumption of the existence of an Ur-Gospel (which was Lachmann's own assumption).[83] Without this assumption, the evidence only proves that Mark occupies some 'medial' position with respect to the other two. (This is certainly true, but a position of relative priority is also a medial one—hence there is nothing logically impossible about the conclusion of Markan priority: if there is a fallacy, it is only in the logic itself, not necessarily in the final result claimed.)[84] Others have sought to refine the argument by claiming that the differences between Matthew's and Mark's orders are explicable on the assumption that Mark is prior,

---

this is due to a personal link between Mark and Peter. The same had been claimed by F.J. Schwarz, *Neue Untersuchungen über das Verwandtsschaftsverhältniss der synoptischen Evangelien* (Tübingen: Laupp, 1844), pp. 275-76. However, quite apart from the problem of how far the speeches in Acts present traditional material and how much is due to Luke's editing, it is doubtful if the Petrine speeches are definite enough to bear this weight. For example, the lack of reference to Jesus' teaching in the speeches is said by Farmer to explain Mark's omission of most of the sayings material (p. 285). Yet this still does not explain why Mark includes some teaching material, and why he has chosen to include precisely what he has. Further, this does not fit very easily with Mark's well-known stress on Jesus as a 'teacher'. (Cf. E. Schweizer, 'Der theologische Leistung des Markus', *EvT* 24 (1964), pp. 337-55 (340-41).

82. Baur, *Kritische Untersuchungen*, pp. 544ff.; for the importance of this argument for Baur, see Fuller, 'Baur versus Hilgenfeld', p. 358; for Farmer, see 'Modern Developments' p. 293.

83. B.C. Butler, *The Originality of St Matthew* (Cambridge: Cambridge University Press, 1951), pp. 63ff.; Farmer, *Synoptic Problem*, p. 50; Stoldt, *Geschichte und Kritik*, pp. 133ff. The ambiguity of the phenomenon had already been noted by Schwarz, *Neue Untersuchungen*, p. 307.

84. Cf. G.M. Styler, 'The Priority of Mark', Excursus IV of C.F.D. Moule, *The Birth of the New Testament* (London: A. & C. Black, 1962), p. 225.

but that the reverse changes are not so easy to envisage.[85] This is, of course, simply a return to Lachmann's own original form of the argument, and this appeal to order was that used later by Holtzmann:

> If one accepts the order of the individual narratives in Mark and places those in Matthew on one page and those in Luke on another, then one can prove step by step that each one of the others presupposes this sequence as original. Herein lies the essential strength of the Markan hypothesis.[86]

Stoldt, referring to this, claims that this is a circular argument:

> The only one who here assumes that the order of Mark is the original is Haltzmann. In doing so he commits an egregious classical *petitio principii*: the proposition that needs to be proven is assumed already proven and is used as evidence.[87]

This is part of a constantly recurring theme in Stoldt's book—that nearly all arguments for Markan priority are circular. This reaches its climax in his consideration of what he calls 'proof from psychological reflection'.[88] Here he deals with the form of argument that seeks to find reasons for the differences between the Gospels in the redactional activity of the later writer. Stoldt asks:

> What do we really know in an objective sense about the Evangelist's motives and mental deliberations which moved and motivated them while they were conceiving their work?[89]

In this way, he says, advocates of the two-document hypothesis have to explain hundreds of extra details in Mark omitted by Matthew and Luke, as well as the other positive minor agreements. He recognizes that the Griesbach hypothesis is not free from this problem, in that the Griesbach hypothesis has to explain why Mark might have omitted the birth stories, but nevertheless the problem is much less.[90] Stoldt points to many of the

---

85. See, for example, W.G. Kümmel, *Introduction to the New Testament* (London: SCM Press, rev. edn, 1975), p. 5.

86. Holtzmann, *Einleitung*, p. 307 [editors' trans.].

87. Stoldt, *Geschichte und Kritik*, pp. 129-30 [editors' trans.].

88. Stoldt, *Geschichte und Kritik*, pp. 184-201. Cf. too Farmer's similar criticisms of the circularity in the arguments of J. Schmid and others, which claim that Matthew and Luke have 'improved' Mark ('Response', p. 420).

89. Stoldt, *Geschichte und Kritik*, pp. 185-86 [editors' trans.].

90. Stoldt, *Geschichte und Kritik*, p. 186. In fact, of course, the problem is of precisely the same proportions: a minor agreement on the two-document hypothesis becomes an instance where Mark has chosen to ignore the common witness of both

contradictory reasons given by scholars in the past, and he claims that the whole method assumes the result to be proved before seeking to make it convincing. 'The whole proof from psychological reflection represents an immense *petitio principii*.'[91]

At the purely formal level, this criticism is probably justified: to assume the Markan order or wording as primary and then to find reasons for Matthew's/Luke's alleged deviations from it is to argue in a circle. Further, the dogmatic statement that the opposite changes are inconceivable is in itself not conclusive: it might be the case that changes were made in this way but that we have not yet discovered the true reasons. Nevertheless, some such form of argument is inevitable. Griesbach's own original argument on order was equally circular—he proposed a source theory and sought to give reasons *why* Mark might have proceeded in the way he is alleged to have done. In fact, if the three Gospels are directly related to each other, then *any* argument from order (including Griesbach's) is in itself, at the purely formal level, logically inconclusive. The facts of the case are undisputed—that is, that there is a close similarity in order among all three Gospels, as well as some disagreement, and that the Matthew–Luke agreements are almost always mediated through Mark. But these facts are open to a number of different interpretations.

In fact, any source theory can be put forward—there is no logical law which excludes any theory of synoptic interrelationships with the degree of finality which would be attained if it could be shown that such a hypothesis led to a self-contradiction of the kind $0 = 1$. One can postulate any hypothesis, and then make a list, in a purely mechanical way, of the changes which the later writer must have made to his source(s). For example, if Luke were prior, Mark second, and Matthew a conflation of both, then one could go through a synopsis showing that Mark must have omitted this from Luke, added that, changed this, retained that, and so forth; then Matthew must have taken this from Luke, that from Mark, ignored Luke here, preferred Mark there, and so on. What is then required if the hypothesis is to be made credible is a presentation of the reasons why the later writer made the changes he is alleged to have done. These must then be rational, consistent with each other and with the facts as they are. The extent to which the reasons given form a

his sources on the Griesbach hypothesis; a common omission by Matthew and Luke becomes an addition by Mark to them. Either way an explanation is required.

91. Stoldt, *Geschichte und Kritik*, p. 201 [editors' trans.].

coherent whole and fit the facts will then be a measure of the credibility of the hypothesis. On the other hand, if the reasons form an incoherent set, then this will be some indication that the underlying source theory is wrong. (It is, of course, no proof of this—the theory could be right but the redactional reasons suggested by its advocates wrong.)

Herein lies the importance of Weiss's arguments against Griesbach over the question of order. The theory of Markan priority can be made credible by appealing to the agreement in order, and to possible reasons why Matthew and Luke should have deviated from Mark's order in the way they are alleged to have done.[92] On the Griesbach hypothesis, the actual path followed by Mark in using his alleged sources alternately can also be traced formally (as was done by Griesbach, and, following him, De Wette, Bleek and Farmer); but what is now lacking is the equivalent series of coherent reasons why Mark should have proceeded in this way, switching between sources precisely when and where he did. Griesbach did try to give reasons, and the importance of Weiss's criticisms is that they show these to be unsatisfactory at many points. It is in this light, also, that one should read the adverse criticisms of the Griesbach hypothesis, often in apparently emotive terms, made by Lachmann, Wilke and others. When Lachmann said that Mark, according to the Griesbach hypothesis, would have been a 'bungling dilettante', and so on, this should probably be read as implying that he could see no coherent pattern in Mark's alleged behaviour. So too, Wilke's comment, that Mark according to the Griesbach hypothesis would be 'not an abbreviator, not an epitomizer, not an excerptor, but a castrator of texts near to hand.' should not be read out of context as a piece of unnecessary abuse.[93] The previous sentence in Wilke's book is necessary to understand his line of thought: 'The combination of words related to other texts cannot be based on intentional choice'. This is not just a comment out of the blue, but is the result of the whole of the previous analysis, which has tried to show that no coherent plan can be discerned in Mark's alleged redaction of Matthew and Luke. At the level of detailed wording (rather than order) no consistent plan emerges—Mark neither consistently conflates, nor abbreviates, nor expands, and so on, and to say in any one particular case, for example, where Mark had abbreviated his sources, that 'Mark wanted to abbreviate' is in itself no reason

92. Usually for reasons similar to those given by Kümmel, *Introduction*, pp. 58-60.

93. Wilke, *Der Urevangelist*, p. 443 [editors' trans.].

beyond being a truism unless it can be shown to be part of a consistent, overall plan.

The result of this historical survey of the fate of the Griesbach hypothesis in the nineteenth century is two-fold. First, there is very little firm evidence that reaction against the scepticism of Strauss and others in the Tübingen school was a significant factor in the general rejection of the Griesbach hypothesis in the mid-nineteenth century. Secondly, other arguments were brought against that hypothesis in a form which was quite independent of the arguments of the Tübingen school, and indeed quite independent of the question of whether the first Gospel to be written was based on eye-witness testimony. Many of these arguments are reversible, or at best indirect, although this is an inevitable feature of almost any arguments used in the study of the Synoptic Problem. Nevertheless, the outstanding problem remains for those who would revive the Griesbach hypothesis today: Can one find a convincing set of reasons for Mark's proceeding in precisely the way he is alleged to have done? What is required today, therefore, is a convincing detailed presentation of what Markan redaction might look like according to the Griesbach hypothesis.

ADDITIONAL NOTE

On the contemporary debate about the Griesbach (or two-Gospel) hypothesis, see my *The Revival of the Griesbach Hypothesis* (SNTSMS, 44; Cambridge: Cambridge University Press, 1983). On past and present appeals to the phenomenon of order, and any alleged circularity, see also my 'The Argument from Order and the Synoptic Problem', *TZ* 36 (1980), pp. 338-54; and 'Arguments from Order: Definition and Evaluation', in C.M. Tuckett (ed.), *Synoptic Studies* (JSNTSup, 7; Sheffield: JSOT Press, 1984), pp. 197-219.

Stoldt's book is now available in English translation: *History and Criticism of the Marcan Hypothesis* (Edinburgh: T. & T. Clark; Macon, GA: Mercer University Press, 1980). Fuller discussion of arguments from order in D.J. Neville, *Arguments from Order in Synoptic Source Criticism: A History and Critique* (Macon, GA: Mercer University Press, 1994). The theory that ideological factors were at work in the establishment of the theory of Markan priority is now also argued in a slightly different way by W.R. Farmer, 'State *Interesse* and Marcan Priority', in F. van Segbroek *et al.* (eds.), *The Four Gospels 1992* (Festschrift F. Neirynck; BETL, 100; Leuven: Peeters/Leuven University Press, 1992), pp. 2477-98, and in his *The Gospel of Jesus: The Pastoral Relevance of the Synoptic Problem* (Louisville: Westminster/ John Knox Press, 1994).

JSNT 20 (1984), pp. 87-107

NORMAN PERRIN AND HIS 'SCHOOL':
RETRACING A PILGRIMAGE

Welton O. Seal, Jr

> It has been a feature of my academic pilgrimage that 'one thing has led to another'. I began with *Life of Jesus research* and that led me to the Son of Man and *New Testament Christology*. The Son of Man is most prominent in the Gospel of Mark and that fact led me to *Markan research and redaction criticism*. In its turn redaction criticism led me to *literary criticism and hermeneutics*, the most recent phases of my interest and concerns.—Norman Perrin[1]

During a relatively brief but highly productive career, Norman Perrin (d. 1976) made a significant contribution to the literature of New Testament scholarship. Addressing vital issues ranging from Life of Jesus research to the interpretation of the Gospel of Mark, Perrin repeatedly challenged his peers with bold positions on methodology and interpretation along the route of his 'pilgrimage' in New Testament research. Several of his students have followed on this road by adopting, implementing, and advancing many of Perrin's positions. After introducing Norman Perrin and his students (who with qualifications may be called a 'school'), I will draw upon the published works of these popular critics to retrace their pilgrimage as it is charted in Perrin's words above.

Norman Perrin and his 'School'

Born in 1920 at Wellingborough, Northants, England, Norman Perrin began biblical study after serving in the Royal Air Force during World

---

1. *A Modern Pilgrimage in New Testament Christology* (Philadelphia: Fortress Press, 1974), p. 1. The italics in the quotation are the emphases of the author of the present article.

War II.[2] First, at Manchester Baptist College and Manchester University, he was instructed by T.W. Manson and earned the BA in 1949.[3] Then, after ordination in the same year by the Baptist Union of Great Britain and Northern Ireland, Perrin began post-graduate work at London University during which time he served as a pastor to Baptist churches in London and South Wales.[4] After receiving the BD in 1952 and the MTh in 1956, he travelled to Germany to pursue the DTheol which he completed under Joachim Jeremias in 1959.[5] In America, while serving at Emory University as Assistant (later Associate) Professor of New Testament Theology and at the Divinity School of the University of Chicago as Associate (later full) Professor of New Testament, Perrin published a total of nine books, over thirty articles, and nearly forty book reviews. Appreciation for his work was attested in 1971 by the publication in his honour of a *Festschrift* or collection of scholarly responses to his writings,[6] and by his election to the Presidency of the Society of Biblical Literature (1972–73).

In his writings Perrin consistently acknowledges indebtedness to and appreciation of his students. In *The Kingdom of God in the Teaching of Jesus*,[7] Perrin thanks his Emory students for proof-reading, and in *Rediscovering the Teaching of Jesus*,[8] he mentions 'the extremely competent help' he received from graduate students at Chicago. Later, reflecting upon his move to Chicago and his work on *Rediscovering the Teaching of Jesus* there from 1964 to 1966, Perrin[9] writes that at this point he was 'beginning to experience what has become a major feature of my academic life: creative interaction in my work with the work of some quite outstanding graduate students'. He cites key students whose

2. 'Memorial Tribute to Norman Perrin, 1920–1976', *Criterion* 16 (1977), p. 4.

3. N. Perrin, Review of W. Beardslee, *Human Achievement and Divine Vocation in the Message of Paul*, in *Emory University Quarterly* 18 (1962), p. 60.

4. 'Memorial Tribute', p. 4.

5. 'Memorial Tribute', p. 7. According to his colleagues, Perrin actually began doctoral study under Ernst Fuchs in East Berlin; however, I have found no reference to this in Perrin's published works. Apparently, it was during his stay in Germany that Perrin encountered the work of Rudolf Bultmann, the scholar who so heavily influenced Perrin's early writings.

6. H. Betz (ed.), *Christology and a Modern Pilgrimage: A Discussion with Norman Perrin* (Claremont, CA: The New Testament Colloquium, 1971).

7. (London: SCM Press; Philadelphia: Westminster Press, 1963), p. 11.

8. (London: SCM Press; New York: Harper & Row, 1967), p. 13.

9. *A Modern Pilgrimage*, p. 7.

work on Christology influenced the development of his own thought in this area or who remained 'in constant discussion with me of my work'. Significant among those mentioned are Dennis Duling (now at Canisius College, Buffalo, NY, Vernon K. Robbins (now at Emory University), Richard A. Edwards (now at Marquette University), John R. Donahue (now at the Jesuit School of Theology, Berkeley, CA), and Werner Kelber (now at Rice University).[10] Additionally, Perrin[11] singles out his graduate assistant Mary Ann Tolbert (now at Vanderbuilt University) for special commendation as 'a gifted and challenging student of the problem of hermeneutics who has contributed a great deal to this volume'. Finally, in *The New Testament: An Introduction*,[12] Perrin offers his most comprehensive acknowledgment and listing of students, and among these two stand out notably: 'Each of them commented on a first draft of the manuscript, Donahue and Kelber in very considerable detail'.

Such close relationships and constant interaction produced shared innovations and commonly asserted opinions among Perrin and several of his students. In a 1972 article, Perrin[13] bases his argumentation on 'a series of assertions' about Mark for which 'the justification comes from the intensive work on the gospel that my students and I have been doing for the past five years or so'. Likewise, at the conclusion of his chapter on Mark in *The New Testament: An Introduction* (pp. 166-67), Perrin writes, 'The insights and ideas represented in this chapter are, however, very largely those of the present writer and his students', and lists six of his own writings and the dissertations of Donahue, Kelber, and Robbins.

Although Perrin never uses the expression 'school' with reference to the work of his students and himself on Mark, such statements along with interdependence in effort, interaction of ideas, and consensus in position indicate that the term 'school' is quite appropriate. Indeed, *The*

10. *A Modern Pilgrimage*, p. x.

11. *Jesus and the Language of the Kingdom* (Philadelphia: Fortress Press, 1976), p. xiii.

12. (New York: Harcourt Brace Jovanovich, 1974), p. vi. Writing of his close involvement with his Chicago students as a group, Perrin once described himself as 'in constant discussion with them in classroom, coffee shop, and office' (*Jesus*, pp. xii-xiii). Later, at a memorial service honoring Perrin, Donahue confirmed from a student's perspective what is evident from Perrin's own statements: 'Norman lived for his students; he lived with them' ('Memorial Tribute', p. 11).

13. 'Historical Criticism, Literary Criticism and Hermeneutics', *JR* 52 (1972), p. 364.

Passion in Mark[14] stands as a clear testimony to the considerable coherence of its authors in terms of methodology and conclusions. Perrin himself is a contributor—along with students Donahue, Kelber, Robbins, and Dewey, and non-students Weeden and Crossan—and he attests to the degree of unanimity in methodology and conclusions exhibited in this collection.[15] Although a broad school of 'kindred minds' centering around Perrin's work could be envisaged to include students and non-students alike, Perrin himself warns against imposing an unwarranted degree of solidarity upon such a group. In expressing his own estimate of non-student Weeden's work, for example, Perrin[16] explains, 'Enthusiasm for Weeden's work at the level of method does not, of course, necessarily carry with it agreement with his conclusions'. But when we limit our purview to the consideration of a 'Perrin school' consisting of Perrin and key students such as Donahue and Kelber, a body of scholarship with numerous and clearly defined lines of interconnection and development comes into focus.

Life of Jesus Research and New Testament Christology (1957–71)

Perrin inaugurated his academic career, and the first stage of his pilgrimage, with the preparation of his doctoral dissertation, later published as *The Kingdom of God in the Teaching of Jesus*. A series of articles followed on the problem of the historical Jesus in anticipation of Perrin's milestone treatment, *Rediscovering the Teaching of Jesus*. In *Rediscovering the Teaching of Jesus* (p. 12) Perrin proposed an investigation of

14. W. Kelber (ed.), *The Passion in Mark* (Philadelphia: Fortress Press, 1968). One reviewer of *Passion in Mark*, R.E. Brown, refers to this group of writers as 'a Chicago school' (*CBQ* 39 [1977], p. 283). W. Schenk may have been the first critic to speak of a Perrin school (Review of J.R. Donahue, *Are You the Christ?*, *TLZ* 100 [1975], p. 839). R. Fortna ('Jesus and Peter at the High Priest's House: A Test Case for the Question of the Relation between Mark's and John's Gospels', *NTS* 24 [1977–78], p. 382) and D.M. Smith ('John and the Synoptics: Some Dimensions of the Problem', *NTS* 26 [1979–80], p. 426) speak of 'Perrin's school' or a 'Perrin school' of Markan redaction criticism.

15. He deems the framing chapters by Kelber and Donahue to be 'important methodological essays' exemplifying in Markan studies 'the self-conscious movement from the narrower redaction criticism to the broader literary criticism which has taken place in America' (Perrin, 'The Interpretation of the Gospel of Mark', *Int* 30 [1976], p. 121).

16. Perrin, 'The Interpretation of the Gospel of Mark', p. 123.

'the whole problem of the formation of christological traditions in the early church', an investigation recounted in the autobiographical *A Modern Pilgrimage* from its beginning in the synoptic tradition to its conclusion in the Gospel of Mark.

In *Kingdom of God* (p. 158) Perrin seeks answers to three questions: '(i) is Kingdom of God an apocalyptic concept in the teaching of Jesus? (ii) is the Kingdom present or future or both in that teaching? and, (iii) what is the relationship between eschatology and ethics in Jesus' teaching?' First, Jesus uses Kingdom of God as an apocalyptic concept in sayings that: (1) proclaim that God's decisive intervention into history and human experience is at hand (Mk 1.15; Mt. 10.7; Lk. 10.9-11); (2) claim Holy War victory over Satan through exorcisms (Mt. 12.28/ Lk. 11.20); (3) explicitly discredit apocalyptic sign-seeking (Lk. 17.20-21); and, (4) speak of the final state of those redeemed by God's intervention (the Beatitudes and sayings about entering and receiving the Kingdom). Secondly, Jesus teaches that the Kingdom is both present and future: present in his interpretation of exorcisms, proclamation of the fulfilment of messianic prophecy, and offering of 'the eschatological forgiveness of sins' (p. 186); future in his expectation of a future consummation in terms of 'judgement, the vindication of Jesus himself, the establishment of the values of God, and the enjoyment of all the blessings to be associated with a perfect relationship with God' (p. 199). The Lord's Prayer clearly manifests this present–future tension characteristic of Jesus' Kingdom of God teaching. Thirdly, Jesus' ethical teaching is eschatological as it assumes a proclamation–response pattern to illustrate the kind of response that enables an individual to enter into the new and perfect relationship with God, which is the ultimate aim of God's intervention into history and human experience.

In a pair of articles published prior to *Rediscovering the Teaching of Jesus*, Perrin draws preliminary conclusions concerning the significance of the historical Jesus for the New Testament evangelists and for contemporary faith. In 'Faith, Fact and History' Perrin[17] advocates the Bultmannian discontinuity between Proclaimer and Proclaimed: 'The evangelists have no interest whatsoever in the factuality of that which they are recording' for 'it does not matter to them in the slightest degree that their presentation of the teaching of Jesus is very different from

17. *Christian Advocate* (Dec. 20, 1962), p. 8. In his *The Promise of Bultmann* (Philadelphia: J.B. Lippincott, 1969), p. 13, Perrin praises this scholar as 'the climax and period of the tradition in which he stands'.

what Jesus had actually said in Galilee and Judea'. However, while Bultmann concluded that the kerygmatic Christ is the sole and proper object for faith, in 'The Wredestrasse Becomes the Hauptstrasse' Perrin[18] admits uncertainty as to 'how we shall ultimately be able to define the true "object" of Christian faith'. In fact, Perrin[19] concludes with J.M. Robinson that knowledge of the historical Jesus may be employed 'to give consent to, to correct, or to interpret our knowledge and understanding of the Lord we experience and proclaim'.

Working under the methodological mottos 'When in doubt, discard' and 'The burden of proof always lies on the claim to authenticity', Perrin opens *Rediscovering the Teaching of Jesus* (pp. 11-12) by proposing a rigorous methodology for reconstructing the teaching of Jesus. Citing the work of such form critics as Haenchen, Käsemann, and Jeremias, Perrin asserts that

> The early church made no attempt to distinguish between the words the earthly Jesus had spoken and those spoken by the risen Lord through a prophet in the community, nor between the original teaching of Jesus and the new understanding and reformulation of that teaching in the catechesis or parenesis of the Church under the guidance of the Lord of the Church (p. 15).

Therefore, the first step of reconstruction must be 'to write a history of the tradition of which a given saying is a part' (p. 32). Thus attained, the earliest form of a saying must be tested by various 'criteria for authenticity'[20] beginning with the foundational *criterion of dissimilarity* which requires that a logion be 'dissimilar to characteristic emphases both of ancient Judaism and of the early church' (p. 39). Next, by implementation of the *criterion of coherence*, 'material from the earliest strata of the tradition may be accepted as authentic if it can be shown to cohere with material established as authentic by means of the criterion of dissimilarity' (p. 43). Finally, according to the *criterion of multiple attestation*, 'a motif which can be detected in a multiplicity of strands of tradition and in various forms' may be declared authentic provided it too passes the fundamental criterion of dissimilarity (p. 46).

18. *JR* 46 (1966), p. 300.

19. Robinson was visiting professor at Göttingen when Perrin was a student there, and he provided 'detailed comments' upon Perrin's dissertation as it was being prepared for publication (*Kingdom of God*, p. 11).

20. For Perrin, 'authentic' means 'going back to Jesus himself'. He credits Bultmann with the invention of the criteria.

Perrin employs this method throughout the remainder of *Rediscovering the Teaching of Jesus* in an effort to produce an 'irreducible minimum of historical knowledge' (p. 12) of Jesus and to estimate its significance for faith. Surviving the tests for authenticity are three 'Kingdom sayings' (Lk. 11.20/Mt. 12.28; Lk. 17.20-21; Mt. 11.12), numerous proverbs and parables, the Lord's Prayer, and the 'acted parable' (p. 102) of Jesus' table fellowship with tax collectors and sinners. Three aspects of Jesus' teaching are substantiated by these traditions: (1) his proclamation of the Kingdom of God; (2) his call for a response in terms of radical single-mindedness, self-denial, and the return of goodness for evil; and, (3) his clear hope for the future consummation of the Kingdom.[21] This historical knowledge of Jesus is significant for faith in several ways. First, it can provide content for the formation of a 'faith-image' of Jesus even though the main source 'will always be the proclamation of the church, a proclamation arising out of a Christian experience of the risen Lord' (p. 244). Secondly, when the believer is faced with varying or contradictory forms of proclamation purporting to be Christian, 'historical knowledge of Jesus validates the Christian kerygma; it does not validate it as kerygma: but it validates it as Christian'. Finally, because of the early Christian equation 'situation in earthly ministry of Jesus = situation in early Church's experience', historical knowledge of Jesus may be used as instruction for believers in any age (p. 248).

In the articles which constitute the first half of *A Modern Pilgrimage*, Perrin sets forth two theses regarding christological origins in support of his conclusion that the apocalyptic Son of man sayings are products of the Church. The first thesis, based on Mk 14.62, proposes that 'the use of Son of man in the New Testament begins in the interpretation of the resurrection of Jesus by Christians in terms of Old Testament texts, specifically Dan 7:13; Ps 110:1; Zech 12:10ff' (p. 5). With word-play as a key developmental feature, early Christian *pesharim*[22] took shape in a four-step procedure:

21. Perrin again denies the authenticity of logia predicting the *timing* of the End (pp. 199-202); but, in a departure from *Kingdom of God*, he declares the apocalyptic Son of man sayings to be products of early Christian theological reflection.

22. Perrin acknowledges that his understanding of early Christian *pesharim* is heavily influenced by B. Lindars's *New Testament Apologetic* (Philadelphia: Westminster Press, 1961), exclaiming that this book 'hit me with what can only be described as the force of a bomb' (p. 4).

1. There is a point of origin in Christian experience or expectation.
2. This experience or expectation is then interpreted in terms of Old Testament passages as in the Qumran *pesharim*. This is the Christian pesher.
3. The Christian pesher can then be historicized, that is, a narrative can be formed from it or it can be read back into the teaching of Jesus.
4. The pesher itself, or its historicization, can then become the basis for further theologizing (pp. 10-11).

Grounded in a study of apocalyptic texts, the second thesis holds that 'with regard to "Son of Man" in ancient Judaism and primitive Christianity...there is no "Son of Man concept" but rather a variety of uses of Son of Man imagery' (p. 26). In ancient Judaism, *1 Enoch* combines the imagery of Daniel 7 and Ezekiel 1 to interpret the translation of Enoch, while *4 Ezra* 13 uses Daniel 7 independently in an apocalyptic midrash on *Psalms of Solomon* 17 to describe the coming of the Messiah. Likewise, early Christianity independently employs Dan. 7.13 as the basis of three exegetical traditions: (1) an exaltation tradition interpreting Jesus' resurrection (as *1 Enoch* used Dan. 7.13 to interpret the translation of Enoch); (2) a passion apologetic interpreting Jesus' crucifixion; and (3) a 'full-blooded apocalyptic use' (p. 35) interpreting the parousia hope. Because 'Christology begins with the interpretation of the resurrection as Jesus' exaltation to the right hand of God as Son of Man' (p. 36), all apocalyptic Son of man sayings[23] are products of the Church. At the fountainhead of these sayings is early Christian apocalyptic speculation based on Ps. 110.1: because Ps. 110.1 includes a promise of ultimate victory making the heavenly residence temporary, 'The exegesis of the verse itself produces the *mar*-Christology and the expectation expressed in *maranatha*' (p. 59). The apocalyptic Son of man expectation, then, was the particular form of *maranatha* ('Our Lord, come!') hope produced when Zech. 12.10-14 and Dan. 7.13 were combined with Ps. 110.1 in early Christian reflection.

Next, recognizing that 'the evangelist Mark is the major figure in the creative use of the Son of Man traditions in the New Testament period' (p. 77), Perrin gives special attention in *A Modern Pilgrimage* to the

---

23. These sayings indude: (1) 'sayings reflecting Dan. 7.13' (Mk 13.26; 14.62); (2) 'judgment sayings' (Lk. 12.8-9 par.; Mk 8.38); and (3) 'comparison sayings' (Lk. 17.24 par.; 17.26-27; 17.28-30 par.; 11.30 par.).

Markan passion predictions and the thrust of Mark's christological lesson. The suffering Son of man sayings, found only in Mark and parallels dependent upon Mark, are Markan creations—but not *ex nihilo*. Behind them stands a long, complex history of early Christian reflection upon the passion, reflection carried out because of: (1) the need to come to terms with the crucifixion of the Messiah; (2) the desire to offer apologetic against Judaism at this point; and (3) the later development of the soteriological significance of the cross for faith (p. 75). Prediction, misunderstanding, and discipleship teaching are the ingredients of the thrice-repeated cycle of Mark's central unit 8.27–10.45. In each passion prediction Jesus teaches true Christology, while the misunderstanding of the disciples embodies false Christology, and Jesus' corrective teaching on discipleship expresses Mark's application of his christological message. In essence, Mark creatively employs the passion predictions[24] to issue the christological and ecclesiological challenge that 'necessary suffering' was 'the way to the salvation of mankind when accepted by Jesus' and remains 'the way to glory for the believer when accepted by him' (p. 93). Moreover, in the overall structure of his Gospel, Mark uses the juxtaposition of messianic titles to teach his christological lesson. After establishing rapport with his readers by introducing Jesus as Christ and Son of God in 1.1 and 1.11, Mark injects the secrecy motif into a traditional miracle cycle to downplay *theios anēr* Christology. Then, through his careful composition of 8.27–10.45, Mark presents 'his own passion-oriented Christology, using Son of Man, and then drawing out its consequences for Christian discipleship' (p. 111). Climactically, at 14.62 Jesus discloses the messianic secret; and at 15.39 the centurion gives a properly informed confession of Jesus as Son of God—suffering messiahship has run its course, Mark's christological lesson is finished.

As *A Modern Pilgrimage* closes, Perrin uses his study of Mark as a vantage point from which to observe the function of Son of man in John. The Johannine Son of man sayings are distinct in that they express 'the Christology of Christ as the descending–ascending heavenly redeemer' developed from the Christology of the hymns at Phil. 2.6-11; 1 Tim. 3.16; and 1 Pet. 3.18-22 (pp. 125-26). In fact, this is the Christology of the whole Gospel (1.1-11; the 'Son [of God]' sayings; cf. 5.25-27 where Son of man and Son of God appear interchangeable).

---

24. By Perrin's analysis, the Markan passion predictions represent an 'apologetic' *(para)didonai* ('to hand over') tradition in the New Testament while Mk 10.45 exemplifies a distinct 'soteriological' use (pp. 94-103).

Surprisingly, however, the Johannine Son of man sayings offer points of comparison with their synoptic counterparts, especially Mk 2.10 and 14.62. Mark 2.10 exemplifies the uniquely Markan ascription of *exousia* ('authority') to the Son of man: Jn 5.27 also imputes *exousia* to the Son of man. Moreover, Mk 14.62 is 'distinctively Markan rather than traditional', and Jn 1.51 'looks extraordinarily like...a translation of Mk 14.62 into a Johannine idiom' (p. 128). In a dramatic break from his earlier view, Perrin concludes that these Markan–Johannine connections 'seem to me to indicate Johannine knowledge of the Gospel of Mark'.

Redaction Criticism and Markan Study (1969–76)

'The Wredestrasse has become the Hauptstrasse, and it is leading us to new and exciting country.' With these enthusiastic words Perrin[25] heralded the advent of redaction criticism and its revolutionary implications for understanding the Gospels. In *What is Redaction Criticism?*,[26] his 1970 exposition of the discipline, Perrin began to equip himself methodologically for his undertaking of Markan study in the 1970s. Then, in a 1971 essay originally intended for release as his next book,[27] Perrin applied his developed, eclectic, critical approach[28] in a thorough-going effort to move 'Towards an Interpretation of the Gospel of Mark';[29] compare his treatment of Mark in *The New Testament: An Introduction* and *The Resurrection according to Matthew, Mark and Luke*.[30] Working closely with Perrin at this stage were Edwards (redaction criticism) and Donahue and Kelber (Markan study).

In *What is Redaction Criticism?* Perrin defines the discipline, defends its validity, and assesses its impact. Redaction criticism is the study of

> the theological motivation of an author as this is revealed in the collection, arrangement, editing, and modification of traditional material, and in the composition of new material or the creation of new forms within the traditions of early Christianity (p. 1).

Redaction criticism, then, can be conducted wherever the employment

---

25. 'Wredestrasse', pp. 297-98.

26. Philadelphia: Fortress Press, 1970.

27. *A Modern Pilgrimage*, p. 116.

28. A blend of redaction criticism, literary criticism, and the search for a literary model (*A Modern Pilgrimage*, pp. 104-108).

29. In Betz, *Christology and a Modern Pilgrimage*, pp. 1-78.

30. Philadelphia: Fortress Press, 1977.

of traditional material can be detected or the special creative activity of the author can be identified. In each pericope, redaction criticism carefully studies first the constituent phrases to discern the evangelist's redactional and compositional contributions to the narrative, and then the setting in the Gospel framework to determine the evangelist's theological purpose for the narrative. In fact, 'the way that redaction criticism is able to make sense of the phenomena demonstrably present in the text is itself a validation of the methodology' (p. 40). Through the work of scholars such as Marxsen, redaction criticism has progressed from the discovery of the theological concerns of the evangelist to the description of the historical situation that produced those concerns. Thus redaction criticism may 'ultimately produce a theological history of earliest Christianity such as it has not yet been possible to write' (p. 39). Since redaction criticism demands recognition that the Gospels offer first-hand information on early Christian theology rather than on the historical Jesus, Life of Jesus research must be undertaken much more cautiously. Moreover, redaction criticism challenges the validity of Life of Jesus theology because it disputes the presupposition that the historical Jesus is 'the locus of revelation and the central concern of Christian faith' (p. 68). Finally, redaction criticism has shown that in the Gospel form Mark created, as in the gospel traditions individually, both the early Christian experience of the risen Lord in their present and the hope for his coming in their future are expressed in stories of the past ministry of Jesus.[31]

Perrin's student Richard Edwards makes an important contribution in *The Sign of Jonah*[32] and *A Theology of Q*[33] by applying redaction criticism to the synoptics, and especially to Q, to ascertain its distinctive theology. Treating the evangelists as 'creative editors',[34] Edwards discerns their theological stance by applying 'emendation analysis', a study of the changes an evangelist makes in a traditional unit, and 'compositional analysis', an examination of the structure or composition of the

---

31. Perrin supports this opinion with a summary of his own redaction-critical investigation of the Son of man sayings in Mark (pp. 77-78), as he does also in his article 'The Literary *Gattung* "Gospel"—Some Observations' (*ExpTim* 82 [1970], pp. 4-7) where he argues that Matthew, Luke, and John were not 'completely true' to the Gospel genre as Mark created it (p. 7).

32. London: SCM Press, 1971.

33. Philadelphia: Fortress Press, 1976.

34. *Sign of Jonah*, p. 20. For support of this view, Edwards cites Perrin's *Rediscovering the Teaching of Jesus*, chapter 1, pp. 15-53.

Gospel as a whole.[35] But redaction criticism of Q must begin with a concentration on the forms employed in its sayings and proceed with an investigation of the themes and emphases present in the forms. Then, by using the 'criterion of dissimilarity' the redaction critic can recognize the distinctive theology of the Q community, the dominant features of which are eschatology, prophecy, and wisdom. The most striking aspect of Q eschatology is the expectation of Jesus' immediate return as Son of man. In fact, Q offers no cosmic apocalyptic expectations as does Mark 13; rather, Q eschatology is marked by careful practical assessment of those actions required of believers in the brief present. Also, Q community members clearly view themselves as prophets who not only participate in prophetic activity under the inspiration of Jesus but who also would likely follow Jesus to the classic prophetic fate of suffering and death. Finally, as 'the source of true wisdom' which will enable the believer 'to survive the judgement when he returns, the members of this community have collected the saying of the judge as a guide for living in these last days'.[36]

In 'Towards an Interpretation of the Gospel of Mark', his most comprehensive treatment of the Gospel, Perrin offers a careful consideration of the structure and purpose of Mark, with particular reference to the relationship between the passion and the parousia. Besides the careful structuring of 8.27–10.45, Mark uses several structural devices to divide his overall work into sense units: (1) geographical references with vital theological and transitional significance; (2) summary statements that are 'essentially transitional in nature rather than simply either beginning or ending a section';[37] (3) two sight-giving stories (8.22-26; 10.46-52) which frame and interpret the central unit 8.27–10.45 and, with built-in geographical references, move the plot to Jerusalem for the Passion; and (4) the obvious sense units in 11.1–16.8 with its 'double-barrelled climax' of apocalyptic discourse and passion narrative, each with its own introduction (pp. 3-5). This twin climax suggests a vital relationship between

---

35. Edwards cites as 'one of the most impressive examples' of composition analysis of Mark, Perrin's 'recognition of a threefold pattern in Mark 8.27–10.45' (*What is Redaction Criticism?*, pp. 40-63). For an example of Edwards's own redaction-critical work with Mark, see his 'A New Approach to the Gospel of Mark', *LQ* 22 (1970), pp. 330-35.

36. *A Theology of Q*, p. 78.

37. This innovation he credits to V. Robbins, 'The Christology of Mark' (doctoral dissertation, University of Chicago Divinity School, 1969), p. 3.

passion and parousia, a suggestion confirmed by Mark in these ways:
(1) the transfiguration is proleptic of the parousia because 9.1 links it to
the passion prediction at 8.31; (2) the apocalyptic discourse moves from
present suffering to future glory; (3) the key redactional Galilee sayings
refer to the parousia in the event to come 'after my resurrection' (14.28)
and by the announcement at the empty tomb (16.7) as Mark summons
believers to follow the risen Lord to Galilee, the locale of the parousia
(pp. 22-30). The purpose, then, behind Mark's carefully constructed
mimetic narrative is to challenge his readers 'to discipleship in the
context of the prospect of the coming of Jesus as Son of Man' (p. 37).

Two of Perrin's later books include sections developing his analy
sis and interpretation of Mark. *The New Testament: An Introduction*
(p. 144) presents Mark as an 'apocalyptic drama' unfolding in three acts:
(1) John the Baptist 'preaches' (1.7) and is 'delivered up' (1.14); (2) Jesus
'preaches' (1.14) and is 'delivered up' (9.31; 10.33); (3) Christians
'preach' (1.1; 13.10) and are 'delivered up' (13.9-13), after which Jesus
will return as the Son of man. Matthew and Luke, recognizing a 'delay
of the parousia', in effect transformed this Markan apocalypse into a
'foundation myth' for the early Church (p. 164). *Resurrection* (p. 25)
argues that Mark is interested in the resurrection only as a prelude to
something else: first, Jesus' immediate state after the resurrection symbolized by the transfiguration story depicting him proleptically 'in heaven
with Moses and Elijah awaiting the moment of his return to earth as Son
of Man'; and secondly, the parousia itself, which Mark expects imminently. The 'totality of discipleship failure', denoted by the action of the
women in 16.8, 'reinforces the contention that there never were any
resurrection appearance stories in the gospel' (p. 31).

With books based on their dissertations under Perrin, Donahue and
Kelber undertake redaction-critical analysis of Mark. Donahue argues in
Are You the Christ?[38] that Mark created the trial narrative (14.53-65)
out of available traditions: (1) the structure of the pericope is dominated
by the Markan literary-theological device of 'intercalation' which here
juxtaposes the disciples' activity with Jesus' words and deeds; (2) Mark's
'insertion' technique also appears in order to stress the significance of
the temple saying at 14.58 by interjecting it between two repetitious
references to false witnesses; and (3) in the High Priest's question and
Jesus' response (14.61-62), Mark carefully groups christological titles in

---

38. SBLDS, 10; Missoula, MT: SBL, 1973.

an exchange that unveils the 'messianic secret', climaxes Mark's christological lesson, and points toward the exaltation and parousia.[39] Because the reasoning for the condemnation of Jesus (14.63-64) discredits the historicity of the trial narrative, Mark has apparently chosen the 'trial form' for a theological purpose: to encourage with the example of Jesus a community actually facing such trials (13.9-13 mentions them explicitly) and to offer them hope of vindication grounded in the exaltation and imminently expected parousia of the Son of man. In *The Kingdom in Mark*, Kelber[40] reconstructs the historical situation of Markan Christianity, a post-70 community traumatized by the destruction of the Jerusalem temple. Mark proclaims the realization of the Kingdom in Galilee (1.14-15) through his literary 'prologue to the parousia' (p. 143): (1) the 'mystery of the Kingdom' (4.1-34) is its marvellous spread to embrace as 'Galilee' both Jewish and Gentile Christians north of Jerusalem (4.35–8.21); (2) as Jesus taught (8.22–10.52), the parousia, anticipated by the transfiguration, lies at the end of a 'way' of suffering; and (3) while attacking the Jerusalem church for its 'mistaken realization of eschatology' (p. 84), Mark uses the apocalyptic discourse (p. 13) to preserve and reinstate for his community an imminent parousia hope.

In *Passion in Mark*, four students along with Perrin present redaction-critical essays that offer, according to Kelber, 'a remarkably coherent view of the theology of Mark's Passion Narrative' (p. xvii). For Robbins the Last Supper story (14.12-25), to be appreciated in connection with the feeding stories of chs. 6–8, represents Mark's efforts 'to defuse a view that Jesus' miraculous powers are the basis for belief and to link the Christian meal with Jesus' suffering and death and resurrection into heaven' (p. 21). Kelber, working with 14.32-42, sees Markan three-fold repetition used to stress the disciples' 'recurrent and incorrigible blindness' to the suffering Son of man Christology summarized at Gethsemane (p. 50). Readdressing the trial scene (14.53-65), Donahue stresses Mark's use of 'royal Christology to interpret the trial and death of Jesus as the suffering of the crucified King' (p. 78) who would be revealed as eschatological king at the parousia when he rebuilds the temple by forming the community of the Kingdom. Perrin sets forth a

---

39. Donahue assigns the creation of the apocalyptic Son of man sayings to Mark (*Are You the Christ?*, p. 151).

40. Philadelphia: Fortress Press, 1974. Kelber dedicates this revision of his dissertation to Perrin 'who during the last decade has prepared the ground for a theology of Mark' (p. xi).

dual function[41] for 14.61-62: (1) retrospective, representing the climax of Markan Christology and the disclosure of the messianic secret; and (2) prospective, as it points ahead to the centurion's confession, interprets the crucifixion/resurrection as the enthronement of Jesus, and anticipates his parousia (p. 81). In the story of Peter's denial (14.53-54, 66-72), Dewey discerns a one-stage account characteristically developed with Markan devices of intercalation and threefold repetition to discredit the Christianity Peter represents (p. 97). Summarizing the consensus of the contributors to *Passion in Mark*, Kelber concludes that 'there exists no appreciable difference between Mark 14–16 and what is known about the literary genesis and composition of Mark 1–13' (pp. 157-58).

Through a series of subsequent publications, Donahue and Kelber further their contribution to Markan study.[42] Donahue's 'Jesus as the Parable of God' presents Mark as a metaphorical portrayal of Jesus by means of realistic narrative, using surprise as a key element, and capable of a variety of interpretations because of its 'open-ended' character. In 'Miracle' Donahue explains that Mark preserves miracle stories of Jesus to emphasize the authority of his teaching but subordinates them to the passion to ward off a false 'theology of miracles' represented by the attitude of the disciples. With 'Mark and Oral Tradition' Kelber proposes a radical break from the conventional Bultmannian form-critical view of the nature of Mark's Gospel by arguing from Gospel themes that Markan 'textuality' stands at odds with early Christian 'orality': (1) by accentuating disciple misunderstanding, Mark discredits the disciples as mediators of oral tradition; (2) in ch. 13 Mark repudiates the early Christian prophets who claimed to represent Jesus in their oral proclamation of realized eschatology; and (3) with an ending bereft of appearance stories, Mark stresses the 'absence' of Jesus. Kelber's 'Redaction Criticism' cites the overarching themes of suffering messiahship and discipleship failure, characterizing Mark as 'a masterpiece in irony' and 'a dramatic mystery story' in which paradox borders on absurdity. Finally, in *Mark's Story*

---

41. Perrin ('The Interpretation of the Gospel of Mark', p. 123) credits Dewey with the discovery of this dual function for several key Markan texts.

42. J. Donahue, 'Jesus as the Parable of God in the Gospel of Mark', *Int* 32 (1978), pp. 369-86 and 'Miracle, Mystery and Parable', *The Way* 18 (1978), pp. 252-62. W. Kelber, 'Mark and Oral Tradition', *Semeia* 16 (1979), pp. 7-55; 'Redaction Criticism: On the Nature and Exposition of the Gospels', *Perspectives in Religious Studies* 6 (1979), pp. 4-16; and *Mark's Story of Jesus* (Philadelphia: Fortress Press, 1979).

of Jesus (p. 9) Kelber interprets the Gospel as 'a dramatically plotted journey of Jesus' which climaxes at the cross but leads back to Galilee (14.28; 16.7) where Jesus himself had founded the ecumenical community of the Kingdom. Never comprehending the logic of the itinerary along the way, the disciples tragically abandon Jesus. Their negative role represents Mark's assessment of the Jerusalem church of his day as he seeks to explain its demise and to offer a manifesto for the ongoing mission in Galilee.

Literary Criticism and Hermeneutics (1971–76)

While his work on Mark spanned the seventies, what dominated these last years of Perrin's career was an interplay of literary criticism and hermeneutics applied to the task of interpreting the teaching of Jesus. The literary-critical approach Perrin advanced is both eclectic, borrowing from the proven historical-critical methods of New Testament scholarship, and innovative, exhibiting the features of thorough-going literary analysis. The latter must give new and careful attention to: (1) the question of literary genre; (2) special themes pursued by each author; (3) the structure of the work, on both the surface level and the deeper levels studied by structuralists; (4) distinctive narrative features; (5) internal literary devices; and (6) protagonists and plot.[43] Through all these, literary criticism seeks to determine the distinctive meaning of the author. Recognizing through literary-critical categories that the Kingdom of God, the focal point of Jesus' message, is 'a major biblical symbol', and that the parables, whose ultimate referent is the Kingdom of God, are 'a most distinct literary form', Perrin[44] re-addressed these topics now because 'they present fascinating problems at the level of hermeneutics'.

43. 'Interpretation of the Gospel of Mark', pp. 121-22.

44. *Jesus and the Language of the Kingdom*, p. 1. While *Jesus* represents Perrin's final, comprehensive treatment of these subjects, it incorporates in rewritten form three earlier articles on the Kingdom of God as symbol ('Wisdom and Apocalyptic in the Message of Jesus', *SBLASP* [1972], pp. 543-72; 'Eschatology and Hermeneutics: Reflections on Method in the Interpretation of the New Testament', *JBL* 93 [1974], pp. 3-14; 'The Interpretation of a Biblical Symbol', *JR* 55 [1975], pp. 348-70) and builds upon work begun in three pieces on parable interpretation and hermeneutics ('The Parables of Jesus as Parables, as Metaphors, and as Aesthetic Objects: A Review Article', *JR* 47 [1967], pp. 340-46; 'The Modern Interpretation of the Parables of Jesus and the Problem of Hermeneutics', *Int* 25 [1971], pp. 131-48; 'Historical Criticism').

Two of Perrin's students have carried forward the work of this final stage of his career, Dennis Duling in *Jesus Christ through History*[45] and Mary Ann Tolbert with *Perspectives on the Parables*.[46]

In 'Towards an Introduction of the Gospel of Mark' (pp. 44-45) Perrin proposes that historical criticism and literary criticism, working in essential conjunction, 'can establish the guidelines of the original intent and natural function of the text' and thus indicate 'what is actually inherent in the text itself as distinct from what can be read into that text by the use of an undisciplined imagination'. But, when exegetical methods offer conflicting results, historical criticism 'should exercise normative influence and control' (p. 42). In 'Historical Criticism' (pp. 363-64), however, while admitting that disregard for authorial intent constitutes 'an act of rape on the text', Perrin still would argue that a written text once circulated 'now exists in its own right, essentially independent of the original author and intended reader, and its potentiality for meaning is limited only by the function of its form and its language'. The only difference now between exegesis and eisegesis is that exegesis recognizes literary criticism as its sole control: 'From the standpoint of interpretive theory, an interpretation of a text may go beyond anything the author intended, but it may not do violence to the nature of the text as a text' (p. 370). Interestingly, Perrin proposes a qualitative distinction between the parables and other biblical texts: because the parables of Jesus seem to be 'such intensely personal texts...the vision and intent of the author remain most important hermeneutical considerations'; but since Mark's Gospel, for instance, 'is not so intensely personal...the author's vision of reality is not therefore so important' (pp. 374-75). Finally, in *Jesus and the Language of the Kingdom* Perrin establishes a methodological balance between historical criticism and literary criticism in hermeneutics. Acknowledging that 'the meaning of a text in its historical context' is the criterion for valid hermeneutics, Perrin urges a movement 'beyond historical criticism to a literary criticism' because a clear 'historical understanding' of a text requires proper 'appreciation of the literary form and language of the text' (pp. 5-9). Clearly, Perrin is not actually going 'beyond historical criticism', but is in fact developing and emphasizing the natural role of literary criticism in establishing a 'historical understanding' of the text.[47] Even when he speaks of literary criticism's

---

45. New York: Harcourt Brace Jovanovich, 1979.
46. Philadelphia: Fortress Press, 1979.
47. When defining the task of 'historical criticism' in *Jesus* (p. 4), Perrin includes

'further and very important potential significance' for hermeneutics, Perrin is actually maintaining essential complementarity between literary criticism and historical criticism: as for the '*new* and *valid* possibilities' literary criticism can offer,

> The possibilities are new because they could not be discerned apart from the literary critical considerations; they are valid because they arise out of the nature and natural force of the literary form and language of the text (p. 9).

Perrin employs literary-critical analysis to support the hermeneutical assertion that in the Church today, as in ancient Judaism and the teaching of Jesus, the Kingdom of God is best interpreted as a 'symbol' used 'to evoke a myth'.[48] In ancient Judaism the Kingdom of God was capable of functioning as a 'tensive symbol' with 'a set of meanings that can neither be exhausted nor adequately expressed by any one referent', even though many Jews considered it in the context of apocalyptic hope as a 'steno-symbol' with a 'one to one relationship to that which it represents'. In fact, in the 'kingdom saying' at Lk. 17.20-21, Jesus rejects apocalyptic sign-seeking with its treatment of myth as allegory and symbols as steno-symbols; rather, 'the Kingdom of God *entos hymōn estin*' ('is in your midst') signifies that for Jesus the myth is true myth and the symbol is tensive.[49] Likewise, the petitions of the Lord's Prayer and the eschatological proverbs of Jesus teach of present experience of the Kingdom while the parables actually 'mediated to the hearer an experience of the Kingdom of God'.[50] Whereas Jesus used the Kingdom of God as a tensive symbol to evoke the myth of God acting as king, early Christians employed it as a steno-symbol to evoke the myth of apocalyptic redemption, identifying Jesus as Son of man and inviting calculations of time and sign-seeking, apocalyptic practices which Jesus rejected. Because of this early Christian 'shift toward steno-symbolism',[51] Jesus'

the responsibility of historical criticism to enable understanding of 'the nature of the text itself as a historical and literary artifact'.

48. *Jesus*, p. 5. Perrin accepts P. Wheelwright's definition: 'Myth is to be defined as a complex of stories—some no doubt fact, and some fantasy—which, for various reasons, human beings regard as demonstrations of the inner meaning of the universe and human life' (p. 22). See below for Perrin's adoption of Wheelwright's terms 'tensive symbol' and 'steno-symbol' (p. 30).

49. Perrin, *Jesus*, pp. 45-46.

50. Perrin, *Jesus*, p. 56.

51. Perrin, *Jesus*, pp. 59-60.

'distinctive use' of the Kingdom of God 'was lost until it was recovered by modern scholarship in the twentieth century'.[52] Jesus' use of the Kingdom of God as a tensive symbol means first that he did not mistakenly predict its coming in his day, and secondly that the hermeneutical task for the Church today is 'to explore the manifold ways in which the experience of God can become an existential reality to man'.[53]

Departing from Perrin's view, Duling, in *Jesus Christ through History* (p. 19), portrays Kingdom of God as an 'eschatological myth' which expresses the 'inevitability of death, destruction, and judgement—but also the possibility of new life beyond death, of a new creation'.[54] In continuity with Jewish usage, Jesus proclaimed the eschatological myth of God's rule, celebrating its coming with his disciples in the ritual of the fellowship meal. But he transformed the myth in three ways: (1) by shifting 'the meaning of the *language*', proclaiming the Kingdom's 'coming'; (2) by altering the '*context*', greatly reducing the 'apocalyptic element' (by, for instance, not describing the Kingdom); and (3) by preaching the Kingdom as already *present* in exorcism and healing, demanding total commitment of disciples and thus injecting a predominant ethical element (p. 22). Indeed, concludes Duling,

> One might suggest that for Jesus the mythical reality which speaks of another time is transformed, in thought, language, and the activity of extra-cultic, or 'secular', living into a reality which includes this world and this time (p. 22).

Finally, after rehearsing an extensive survey of modern parable study, Perrin concludes in *Jesus and the Language of the Kingdom* (p. 202) that accurate interpretation of the parables of Jesus depends upon literary-critical recognition of their nature as 'simile' or 'metaphor'. As simile, the parable is illustrative ('the Kingdom of God is *like*...') and 'teases the mind into recognition of new aspects of the reality mediated by the myth of God active as king'. As metaphor, the parable 'contrasts two fundamentally different categories of reality' ('the Kingdom of God *is*...') and 'produces a shock which induces a new vision of world and new possibilities...for the experiencing of that existential reality which the myth mediates'. Because of this 'open-ended' nature, the parables

---

52. 'Interpretation of a Biblical Symbol', p. 362.
53. 'Eschatology and Hermeneutics', p. 13.
54. Duling is following the interpretation of M. Eliade (*Myth and Reality* [New York: Harper & Row Torchbook, 1963], chapter 4).

function like 'tensive symbols' with unlimited potentiality for meaning (p. 134). Thus Perrin claims that

> Parables as parables do not have a 'message'. They tease the mind into ever new perceptions of reality; they startle the imagination; they function like symbols in that they give rise to thought (p. 106).

In *Perspectives on the Parables* Tolbert attempts to deal creatively with the phenomenon of multiple interpretations by proposing a literary-critical 'option for modern scholarship to explore', because 'establishing what a parable meant for Jesus or for the early church, even when that is possible, does not necessarily illuminate what it can mean today' (p. 93). The hermeneutical task is difficult because the biblical texts are ancient and culturally alien, and is urgent because these materials are canonically authoritative. Moreover, parable interpretation is complicated by the fact that capable scholars using similar methods reach different understandings of the message of each parable, understandings which, however, seem to cohere with the 'personal theological or philosophical orientation of the individual interpreter' (p. 24). Tolbert surmises that 'the parable form itself must in some way be open to multiple interpretations' and that 'the diverse interpretations are not all equally valid' (p. 30). In sum, for Tolbert parable interpretation is an 'art' in which the interpreter becomes 'cocreator' of the parable, and it includes three interacting ingredients: 'the parable story itself, the context into which it is placed by the interpreter, and the personal insight, sensitivity, and creativity of the individual interpreter' (p. 126).

Conclusion

With the 'pilgrimage' motif, Perrin[55] symbolized a personal conviction that his scholarly work constituted a carefully methodical progression: 'one thing has led to another'. Therefore, Perrin viewed his resultant approach to New Testament study as an interlocking whole. This approach has garnered plaudits from many, such as the contributors to *Christology and a Modern Pilgrimage*. At the same time, scholars such as E. Best, J.D. Kingsbury, and R.T. Fortna[56] have challenged various

---

55. *A Modern Pilgrimage*, p. 1.

56. See, e.g., E. Best, *Following Jesus: Discipleship in the Gospel of Mark* (JSNTSup, 4; Sheffield: JSOT Press, 1981); J. Kingsbury, 'The "Divine Man" as

aspects of Perrin's approach. Clearly, Perrin's pilgrimage has stimulated significant scholarly discussions of vital issues in New Testament criticism. A verdict as to the enduring value of Perrin's pilgrimage must await the outcome of these discussions.

the Key to Mark's Christology—The End of an Era?', *Int* 45 (1981), pp. 243-57; Fortna, 'Jesus and Peter'.

JSNT 30 (1987), pp. 21-37

GOSPEL CHRISTOLOGY: A STUDY OF METHODOLOGY

Larry Chouinard

Introduction

Christological conclusions based on the synoptic tradition are directly related to the assumptions associated with one's methodology. Throughout the Middle Ages, exegesis was largely an effort to assure that interpretation of Scripture squared with the tradition of the Church. The dominance of Augustinian allegory, and the tendency to strain Scripture through the theology of the Latin Fathers, assured the desired results.[1] With the rise of Renaissance humanism a renewed interest was stirred in the study of antiquity, especially the literature of the Graeco-Roman world. The Renaissance's interest in history produced an historical consciousness and linguistic sensitivity which gave the initial impulse to a critical evaluation of ancient literature. Reacting to the exegetical imagination of medieval interpreters, the new consciousness focused to a large degree on the informational value of ancient texts. The tendency of many thinkers of the Enlightenment was to subject historical sources to the rigid demands of reason apart from the dogma of ecclesiastical authority. The result was a low estimation of the reliability of the biblical text, since its world view seemed so inferior to the contemporary perspective.[2] Driven by an intense 'struggle against the tyranny of dogma',

1.　See B. Smalley, 'The Bible in the Middle Ages', in D. Nineham (ed.) *The Church's Use of the Bible* (London: SPCK, 1963); and also her book, *The Study of the Bible in the Middle Ages* (Oxford: Blackwell, 1952).

2.　For helpful surveys of the period, see W.G. Kümmel, *The New Testament: The History of the Investigation of its Problems* (trans. S.M. Gilmour and H.C. Kee; Nashville and New York: Abingdon Press, 1972); D.C. Duling, *Jesus Christ through History* (New York: Harcourt Brace Jovanovich, 1979), and especially the insightful treatment of H.W. Frei, *The Eclipse of Biblical Narrative: A Study in*

and by a thorough-going rationalism, critics such as Hermann Samuel Reimarus (1694–1768) and H.E.G. Paulus (1761–1851), sought to reconstruct a purely historical conception of the life of Jesus, free from the 'simple-minded supernaturalism' of the first century.[3] As Schweitzer has shown, the agenda initiated by rationalistic concerns largely determined the course of the subsequent quest to recover the historical Jesus. Some fifty years later David Friedrich Strauss (1808–1874) acknowledged his debt to Reimarus, and reconstructed his *Life of Jesus* based on his view of myth and Hegel's idealism. Although subsequent 'lives of Jesus' were fashioned out of the same historical skepticism characterizing Reimarus and Strauss, post-Straussian critics reconstructed the life of Jesus according to their own projected values. While the extreme skepticism of most liberal authors limited their influence, the basic historical questions raised by their studies established the course for scholarly evaluations of the sources for Jesus' life and teachings.

Concurrent with attempts in the nineteenth century to recover the historical Jesus, scholarly investigation sought not only to analyze, but also to evaluate the historical worth of the sources behind the Gospel presentation of Jesus. For many scholars Source Criticism provided an answer to the historical skepticism of earlier research. While it is difficult to date precisely when Markan priority became generally accepted, by the end of the nineteenth century 'scholars were almost unanimously agreed that St. Mark was the earliest of the Gospels'.[4] It was hoped that from Mark's Gospel a fairly reliable picture of Jesus could be reconstructed. However, in the minds of many scholars, William Wrede's work entitled *The Messianic Secret in the Gospels* thoroughly dismissed Mark as a simple historical document. In Bultmann's estimation Wrede established that 'Mark is the work of an author who is steeped in the theology of the early Church, and who ordered and arranged the traditional material that he received in the light of the faith of the early Church'.[5] Wrede

Eighteenth and Nineteenth Century Hermeneutics (New Haven and London: Yale University Press, 1974).

3.   See the survey of A. Schweitzer, *The Quest of the Historical Jesus: A Critical Study of its Progress from Reimarus to Wrede* (New York: Macmillan, 9th printing, 1968), pp. 13-67.

4.   S. Neill, *The Interpretation of the New Testament: 1861–1961* (London: Oxford University Press, 1964), p. 115.

5.   R. Bultmann, *History of the Synoptic Tradition* (trans. J. Marsh; New York: Harper & Row, 1963), p. 6.

marks the shift from the quest for the historical Jesus to the quest for the historical community.

While few scholars of the nineteenth century argued that the biblical narratives were religiously meaningless, the relationship of *meaning to historical factuality* divided biblical scholars.[6] For some, religious significance was intimately connected to the factuality of the events recorded in Scripture. Others entertained the notion that the biblical narratives could be factually erroneous and yet religiously meaningful. Motivated by historical interests, both left- and right-wing exegetes sought to penetrate the biblical sources to measure the accuracy of the biblical world by the real world. The result was that the Gospel narratives were forced to fit either the mythological categories of nineteenth-century liberals, or a strained historical reconstruction of events by conservatives. In either case, the narrative form of the Gospels was *eclipsed* by modern concerns.

Christological investigations were also confined to the historical arena, as scholars sought to reconstruct the historical process whereby christological categories developed in the early Christian communities. The procedure begins by first establishing an 'historical context of meaning',[7] in order to fit the New Testament documents within an historical and cultural context.[8] Once the Gospels are aligned within a precise cultural

6. Frei, *Eclipse*, pp. 118-22.

7. J.D.G. Dunn ('In Defence of Methodology', *ExpTim* 95 [1984], p. 296) insists on the importance of establishing an historical context whereby the language used in the New Testament might be understood. While his approach is valid, in my opinion he claims too much when he assumes that verbal parallels in literature contemporary with the New Testament necessarily provide the meaning intended by the New Testament text. However, Dunn sufficiently demonstrates the exegetical weakness of R.G. Gruenler's critique of his work: see Gruenler, *New Approaches to Jesus and the Gospels* (Grand Rapids: Baker, 1982), especially pp. 88-107; and also the criticisms coming from the D. Guthrie Festschrift, *Christ the Lord* (ed. H.H.Rowden; Leicester: IVP, 1982), and A.T. Hanson, *The Image of the Invisible God* (London: SCM Press, 1982), see chapter 3. However, see the much more substantial critique of Dunn offered by C.R. Holladay, 'New Testament Christology: Some Considerations of Method', *NovT* 25 (1983), pp. 257-78. Dunn's response to Holladay is found in 'Some Clarifications on Issues of Method', *Semeia* 30 (1984), pp. 97-104.

8. The efforts were initially stimulated by W. Bousset, *Kyrios Christos: A History of the Belief in Christ from the Beginnings of Christianity to Irenaeus* (trans. J.E. Steeley; Nashville: Abingdon Press, 1970, 1st German edn, 1913). Bousset's work has been foundational for the study of New Testament Christology throughout this century. However, see the critique by L.W. Hurtado, 'New Testament Christology: A Critique of Bousset's Influence', *TS* 40 (1979), pp. 306-17.

and developmental framework, christological categories are given contemporary significance. As Larry Hurtado points out, 'the lines of influence were almost certainly from non-Christian groups and sources to
Christian ones'.[9] It follows that the content of christological concepts
contained in the Gospel narratives is determined by factors outside the
Gospel narratives. Without disputing the value of establishing the Graeco-
Roman context of early Christianity, we must avoid the assumption that
the meaning of a term or concept in the New Testament can be determined solely on the basis of its occurrence in contemporary literature.
The post-Enlightenment preoccupation with historical and cultural matters has often pushed scholarly research away from a textual referent for
meaning, and has driven a wedge between the person of Jesus and
Christology.

Without doubting the value of excavating the earliest layers of tradition, and reconstructing the hypothetical stages of composition, or the
working of impersonal cultural factors, exegesis must begin with the
realization that the Bible possesses a 'verbal reality'[10] which must be
given priority in the quest for meaning. Contemporary research has
supplemented the concerns of historical criticism with an appreciation of
the rhetorical and literary form of the Gospel narratives. While the
methodology of the two disciplines differs, they are, in the words of John
Crossan, the 'twin axes...upon which biblical criticism will hereafter
unfold'.[11] Using the techniques of literary or narrative criticism, the
Gospel text is restored as the starting point for Christology. An historical,
reconstructed Jesus often bypasses the Gospel narratives as a valid reference point for knowing the figure of Jesus. Historical research seeks a
Jesus removed from the pietistic embellishments of the early Church as
reflected in the Gospel narratives. The historical paradigm organizes its
interpretation of the text, and elucidates christological categories, by

9. L.W. Hurtado, 'The Study of New Testament Christology: Notes for the
Agenda', in *SBLSP* (ed. K.H. Richards; Chico, CA: Scholars Press, 1981), p. 189;
see also H.C. Kee, 'Christology and Ecclesiology: Titles of Christ and Models of
Community', in *SBLSP* (ed. K.H. Richards; Chico, CA: Scholars Press, 1982),
pp. 227-42.

10. The terminology of G.A. Kennedy, *New Testament Interpretation through
Rhetorical Criticism* (Chapel Hill and London: University of North Carolina Press,
1984), p. 159.

11. J.D. Crossan, 'Perspectives and Methods in Contemporary Biblical Criticism',
BR 22 (1977), p. 45.

locating meaning in events outside the text, rather than in the development of thought and structure within the text itself. While historical research is valuable for tracing the lines of congruence or divergence between Christian religious expressions and those of the Graeco-Roman or Jewish traditions, the literary paradigm is logically prior to the historical analysis.[12] The text, in relationship to itself, and understood in its wholeness, must predominate in the exegetical process. Roland M. Frye provides a helpful proposal for future christological research:

> My proposal is that *first* we use the readily available techniques of secular literary-historical criticism for bringing the character of Jesus to life literarily, *then* we compare the figure (or figures) of Jesus emerging from the four Gospels (each with its distinctive presentations and emphases), and *finally* we may be able to better assess the historical figure who lies behind the four characterizations and his relevance to us: we can only get back to the Jesus of history through the Jesus of literature.[13]

Contemporary christological research has largely been stimulated by the effort to establish a conceptual setting for christological meaning. Attempts to describe the rise of early Christology and its subsequent development need to be supplemented with a sensitive appraisal of Gospel narrative as a valid reference point for christological conclusions. The failure to begin with the New Testament text bypasses the most valuable source we have for determining the significance of christological titles and concepts. In this paper I propose to examine the methodology of narrative criticism as a viable supplement to the historical-critical approach to Gospel Christology.

Narrative Christology

In his presidential address at the annual meeting of SBL in 1968, Professor James Muilenburg called attention to 'the perils involved in too exclusive employment of form-critical methods', and particularly 'that there are other features in the literary compositions which lie beyond the province of the *Gattungsforscher*'.[14] He proposed that greater emphasis

12. See the observations by P.R. Keifert, 'Interpretive Paradigms: A Proposal Concerning New Testament Christology', *Semeia* 30 (1984); Crossan, 'Perspectives and Methods', p. 45.

13. R.M. Frye, 'Literary Criticism and Gospel Criticism', *TTod* 36 (1979–80), p. 219.

14. J. Muilenburg, 'Form Criticism and Beyond', *JBL* 88 (1969), pp. 1-18; see

should be given to the nature of Hebrew rhetoric and the structural patterns exhibited in a Hebrew literary composition. Muilenburg labelled such an effort *rhetorical criticism* and largely confined his efforts to the text of the Old Testament. In recent years some of the most insightful writing about the biblical text has come from scholars trained in the field of literature. Robert Alter described a literary analysis as the 'minutely discriminating attention to the artful use of language, to the shifting play of ideas, conventions, tone, sound, imagery, syntax, narrative viewpoint, compositional units, and much else; the kind of disciplined attention, in other words, which through a whole spectrum of critical approaches has illuminated, for example, the poetry of Dante, the plays of Shakespeare, the novels of Tolstoy'.[15] In 1974 Hans Frei of Yale University published a book entitled *The Eclipse of Biblical Narrative*. His thesis was that biblical scholarship in the eighteenth and early-nineteenth centuries sacrificed the meaning attached to the biblical text in their effort to reconstruct the real world events by penetrating the biblical depiction. In Frei's estimation, the preoccupation with historical concerns has blurred the picture of Jesus because it has been assumed that what the Gospels mean can be separated from the way in which that meaning is expressed.[16] Frei's meticulous study highlights the real value of suspending historical questions and other issues until the literary dimension of the text is given full consideration.

In the classic expressions of form criticism meaning shifted from the flow of the biblical narrative to pericopes pre-formed within an anonymous community. In 1939 Martin Dibelius published a book on the life of Jesus, based on what he considered to be the earliest traditional sources.[17] He reaffirms the conclusions of his earlier work (i.e. *From Tradition to Gospel*), that the Gospels were non-literary works, and the evangelists merely framed and combined material that 'was already in circulation in the communities before the composition of the Gospels', which 'consisted of narratives, sayings, and other bits of discourse

also D. Greenwood, 'Rhetorical Criticism and Formgeschichte: Some Methodological Considerations', *JBL* 89 (1970), pp. 418-26.

15. R. Alter, *The Art of Biblical Narrative* (New York: Basic Books, 1981), pp. 12-13.

16. Frei, *Eclipse*, pp. 222ff.

17. *Jesus* (trans. C.B. Hendrick and F.C. Grant; Philadelphia: Westminster Press, 1949).

(including the parables), and the Passion story'.[18] All christological categories are relegated to the post-Easter community wherein meaning is to be found. For Bultmann, the narrative-story actually got in the way of a meaningful encounter with Jesus because it was studded with mythological categories.[19] The result was a 'storyless theology',[20] wherein the text is rewritten (or demythologized) to conform to the presuppositions of a particular school of critics.[21] In the final analysis, Dibelius attributes to the evangelist only 'relatively independent minor adjustments to the traditions, while Bultmann insists that the composition of the Gospels 'involves nothing in principle new, but only completes what was begun in the oral tradition'.[22] What formal literary features he did distinguish are dismissed as only 'ornamental'.[23] It follows that christological meaning can be ascertained only by a study of the *Sitz im Leben* from which the christological perspective arose. Meaning has shifted from the text to a hypothetical historical reconstruction of a Gospel's *Sitz im Leben*. And it was assumed that understanding of a text could be exhausted by tracing its origin, to determine the background of its formal features.[24]

Source- and redaction-critical efforts often resulted in the fragmentation of the text in the effort to separate tradition from redaction.

18. Dibelius, *Jesus*, pp. 16, 21. Cf. M. Dibelius, *From Tradition to Gospel* (trans. B.L. Woolf; London: Ivor Nicholson and Watson, 1934).

19. See R. Bultmann, *Jesus Christ and Mythology* (New York: Scribner's, 1958), esp. pp. 35ff.

20. The words of M.B. Miller, 'Restoring the Story', *Word World* 3 (1983), pp. 284-93.

21. R.M. Frye, 'A Literary Perspective for the Criticism of the Gospels', in D.G. Miller and D.Y. Hadidian (eds.), *Jesus and Man's Hope* (Pittsburgh: Pittsburgh Theological Seminary, 1971), II, p. 197. Frye notes that 'if we play fast and loose with the literary text in order to eliminate or ignore whatever does not accord with stereotyped twentieth-century views, then we have abandoned anything which might legitimately be regarded as literary criticism'. R.C. Tannehill ('Synoptic Pronouncement Stories: Form and Function', *SBLSP* [Chico, CA: Scholars Press, 1980], pp. 51-56), compares the work of Bultmann with current interest in the form and function of the text.

22. Bultmann, *History*, p. 321.

23. Bultmann, *History*, pp. 69-70.

24. See the critique of Bultmann by R.C. Tannehill, *The Sword of his Mouth* (Philadelphia: Fortress Press, 1975), p. 9. It is interesting to compare this approach with earlier linguistic studies which assumed that the meaning of words could be ascertained by tracing their etymology; see J. Barr, *The Semantics of Biblical Language* (Oxford: Oxford University Press, 1961).

Traditional minor forms are considered to be 'incidental to the redaction that revealed the theology of the evangelists'.[25] The redaction critic asks questions of the text in order to ascertain the theological intentions of the evangelist, and the *Sitz im Leben* of his Gospel. A literary critic accepts the text as a given and looks at it from the point of view of the author's or editor's means of expression and how it would be perceived by a contemporary reader. Efforts to separate tradition from redaction often do so at the expense of losing the comprehensive unity of a Gospel composition which embraces all of its parts and particulars. Slight literary and stylistic variations are often attributed to the 'carelessness of popular journalism',[26] or 'editorial fatigue',[27] as the evangelist attempts to integrate his sources into a coherent whole. The literary integrity of his work is established only by a holistic examination, in which all the parts contribute to an appreciation of the finished work. The hypothetical sources employed by the evangelist have been fully integrated into a coherent flow of narrative which exhibits its own internal structure.

The revival of literary concerns has been largely the result of an increasing interest in the rhetorical or literary art of the biblical stories. From the field of literature, and other disciplines concerned with language, new approaches to the biblical text have brought a fresh and imaginative perspective to biblical study. By the use of insights from sophisticated techniques from the field of literature, scholars 'have deemphasized the historical-biographical approach to literature and have turned to a study of the literary form and how it works'.[28] Terminology

25. V.K. Robbins, *Jesus the Teacher: A Socio-Rhetorical Interpretation of Mark* (Philadelphia: Fortress Press, 1984), p. 8; see also the critique by N. Petersen, *Literary Criticism for New Testament Critics* (Philadelphia: Fortress Press, 1978), pp. 17-20; and D.O. Via, *Kerygma and Comedy in the New Testament* (Philadelphia: Fortress Press, 1975), pp. 71-78.

26. H.J. Held, 'Matthew as Interpreter of the Miracle Stories', in *Tradition and Interpretation in Matthew* (Philadelphia: Westminster Press, 1963), p. 167.

27. R.H. Gundry, *Matthew: A Commentary on his Literary and Theological Art* (Grand Rapids: Eerdmans, 1982), p. 10.

28. W.A. Beardslee, *Literary Criticism of the New Testament* (Philadelphia: Fortress Press, 1970), p. 7. K.R.R. Gros Louis ('Some Methodological Considerations', in K.R.R. Gros Louis [ed.], *Literary Interpretations of Biblical Narratives* [Nashville: Abingdon Press, 1982], p. 14) remarks, 'Our approach is essentially ahistorical; the text is taken as received, and the truth of an action or an idea or a motive, for literary criticism, depends on its rightness or appropriateness in context.

such as 'story', 'role of narrator', 'implied reader', 'point of view', 'plot', 'settings' and 'fiction' have now become as commonplace as the historically oriented language of twenty years ago.[29] Within this new conceptual framework christological discussions have been content to recognize that 'the Jesus of history is now available to us only through the Jesus of literature'.[30]

Although a detailed treatment of the methodological procedures for ascertaining Gospel Christology within a literary emphasis of synoptic tradition has yet to be published,[31] various articles and monographs have used literary techniques to elucidate the Gospel portrayal of Jesus.[32] Fundamental to the study of the narrative within a Gospel is the recognition that the Gospels are 'autonomous stories about Jesus'. It follows that 'in narrative study, we cannot legitimately use the other Gospels to "fill out" or "fill in" some unclear passage' in the Gospel we are studying.[33] The study of narrative emphasizes the unity of the text by highlighting the 'connecting threads of purpose and development which bind the story togther'.[34] This contrasts with what has been termed the 'excavative'[35] approach which assaulted the unitary character of the Bible by breaking it up into as many pieces as possible, and attempting to link those pieces to their original life setting. Rather than assuming that the evangelists have 'simply collected traditions, organized them,

Is it true, we ask, not in the real world but within the fictive world that has been created by the narrative?'

29. K. Stendahl ('The Bible as a Classic and the Bible as Holy Scripture', *JBL* 103 [1984], pp. 3-10), documents some of the possible philosophical, literary, and cultural factors that may have contributed to this shift of terminology.

30. R.M. Frye, 'The Jesus of the Gospels: Approaches through Narrative Structure', in *From Faith to Faith: Essays in Honor of Donald G. Miller* (Pittsburgh: Pickwick Press, 1979), p. 75.

31. However, see the collection of essays entitled 'Christology and Exegesis: New Approaches', *Semeia* 30 (1984).

32. Most efforts have been devoted to the study of Mark's text: D. Rhoads and D. Michie, *Mark as Story* (Philadelphia: Fortress Press, 1982); R. Tannehill, 'The Gospel of Mark as Narrative Christology', *Semeia* 16 (1979), pp. 57-93; J.D. Kingsbury, *The Christology of Mark's Gospel* (Philadelphia: Fortress Press, 1983). For further biographical references to studies on Mark, see Rhoads and Michie, *Mark as Story*.

33. Rhoads and Michie, *Mark as Story*, p. 3.

34. Tannehill, 'Narrative Christology', p. 60.

35. The term is used by Alter, *Biblical Narrative*, p. 13; Tannehill ('Synoptic Pronouncement', p. 51) refers to form-critical efforts as 'textual archaeology'.

made connections between them and added summaries', literary critics insist that 'the author has told a story, a dramatic story, with characters whose lives we follow to the various places they travel and through the various events in which they are caught up'.[36] In literary terminology, the 'evangelists' are 'narrators' whose intent is to narrate 'the story with certain loaded words, in a certain order, and with various rhetorical techniques',[37] in order to encourage a certain response from the reader. If one is to appreciate the story told by the narrator, one must abandon 'historical inhibitions' created by modern concerns for facticity and accuracy, and enter into the 'story-world' created by the author.[38] The shift in the conceptual framework by which one approaches the Gospels is noted by John Collins:

> It has become apparent that the biblical stories are not predominantly history but rather fiction, which may incorporate historical data. These fictions are *history-like* in the sense that they represent human experience in its historical condition. They are specific and concrete, not general and abstract. They do not provide absolute truths, but frustrations of human experience. The power of such stories is that we can easily identify with them. For this reason they are more accessible and dynamic than abstract theological formulations. Narrative theology, however, neither provides proof nor furnishes fact. Its value must be constantly validated in our own experience.[39]

Most contemporary christological discussions have neglected to see that the Gospels are narrative whose content is inseparable from their form. By a literary analysis of the text, literary critics have sought to clarify the kind of impact that the Gospels were intended to have on their original

36. D. Rhoads, 'Narrative Criticism and the Gospel of Mark', *JAAR* 50 (1982), p. 413.

37. Rhoads and Michie, *Mark as Story*, p. 39.

38. In the words of Petersen (*Literary Criticism*, pp. 24-39), we must stop seeing the texts as 'windows' through which we see the 'real-world events' of Jesus' day. We commit the 'referential fallacy' when we assume that the world created by the author corresponds precisely to earlier historical events.

39. J.J. Collins, 'The Rediscovery of Biblical Narrative', *Chicago Studies* 21 (1982), pp. 57-58. H. Frei (*The Identity of Jesus Christ* [Philadelphia: Fortress Press, 1967], p. xiv) reminds us that 'we cannot have what they (the Gospels) are about (the "subject matter") without the stories themselves. They are history-like precisely because like history writing and the traditional novel and unlike myths and allegories they literally mean what they say. There is no gap between the representation and what is represented by it.'

readers.[40] The reader's evaluation of the person of Jesus is controlled by the narrator, by having him speak and act, and by noting how others responded to him. Tannehill provides a treatment of the person of Jesus by means of an investigation of the narrative composition of the Gospel of Mark. He lays the groundwork for his investigation by noting:

> In the Gospel of Mark there is little description of the inner states of the story characters. Instead, characterization takes place through the narration of action. We learn who Jesus is through what he says and does in the context of the action of others. Therefore, the study of character (not in the sense of inner qualities but in the sense of defining characteristics as presented in the story) can only be approached through the study of plot.[41]

Within the narrative-story what Jesus *says* does disclose something about himself and his purpose. His conduct is illustrative of his person, and is narrated by the author to elucidate a particular response. Within the narrative the author has developed his Christology in the context of certain role relationships that Jesus sustains to other persons. The narrative development of a Gospel Christology begins to take form when we observe how various people and groups respond to Jesus, and the relationship that Jesus sustains to them.

A significant contribution of the literary approach to Christology involves the treatment of christological titles. Since the days of Bultmann the assumption has prevailed that New Testament Christology involved the study of titles within chronological and geographical categories. As noted by Keck, 'scholars turned New Testament christology into paleontology of christological titles'.[42] Literary critics have insisted that the significance of christological titles must be unfolded within the confines of the developing narrative.[43] The christological investigations of Cullmann, Hahn, Fuller, and even Dunn offer little help in understanding how a narrator meant a title to be understood within the flow of his

40. For discussion on the concept of reader, see R.M. Fowler, 'Who is the Reader of Mark's Gospel', in *SBLSP* (ed. K.H. Richards; Chico, CA: Scholars Press, 1983), pp. 31-53.

41. Tannehill, 'Narrative Christology', p. 58.

42. L.E. Keck, 'Jesus in New Testament Christology', *Australian Biblical Review* 28 (1980), p. 8.

43. See Tannehill, 'Narrative Christology', p. 58; Rhoads and Michie, *Mark as Story*, pp. 104-105. Kingsbury (*Christology of Mark*, p. 53 n. 34) notes that 'it is particularly literary critics who rightly warn against an approach to the christological task with the study of the titles of Jesus'.

narrative.[44] One must also avoid the assumption that an examination of titles within the narrative exhausts the Christology of a Gospel. The preoccupation with titles has often caused a failure to grasp the rich detail of a Gospel's christological presentation. Often at important structural junctures, decisive things are narrated about Jesus without the use of a title. For instance, Matthew's Sermon on the Mount is brimming with christological implications, and yet there are no explicit christological references.[45]

Literary criticism challenges the reader to discover the figure of Jesus by following the literary sense of the narrative itself. This is a decisive improvement over a methodology that brings its own categories and terms to the text. Literary criticism does not concern itself directly with historical questions such as the Gospel's *Sitz im Leben* and traditions a writer may have used. However R. Alter cautions modern critics against taking over some modern literary theory and imposing it upon 'ancient texts that in fact have their own dynamics, their own distinctive conventions and characteristic techniques'.[46] This anachronistic fallacy can be avoided by isolating literary forms and techniques common to the culture from which a New Testament document comes. Vernon Robbins and George Kennedy have analyzed New Testament literary forms in the light of various rhetorical devices in the Graeco-Roman world.[47] Another objection to current literary methods involves the observation that the paradigm shift from 'history' to 'story' may be an over-reaction to the negative results of historical research. It may be that for some, literary concerns function as the last refuge for scholars who still consider the Bible worth their attention. As Stendahl notes, the Bible retains the designation 'classic', but has lost its normative and sacred

44. O. Cullmann, *The Christology of the New Testament* (trans. S.C. Guthrie and C.A.M. Hall; Philadelphia: Westminster Press, 1963); F. Hahn, *The Titles of Jesus in Christology* (trans. H. Knight and G. Ogg; London: Lutterworth, 2nd edn, 1969); R.H. Fuller, *The Foundation of New Testament Christology* (London: Lutterworth, 1966); J.D.G. Dunn, *Christology in the Making* (Philadelphia: Westminster Press, 1980). Since the work of M. Hengel, *Judaism and Hellenism* (trans. J. Bowden; 2 vols.; Philadelphia: Fortress Press, 1974), it is no longer possible to delineate clear lines of cultural distinction between Judaism and Hellenism.

45. R.A. Guelich (*The Sermon on the Mount: A Foundation for Understanding* [Waco, TX: Word Books, 1982], p. 27) asserts 'above all else, the Sermon on the Mount makes a christological statement'.

46. Alter, *Biblical Narrative*, p. 15.

47. Robbins, *Jesus the Teacher*; Kennedy, *New Testament Interpretation*.

dimension.[48] No doubt, philosophical and cultural factors may have contributed to the shift from 'history' to 'story'; but it must be observed that the 'tools' of literary criticism are neutral, and literary critics come from a wide variety of theological approaches; therefore, the methodology does not assume historical conclusions. In addition, it was literary critics who rightly reminded us that in order for the text to be normative there must be the recognition that some readings of the text are not normative.[49] By its very nature, 'the text limits the bounds of acceptable interpretation'.[50] Without the literary method the normative value of the Bible could not be appreciated.

Conclusion: A Paradigm for Synoptic Christology

The domination of christological research by historical concerns has created a tendency to read into the Gospel narratives categories and concerns not inherent within the text. The preoccupation with the cultural and textual relationships of various titles often results in the straining of the Christian understanding and use of a term through the conceptual categories of supposed pre-Christian antecedents. It has been thought that if one can determine the sociological setting from whence a title emerged, the content associated with that title can be read into a Gospel coming from the same cultural environment. Kingsbury rightly objects by pointing out concerning Mark's Gospel that 'any thesis that dictates that the interpretive key to Mark's christology is to be found outside the Second Gospel may be said to be suspect from the outset'.[51] The content of the titles must emerge from the narrative flow of the Gospel, and not by imposing an artificial scheme based on chronological stages linked with geographical localities.

Most form and redaction critics assume that the use of a christological title within the Gospel narrative is the evangelist's (or church's) way of

48. Stendahl, 'The Bible as a Classic', pp. 3-10.
49. W. Booth, 'Preserving the Exemplar' (*Critical Inquiry* 3 [1977], p. 413), raises the question, 'Are we right to rule out at least some readings?' He responds that literary analysis demands that we do. G. Stroup (*The Promise of Narrative Theology: Recovering the Gospel in the Church* [Atlanta: John Knox Press, 1981], pp. 248ff.) shows how Scripture can be authoritative in narrative theology.
50. M. Root, 'Dying He Lives: Biblical Image, Biblical Narrative and the Redemptive Jesus', *Semeia* 30 (1984), pp. 155-69.
51. Kingsbury, *Christology of Mark*, p. 41.

making what is *implicit* within Jesus' ministry an *explicit* expression of christological commitment. However, this conclusion assumes *a priori* that the author intended that every title within his Gospel be read through the eyes of a post-resurrection experience.[52] Such methodology does not take seriously the narrative-story told by the author. Within a narrative-plot, the narrator may want the reader to see a title on more than one level. In order to follow the story, as developed by the narrator, it may be necessary to see the use of a title from the limited perspective of the one who uses it. The assumption that all explicit christological references were the creation of a believing community, pushed back into the earthly ministry of Jesus,[53] overlooks the possibility that the evangelists expect their readers to interpret the titles contextually; for example, when the crowd addresses Jesus as 'Son of David' in Mt. 21.9, certainly the content associated with the title by the crowd differs from the 'evaluative point of view' of the narrator as suggested in Mt. 1.1. When Peter affirms that Jesus is 'the Christ, the Son of the living God' (16.16), his level of perception, within the narrative-plot of the Gospel, is not to be equated with God's evaluation of his Son in 3.17, or Jesus' perception of his Sonship as suggested in 11.25-27. In the words of Kingsbury, the confessions are often 'correct' but 'insufficient'.[54] The author gives content to the titles by narrative scenes that explain in what sense the title has application to Jesus.[55] Only a holistic reading of the text will enable

52. G.M. Styler ('Stages in Christology in the Synoptic Gospels', *NTS* 10 [1963–64], p. 401 n. 1) observes that 'the use of a title establishes that some Christology is intended. But the titles are wide, and admit of varieties of interpretation. The high-sounding title Messiah if intended in an exclusively nationalist and political sense, would yield a comparatively *low* Christology.' One wonders what kind of Christology emerges in the Gospel narratives if the titles were removed.

53. In J.D. Kingsbury's treatment of Matthean Christology he affirms that 'Matthew depicts Jesus throughout his Gospel after the fashion in which his church knows him' (*Matthew: Structure, Christology, Kingdom* [Philadelphia: Fortress Press, 1975], pp. 32-33). It is interesting to note his effort to rebut H. Frankemölle's study on Matthew's Gospel (*Jahwebund und Kirche Christi* [NTAbh, 10; Münster: Aschendorff, 1974]). Frankemölle argues that Matthew operates 'fictionally' with the immediate past in his interest to overshadow the early Jesus by the exalted Lord of the Church. Kingsbury (pp. 37-39) grants a 'high degree of assimilation between the past and present' but denies that Matthew has 'reduced his sense of history to the single point of the present'.

54. Kingsbury, *Christology of Mark*, pp. 97, 102ff.

55. E.g. Peter's confession in 16.16 is put in the proper light by the next scene which depicts Jesus as the Suffering Son (16.21-23).

the reader to arrive at the same 'evaluative point of view' entertained by the narrator.

While the tool of redaction criticism helps the student to see the particular emphasis of the evangelist over against his sources, it must not be assumed that the identification of editorial skills sufficiently details logical concerns. Often the ambition to separate redaction from tradition results in a fragmented text, wherein meaning is sought in the pieces and not in an integrated text. Stein notes that '*Redaktionsgeschichte* seeks not the total theology of the evangelists but primarily their uniqueness in relation to their sources'.[56] For this reason redaction studies are limited in their capacity to appreciate how the evangelist's use of sources contributed to the overall emphasis of his work. Furthermore, an investigation of the theology of an evangelist demands that we first work through his narrative to ascertain his understanding before working with synoptic parallels. The evangelist's redactional activity must be seen as but a single facet in ascertaining the christological emphasis of a given Gospel.

Although the historical level is not the primary emphasis within a literary examination of Gospel Christology, it should not be assumed that the evangelists had no sense of the historical. Ultimately, the *truth* of Christology rests on the integrity of time-place events. Gospel writers did not 'create *ex nihilo*' nor do they do their 'work in a vacuum'.[57] It is amazing how readily many scholars have concluded that the Gospels reflect no interest in historical matters. It is a giant leap from the premise that the Gospels depict historical events differently and lack the precision for detail of a scientific treatise, to the claim that the Gospels have little informative value and merely provide images and stories which will illuminate areas of experience. Without an historical foundation giving rise to the 'story' told by the evangelists, the narrative is open to limitless forms and radically different conclusions. However, Petersen is correct when he observes:

> It is a literary problem to grasp the narrative's world and the events that transpire in it; it is an historical problem to determine the relationship, if any (cf. fairy tales and novels), between the narrative's world and the real-world events to which it may or may not refer. In either case, we must start with the narrative world, lest we lose it by assuming that it refers to

---

56. R.H. Stein, 'What is *Redaktionsgeschichte?*', *JBL* 88 (1969), p. 53.

57. The words of D.A. Hagner, 'Interpreting the Gospels: The Landscape and the Quest', *JETS* 24 (1981), p. 33.

real-world events we know about from other sources than the narrative we are trying to understand.[58]

Hence, a literary study of the text forces the exegete to address the question of 'textual compositeness', before the 'judging (criticizing) of biblical texts in terms of their value as evidence for the real world events to which they refer'.[59] Within this 'literary world' we must recognize that christological concerns transcend the *Sitz im Leben* of the historical Jesus. The narrator uses the time frame of Jesus' ministry to bring his readers into a heightened awareness of the significance of Jesus for their own time frame. Since the evangelist is not merely recording biographical details, his use of history will serve his theological interest. The narrator does see the earthly Jesus in light of the Risen Christ. However, it does not take seriously the story-plot to contend that the evangelist intends his readers to hear the voice of the Risen Lord every time the earthly Jesus speaks. The story takes seriously the time frame of the earthly Jesus and the glorification which is to come. The narration is constructed so as to reveal a continuity between the earthly Jesus and the Risen Christ, but not a total absorption of the one into the other. The story is told from the perspective of a post-Easter commitment, to challenge the readers to adopt a heightened awareness of the significance of Jesus.

Scholarly appraisals of Synoptic Christology have stressed that christological categories conceived by the evangelists were not so much motivated by ontological concerns as by functional concerns, to depict God's activity in Jesus as expressed in his teaching and deeds. Christology is directly related to ecclesiastical and ethical interests. The presentation of the Kerygma in narrative form enabled the evangelists to tie Christology to the practical affairs of everyday life. The Synoptics are not primarily concerned to convince their readers of the validity of applying a particular title to Jesus. The communities of the evangelists already accept and use the titles. The evangelists are concerned to relate the person of Jesus in terms that will attract the readers to identify with Jesus. It is not sufficient to affirm that Jesus is the Son of God without demonstrating how sonship is expressed. In this way Christology moves out of the abstract into the practical. The readers are asked to identify with Jesus

58. N.R. Petersen, 'Point of View in Mark's Narrative', *Semeia* 12 (1978), p. 101.

59. N.R. Petersen, 'Literary Criticism in Biblical Studies', in R.A. Spencer (ed.), *Orientation by Disorientation* (Pittsburgh: Pickwick Press, 1980), p. 41.

and confront situations in the way that he did. However, as Fuller points out: 'Functional christology inevitably raises ontological problems'.[60] The person of Jesus is wrapped up in his words and deeds, and, therefore, ontological questions are never very far beyond functional concerns.[61]

The Christology of a Gospel is not limited to one theme or title. The narrator unfolds his estimation of Jesus as the story unfolds. A christological investigation of the Synoptic Gospels must take seriously the rich and varied avenues through which a writer leads his readers into an awareness of the significance of Jesus.[62]

60. R.H. Fuller and P. Perkins, *Who Is this Christ? Gospel Christology and Contemporary Faith* (Philadelphia: Fortress Press, 1983), p. 9.

61. Styler ('Stages in Christology', pp. 404-406) detects the beginning of ontological concerns in Matthew's Gospel.

62. See now L. Chouinard, 'Changing Paradigms for Interpreting the Gospels: Literary Criticism and Biblical Narrative', *ResQ* 35 (1993), pp. 71-79.

JSNT 16 (1982), pp. 24-44

LITERARY CRITICISM AND THE NEW TESTAMENT CANON

Robert M. Grant

This essay will deal not with the 'religious' reasons for the creation, existence, and recognition of a New Testament canon or, for that matter, an Old Testament one, but with the literary-historical questions which inevitably arose when the limits of the canon were being considered. Some of the questions had to do with usage. Were the books still in use? Had they been used in earlier periods? Such questions are especially prominent in the *Church History* of Eusebius. Others had to do with origins. Had presumed authors really written the books ascribed to them? Friends and foes of various books necessarily turned to the literary criticism already well known in the Graeco-Roman schools and often employed in regard to just such questions about acceptable or non-acceptable literature.

Our purpose is to show first the similarity (not identity) between the 'approved' if not really 'canonical' literature read in the schools and the 'acknowledged' and gradually 'canonized' literature read in the churches (and studied in Christian schools); secondly, the similar criteria used to judge this literature; and thirdly, the identical methods of literary and historical criticism employed in the schools. Obviously the canon was partly shaped by the conclusions of teachers in schools—sometimes bishops, sometimes not.[1]

1. Some problems discussed: my *The Formation of the New Testament* (London: Hutchinson, 1965). Inadequate correlation: my 'Historical Criticism in the Ancient Church', *JR* 25 (1945), pp. 183-96. Need for criticism: A. Gudeman, 'Literary Frauds among the Greeks', in *Classical Studies in Honor of H. Drisler* (New York: Macmillan, 1894), pp. 52-74; *idem*, 'Literary Frauds among the Romans', *TAPA* 25 (1894), pp. 140-64; G. Bardy, 'Faux et fraudes littéraires dans l'antiquité chrétienne', *RHE* 32 (1936), pp. 5-23, 275-302; also F.H. Kettler, 'Funktion und Tragweite der historischen Kritik des Origenes an den Evangelien', *Kairos* 15

Perhaps we can begin *in medias res* by looking at what Josephus has to say about both kinds of literature toward the end of the first century. In his treatise *Contra Apionem* (1.38–42) he describes the content and the criteria for the Old Testament canon. We paraphrase. Our books, the ones which are rightly credited (δικαίως πεπιστευμένα) are only twenty-two in number (and do not include apocalyptic books of the Qumran type); they contain a record of all history (and are thus comparable to the universal histories of some Greeks). There are five books of Moses, thirteen books of the prophets up to the time of Artaxerxes and Esther, and four books with 'hymns to God and precepts for the conduct of human life'. Textual criticism is unnecessary, for there have been no additions, deletions, or alterations. The accepted books end with Esther because, though histories have been written, they do not deserve 'equal credit because there has not been an exact succession of prophets' inspired to write. Obviously Josephus is passing over problems which he prefers not to discuss.

When he speaks of the antiquity of Homer he again leaves out the context. 'Among the Greeks there is no acknowledged (ὁμολογούμενον) writing older than the poetry of Homer' (*Apion* 1.12). This comes out of the discussion of correct Greek among grammarians. The school of Pindarion, cited by Sextus Empiricus (*Adv. Math.* 1.202-208), claimed that ordinary usage and Homer were to be followed; his poetry was approved and most ancient: 'no poem older than his poetry has come down to us'. In reply the Sceptics noted that usage differed from Homer and that 'it is not acknowledged (ὁμολογεῖται) by all that Homer is the most ancient poet; for some say that Hesiod was earlier, as well as Linus, Orpheus, and Musaeus, and very many others'.[2] Homer, though Josephus certainly would not have admitted it, was virtually the Moses of the Greeks.

In 1952 and again in 1965, Roger Pack of the University of Michigan analyzed Greek and Latin literary papyri, in the second edition discussing about three thousand of them.[3] The sheer number of these papyri

(1973), pp. 36-49. Note that some materials are not usable for the second century: E. Gutwenger, 'The Anti-Marcionite Prologues', *TS* 7 (1946), pp. 393-403; A.C. Sundberg, Jr, 'Canon Muratori: A Fourth-Century List', *HTR* 66 (1973), pp. 1-41.

  2.   Cf. R. Pfeiffer, *History of Classical Scholarship* (Oxford: Clarendon Press, 1968), I, pp. 11, 42.

  3.   *The Greek and Latin Literary Texts from Greco-Roman Egypt* (Ann Arbor: University of Michigan Press, 1965).

and their rather random character point to their value as a statistical sample. They come from Hellenistic and Roman Egypt, from the age of the Ptolemies up to and beyond the end of the Roman empire. And they show us that once settled in the Hellenistic age, the reading tradition imposed by schoolmasters continued virtually unchanged to the end. If we limit our investigation to the authors for whom there are more than ten papyrus fragments, we find an overwhelming concentration of evidence for those viewed as somehow 'classical' in antiquity. There are more than twelve hundred such fragments and half of them come from the *Iliad* (487) and the *Odyssey* (138). Two more epic poets are represented, Hesiod from early times (59) and, less important, Apollonius of Rhodes from the third century BCE (15).[4] Archilochus is the only iambic poet to be found (16), while from tragedy come Aeschylus (30), Sophocles (20) and the more popular Euripides (77)—along with many unidentified fragments. Fragments also flourish for comedy, but Aristophanes is the most popular (44), followed at a distance by the third-century Menander (28). The lyric poets too come from ancient times: Pindar (45), Alcaeus (22), Sappho (18), and Bacchylides (11). Finally, the Hellenistic bucolic poet Theocritus meets us thirteen times. Of these poets there are a thousand fragments in all, and only a tenth of them come from the third century BCE poets. All the rest come from older authors, with nearly sixty per cent of the poetic papyri coming from Homer.

There is an equally marked concentration on the older authors when we look at prose writers. From among historians come Thucydides (33), Herodotus (23), and Xenophon (23 historical fragments). Philosophy is represented by Plato (44) and Aristotle (15), rhetoric by Demosthenes (82) and Isocrates (42), along with many anonymous fragments.

In other words, what we see from the sample offered by the papyri is that in Hellenistic and Roman times the dominance of the literature handed down from the fifth and fourth centuries BCE continued, and no new literature was read in the schools (if our cut-off number of ten be fairly reasonable) during this period. The emphasis was on tradition from a remote and 'classical' past.

Beyond this, however, stood the importance of the selection that had been made from among the authors of this literature. Homer was not the only epic poet; he was simply the only one (with Hesiod) whose works were read in the schools. The situation is especially clear as

---

4.   Seventy-nine fragments of unidentified epic verse simply reinforces the emphasis on epic poetry.

regards tragedy and comedy, for which lists of victors in contests at Athens, for example, and Magnesia in Ionia are preserved on stone; local victories, even at Athens, did not mean that one's poems would be read in school. A list of tragic poets with the number of their plays, preserved on a scrap from the late third century BCE, is significant because none of the plays survived, even in fragments.[5] To be listed was not enough. One had to be compared with the great authors of the past. At the Dionysiac festival in Athens in the year 340 the comic actors turned to an 'ancient drama'.[6] A century or so later at Magnesia the winners of the dramatic prizes are singled out as having presented 'new dramas'.[7] The fact that it was worth noting at all is significant. Throughout the Hellenistic age students noted that there were three tragic poets: Aeschylus, Sophocles, Euripides.[8] The names of the approved comic poets emerged later, but in the Roman period only Aristophanes and Menander were generally recognized. The influence of even later schoolmasters accounts for the survival of eleven plays of Aristophanes in manuscript form, none from Menander. The teachers liked the way Aristophanes used Greek.

It should be pointed out, however, that in early Christian times reading was not limited to these eleven plays or to the now extant 'canonical' plays of Aeschylus, Sophocles, and Euripides. We possess complete only seven plays by Aeschylus, another seven by Sophocles, nineteen by Euripides. Apparently ten of Euripides' plays were selected for school reading about CE 200. In early Christian times it is likely that many more witnesses to classical tragedy existed, for the three wrote about three hundred tragedies in all. What seems to have been important in earlier times was the authorship of the plays, not so much particular dramas. Thus philosophical and other critics of literature attack it not by naming books but by naming authors.

The 'canonical' lists that we have are inclusive rather than exclusive. That is to say, they contain the names of more authors than those usually read in a Hellenistic-early Roman school.[9] A better guide for early

---

5.   *P. Tebt.*, p. 695.

6.   *SIG³* 134, p. 1078.

7.   *SIG³* 134.2, p. 1079.

8.   O. Kroehnert, *Canonesne poetarum scriptorum artificum per antiquitatem fuerunt?* (Königsberg: O. Kroehnert, 1897), pp. 24-25.

9.   Cf. H. Rabe, 'Die Listen griechischer Profanschriftsteller', *RhMus* 65 (1910), pp. 339-44.

Christian times may be provided in the writings of such teachers as
Dionysius of Halicarnassus and Quintilian. In his treatise *On imitation*,
Dionysius lists twelve poets, notably Homer, Hesiod, Pindar, the three
tragic poets, and, for comedy, Menander. Prose writers begin with the
historians Herodotus, Thucydides, Philistus, Xenophon, and Theopompus.
Then comes Xenophon again, this time as a philosopher, along with
Plato and Aristotle. Finally there are six orators, including Isocrates and
Demosthenes.[10] Quintilian's comments are more significant. He tells us
that 'the old teachers of grammar'—by which he means the critics of
early Alexandria—not only rejected lines or whole books as not written
by their presumed authors, but drew up lists from which some authors
were completely excluded.[11] In reviewing such a list of Greek authors he
explains that the Hellenistic poet Apollonius of Rhodes 'is not admitted
to the lists drawn up by the teachers of grammar because the critics of
the poets, Aristarchus and Aristophanes, included none of their contemporaries'.[12] The critics whom Quintilian names were two heads of the
Hellenistic library at Alexandria, both of them renowned for their work
in editing and criticizing poetic texts. Apparently both of these scholars
created lists of the best poets and then proceeded to produce editions
and commentaries; or perhaps it was the other way around: editions first,
lists later. Quintilian follows Aristarchus when he mentions 'three writers
of iambics' and presumably does so when he speaks of 'the nine lyric
poets'.[13] Though he prefers these 'canonical' lists, he is quite ready to
admit that anyone could 'if he chose, copy a catalogue of such poets
from some library'.[14] Presumably just because Menander's plays were
so numerous he names six of them as especially admirable for teaching
oratory.[15] Among the orators themselves, he knows of something like a
canon of ten Athenians who flourished in the early fourth century. This
list may just have been settled at the beginning of the second century
CE.[16]

10. H. Usener, *Dionysii Halicarnassensis Librorum de Imitatione reliquiae*
(Bonn: M. Cohen, 1889), pp. 19-30.
11. Quintilian 1.4.3.
12. Quintilian 10.1.54.
13. Quintilian 10.1.59-61.
14. Quintilian 10.1.57.
15. Quintilian 10.1.70.
16. Quintilian 10.1.76; cf. A.E. Douglas, 'Cicero, Quintilian, and the Canon of
Ten Attic Orators', *Mnemosyne* 4.9 (1956), pp. 30-40.

We might suppose that the lists of approved authors had something to do with libraries, but the statement of Quintilian already indicates that non-canonical authors were to be found in them. Indeed, the lists and the library catalogues cannot have been correlated, for the lowest figure for the number of books at Alexandria was a hundred thousand; at Pergamum it was said there were twice as many.[17] An early Alexandrian catalogue (by Callimachus) contained items like this: 'Writers on dinners: Chaerephon; dedicated to Pod'. The book began, 'Since you have often bidden me', and contained 375 lines.[18] Obviously there was nothing canonical about inclusion in a library.

On the other hand, there was a connection between inclusion and the desirability, or presumed desirability, of books. The Hellenistic Jewish author who produced the *Letter of Aristeas to Philocrates* on the origins of the Greek version of the Old Testament obviously wanted this version included in the library at Alexandria. He reports a most unlikely conversation between the first Ptolemy and his Peripatetic book-hunter. The king asked how many books there were, and the reply was that there were over two hundred thousand, with half a million more expected shortly. Could the purchase of books 'on Jewish customs' be justified? The king thought it could, and proceeded to write to the high priest in Jerusalem so that a translation could be arranged.[19] Hence came the Septuagint. As Jerome, himself a translator, noted, the work was no more a miracle than Cicero's translations from Greek. According to the letters supposedly exchanged at the time, the translation was to cover the Pentateuch. This seems to correspond with the reality: the Pentateuch was the first part of the Old Testament to be translated.

At the beginning, obviously enough, no questions of 'canonicity' needed to be raised by anyone. As the Law, the Pentateuch was canonical for Jews; no choices had to be made. It was helpful for some readers to believe that the translators had worked independently and had agreed miraculously. Jerome, who knew something about translating, ridiculed the notion and pointed out that neither Aristeas nor Josephus mentioned it. Unfortunately some early Christians found it attractive. They followed Philo, and their numbers included Irenaeus, Clement of Alexandria, and Pseudo-Justin, who claimed to have visited the ruins of the translators'

17. Cf. F.G. Kenyon and C.H. Roberts, 'Libraries', *OCD* (Oxford: Clarendon Press, 2nd edn, 1970), p. 607.
18. Athenaeus 244A; cf. 585B.
19. Aristeas, *Epistle* 9–11 (Eusebius, *P.E.* 8.2.1-4).

separate cells. Justin himself, while given to odd fancies, did not reflect this one; nor did Tertullian.[20]

As the translation of the Old Testament came to be extended beyond the Pentateuch, various books became attached to the Greek Bible, not all of which had been present in Hebrew and in Palestine. A.C. Sundberg, Jr, has shown that both in Alexandria and in Jerusalem Jews clearly recognized the Law and the Prophets as canonical categories. To these groups they attached an indefinite number of other books, often called the Writings. At the so-called Council of Jamnia toward the end of the first century of our era, the rabbis present decided to accept Ezekiel, Proverbs, the Song of Songs, Ecclesiastes, and Esther; but not Sirach or 'any other books written after his time'. There was a definite theory that after the time of Ezra prophetic inspiration had come to an end. The theory is expressed both in the Babylonian Talmud and by Josephus, and the kind of list one would consequently expect is given by the early Christian writers Melito and Origen.[21]

We seem to have travelled far from the Graeco-Roman books with which we began, and we should now explain some of the ways in which the 'canonical' questions are similar. The place to start is in Quintilian's comment on the Alexandrian teachers of grammar, that is, of philology and literature. The old-time grammarians, he said, rejected lines and books and even omitted some authors (indeed, most authors) from their approved list. What this means is that in the time of the Alexandrian librarians the study of philology was developed. Analysis, primarily logical but sometimes involving the comparison of manuscripts, took place for books and parts of books. There was a search for internal and external consistency. We sometimes think of the grammarians' so-called canon as simply involving matters of aesthetic taste or moral judgment. Certainly these criteria were present. Quintilian explains that even authors of whom he approves are not always suitable for young readers. 'The Greek lyric poets are often licentious', he says.[22] But they were obviously not all-important. What mattered most was a strong critical sense

20. Jerome, *Praef. in Pentateuchum* (*PL* XXVIII, pp. 181-82); Philo, *Vit. Mos.* 2.37; Irenaeus, *Adv. haer.* 3.21.2; Clement, *Strom.* 1.149.2; Ps.-Justin, *Coh.* 13. Different: Justin, *Apol.* 1.31.4; Tertullian, *Apol.* 18.5-8.

21. A.C. Sundberg, Jr, *The Old Testament of the Early Church* (Harvard Theological Studies, 20; Cambridge, MA: Harvard University Press, 1964), p. 114; cf. Eusebius, *H.E.* 4.26.12-14; 6.25.1-2.

22. Quintilian 1.8.6.

expressing itself in *krisis*, judgment. What judgment was able to determine, at least to the satisfaction of the judge, was whether or not works or parts of works belonged to particular authors. For example, Homer had long been credited with many of the poems of the 'epic cycle', in spite of criticisms raised by Herodotus, Aristotle, and others. In the early Roman period the critics won and people hardly ever cited the poems as Homer's. Instead, they used expressions such as 'He who wrote the *Titanomachy*', that is, the anonymous author of the *Titanomachy*. In just this period the study and use of critical methods flourished to such a degree that when one looks at a compendium like that of Diogenes Laertius on philosophy it is really remarkable to find how much discussion there is of who wrote what. Diogenes was no innovator, but he pulled together what earlier pioneers had achieved, including a work on *Men of the Same Name*. Given the confusion often present in the philosophical tradition, this must have been helpful. (Something like it could have been used among early Christians.)

The basic method was literary and it was employed for literary works. Thus scholia tell us that by means of literary criticism one can tell what is similar, what dissimilar, what genuine, what spurious. Sometimes they add examples of spurious works: the *Antigone* ascribed to Sophocles (actually by his son), the epic *Cypriaca* and the *Margites* ascribed to Homer, the *Divinations* and the treatise *On birds* ascribed to Aratus, and the *Aspis* of Hesiod.[23] From the second century of our era we have a couple of examples of the use of the method by the famous physician Galen. In discussing a work of Hippocrates, Galen reports that 'people say that this writing is not his, for there are errors in its grammar'. Galen himself does not accept this as a criterion: 'I personally think that one must not judge or condemn the compositions of ancient and celebrated authors on the basis of diction, but rather in relation to thoughts and ideas'.[24] On the other hand, he was pleased when at Rome he was 'in the Sandalarion, where many of the Roman booksellers are', and 'saw some persons questioning whether a book being sold was mine or by someone else; for it bore the title *Galen physician*'. A bystander with some training in literature looked at it, read the first two lines (aloud),

23. Texts cited by G.B. Pecorella, *Techne Grammatike* (Bologna: Cappell, 1962), p. 71.

24. Galen, *Comm.* 1.2 in *Hippocr. de humor.* (16.65 Kühn); cf. L.O. Bröcker, 'Die Methoden Galens in der literarische Kritik', *RhMus* 40 (1885), pp. 415-38 (433).

and rejected it. 'This diction is not Galen's and the book bears a false title.'[25] The comparative methods involved have not changed much through the centuries. I need refer only to the refinements produced by computer analysis, still based on the common-sense observations indispensable for judgments on authorship.[26]

Among Hellenistic Jews such methods were not often employed, if at all. The desire to praise the Bible clearly stood first. Philo says that there is a marvellous ending for the holy Scriptures (he means the end of the Pentateuch). When Moses was already being taken up, 'the divine spirit fell upon him and he prophesied, with discernment while still alive, the story of his own death and told before the end came how he died...'[27] Josephus too insists that 'he has written of himself in the sacred books that he died'. Neither of these Hellenists was willing to face the problem. Yet rabbis in Palestine urged that it was Joshua who wrote about the death of Moses, not Moses himself. One would think that such a conclusion made more sense. Usually Philo allegorizes, however, when difficulties arise. And the questions about canon that arose at Jamnia were entirely theological. Josephus knows about the Jamnian canon, it would appear. He knows about theories on the transmission of the Homeric poems. But he does not refer to any theories about the biblical authors.[28]

It is therefore all the more significant that when Christians began to discuss the books that were to form parts of their own canon (after the question had first been raised at Jamnia), they maintained a sober concern for historical and literary information. This was the case in what we know of the writings of Papias of Hierapolis in Phrygia, who apparently wrote soon after the beginning of the second century. Papias tells us nothing about the origins of the Gospels according to Luke and John. His statements, as quoted by Eusebius, have to do only with Mark and Matthew. In order to understand them it is necessary to begin with the preface to the Gospel of Luke as it now stands:[29]

25. Galen, *De libris suis* (19.8-9 Kühn; 91–92 Müller).

26. Cf. A.Q. Morton and A.D. Winspear, *It's Greek to the Computer* (Montreal: Harvest House, 1971).

27. *Vit. Mos.* 2.290-91.

28. *Ant.* 4.326; so also regrettably Origen, *Princ.* 4.2.2; *Num. hom.* 26.3; *C. Cels.* 2.54.

29. Cf. H.J. Cadbury, *The Making of Luke–Acts* (New York: Macmillan, 1927); E. Plümacher in *RE* Sup. 13.235-65.

> Inasmuch as many have undertaken to compile a narrative of the things
> which have been accomplished among us, just as they were delivered to
> us by those who from the beginning were eyewitnesses and ministers of
> the word, it seemed good to me also, having followed all things accurately
> for some time past, to write an orderly account for you, most excellent
> Theophilus, that you may know the truth concerning the things of which
> you have been informed (Lk. 1.1-4).

One suspects that Luke views his predecessors, whether many or few,
without enthusiasm. His own informants were eyewitnesses and he proposes to give an account characterized by accuracy, order, and truth.
Look at what Papias says an 'elder' told him about Mark:

> Mark became Peter's interpreter and wrote *accurately* what he remem-
> bered of the things said or done by the Lord, though by no means in
> *order*. For he had not heard the Lord nor followed him, but later, as I said,
> he followed Peter, who used to provide teaching as necessity demanded,
> without making anything like an *ordered arrangement* of the Lord's
> oracles. Therefore Mark made no mistake in thus writing down some
> things as he remembered them. He took care about one thing, to omit
> nothing he had heard and to make no false statements in his record.

From this account one would judge that Papias's elder was acquainted
with the preface to Luke, that he regarded it as referring to Mark, that
he admitted the truth of Luke's accusations as referred to Mark, and
that he thought some defence of Mark was possible.[30] We are entirely in
the realm of literary and historical criticism. Just as Luke had viewed his
own work as a Hellenistic history, so Papias's elder viewed both Mark
and Luke in the same light.

The words of the elder about Matthew are harder to explain, but
clearly while Mark was not an orderly book that of Matthew was.
'Matthew drew up the *logia* in the [or, a] Hebrew dialect, but [or, and]
each person translated them as he was able.' Lots of problems here.
Fortunately they do not make much difference for our purposes. We
could ask whether *logia* are, as usual, 'oracles' or, instead, and as in
Irenaeus, 'words'—specifically the sayings of Jesus. We could ask about
Hebrew or Aramaic. And we could ask whether Papias did or did not
think it a good thing that there were various versions of Matthew in
circulation (or so it would appear; according to Eusebius he told a story
also contained in the Matthew-like *Gospel according to the Hebrews*).[31]

---

30. Eusebius, *H.E.* 3.39.15. On Papias and Luke, *ATR* 25 (1943), p. 218.
31. Eusebius, *H.E.* 3.39.16-17.

Our only point is that though Papias liked oral tradition better than
books, he knew about books and himself wrote down what he 'learned
well and remembered well'.[32] In other words, his situation in his own
time was much like what he thought Mark's had been.

We should note that while Papias certainly believed in miracles, when
he dealt with the books of the Christian Church he made no mention of
inspiration and indeed rather went out of his way to avoid it especially
when discussing Mark. The point will prove important when we come to
Clement of Alexandria, whose very different accounts of Mark supposedly agree with Papias, according to Eusebius.[33]

Between Papias and our next witness, Justin, 'falls the Shadow', the
historical crisis provoked by Marcion. Marcion, who came to Rome from
Pontus perhaps in 137, insisted that the apostles, apart from Paul, wrote
nothing. He did not and could not transmit or invent piquant bits of
biography or literary criticism. But the essence of his treatment of what
he called the *Gospel* and the *Apostle* was literary in nature. It eventuated
in a strictly literary-historical theory about the books used by ordinary
Christians though not by himself. (He never explained where his books
came from.) His own books had been interpolated by protectors of
Judaism from apostolic times onward, and it had been his own burden-
some task to rid his version of the interpolations.[34] The immediate
response of the churches seems to have been to excommunicate him (at
Rome) and otherwise to maintain total silence in the face of such
effrontery.

Within a decade or so, however, the normal philological approach,
combined with increased emphasis on divine inspiration, could be employed; and it was employed at Rome by the apologist Justin Martyr. As
we have said, Justin did not lay emphasis on the inspiration of the
Septuagint version of the Old Testament. He did not need to do so, for
he spoke of the prophets as those through whom the prophetic Spirit
foretold future events, men who collected the prophecies in books which
were then preserved by later kings among the Jews.[35] (This sounds like
an echo of the account in Deuteronomy.) Justin had learned this, he says,
from an old Christian who converted him and taught that the prophets

32. Eusebius, *H.E.* 3.39.3.
33. Eusebius, *H.E.* 2.15.2.
34. A. von Harnack, *Marcion* (TU, 45; Leipzig: Teubner, 2nd ed, 1924), pp.
35-73.
35. Justin, *Apol.* 1.31.1.

were filled by the Spirit.[36] He knew of problems in the Greek Old
Testament text, however. Jewish teachers claimed that the 'virgin' of
Isa. 7.14 was a mistranslation for 'young woman'. They also argued that
at other points the translation was inaccurate and that some passages
had been interpolated by Christians for the sake of their predictive
value.[37] These Jewish teachers thus attacked the Old Testament version
of ordinary Christians just as Marcion was attacking the Gospels and
epistles. In the crossfire all that Christian teachers could do was reiterate
their ideas about how the Gospels originated.

Justin is very definite, but his definite categories emerge only when he
discusses the Eucharist or the exegesis of Psalm 22. At these points
(*Apol.* 1.66–67 and *Dial.* 100–107) he insists upon calling the Gospels
'the *memorabilia* or reminiscences of the apostles'. The term clearly
comes from the title of Xenophon's well-known *Memorabilia* (Greek
Apomnēmoneumata), his reminiscences about Socrates. Whether directly
or not, Justin refers to this work in his own *Second Apology*.[38] The title
implies the presence of eyewitness testimony, though Justin is quite
ready to state that the *memorabilia* were written by the apostles and
their followers—presumably pointing to the apostolic Matthew and John
and the sub-apostolic Mark and Luke.[39] In addition, he explicitly refers
to the *memorabilia* of Peter when he quotes Mk 3.16-17. This implies
that, as we should expect, he knows about the connection between Mark
and Peter.[40] We know that Justin was interested in literary categories,
for just before quoting sayings of Jesus he says that 'his words were
brief and concise, for he was no sophist but his speech was a power of
God'.[41] Once more, though the Gospels may well be inspired, the
emphasis is entirely on their human composition.

According to Eusebius, Justin's some time pupil Tatian 'ventured to
paraphrase some words of the apostle [Paul], as though correcting their
style'. Certainly he was willing, indeed eager, to treat the Gospels like
any other books and in fact as one book, for he created a *Diatessaron*
or compend of the four Gospels which he found in circulation at Rome
or in the East. Beyond that, he produced a book, perhaps after becoming

36. Justin, *Dial.* 7.1.
37. Justin, *Dial.* 68.7; 71.1-2; 72–73.1.
38. *Apol.* 2.11.2-5; cf. Diogenes Laertius 2.48 and 57.
39. *Dial.* 103.8.
40. *Dial.* 106.3 (cf. Clement, *Strom.* 5.82.4).
41. *Apol.* 1.14.5 (cf. 1 Cor. 1.18-24).

a heretic, perhaps not, of *Problems*. In it 'he undertook to set forth what was unclear and hidden in the divine scriptures'.[42] Unfortunately we know nothing about it.

The most vigorous statement about inspiration to be found in the second century comes from Theophilus, bishop of Antioch around 180. In the Septuagint the prophets are sometimes called 'bearers of the Spirit', and the early Christian prophet Hermas extends the term to include his own group.[43] Theophilus uses it when speaking of the prophets, 'men of God... inspired and made wise by God himself', and when referring to 'the holy scriptures and all the bearers of the Spirit, one of whom, John...' with a quotation from the first verse of the Gospel.[44] Why is John a Spirit-bearer? It looks as if Theophilus were treating him as the seer who was 'in the Spirit on the Lord's day' (Rev. 1.10) and the author who recorded the promise that the Holy Spirit would 'teach and remind' of everything that Jesus said (Jn 14.26).[45] Theophilus thus acknowledges the inspiration of both Gospel and Apocalypse and, in addition, their common authorship. He thus anticipates the views which Irenaeus of Lyons was to make more popular.

Irenaeus explicitly attacks the mass of gnostic books in circulation in his time. These writings, he says, are secret and spurious, composed by the Gnostics themselves.[46] Evidently he thinks he can supply criteria for separating the spurious from the genuine; and since he can criticize his opponents for composing, they must have claimed something like antiquity for their documents. When he himself deals with the Gospels of the Church he adds almost nothing to what Papias said, except that Mark wrote after the 'exodus', presumably death as recorded in *1 Clement* (which Irenaeus knew), of Peter and Paul. John was the Lord's disciple who published his Gospel while living at Ephesus in Asia.[47] Irenaeus could argue that there had to be four Gospels because there were four corners of the earth and four principal winds; unfortunately this scheme is what the naturalist Pliny had already called 'a dull-witted system'.[48] It does not seem very cogent to us. Irenaeus is better when he tries to

---

42. Eusebius, *H.E.* 4.29.6; 5.13.8.
43. Hos. 9.7; Zeph. 3.4; *Hermas, Mand.* 11.16.
44. Theophilus, *Ad Autol.* 2.9 and 22.
45. Rev. 12.9 echoed in *Ad Autol.* 2.28; Jn 14.26 echoed in 3.11.
46. Irenaeus, *Adv. haer.* 1.20.1.
47. *Adv. haer.* 3.1.1.
48. *Adv. haer.* 3.11.8; cf. Pliny, *N.H.* 2.119.

prove that Luke the companion of Paul wrote the Acts and relies on the 'we-passages' just as modern scholars have for many years relied on them. Of course the name 'Luke' has to come from 2 Timothy and Colossians.[49] For Irenaeus, John the Lord's disciple wrote both Revelation and the Fourth Gospel. Since Matthew was at least sometimes inspired, we may assume that all the evangelists were inspired; but Irenaeus does not seem to make much of the point.[50]

A very important notice comes from Irenaeus's contemporary Serapion, bishop of Antioch a decade or so after Theophilus. We possess part of a letter 'on the so-called Gospel according to Peter' in which Serapion recounted his problems in regard to this apocryphal document.[51] He begins with appropriate praise of the apostles but adds that 'as men of experience [or even, 'as experts'] we avoid the writings falsely composed in their name, since we know that we [Christians] do not accept such things'. He had paid a visit to a small church near Antioch and when someone brought the Gospel to his attention he did not 'go through it' since he supposed the parishioners were orthodox. He said to them, 'If this is the only thing that seems to produce mean-spiritedness among you, go ahead and read it [in church]'. When he got back to Antioch he was informed about the real problems. He took counsel with learned heretics. He or an assistant went through the book and finally concluded that (a) most of it reflected the correct teaching of the Savior, but that (b) some distortions had been added. He noted these (his notes are lost) for the benefit of the congregation. He was planning to visit them again in the near future. Was he going to discuss this Gospel again? We do not know. In any event, it is obvious that he regarded it as neither fully genuine nor fully spurious but as mixed, containing interpolations. Thanks to his counsellors on heresy, he could tell what they were.

We now pass to another great city, Alexandria, the home of the school, and find Clement well aware of the elaborate discussions of Orphic literature that were current in his day. Practically nothing was written by Orpheus himself; almost all by others, whose names were handed down in the Orphic tradition.[52] This was one of the settings in which Clement thought and wrote. Another was, of course, the mixed situation in which

49. Irenaeus, *Adv. haer.* 3.14.1.

50. *Adv. haer.* 3.16.2; cf. 2.28.2 (all Scriptures spiritual).

51. Eusebius, *H.E.* 6.12.2-6.

52. Clement, *Strom.* 1.131.1-5; O. Kern, *Orphicorum Fragmenta* (Berlin: Weidmann, 1922), Test. 222.

orthodoxy and heresy were disentangling themselves. We are fortunate enough, perhaps, to have three accounts of Mark from Clement's stylus. Since they do not agree, we may be able to see some development—or we could if we knew the sequence of his works. Perhaps we should simply describe his views. Two come from Eusebius and are inconsistent; a third was discovered by Morton Smith at St Saba near Jerusalem.[53] Finally I give them in the order of progressive strangeness, though this criterion is a bit subjective.

The first version is this: 'When Peter was publicly preaching the word at Rome and in the Spirit expressing the gospel, the many who were present called upon Mark, who had followed him for a long time and remembered what had been said, to write his words down. He did so and gave the Gospel to those who asked him. When Peter learned of this he neither forbade it nor encouraged it.' This is roughly the story as given by Papias but it contains two novelties. First, Peter was an inspired preacher, not guided by his circumstances. Secondly, Mark was not inspired at all and Peter made no comment on his book. This is hardly fulsome praise of Mark, and it may be what Clement—who rarely used the book—first wrote.

The second version, according to Eusebius from the same book by Clement, is this: 'The hearers of Peter...with all sorts of encouragement urged Mark, a follower of Peter...to leave them a written memorial of the oral teaching transmitted to them. They did not cease until they persuaded him... The apostle, knowing what had been done...' But wait: just here the whole story changes. 'Knowing by revelation of the Spirit what had been done, was pleased at the zeal of the men and approved the writing for reading in the churches.' If one did not know Eusebius one could not believe that he thought Clement wrote both accounts and in the same book. Conceivably one comes from an epitome, or both.

The third version, presumably from a letter of Clement to a certain Theodore, is not much stranger than what we have already encountered. Clement begins by claiming that his heretical opponents, the Carpocratians, combine true, false, and mixed elements in their comments. Then he goes on to differentiate three Gospels according to Mark. (a) 'During Peter's stay in Rome Mark wrote an account of the Lord's doings, not, however, declaring all of them nor yet hinting at the

53. Eusebius, *H.E.* 6.14.5-7; 2.15.1-2; M. Smith, *Clement of Alexandria and a Secret Gospel of Mark* (Cambridge, MA; Harvard University Press, 1973). I copy his translation (pp. 446-47).

secret ones, but selecting what he thought most useful for increasing the faith of those who were being instructed.' This is not very different from anything we have encountered earlier. (b) 'But when Peter died a martyr, Mark came over to Alexandria, bringing both his own notes and those of Peter, from which he transferred to his former book the things suitable to whatever makes for progress toward knowledge. Thus he composed a more spiritual Gospel for the use of those who were being perfected. Nevertheless, he yet did not divulge the things not to be uttered, nor did he write down the hierophantic teaching of the Lord, but to the stories already written he added yet others and, moreover, brought it certain sayings of which he knew the interpretation would, as a mystagogue, lead the hearers into the innermost sanctuary of that truth hidden by seven veils. Thus, in sum, he prepared matters, neither grudgingly nor incautiously, in my opinion, and, dying, he left his composition to the church in Alexandria, where it even yet is most carefully guarded, being read only to those who are being initiated into the great mysteries.' Since all we know about this book comes from Clement's own account, all we can say about it is that in the *Hypotyposes* he stated that John wrote a spiritual Gospel;[54] presumably, this version of Mark in some ways resembled John. How much is metaphorical in Clement's language about hierophantic teaching, mystagogue, innermost sanctuary, seven veils, and great mysteries remains a question; presumably the language reflects the Alexandrian inner group rather than the Gospel Mark left— criticized as unhelpful without special exegesis. (c) Last of all, the heretic Carpocrates 'so enslaved a certain presbyter of the church in Alexandria that he got from him a copy of the secret Gospel, which he both interpreted according to his blasphemous and carnal doctrine and, moreover, polluted, mixing with the spotless and holy words utterly shameless lies. From this mixture is drawn off the teaching of the Carpocratians.' Since the Carpocratian Gospel is so difficult to deal with, Clement advises his reader to deny the existence of the expanded version of Mark, or at least to deny that it was written by Mark. Clement goes on to discuss whether or not certain passages, questioned by Theodore, are contained in the secret book.

For our purposes the importance of Clement's account of these three versions of Mark lies in the fact that here, most unusually, we are given some kind of explanation of how divergent forms of one Gospel could

54. Eusebius, *H.E.* 6.14.7.

arise. We need not take Clement's account literally, though we are in no position to interpret the origins of two unknown books for ourselves. What seems especially noteworthy is that Mark wrote a spiritual Gospel by taking from his notes 'things suitable to whatever makes for progress toward knowledge'. Even if the knowledge was spiritual, as presumably it was, there is no hint of inspiration in Mark's original text, his revised version, and (naturally) in Carpocrates' interpolations. The discussion takes place on the level of literary composition, just as if Mark were a book like the *Acts of Paul*, according to Tertullian written by a second-century presbyter who confessed that he wrote out of love for the apostle.[55] Elsewhere Clement refers to the *Gospel according to the Egyptians* as not among the four Gospels 'handed down to us', but one wonders who 'we' are.[56]

After Clement's time interest in Mark tended to die down. Synthesis took the place of analysis. Hippolytus added the apparently valueless detail that Mark was 'stump-fingered'.[57] Origen reached the certainly valueless conclusion that Mark wrote 'in accordance with Peter's instructions'.[58] It was a time of synthesis. In Book 3 of his *Church History* Eusebius could write that 'the cause for the writing of Mark's Gospel has been explained above'. By 'above' he referred to a passage in Book 2 where he had said that Clement agreed with Papias. He was to come back to Clement's views in Book 6 and there give yet another account; and to Origen in the same book, without comment.[59] Perhaps 'synthesis' is too lofty a word. 'Juxtaposition' might do as well. Some sort of legend has been created. It is true that certain aspects of the textual history of Mark raise questions like those discussed by Clement, but it seems certain that he knew nothing about them.[60]

Eusebius has something to say about heretical Gospels in the names of the apostles: Peter, Thomas, and Matthias. He says that no ecclesiastical author ever referred to them. (When he himself refers to a phrase from

55. Tertullian, *De baptismo* 17.5.
56. Clement, *Strom.* 3.93.1.
57. Hippolytus, *Ref.* 7.30.1; this reminds us of the details about the lives of the philosophers supplied by Diogenes Laertius. P. Carrington compared it with a local Quebec tradition about the large feet of Bishop Mountain (1942; going back ninety years).
58. Eusebius, *H.E.* 6.25.5.
59. Eusebius, *H.E.* 3.24.14; 2.15.2; 6.14.6; 25.5.
60. Justin may know the interpolated Mk 16.19 (*Dial.* 108.2).

Thomas he does not identify it.[61]) In addition, the 'character of the expression' differs from the apostolic usage (hard to prove!) and the content in idea and intent differs from true orthodoxy.[62] To prove, then, that Gospels should or should not be accepted one must rely on precedent and on literary-theological analysis.

We now turn back to one of the 'great debates' that flourished in the second century and later. This one was precipitated by the rise of the Montanists, a group which expected the descent of the new Jerusalem in reliance on the book of Revelation and regarded its leader as the Paraclete foretold in the Gospel of John. Apparently in Phrygia, the heartland of Montanism, alarmed Christians thought they should jettison the books used by the Montanists rather than reinterpret them. They argued, as their Roman colleague Gaius was to argue a few decades later, that both books ascribed to John were unacceptable, since neither was his. Then they compared the sequence of events (meaning 'order') in John with that found in the Synoptic Gospels; as for the Apocalypse, they must have written more than that its accounts of seven angels and seven trumpets were meaningless and that there was no church in Thyatira for John to address with a letter. We do not know what more they said, however.[63] What Gaius said, in agreement with them, is clear enough. He spoke of the heretic Cerinthus as writing an apocalypse—with the same content as our Revelation—'as if from a great apostle'.[64] The apostle is evidently John. In his early teaching Origen steadfastly rejected such theories, but when he got older he could refer to 'the Apocalypse said to be John's'.[65] This kind of expression means that he shares the doubts of others but is not quite certain about them.

From Dionysius, bishop and former school head at Alexandria, we obtain our most complete picture of the kind of analysis involved.[66] He

---

61. *Paganisme, Judaisme, Christianisme: Influences et affrontements dans le monde antique: Mélanges offerts à Marcel Simon* (Paris: E. de Boccard, 1978), p. 198; cf. *H.E.* 2.13.7.

62. Eusebius, *H.E.* 3.25.7.

63. Epiphanius, *Haer.* 51.3–8; 32–34.

64. Eusebius, *H.E.* 3.28.2.

65. Origen, *De pascha*; O. Guéraud and P. Nautin, *Origene sur la Pâque* (Paris: Beauchesne, 1979), 119.23; cf. R.M. Grant, *Eusebius as Church Historian* (Oxford: Clarendon Press, 1980), p. 141.

66. Eusebius, *H.E.* 7.24–25; cf. F.H. Colson, in *JTS* 25 (1923–24), pp. 365-74. The question was basically that raised by the 'dividers' in regard to *Iliad* and *Odyssey*; cf. J.W. Kohl, *De chorizontibus* (Darmstadt: Benderi, 1917); in *Neue Jahrbücher* 47

refers to some predecessors as rejecting the Apocalypse and refuting it by proving it unrecognized earlier and inconsistent (*asyllogiston*); also bearing a false title. It was not by John, nor a revelation, nor written by an apostle or a saint or a churchman—but by Cerinthus. Obviously Dionysius has Gaius of Rome in mind. He himself yields to majority opinion and refuses to reject the book, preferring to say that he cannot understand it. With Origen, he holds that it cannot be taken literally. Critical questions, however, must be set and answered literally. Dionysius proceeds to use all sorts of conventional school terms for determining the authenticity of books or parts of books. One must rely on usage, the forms of the words, and the general construction of the books. In addition, one must consider the thoughts, words and arrangements used in them. Dionysius therefore undertakes a vocabulary analysis of the Gospel and First Epistle of John as against the Apocalypse. It is not altogether accurate, but in general it seems persuasive. The Greek of the Gospel, too, is quite different from that of the Apocalypse with its barbarisms and errors in grammar.

Obviously Dionysius marks the high water-mark of ante-Nicene grammatical analysis, at least in so far as it has been preserved for us. We should add that this kind of study was exceedingly widespread. Roman Adoptionists spent much time revising and correcting texts and dealing with 'syllogistic' consistencies in documents or the lack of them.[67] Julius Africanus explained to Origen that the story of Susannah, more ridiculous than Greek comic poetry, was clever but recent and forged. Its historical background was not historical and its play on words was based on Greek, not Hebrew. Origen simply denied that Africanus could be right and insisted that the text was canonical.[68] Apparently Irenaeus rejected the Pauline authorship of Hebrews; so did Gaius of Rome.[69] It did not bear the title 'of Paul', and Clement therefore carefully explained that (a) Paul was aware that the Lord was sent to the Hebrews, Paul to the Gentiles; he modestly omitted his name; or (b) Paul was aware that the Hebrews were suspicious of him and wisely omitted it. And (c) Paul wrote in Hebrew but it was translated into Greek by Luke and therefore

(1921), pp. 198-214; M. Fuhrmann, in *RE* 15 A (1967), p. 1540.

67. Eusebius, *H.E.* 5.28.13-19; cf. R. Walzer, *Galen on Jews and Christians* (London: Oxford University Press, 1949), pp. 75-86.

68. M.J. Routh, *Reliquiae Sacrae* (5 vols.; Oxford: Typographeo Academico, 2nd edn, 1846), II, pp. 225-28 and 328.

69. Grant, *The Formation of the New Testament*, p. 154; Eusebius, *H.E.* 6.20.3.

has the same stylistic coloration as the book of Acts.[70] Origen, preaching on Hebrews, put the difficulties more clearly. 'Everyone who is able to discern differences of style' can tell that the Greek of Hebrews is better than Paul's. The thoughts, however, are 'admirable and not inferior to the acknowledged writings of the apostle'. What to conclude? 'The thoughts are the apostle's [surely not the correct conclusion to draw] but the style and composition belong to one who remembered the apostolic teachings and, as it were, made short notes on what his teacher said.' On this basis it could be vaguely allowed that the epistle was Paul's. But Origen insisted that 'who wrote the epistle, God knows what is true'—even though traditions have existed that it was written by either Clement of Rome or Luke.[71] Like other early Christians, Origen treated 2 Peter as questionable and 2–3 John as possibly not genuine.[72]

All this evidence shows that in the formation of the New Testament canon as well as in the history of exegesis, what was taught about literary criticism in schools both pagan and Christian was extremely important. This is not to say that it took the place of theological ideas about content. Origen holds, rather traditionally, that the four Gospels are the 'elements' of the faith of the Church, while the 'first-fruits' of the Gospels is the one according to John. 'No one can catch its meaning unless he [too] reclines on the bosom of Jesus and receives Mary from John to be his own mother'—becoming another John and, indeed, another Jesus.[73] But apart from such theological considerations, pagans and Christians raised the same literary questions and, indeed, about much the same literature. In discussing the so-called *Preaching of Peter* Origen notes that it can be classified as 'genuine or spurious or mixed' (i.e., interpolated).[74] Just so in the school of Plotinus the Neoplatonist scholars denounced the recent gnostic forgeries of the type found at Nag Hammadi. Porphyry himself wrote against the book of Zoroaster to prove that it was spurious, recent, and forged by those who supported the gnostic sect or, should we say, heresy.[75] Pagan and Christian alike relied on literary criticism in an age of forgery.

70. Eusebius, *H.E.* 6.14.2-4.
71. Eusebius, *H.E.* 6.25.11-14.
72. Eusebius, *H.E.* 6.25.8-10.
73. Origen, *Ioh. comm.* 1.4.
74. Origen, *Ioh. comm.* 13.17.
75. Porphyry, *Vit. Plot.* 16.

JSNT 50 (1993), pp. 85-103

CONVERGING IDEOLOGIES:
BERGER AND LUCKMANN AND THE PASTORAL EPISTLES

David Horrell

Introduction

In the last twenty years or so New Testament studies have been
influenced by a wide variety of new interpretative methods, among
which sociological perspectives have been prominent. While a considerable range of social-scientific approaches have been employed, both
sociological and anthropological, the 'sociology of knowledge' has been
of notable influence. In 1975 Nineham suggested that the sociology of
knowledge offered great potential as a 'partner' for theology,[1] and in
1980, reviewing the state of sociological interpretation of the New
Testament, Scroggs stated that 'For some of us...the single most important approach within the field of sociology comes from the sociology of
knowledge'.[2] From this area of sociology the most influential work has
almost certainly been Berger and Luckmann's *The Social Construction
of Reality*, first drawn upon, to my knowledge, by Wayne Meeks, but
employed since in a variety of works.[3] Also influential is *The Social*

1.   D. Nineham, 'A Partner for Cinderella?', in M. Hooker and C. Hickling
(eds.), *What about the New Testament? Essays in Honour of Christopher Evans*
(London: SCM Press, 1975), pp. 143-54.
2.   R. Scroggs, 'The Sociological Interpretation of the New Testament: The
Present State of Research', *NTS* 26 (1980), pp. 164-79 (175). Assessments of the
sociology of knowledge in relation to New Testament study are offered by K. Berger
('Wissensoziologie und Exegese des Neuen Testaments', *Kairos* 19 [1977], pp. 124-
33) and H.E. Remus ('Sociology of Knowledge and the Study of Early Christianity',
SR 11 [1982], pp. 45-56).
3.   P.L. Berger and T. Luckmann, *The Social Construction of Reality*
(Harmondsworth: Penguin Books, 1967). N.B. page numbers are quoted from the

Reality of Religion, authored by Berger alone, which elaborates Berger and Luckmann's theoretical perspectives specifically in relation to religion.[4] The primary aim of this essay is to raise critical questions in relation both to Berger and Luckmann's theory and to the Pastoral Epistles.[5] This dual focus arises from the work of Margaret MacDonald in her book *The Pauline Churches*, which uses Berger and Luckmann's theory as a fundamental resource with which to understand the process of institutionalization.[6] I will suggest that a number of critical issues need to be considered when using Berger and Luckmann's sociological theory and that these issues are particularly crucial in relation to the Pastoral Epistles. It is possible that using Berger and Luckmann as a theoretical perspective with which to interpret the Pastorals results essentially in a confirmation of the ideology of the Pastoral Epistles, and a failure to raise the kind of questions essential to any genuinely critical sociological inquiry.

As Berger and Luckmann comment: 'The term "ideology" has been

Penguin edition which differs from the American original (New York: Doubleday, 1966); W.A. Meeks, 'The Man from Heaven in Johannine Sectarianism', *JBL* 91 (1972), pp. 44-72 (70); P.F. Esler, *Community and Gospel in Luke–Acts: The Social and Political Motivations of Lucan Theology* (SNTSMS, 57; Cambridge: Cambridge University Press, 1987), pp. 16-23; M.Y. MacDonald, *The Pauline Churches: A Socio-Historical Study of Institutionalization in the Pauline and Deutero-Pauline Writings* (SNTSMS, 60; Cambridge: Cambridge University Press, 1988), pp. 10-18.

4. P.L. Berger, *The Social Reality of Religion* (London: Faber & Faber, 1969). For use of sociology of knowledge perspectives drawing on Berger's work, see J.G. Gager, *Kingdom and Community: The Social World of Early Christianity* (Engelwood Cliffs, NJ: Prentice-Hall, 1975), pp. 9-12; H.C. Kee, *Christian Origins in Sociological Perspective* (London: SCM Press, 1980), pp. 23-25, 30-53; G. Theissen, 'Christologie und soziale Erfahrung. Wissenssoziologische Aspekte paulinischer Christologie', in *Studien zur Soziologie des Urchristentums* (WUNT, 19; Tübingen: Mohr [Paul Siebeck], 2nd edn, 1983; 3rd edn, 1988), pp. 318-30.

5. Taking up the arguments of Prior, Murphy O'Connor has recently argued against the assumption that the three 'Pastoral' Epistles constitute a corpus from a common pen. 2 Timothy, he argues, is significantly different. I am not entirely convinced that, given the similarities, the differences cannot as well be accounted for as emanating from the different character of the letters within the small corpus, but their arguments deserve closer attention than is possible here. See M. Prior, *Paul the Letter Writer and the Second Letter to Timothy* (JSNTSup, 23; Sheffield: JSOT Press, 1989), pp. 61-67, 168; J.M. O'Connor, '2 Timothy Contrasted with 1 Timothy and Titus', *RB* 98 (1991), pp. 403-18.

6. MacDonald, *Pauline Churches*, *passim*, esp. pp. 10-18, 235-38.

used in so many different senses that one might despair of using it in any precise manner at all'.[7] Its use in this essay therefore requires some clarification. The word 'ideology', Thompson points out, is used in 'two fundamentally differing ways' in contemporary thought.[8] One is based on what may be termed a 'neutral' conception of the term, and uses 'ideology' as a descriptive term to refer to any system of thought or belief. The second is based on a 'critical' use of the term, and links ideology 'to the process of sustaining asymmetrical relations of power—that is, to the process of maintaining domination'.[9] Following Thompson and Giddens I shall use the term throughout in this critical sense. For Thompson, as for Giddens, 'To study ideology...is to study the ways in which meaning...serves to sustain relations of domination'.[10]

Berger and Luckmann's Project

Berger and Luckmann's project consists of an attempt to understand social reality as a human construction:[11] the reality which people generally take for granted as 'the way things are', is in fact a human product. Every human society represents an enterprise of 'world-building' in which behaviour and interaction are shaped by socially constructed norms giving order and meaning to life.[12] The construction of social worlds is a human attempt to make life meaningful in the face of the ever-present threat of chaos, anomy and death.[13]

7.   Berger and Luckmann, *Social Construction*, p. 228 n. 100.

8.   J.B. Thompson, *Studies in the Theory of Ideology* (Cambridge: Polity Press, 1984), p. 3.

9.   Thompson, *Studies in the Theory of Ideology*, p. 4.

10.   Thompson, *Studies in the Theory of Ideology*, pp. 4, 130-31, 134, 141, 146 (note the general discussion on pp. 126-47). Cf. A. Giddens, *Central Problems in Social Theory* (London: Macmillan, 1979), pp. 6, 191, 193. See further the discussion of modes of ideology in Thompson, *Studies in the Theory of Ideology*, p. 131, and Giddens, *Central Problems*, pp. 193-96.

11.   Cf. Berger and Luckmann, *Social Construction*, p. 13. For the discussion that follows, see now D.G. Horrell, *The Social Ethos of the Corinthian Correspondence: Interests and Ideology from 1 Corinthians to 1 Clement* (SNTW; Edinburgh: T. & T. Clark, 1996), pp. 39-59.

12.   Cf. Berger, *Social Reality*, p. 3; P.L. Berger and S. Pullberg, 'Reification and the Sociological Critique of Consciousness', *New Left Review* 35 (1966), pp. 56-71 (62).

13.   Berger and Luckmann, *Social Construction*, p. 121: 'All societies are

Berger and Luckmann identify three inseparable moments in the dialectical process by which human beings produce society which produces human beings: externalization, objectivation and internalization.[14] In a Feuerbachian sense society is a human projection which is externalized such that it becomes, for each individual, objectified.[15] Thus, 'society confronts man as external, subjectively opaque and coercive facticity'.[16] Through the process of socialization, each individual 'internalizes' this social world, making it their own. This process of internalization is generally unconscious and hidden from critical scrutiny: 'The social world intends, as far as possible, to be taken for granted. Socialization achieves success to the degree that this taken-for granted quality is internalized.'[17]

Every social construction of reality requires legitimation, 'that is, ways by which it can be "explained" and justified'.[18] The most comprehensive level of legitimation is offered by 'symbolic universes', 'bodies of theoretical tradition' that 'encompass the institutional order in a symbolic totality'.[19] These symbolic universes have a definite social significance: 'They are sheltering canopies over the institutional order as well as over individual biography. They also provide the delimitation of social reality; that is, they set the limits of what is relevant in terms of social interaction.'[20] It is on such a level that religion is generally to be understood; as a 'sacred canopy' which legitimates the social order upon which a society is built and as a fundamental provider of meaning.[21]

Such a hasty sketch can hardly do justice to the breadth and value of Berger and Luckmann's work, and the critical questions which follow should be seen as an attempt to refine and redirect the use of their

constructions in the face of chaos'. Cf. Berger, *Social Reality*, pp. 52, 53-80.

14. Berger and Luckmann, *Social Construction*, pp. 78-79, 149; Berger, *Social Reality*, pp. 3-4, 81-85. Cf. also MacDonald, *Pauline Churches*, pp. 10-11.

15. Cf. Berger, *Social Reality*, pp. 89 and 203 n. 20 for his use of the term 'projection' and its derivation from Feuerbach.

16. Berger, *Social Reality*, p. 11.

17. Berger, *Social Reality*, p. 24. Cf. Berger and Luckmann, *Social Construction*, pp. 149-82.

18. Berger and Luckmann, *Social Construction*, p. 79; see further pp. 110-46.

19. Berger and Luckmann, *Social Construction*, p. 113; see further, pp. 113-22.

20. Berger and Luckmann, *Social Construction*, p. 120.

21. The American title of Berger's book on religion (*The Social Reality*) was *The Sacred Canopy*, first published in 1967. See further Berger, *Social Reality*, esp. pp. 26-28, 32-52, 87-101.

theory, and not as a rejection of it. Their development of the idea that 'reality' is socially constructed by human beings is of fundamental importance, although it raises difficult questions for any theology which seeks to speak of objective truth or ultimate reality.[22] Their focus on legitimation, taken up particularly by Esler,[23] is also of profound value: a consideration of the ways in which any ordering of reality is sustained, explained and justified is deeply significant, particularly, I would suggest, when brought more explicitly into connection with the issues raised below.

Critical Concerns

My first concern arises from the extent to which Berger and Luckmann stress the objectivity which the social world attains. While they appreciate the dialectical way in which human beings simultaneously produce and are produced by society,[24] and stress society's humanly constructed nature,[25] their concepts of externalization and objectivation lead to a

22. Berger himself shows considerable interest in these theological questions. See particularly the appendix in *Social Reality*, pp. 179-88 and the remarkable book in which Berger attempts a theological 'reply' to his own sociological perspectives, *A Rumour of Angels* (Harmondsworth: Penguin Books, 1970). The theological interest and implications of Berger's work are discussed by D. Cairns ('The Thought of Peter Berger', *SJT* 27 [1974], pp. 181-97) and R. Gill ('Berger's Plausibility Structures: A Response to Professor Cairns', *SJT* 27 [1974], pp. 198-207). See further R. Gill, *The Social Context of Theology* (London: Mowbray, 1975), pp. 29-34, and *idem*, *Theology and Social Structure* (London: Mowbray, 1977), pp. 16-22.

23. Esler, *Community and Gospel*, pp. 16-23.

24. Berger and Luckmann, *Social Construction*, pp. 78-79, 208-209; Berger, *Social Reality*, pp. 3, 18-19, 189 n. 2. Cf. MacDonald, *Pauline Churches*, pp. 10-11. They share this concern with a number of modern attempts to reformulate the relationship between human action and social structure: see overviews in R. Bhaskar, *The Possibility of Naturalism* (Brighton: Harvester, 1979), pp. 39-47; D. Gregory, 'Human Agency and Human Geography', *Transactions of the Institute of British Geographers* NS 6 (1981), pp. 1-18 (11); A. Pred, 'Social Reproduction and the Time-Geography of Everyday Life', in P. Gould and G. Olsson (eds.), *A Search for Common Ground* (London: Pion, 1982), pp. 157-86 (158-63).

25. Cf. Berger and Luckmann, *Social Construction*, pp. 69-70, 78; Berger, *Social Reality*, pp. 6-9; Berger and Pullberg, 'Reification', p. 62. See further the discussion by B.C. Thomason, *Making Sense of Reification: Alfred Schutz and Constructionist Theory* (London: Macmillan, 1982), pp. 114-61. Alienation, according to Berger, occurs when people 'forget' that they are the producers of their own social world; see

view of the social order as *external* to human activity. Thus, 'An institutional order is experienced as an objective reality'.[26] 'Social structure
is encountered by the individual as an external facticity.'[27] 'Above all
society manifests itself by its coercive power. The final test of its objective reality is its capacity to impose itself upon the reluctance of individuals.'[28] In my opinion, this formulation obscures the extent to which
social order is continually reproduced only in and through the activities
of human subjects, and hence neglects the important relationship between
reproduction and transformation.[29] Berger, for example, illustrates the
social world's objectivity with a reference to language, whose 'rules are
objectively given'.[30] While partially true, quite obviously, one may contrast this emphasis with Giddens's use of the linguistic illustration as an
analogy of social structure: for Giddens, every use of language both
draws upon the rules of that language *and* at the same time reproduces
them.[31] Thus, in every act of reproduction the possibility of transformation is at hand.[32] Language, like society, is not simply objectively

Social Reality, pp. 81-101; Berger and Pullberg, 'Reification', pp. 61, 64.

26. Berger and Luckmann, *Social Construction*, p. 77.

27. Berger and Pullberg, 'Reification', p. 63.

28. Berger, *Social Reality*, p. 11; cf. also pp. 24-25.

29. This concern is at the heart of Giddens's 'structuration theory', probably the
most influential contemporary attempt to theorize adequately the relation between
action and structure in social life. See esp. Giddens, *Central Problems*, and *idem,
The Constitution of Society* (Cambridge: Polity Press, 1984). A number of recent
books are devoted to critical discussion of Giddens's work, including D. Held and
J.B. Thompson (eds.), *Social Theory of Modern Societies: Anthony Giddens and his
Critics* (Cambridge: Cambridge University Press, 1989); J. Clark, C. Modgil and
S. Modgil (eds.), *Anthony Giddens: Consensus and Controversy* (London: The
Falmer Press, 1990); C.G.A. Bryant and D. Jary (eds.), *Giddens' Theory of
Structuration: A Critical Appreciation* (London: Routledge, 1991).

30. Berger, *Social Reality*, p. 12. Cf. Berger and Pullberg, 'Reification', pp. 63-
64.

31. See A. Giddens, *Profiles and Critiques in Social Theory* (London: Macmillan,
1982), p. 37; *idem, New Rules of Sociological Method* (London: Hutchinson, 1976),
pp. 103-104, 118-29, 161; *idem, Constitution*, p. 24.

32. Giddens, *New Rules*, p. 128: 'Every act which contributes to the reproduction
of a structure is also an act of production, a novel enterprise, and as such may initiate
change by altering that structure at the same time as it reproduces it—as the meanings of words change in and through their use'; *idem, Central Problems*, p. 210:
'with a conception of structuration, the possibility of change is recognised as inherent
in every circumstance of social reproduction'.

'given', but is reproduced and transformed in and through ongoing human activity. Such a shift in emphasis is, I believe, of considerable socio-political significance.

The concept of an externalized and objectified social world gives rise to a second concern: namely, that, with such a conceptualization of the dominant social order, critique and alternative, indeed *change* itself, are all too easily conceived of as threatening and destructive.[33] Ideally, individuals are 'successfully socialized' into the 'reality' which confronts them as 'objective'. The dominant social order requires legitimation and maintenance: its continuance provides security against chaos and anomy. Such a theory can easily form a legitimation of the status quo, suggesting that its maintenance and continuation are essential for human wellbeing. Challenges to the social order are portrayed as marginal activities which threaten to cause chaos, and increase the need for legitimation. Berger and Luckmann speak, for example, of the 'problem' caused by 'deviant versions of the symbolic universe'.[34] Note, too, Berger's description of threats to the social world:

> All socially constructed worlds are inherently precarious... they are constantly *threatened* by the human facts of self-interest and stupidity. The institutional programmes are *sabotaged* by individuals with conflicting interests. Frequently individuals simply forget them or are incapable of learning them in the first place. The *fundamental processes of social control*, to the extent that they are successful, *serve to mitigate these threats*.[35]

The idea that the continuance of the social order is necessary for the wellbeing of society is all the more dangerous given the insistence that the social world intends, as far as possible, to remain unquestionable. 'It is not enough', Berger writes, 'that the individual look upon the key meanings of the social order as useful, desirable, or right. It is much better (*better, that is, in terms of social stability*) if he looks upon them

---

33. Berger and Luckmann, *Social Construction*, p. 121: 'The constant possibility of anomic terror is actualized whenever the legitimations that obscure the precariousness [of all societies] are threatened or collapse'. The analysis of 'de-reification' is deemed to be beyond the framework of their concerns (p. 109), though on this, see Berger and Pullberg, 'Reification', pp. 69-70.

34. Berger and Luckmann, *Social Construction*, p. 124.

35. Berger, *Social Reality*, p. 29, my italics; see further pp. 29-32. Cf. Berger and Luckmann, *Social Construction*, p. 87.

as *inevitable*, as part and parcel of the universal nature of things.'[36]

But is such a presentation of the way society works best necessarily true, or is it in danger itself of ideologically legitimating the dominant social order? Think, as an example, of certain environmental pressure groups, whom some, as in Berger and Luckmann's theory, might portray as a 'threat' to the stability of society. Is it not equally possible to argue that such pressure groups have actually played a *positive* role in the ongoing *reconstruction* of social reality, so that almost all of us, albeit to greater or lesser degrees, are more 'environmentally aware'? The issue of the *portrayal* of 'opponents' and alternatives is important in relation to the Pastoral Epistles.

The danger that Berger and Luckmann's work may be taken as offering theoretical legitimation of the status quo is furthered by their insufficient critical attention to issues of ideology and interests. Thus, my third concern may be summarized by Giddens's observation that 'their approach...completely lacks a conception of the critique of ideology'.[37] In other words, there is no adequate consideration of the ideological dimensions of the construction of social reality: whose interests are served by the social order and how are inequalities and exploitation concealed as 'natural' in such a construction of 'reality'? Any consideration of the 'construction' of social reality must give due attention to the ways in which the dominant reality which is constructed may reflect the interests of certain groups and legitimate and conceal the exploitation of others. Moreover, the emergence and sustenance of a dominant social order is inextricably connected to the issue of power. As Berger and Luckmann themselves comment, 'He who has the bigger stick has the better chance of imposing his definitions of reality'.[38]

In short, Berger and Luckmann's theory, for all its strengths, is itself in danger of being ideological. It offers a theoretical formulation with which the exploitation and domination sustained by a social order may be legitimated and 'taken for granted' by the individuals who are socialized into it, but fails critically to penetrate the interests and exploitation which such an order may sustain. Moreover, alternatives and critiques of such orders are portrayed as a threat to the wellbeing of all, bringing potential chaos.

36. Berger, *Social Reality*, p. 24, my italics. Cf. Berger and Luckmann, *Social Construction*, pp. 77-85, 149-57.

37. Giddens, *Central Problems*, p. 267 n. 8.

38. Berger and Luckmann, *Social Construction*, p. 127.

The Pastoral Epistles

Turning now to the Pastoral Epistles, I suggest that three very similar areas of critical questioning are required for the development of a sociological interpretation of these letters.

My first concern is with the way in which the Pastoral Epistles present Pauline teaching as an objective 'thing' which they are concerned to guard, protect and pass on. They express a clear concern with 'sound teaching', and Timothy is urged to 'guard the deposit' (1 Tim. 6.20; 2 Tim. 1.14).[39] The Paul of the Pastorals declares that 'you have an example of sound words which you heard from me...' (2 Tim. 1.13; cf. 2.2). In Berger and Luckmann's terms, used by MacDonald, the Pastorals are primarily engaged in protecting and sustaining a symbolic universe which was created in the earlier years of Pauline Christianity.[40] The critical point is almost identical to that raised in connection with Berger and Luckmann's presentation of the social order as 'objectified': namely, that the claim of the Pastorals to be preserving and protecting 'sound teaching', which is the deposit of Paul himself, obscures the extent to which these epistles evidence a development and transformation of Pauline Christianity.[41] Berger and Luckmann's notion that a symbolic order is being protected tends merely to confirm the view which the author of the epistles seeks to promote. But it is not only the 'opponents' who are 'corrupting', or, more neutrally, 'changing' the faith, as our author would have us believe. Pauline Christianity cannot simply be 'guarded' or 'protected', but must be reproduced in the light of new situations and contexts. The Pastorals urge upon their readers particular forms of social conduct and respectable behaviour, which, at the very least, reflect changes of emphasis from the advice we find Paul himself giving. Women have now been excluded from leadership and are urged

39. Note the uses of ὑγιαίνω and ὑγιής in 1 Tim. 1.10; 6.3; 2 Tim. 1.13; 4.3; Tit. 1.9, 13; 2.1, 2, 8. See M. Dibelius and H. Conzelmann, *The Pastoral Epistles* (Philadelphia: Fortress Press, 1972), pp. 24-25. A general concern for right teaching to oppose the false is a major interest in these epistles: see, for example, 1 Tim. 1.3-11; 4.1-16; 6.3-5; 2 Tim. 2.14-26; 3.1-15; 4.3-5; Tit. 1.10-14; 3.8-11.

40. Cf. MacDonald, *Pauline Churches*, pp. 159, 203-204, 220, 228, 235-36 (esp. 203-204 and 228).

41. MacDonald (*Pauline Churches*) does not deny such transformation and development (see, e.g., pp. 159, 236), but the primary level of interpretation is based upon the idea of protecting and sustaining the community.

to fulfil the role of housewife and mother, a subordinate position legitimized by the stories of creation and fall (1 Tim. 2.11-15).[42] Younger widows are urged to remarry, and there is little sign of the encouragement of singleness which we find in Paul's writing (1 Tim. 5.14; cf. 1 Cor. 7, esp. vv. 39-40). Slaves are urged to be submissive, respectful and pleasing to their masters (1 Tim. 6.1-2; Tit. 2.9-10). Christian masters are especially worthy of good service, because they are beloved believers (1 Tim. 6.2).[43] A religious legitimation is produced to undergird this exploitation; the slaves are to honour their masters 'so that the name of God and the teaching may not be slandered' (1 Tim. 6.1).[44] It is notable, of course, that the author addresses no reciprocal instruction to Christian slave-owners.[45] Could he not at least have added something like: 'And masters, treat your slaves fairly and justly; do not abuse them because they are believers, in order that you may be a good witness to outsiders'

42. See also 1 Tim. 5.11-15 (esp. v. 14); Tit. 2.3-5, where the older women are to teach the younger women to love and submit to their husbands and work in the house (οἰκουργούς).

43. J. Roloff (*Der erste Brief an Timotheus* [EKKNT, 15; Zürich: Benziger Verlag; Neukirchen–Vluyn: Neukirchener Verlag, 1988], pp. 323-34) comments, 'Nicht obwohl, sondern vielmehr *weil* die Herren Christen sind, muß man ihnen dienen, und zwar ohne Vorbehalt und Einschränkung'. Most commentators mention the different addressees of v. 1 (to slaves with non-Christian owners, or a general instruction to all slaves), and v. 2 (specifically to those slaves with Christian owners): e.g. C.K. Barrett, *The Pastoral Epistles* (New Clarendon Bible; Oxford: Clarendon Press, 1963), p. 82 (though Barrett argues that this section is addressed 'to elders who are slaves'); A.T. Hanson, *The Pastoral Epistles* (NCB; London: Marshall, Morgan & Scott, 1982), p. 105; J.N.D. Kelly, *The Pastoral Epistles* (BNTC; London: A. & C. Black, 1963), p. 131; Roloff, *Timotheus*, p. 320.

44. This idea is an echo of Isa. 52.5b (LXX), also cited in Rom. 2.24.

45. Noted, for example, by S. Schulz, *Neutestamentliche Ethik* (Zürcher Grundrisse zur Bibel; Zürich: Theologischer Verlag, 1987), p. 608; W. Schrage, *Ethik des Neuen Testaments* (Grundrisse zum Neuen Testament, 4; NTD; Göttingen: Vandenhoeck & Ruprecht, 5th edn, 1989), p. 273; D.C. Verner, *The Household of God: The Social World of the Pastoral Epistles* (SBLDS, 71; Chico, CA: Scholars Press, 1983), pp. 140-41. As well as in Col. 3.18–4.1 and Eph. 5.21–6.9, a certain reciprocity is found in *Did.* 4.10-11 and *Barn.* 19.7.

The naivete with which exegetes reiterate the ideology of the author is sometimes remarkable: referring to Tit. 2.9-10, Quinn comments that the slaves in view here belong to Christian households and can therefore 'be directed "to be subject...in all matters", *with the presumption that the Christian master or mistress would not command unchristian acts*'! (J.D. Quinn, *The Letter to Titus* [AB, 35; Garden City, NY: Doubleday, 1990], p. 146, my emphasis).

(cf. Col. 4.1)? The absence of any such counterbalancing statements, as are at least found in the still socially conservative codes of Col. 3.18–4.1 and Eph. 5.21–6.9, renders the Pastorals' teaching even more open to the label 'ideological'; in that it presents the Christian faith in such a way as to reinforce the exploitative domination of one social group and to serve the interests of another, while simultaneously concealing such partisan interests. Once more, we must note that no such calls for the subordination of slaves are found in the undisputedly genuine Pauline letters.[46] Indeed, the slave owner Philemon is specifically urged to receive Onesimus 'no longer as a slave, but more than a slave, a beloved brother' (v. 16). Paul certainly was no particular champion of emancipation, but the change in emphasis is nonetheless significant.[47]

An important question, of course, is *why* the Pastoral Epistles address the subordinate members of the household without reciprocal instruction to the 'superior' members. It is often argued that the Pastorals' instruction of women and slaves should be seen against the background of real or potential 'emancipatory movements',[48] which the author saw as

46. The debate over the implied meaning of μᾶλλον χρῆσαι in 1 Cor. 7.21 is obviously relevant here, although a whole article and more could be devoted to the discussion of this topic. However, recent scholarship seems increasingly to favour the 'use freedom' interpretation. See esp. S.S. Bartchy, ΜΑΛΛΟΝ ΧΡΗΣΑΙ: *First-Century Slavery and the Interpretation of 1 Corinthians 7.21* (SBLDS, 11; Missoula, MT: Scholars Press, 1973); P. Trummer, 'Die Chance der Freiheit: Zur Interpretation des μᾶλλον χρῆσαι in 1 Kor 7,21', *Bib* 56 (1975), pp. 344-68; G. Dawes, '"But if you can gain your freedom" (1 Corinthians 7: 17-24)', *CBQ* 52 (1990), pp. 681-97 (689-94); Horrell, *Social Ethos*, pp. 184-95.

47. On the ambiguity of Paul's position and the reasons for such ambiguity, see J.M.G. Barclay, 'Paul, Philemon and the Dilemma of Christian Slave-Ownership', *NTS* 37 (1991), pp. 161-86.

48. In relation to the Pastoral Epistles, see P.H. Towner, *The Goal of our Instruction: The Structure of Theology and Ethics in the Pastoral Epistles* (JSNTSup, 34; Sheffield: JSOT Press, 1989), pp. 38-45, 212, 243-44; Verner, *Household*, pp. 175-80, 185-86, who argues that it is women's emancipation which is particularly problematic for the author of the Pastorals. Note also Dibelius and Conzelmann, *Pastoral Epistles*, p. 116. There is a wider debate about the extent to which Pauline teaching (in 1 Cor. 7; Col. 3.18–4.1, as well as in the Pastorals) is a reaction to emancipatory movements among women and slaves; argued, for example, by R. Gayer, *Die Stellung des Sklaven in den paulinischen Gemeinden und bei Paulus* (Europäische Hochschulschriften, 23.78; Bern: Herbert Lang; Frankfurt: Peter Lang, 1976), pp. 112-222, esp. 154-68, 210-12; J.E. Crouch, *The Origin and Intention of*

dangerous to the life of the Church. The way these movements are described by New Testament scholars sometimes reflects an assumption that they were indeed 'problematic' and that the canonical author was clearly 'right' to oppose them.[49] While this may or may not be deemed to be the case, we should be more cautious, it seems to me, about reiterating the perspective of the canonical author. The 'rightness' implied by canonicity perhaps needs to be resisted in the interests of a sympathetic historical understanding of those whose emancipatory movements were repressed. Certainly the Pastorals are not merely guarding and reproducing older Pauline teaching, but are enmeshed in the struggles and problems of their own particular situation.

My second point relates closely to the second concern raised in connection with Berger and Luckmann's work. As Berger and Luckmann's theory tends to portray anything which opposes the dominant social order as a threat, so the Pastoral Epistles are a concentrated attempt to stigmatize and marginalize alternatives; to portray them as destructive, threatening and worthless, using a host of conventional pejoratives.[50] The convergence between Berger and Luckmann's theoretical perspective as MacDonald employs it and the perspective of the epistles themselves is

the *Colossian Haustafel* (FRLANT, 109; Göttingen: Vandenhoeck & Ruprecht, 1972), pp. 120-51.

49. So Towner, *The Goal*, p. 43: 'Women and slaves had adopted an attitude of emancipation which can be linked to the over-realized eschatology that was in the air'; p. 42: 'As we will see...the appropriate solution to the social disruption occurring in the communities was to be found in adherence to social structures such as the family'; p. 198: 'Perverted conduct, which included a tendency to engage in behaviour that challenged the given social structure, would do nothing but engender criticism and disgust among outsiders'.

A. Padgett, 'The Pauline Rationale for Submission: Biblical Feminism and the *hina* Clauses of Titus 2.1-10', *EvQ* 59 (1987), pp. 39-52 (50-52): 'It was therefore necessary to yield the right of women Christians to equality with men, so that the gospel could go forth... The Pastorals make a choice between two evils: the destruction of the church as a whole, including women and slaves; or the suffering of women and slaves for the sake of the church and her good news.'

Cf. also Crouch, *Origin*, pp. 160-61 n. 32; B. Witherington III, *Women in the Earliest Churches* (SNTSMS, 58; Cambridge: Cambridge University Press, 1988), p. 118.

50. See 1 Tim. 1.3-11; 4.1-5; 6.3-10; 2 Tim. 2.14-26; 3.2-9; Tit. 3.9. On the conventional nature of the polemic in the Pastorals, see esp. R.J. Karris, 'The Background and Significance of the Polemic of the Pastoral Epistles', *JBL* 92 (1973), pp. 549-64; also Dibelius and Conzelmann, *Pastoral Epistles*, pp. 21, 115-16.

again most noteworthy. The idea that he (as I think we may safely assume) was engaged in protecting the symbolic universe or stabilizing the life of the community would, I think, have met with the author's approval.[51] Berger and Luckmann's approach essentially confirms the author's viewpoint; the alternatives are dangerous and threatening.

But a genuinely critical inquiry must surely be most wary of adopting such a viewpoint. Lacking direct textual evidence of any opponents' defence or even teaching, we should at least be open to the possibility that they equally saw themselves as exponents of the true gospel, and as faithfully continuing the Pauline tradition. We must consider carefully what it means to describe them as a threat.

The Pastorals are clearly engaged in a dynamic and significant struggle within the church. The polemic used, however conventional, shows that. Schlarb's recent book opens with a statement to this effect: 'The Pastoral Epistles are evidence of a massive and intensive dispute with false teaching and false teachers, with heresy and heretics'.[52] But what is the nature of the struggle evidenced by the Pastoral Epistles? Is it *primarily* a theological or doctrinal argument, or is it a struggle between social groups with conflicting interests? One of the most notable points about the opposition to false teaching in the Pastorals is that the *doctrines* and *teachings* of the opponents are scarcely mentioned.[53] It is *social conduct* which seems to be the author's primary concern. As Verner notes,

> in Titus 2.1, Titus is urged to teach 'that which befits sound teaching'. In this case the content of the teaching turns out to be the station code of 2.2-10. Similarly, the exhortation 'teach and urge these things' in 1 Tim. 6.2b follows the instructions regarding various groups in the church in 5.3-6.2a.[54]

Moreover, the qualities required of church leaders focus largely upon social conduct and good household management.[55] But if one of the

---

51. Cf. MacDonald, *Pauline Churches*, pp. 159, 213-14, 220, 228, 236.

52. E. Schlarb, *Die gesunde Lehre: Häresie und Wahrheit im Spiegel der Pastoralbriefe* (Marburger theologische Studien, 28; Marburg: Elwert, 1990), p. 14.

53. Cf. MacDonald, *Pauline Churches*, pp. 226-27; Hanson, *Pastoral Epistles*, pp. 25-26. For attempts to reconstruct the position and doctrines of the opponents, see, for example, Roloff, *Timotheus*, pp. 228-39; Dibelius and Conzelmann, *Pastoral Epistles*, pp. 65-67; and Schlarb, *Die gesunde Lehre*, which essentially assumes the Pastorals' view: that the opposition are heretical, false teachers.

54. Verner, *Household*, p. 158.

55. See 1 Tim. 3.1-13; Tit. 1.6-11. Cf. Verner, *Household*, pp. 147-60, esp.

author's primary concerns was to oppose *social* conduct of which he disapproved, the conduct of women, for example, who claimed the authority to teach and the right to remain unmarried, and possibly that of slaves too, who saw some significance in the notion that they and their masters were ἀδελφοί, then we must surely locate the Pastoral Epistles on one side of a social struggle, even a class-based struggle within the early Church. The fact that the socially conservative side may have won the day and emerged as 'orthodox' and canonical is not necessarily to be explained by the assertion that they were the ones 'protecting' the community and its symbolic universe, but may connect in a more insidious way to differentials of power and influence.

Thirdly, and finally, any critical sociological approach must, it seems to me, raise the questions of interests and ideology in connection with every social construction of reality. We must be prepared to ask of each text preserved for us, including the Pastoral Epistles, 'whose interests are reflected here and at what cost to whom?' Conflicting forms of the faith must be analysed, not only as theological arguments, but also as expressions of the interests of particular social groups and as forms of power struggle.

We may thus ask about the extent to which the Christian faith promoted by the Pastoral Epistles is becoming ideological; that is to say, about the extent to which the theological and evangelical resources of the Christian faith are being used to support and justify forms of social domination. The missionary and apologetic motives are certainly explicit in the Pastoral Epistles,[56] and as we have already noted theological resources from the stories of creation and fall are used to legitimate a particular conception of woman's role. It is interesting to note how in 1 Pet. 2.18-25 Christ's sufferings are used as a theological resource to encourage slaves to bear even unjust suffering, again with no reciprocal exhortation addressed to the slave-owners.

A potentially subversive faith has come in the Pastoral Epistles quite

---

p. 159; Towner, *The Goal*, p. 241: 'the approved conduct was that which was respectable both inside and outside the Christian community'.

56. See 1 Tim. 3.7; 5.14; 6.1; Tit. 1.6; 2.5-10; 3.1-2. On 1 Tim. 6.1 Barrett (*Pastoral Epistles*, p. 82) writes, 'The decisive motive is missionary'. On Tit. 2.9-10 Quinn (*Titus*, p. 149) comments, 'The purpose for this thoroughgoing reliability [of slaves] is missionary in character'. The missionary motive for the Pastorals' teaching is (over)stressed by Towner, *The Goal*, pp. 145-257, esp. 222, 232-33, 241, 244, 253-57.

clearly to add new religious legitimation to the social roles traditionally prescribed for the household context. It has thus become to some extent a religious ideology which supports and legitimates the forms of domination upon which Graeco-Roman society depended. Certainly this is not all that the Pastoral Epistles are: among their various elements they preserve many credal formulations,[57] they evidence a system of care for the most needy widows in the community,[58] and they offer a critique of the love of, and desire for, money (1 Tim. 6.6-10, 17-19). Those who would follow in Paul's apostolic tradition are also told of the suffering that faces them (2 Tim. 2.3-13; 3.12; 4.5). Clearly the Pastorals do not merely reproduce dominant cultural values, nor do they advocate shrinking from suffering in favour of a quiet and peaceful life.[59] However, there is no condemnation of the dominant social order; no declaration that the word of the cross is a demonstration that the powers that be are being destroyed through God's deliberate choice of the weak, foolish nobodies (1 Cor. 1.18-29); no particular criticism of those who are rich.[60] As MacDonald points out in relation to this last point, in 1 Tim. 6.17-19, 'the author is not instructing the wealthy to divest themselves of their riches, but is exhorting them on how to be rich…a question of attitude'.[61] There is nothing to negate or contradict the ideological elements within these epistles.

Such a view of the Pastoral Epistles naturally raises a host of ques-

57.   E.g. 1 Tim. 2.5-6; 3.16; 6.15-16; 2 Tim. 1.9-10; 2.11-13; Tit. 3.4-7.

58.   1 Tim. 5.3-16. See the discussion in MacDonald, *Pauline Churches*, pp. 188-89 and Verner, *Household*, pp. 161-66.

59.   R.M. Kidd (*Wealth and Beneficence in the Pastoral Epistles* [SBLDS, 122; Atlanta: Scholars Press, 1990]) argues against the idea that the Pastorals represent a particularly *bürgerlich* form of Christian faith, giving close attention to the themes of cultural accommodation and unheroic conservatism: see esp. pp. 111-94.

60.   On wealth and the wealthy Verner (*Household*, p. 175) argues that the ethic promoted by the Pastorals 'encourages an essentially static social situation'. For a different view, namely that the opponents are among the wealthy, see L.W. Countryman, *The Rich Christian in the Church of the Early Empire: Contradictions and Accommodations* (Texts and Studies in Religion, 7; New York: Edwin Mellen, 1980), pp. 152-54, 166-73, and Kidd, *Wealth*, pp. 75-77, 97-100.

61.   MacDonald, *Pauline Churches*, p. 200. There is debate as to whether the same group (the rich) are addressed also in vv. 9-10. It seems to me most likely that here those seeking to *become* rich are in view; so also MacDonald, *Pauline Churches*, pp. 198-99; Verner, *Household*, pp. 174-75; otherwise Kidd, *Wealth*, pp. 95-97. Barrett (*Pastoral Epistles*, p. 85) comments that 'the author is careful not to condemn those who are rich (v. 9), or riches (v. 10)'.

tions, not least, to what extent, if at all, such a social ethos is to be found in the thought of Paul himself. Following Theissen, some would argue that a 'love-patriarchal' ethos runs throughout the Pauline corpus, although it is more clearly evident in the later epistles.[62] While some contrasts may be drawn, one might indeed argue that many of the ideas developed strongly in the Pastorals find at least an embryonic form in Paul's own letters. 1 Corinthians 11, especially vv. 8 and 9, uses the creation story to develop a somewhat hierarchical relation between the sexes;[63] 1 Cor. 7.20-24 and Philemon certainly allow the interpretation that a Christian may contentedly remain a slave, given the knowledge that they are somehow 'free in the Lord' and a valuable brother or sister; 1 Thess. 4.11 urges the ideal of living quietly (ἡσυχάζειν) in order, partly, to be εὐσχημόνως πρὸς τοὺς ἔξω (v. 12); and, of course, Rom. 13.1-7 urges all Christians to submit to the governing authorities, a passage clearly echoed by Tit. 3.1 (cf. also 1 Pet. 2.13-17).[64]

But given that the Pastorals represent a strong development of such themes, the major question, of course, concerns the reasons for such a development.[65] An exploration of this question, I suggest, must take into consideration both 'internal' and 'external' factors. The presence within Pauline congregations from the start of socially prominent, wealthy householders may not be without significance for the development of Pauline teaching, particularly after the death of the apostle himself.[66] To

62. See G. Theissen, *The Social Setting of Pauline Christianity* (Edinburgh: T. & T. Clark, 1982), pp. 107-108; MacDonald, *Pauline Churches*, pp. 43-44, 121, 202; Kidd, *Wealth*, pp. 177-81. For a critique of the 'love-patriarchalism' thesis, see now Horrell, *Social Ethos*, esp. pp. 126-98.

63. I take 1 Cor. 14.34-35 to be an interpolation. I recognize that a lengthy discussion would be needed to justify this fully, but see esp. G.D. Fee, *The First Epistle to the Corinthians* (NICNT; Grand Rapids: Eerdmans, 1987), pp. 699-708; G. Fitzer, *Das Weib schweige in der Gemeinde* (Theologische Existenz Heute, 110; Munich: Chr. Kaiser Verlag, 1963); Horrell, *Social Ethos*, pp. 184-95.

64. Cf. now D.G. Horrell, 'The Development of Theological Inquiry in Pauline Christianity: A Structuration Theory Perspective', in P.F. Esler (ed.), *Modelling Early Christianity: Social-Scientific Studies of the New Testament in its Context* (London: Routledge, 1995), pp. 224-36.

65. Cf. also Horrell, *Social Ethos*, pp. 285-91.

66. The thesis that there were at least a minority of well-to-do Christians within the Pauline communities has effectively replaced the 'old consensus' that Pauline Christianity was initially a movement among the lower classes. Overviews of the considerable discussion can be found in W.A. Meeks, *The First Urban Christians: The Social World of the Apostle Paul* (New Haven: Yale University Press, 1983),

what extent did such people take the positions of leadership within the Church and increasingly formulate teaching which reflected their social interests? The requirements laid down for church leaders in 1 Tim. 3.1-13 (cf. Tit. 1.5-9) restrict leading functions to those who govern their households well. Non- (male) householders, it seems, would be disqualified from such positions.

However, the Pastorals also suggest that external factors were of considerable influence. The prominence of the missionary and apologetic motives suggests that at least some of the believers were concerned that the faith should not be viewed as a subversive threat, as undermining the fabric of society, due in part to the threat and experience of persecution. The pressure of suspicion and persecution should not be underestimated. But if persecution was a major cause of the development in Pauline Christianity, whereby its eventually 'orthodox', canonical form was becoming to some extent a religious ideology, legitimating and sustaining the forms of domination upon which society rested, then would we not have to acknowledge that such persecution had indeed achieved its aim? Persecution may have played a significant part in transforming a dangerous new religious movement into one which encouraged the subordinate to remain subordinate, prayed for kings and all those in high places (1 Tim. 2.1-2), and generally offered support and legitimation to the established social hierarchy. Perhaps the power of Rome was such that a new religion growing as Christianity was growing could only survive in the long term by transforming itself in this way. That Pauline Christianity could become such an ideology may not be insignificant for understanding its eventual adoption as the official religion of the empire.[67] Perhaps, as Bauer suggested, 'the Roman government finally came to recognize that the Christianity ecclesiastically organized from Rome was flesh of its flesh, came to unite with it, and thereby enabled it

pp. 51-73; B. Holmberg, *Sociology and the New Testament: An Appraisal* (Minneapolis: Fortress Press, 1990), pp. 21-76; Kidd, *Wealth*, pp. 35-75. Important influences upon this new consensus are E.A. Judge, *The Social Pattern of the Christian Groups in the First Century* (London: Tyndale Press, 1960), esp. pp. 59-60, and Theissen, *Social Setting*, pp. 69-119 (an essay originally published in 1974).

67. This idea may, I believe, add a significant new dimension to Theissen's thesis that the love-patriarchal ethos of Pauline Christianity was a significant factor in its eventual adoption as the religion of the empire. See Theissen, *Social Setting*, pp. 107-10, 138-40, 163-64.

to achieve ultimate victory over unbelievers and heretics'.[68]

Conclusion

Given the unavoidable ways in which theoretical perspectives influence and shape interpretation, it is important to look critically at those we adopt and to consider their possible shortcomings and omissions. It may certainly be possible to use a sociological theory 'heuristically', as long as we acknowledge that it nevertheless puts a definite shape upon our inquiry, leading us to ask some questions in certain ways, while omitting others. Critical consideration of our interpretative perspectives is therefore always important. I hope to have raised questions which at least need to be borne in mind when using Berger and Luckmann's theory in New Testament research. A sociological approach based primarily upon it may ignore or misinterpret some of the issues that should be central to critical sociological inquiry. This is especially the case when the object of study is texts like the Pastoral Epistles, whose ideology converges so closely with that of Berger and Luckmann's theory. To interpret the Pastorals from the perspective of Berger and Luckmann's theory is to use a theoretical framework which easily reiterates and legitimates the perspective of the epistles, and thus fails to penetrate them critically. As Castelli points out, the failure to raise the critical questions that relate to the issue of power results in an uncritical reinscription of the power relations asserted by the text.[69] A critical sociological investigation of the New Testament must, I believe, raise the kinds of questions I have dealt with above, and must address them both to the theoretical perspectives which we adopt and to the texts themselves.

Adopting such a critical approach, I have tentatively suggested that we may discern in the Pastoral Epistles the beginnings or the development of ideological dimensions within Pauline Christianity. The symbolic universe of Pauline Christianity in the Pastorals does indeed have the potential to become a 'sheltering canopy over the institutional order'. *For whatever reasons*, this form of Christian faith offers religious motives and theological justifications for the subordination of particular social groups, predominantly women and slaves. The enduring influence

68. W. Bauer, *Orthodoxy and Heresy in Earliest Christianity* (London: SCM Press, 1972), p. 232.

69. E.A. Castelli, *Imitating Paul: A Discourse of Power* (Louisville, KY: Westminster/John Knox Press, 1991), pp. 23-33.

of such religious legitimations can scarcely be estimated, for, as Berger remarks, 'Religion legitimates social institutions by bestowing upon them an ultimately valid ontological status'.[70] When undergirded by religion, the social order becomes rooted not only in human design, but in the will of God.[71]

---

70. Berger, *Social Reality*, p. 33.
71. Cf. Berger, *Social Reality*, p. 37.

JSNT 30 (1987), pp. 103-19

'SOCIAL LOCATION OF THOUGHT' AS A HEURISTIC CONSTRUCT IN NEW TESTAMENT STUDY

Richard L. Rohrbaugh

It was expected, and entirely appropriate, that the work of the last decade on the social world of early Christianity would eventually encourage and enhance our capability for what John Elliott has called 'sociological exegesis'. By this term Elliott means the

> analysis, interpretation, and synthesis (correlation) of (1) the literary, sociological and theological features and dimensions of the text (I Peter) and (2) this text's relation to and impact upon its narrower and wider social contexts.[1]

In good sociological fashion, Elliott assumes that these varied correlations exist and that elucidation of them will help us understand the text more clearly as an expression of actual lived Christian experience.

Yet tracing the correlations between thought and social context, a notoriously difficult task in the sociology of knowledge, quickly raises a host of thorny questions that any complete study of the matter would have to explore. For example, we would have to ask what mechanisms or processes explain why certain groups adopt certain ideologies and not others, and whether social location is really a reliable predictor of ideological stance. We would want to know if the relationship between belief and social structure is causative. Or dialectical? Or symmetrical? What is the relation between social structure and the distribution of belief? These and other questions like them must be looked at as the work of sociological exegesis continues. But the fundamental question underlying these others, one which I propose to explore in what follows, is simply: What

---

1. J.H. Elliott, *A Home for the Homeless: A Sociological Exegesis of I Peter* (Philadelphia: Fortress Press, 1981), p. 8.

do we mean by a social location of thought? Without clarity on that starting point, drawing correlations will be a doubtful enterprise indeed.

I

Ours is thus a problem in the sociology of knowledge. Moreover, it should be clear from the beginning that if the patterns and distribution of belief were isomorphous with the social structure, there would be no theoretical debate on the manner and means of their relation. On the other hand, if belief and social structure were totally uncorrelated, there would likewise be no such problem. In fact, social structures and belief do frequently seem to be related, though as social theorist Barry Barnes has noted, it is usually in 'a complex and apparently unsystematic way'.[2] It is thus the seeming fact of such correlations, rendered problematic by their obvious complexity and irregularity, out of which emerges the necessity of a sociology of knowledge.

The working principles of any sociology of knowledge, of course, all derive from the basic insight that thought is a *social* act. Thus all sociologists of knowledge assume that there is a relation between thought and the social conditions under which it occurs. It is asserted that social groups and processes which qualify as genuine social locations of thought (the focus of the discussion below) can be correlated with idea-clusters or belief-systems because social situations provide the environment in which beliefs and ideas are generated, expressed, and understood. There is thus a so-called social base—what Karl Mannheim first called an 'existential base'—underlying any particular way of thinking as if a substructure of social conditions is the foundation on which the superstructure of thought can be said to rest.

Those familiar with the Mannheimian contours of this basic approach to the sociology of knowledge, justified perhaps in the frequent recognition of Mannheim's fundamental place in the sub-discipline,[3] will also recognize that critics of Mannheim's formulation of sociology of knowledge theory are legion. Phenomenologists such as Peter Berger and Thomas Luckmann, together with some Marxists, complain that

2.   B. Barnes, *Interests and the Growth of Knowledge* (London: Routledge & Kegan Paul, 1977), p. 54.

3.   For an extensive exposition of the 'conventional position' in the sociology of knowledge, see N. Abercrombie, *Class, Structure and Knowledge: Problems in the Sociology of Knowledge* (New York: New York University Press, 1980), pp. 53-55.

conventional sociology of knowledge is too intellectualized, treating only the articulate, usually literary, beliefs of a small segment of society while leaving out the everyday, often vague, but nonetheless critical knowledge *everyone* requires in order to function in the world. Others argue that the notion of 'idea clusters' or 'system of belief' is hard to define and frequently lacks clear parameters. Still others assert that no clear understanding of the relation between an individual and the social location of the person's thought exists in the conventional view. Without this we are in danger of a kind of social determinism that is unable to account for the endless differentiations of the human mind. Such controversies are important for theoretical clarity, of course, but our present interest in the social locations with which thought is said to correlate draws attention elsewhere.

Let us begin with the idea of social location itself, that is, the substructure on which the superstructure of ideology or belief is said to rest. Of what does this social base for knowledge or belief consist, and how is it to be identified? What characteristics qualify a group or process as a social location of thought? Is it possible to designate a social location of thought in a clear and distinct way?

It is widely recognized, of course, that Marxist theorists see social class—itself a notoriously difficult concept to specify in our own society, to say nothing of antiquity—as the key social location of thought.[4] Mannheim, though refusing to see class as singularly decisive, acknowledged its crucial role in the group struggles for dominance that characterize social interaction. Yet he was also interested in other groups, other social locations of thought, particularly those constituted by passing generations.[5] Merton notes that not only groups (classes, generations, occupational groups, sects, etc.) but also processes such as competition or conflict can themselves provide a social base for certain types of thinking.[6] In fact Mannheim, like many social theorists, recognized that

4.   For a discussion of the complexities involved in the use of the term 'class' in Roman antiquity, see R.L. Rohrbaugh, 'Methodological Considerations in the Debate over the Social Class Status of Early Christians', *JAAR* 52.3 (1983), pp. 519-46.

5.   K. Mannheim, 'On the Interpretation of Weltanschauung', in P. Kecskemeti (ed.), *Essays on the Sociology of Knowledge* (London: Routledge & Kegan Paul, 1959), pp. 276-322.

6.   R.K. Merton (*Social Theory and Social Structure* [New York: Free Press, 1968], p. 514) lists the following as social bases of knowledge: 'social position, class, generation, occupational role, mode of production, group structures (university,

the number of social locations is contingent, making it impossible to list all of the likely social processes or groups that provide the context of a given belief.

The result is that a *specific* social location is frequently difficult to define, often overlapping with other locations, and thereby difficult to correlate with particular ideas or beliefs. In fact, Nicholas Abercrombie and Brian Longhurst argue that 'the root difficulty in interpreting Mannheim's work lies in the concept of social location itself. In general, he does not offer any sociological theory of how social locations are constructed.'[7] They argue that this omission is crucial because without *some* understanding of what constitutes a social location one 'cannot explain why specific forms of knowledge are associated with specific social locations'.[8]

II

In any review of the work of either sociologists or New Testament scholars, it quickly becomes obvious that some social locations are easier to specify than others. For example, groups designated by gender—female and male—have clear and identifiable boundaries. If patterns of thought can be found that appear to be gender-specific, the relationship between thought and social location might then be clear. Similarly sharp boundaries can frequently be found in distinctions such as citizen and non-citizen, Jew and Gentile, slave and free. These distinctions are easy to make because the groups involved are, by definition, mutually exclusive: one cannot be female *and* male, Jew *and* Gentile, slave *and* free.

As New Testament scholars think about additional social groups and social locations, however—particularly those that do not fall neatly together as do gender and race, or those such as sect which have been studied with the help of carefully developed comparative models—how are we to know what counts as a group? How are we to handle the complexities created by the overlapping character of group participation? How do we treat both groups and beliefs that are much like slices,

bureaucracy, academies, sects, political parties), "historical situation", interests, society, ethnic affiliation, social mobility, power structure, social processes (competition, conflict, etc.)'.

7.   N. Abercrombie and B. Longhurst, 'Interpreting Mannheim', *Theory, Culture and Society* 2 (1983), p. 10.

8.   Abercrombie and Longhurst, 'Interpreting Mannheim', p. 10.

perhaps arbitrarily demarcated, taken out of continua lacking recognizable breaks or divisions?

For example, are ascetics a group, an identifiable social location of thought, as John Gager assumes in his recent analysis of ancient ascetic attitudes toward the body and the body-politic?[9] In setting up his group for study, Gager himself notes that it is necessary to distinguish between 'the ascetic nostalgia of figures like Augustine, Athanasius, and John Chrysostom', a milder form of this type of belief, and the 'more pronounced expressions of ascetic behavior, especially among the monks of Syria and Egypt in the fourth century'.[10] Gager realizes that in order to see this latter group as discrete, that is, as a particular and identifiable social location of thought, something in addition to their asceticism is necessary. Hence he points to the behavior, their flight to the desert. It is not just their ascetic attitude toward the body, which many urban Christians shared, but their physical separation from both city and ecclesiastical entanglement in it which makes the desert ascetics distinguishable from their urban sympathizers. It is thus as 'protest movement' that Gager believes this group of ascetics is to be understood. Following Mary Douglas, he then asserts that their use of ascetic language about the body is to be explained as parallel and appropriate to their denial of the body-politic.

To the sociologist of knowledge several problems immediately appear. First, who were these ascetic protesters *before* they became ascetic protesters? That is, what social conditions made protest plausible in general, and ascetic protest plausible in particular? Protest movements in that period took a variety of forms other than ascetic flight to the desert, not least of which was the socio-theological contentions of Arius. Asceticism took multiple forms as well. The problem thus expands into a complex web of interrelationships between these different positions. It thus becomes impossible to predict the likelihood of a given protester being an ascetic or a given ascetic being a protester without taking into account variables other than protest and asceticism. We are compelled to ask why these particular ascetics chose to protest 'both the city as such *and* Christianity as the religion of the city' while others did not.

The complexity of these overlapping interactions is such that definitions of 'group' easily acquire a highly selective quality. For example,

9.   J. Gager, 'Body-Symbols and Social Reality: Resurrection, Incarnation and Asceticism in Early Christianity', *Religion* 12 (1982), pp. 356-59.
10.   Gager, 'Body-Symbols', p. 357.

what accounts for the fact that Antony, Athanasius and Arius, all users of body-language, all Egyptian, though the former from Coma in middle Egypt and the latter two from Alexandria, responded so differently to the situation of Church and society in the fourth century? Antony protested and fled to the desert. Arius also protested, but became embroiled in controversy that was not only theological but political as well, moving into the political mainstream when Constantius II appointed Arian bishops and exiled those who refused to depose Athanasius.[11] Athanasius, on the other hand, did not protest the entanglement of Church and city, being deacon to the bishop, Alexander of Alexandria. Yet Athanasius saw Antony as the heroic pattern of anchorite life, taking pains to portray him as an anti-Arian model of theological orthodoxy.[12]

Our situation is now difficult. Do we lump Antony and Athanasius together because of their asceticism? Or Antony and Arius together because of their protest? Or Athanasius and Arius together because of their involvement in the socio-ecclesiastical system? What common denominators of social experience do we choose here in order to designate a social location of thought? Gager has chosen a type of thinking, asceticism, and a type of behavior, flight to the desert, and thereby isolated Antony. This may, of course, be a legitimate exercise representing no more than choice of an angle from which to look at the events. Yet several important observations can be made concerning this construction of a group.

First, most social theorists of today would insist, as Mannheim puts it, that

> a human situation is characterizable only when one has also taken into account those conceptions which the participants have of it, how they experience their tensions in this situation and how they react to the tensions so conceived.[13]

We cannot interview Antony; moreover the corpus of his extant writings

---

11. As Mary Douglas notes in her own analysis of the Arian controversy, once Arian bishops were in power the respective theological statements became little more than code words for the struggle between two political factions (*Natural Symbols: Explorations in Cosmology* [New York: Random House, 1973], p. 197).

12. See James Robinson's suggestion that Athanasius's portrayal of Antony and the anchorite movement as orthodox may have been anachronistic in J.M. Robinson (ed.), *The Nag Hammadi Library* (San Franscisco: Harper & Row, 1977), p. 18.

13. K. Mannheim, *Ideology and Utopia: An Introduction to the Sociology of Knowledge* (New York: Harcourt and Brace, 1968), p. 40.

amounts to no more than eight letters. It is therefore somewhat less than certain if Antony should be isolated in this *as opposed to some other fashion*, and whether his intensely individualistic quest for spiritual perfection should be equated with the kind of social protest of which Gager and Douglas speak. To do so one must make assumptions not only about how Antony construed the tensions to which he was reacting, but also about the tensions that may have generated his responses of which we know nothing. Our explanations tend to be for the (perhaps accidental) remains in the historical record, the place of which we simply do not know in relation to the rest of Antony's experience or the full character of the situation.

Secondly, it is perilously easy to construct social locations without taking into account the overlapping character of social groups. As James Boon points out in a critical review of Mary Douglas's recent work, group analysis inherently 'inhibits perception of overlapping memberships and complex standards of value'.[14] Or as Peter Steinfels suggests, also in reference to Douglas's method of designating groups, it may be little more than 'a terribly complicated way of oversimplifying everything'.[15] Group designation, like all theoretical constructs, simplifies a complex situation for analytical purposes, thereby obscuring some things at the same time that it highlights others. Both the paucity of data and our distance from the agrarian world (socially and historically) entice us in this direction as well, since it is always easier to paint at a distance with broad brush and indistinct strokes.

Thirdly, when separating out a single group for observation, it is easy to forget that groups are not only internally defined, but also defined externally by their relation to other groups. What a group is sometimes most clearly seen as is precisely the fact that it is not part of some other group. The matter of asceticism illustrates this clearly. Again in reference to Mary Douglas's study of ascetics, James Boon criticizes her disregard for the way 'something outside society's categories can still be inside cultural values...how society can be strengthened by being denied'.[16] He cites Louis Dumont's work on Indic asceticism as an illustration of what he calls the dialectical quality of culture, as a result of which 'societies do

14. J. Boon, 'America: Fringe Benefits', *Raritan Review* (1983), p. 115.

15. See P. Steinfels's review of *Natural Symbols* and *Purity and Danger* in *Commonweal* 93.2 (1970), p. 50.

16. Boon, 'America', p. 108.

not necessarily quash but possibly perpetuate their own antitheses'.[17] Boon thus suggests that there is an *institutionalized expectation* that not only asceticism, but also independent ascetics will appear. These ascetics thus need to be understood not only vis-à-vis other ascetics, but over against the society of which they are the antithesis as well. Whether this in any way illuminates the relationship between Antony and Athanasius is difficult to say, but at a minimum it suggests a somewhat different understanding of the tensions involved in the events of the fourth century than that proposed by Douglas and Gager.

Fourthly, as phenomenologists have frequently reminded us, conventional sociology of knowledge has concentrated on theoretical thought or, what is worse, the written ideas of intellectuals, instead of the common-sense 'life-world' of everyday experience.[18] It is these provinces of *finite* meaning, as Berger and Luckmann call them—the views of Antony, Arius, and Athanasius would be examples—on which scholars focus as if articulate ideas are those that structure consciousness and thereby provide the key to understanding social tensions and reactions.[19] Were we to have a phenomenological analysis of the social locations of ancient thought, which would of course require interviewing the participants as Mannheim asserts is necessary, we might learn that the situation of Antony was quite different than we suspect.

Finally, generalizations about groups come more easily when yet another type of complexity is not in view. Merton, complaining about the lack of precision in Mannheim's own concept of group, and quite contrary to Mary Douglas's overstated notion that there exists among humans 'a drive to achieve consonance in all levels of experience',[20] points out how abstractly *conflicting* social values are often integrated *within a single group*.[21] Lewis Feuer even describes at some length how conflicting groups have used the same ideology for *exactly opposite*

17. Boon, 'America', p. 108.

18. While we cannot go into the debate between the phenomenologists and the conventional position on this point, we may note that it centers around what phenomenologists see as the 'deterministic' quality implied in the conventional notion that the individual is the product of social forces. For a discussion of this, and the fact that Berger and Luckmann escape this determinism less successfully than is often supposed, see Abercrombie, *Class, Structure and Knowledge*, pp. 133ff.

19. P. Berger and T. Luckmann, *The Social Construction of Reality: A Treatise in the Sociology of Knowledge* (Garden City, NY: Doubleday, 1966), pp. 24-25.

20. Douglas, *Natural Symbols*, p. 95.

21. Merton, *Social Theory*, p. 556.

purposes.[22] Such complexities add to our problem, not least because of over-easy assumptions about how everything ought to 'fit together' logically and consistently. Things do not, obviously, as the critics of Douglas have often pointed out.

Such problems of group definition, of course, are not unique to John Gager's discussion of early Christian asceticism. Before we attempt to sum up our comments on social location, therefore, a brief look at Wayne Meeks's use of the concept in his recent study of Pauline Christianity will illustrate additional difficulties in this kind of approach.[23]

Meeks begins by describing as fully as possible what he calls the social milieu and internal social forms of the Pauline Christian communities.[24] His discussion of social milieu consists mostly of description of the urban environment of the empire and the possible place of the Pauline Christians in it. That is, it is primarily social description. No *systematic* account is given of the symbolic universe inhabited by these Graeco-Roman urbanites, though scattered comments frequently suggest that their world was not unlike that of twentieth-century Americans.[25] In thus attempting to think about the social meaning of Pauline thought, Meeks identifies the Pauline Christians as a 'group', a subset of the wider culture, whose distinctive thought should correlate with social location. Immediately our problem of group identification begins to appear.

22. L.S. Feuer, *Ideology and Ideologists* (Oxford: Blackwell, 1975).

23. W. Meeks, *The First Urban Christians* (New Haven: Yale University Press, 1983).

24. Meeks's use of the term 'correlation' is sometimes less than clear. For much of his discussion of the matter he asserts an intention of showing the correlation between 'stated beliefs and social forms' in the Pauline communities (p. 164), a correlation he sees evident in consistency of belief and social practice. He characterizes this self-consistency with the sociological term 'correlation', yet self-consistency is *not* what sociologists mean by a correlation between thought and social *location*. The sociologist is asking how people come to think and act, *self-consistently or otherwise*, in ways that correlate with their position in a social order. Moreover, this technical use of the term correlation likewise appears in Meeks's work, underlying his attempt to show the appeal of Christian *communitas* for rootless and dissatisfied persons (*Urban Christians*, pp. 74ff.).

25. For example, see Meeks (*Urban Christians*, p. 104), and my comments thereon below. As another example, note also the illustrative list of social locations (*Social Theory*, n. 4) provided by Merton. Such groups are clearly significant in our society, yet it is not difficult to see that this list has emerged from the *Weltanschauung* of the western, academic, industrial world. A list drawn up by someone in antiquity would undoubtedly look much different.

For example, who are these Pauline Christians and by what criteria do we call them a group? In fact, it is difficult to know if they *are* a group—in the technical sense of social location—at all. Meeks's own social description of Pauline Christians inevitably makes this problematical. He acknowledges that those who appear in the texts are atypical and thus the best picture we are able to present is 'fragmentary, random, and often unclear'.[26] Nonetheless, Meeks argues that we can impressionistically describe these communities as ones in which Jew and Gentile, slave and free, urbanites and new arrivals to the city, women and men of widely varying social status all mixed together. On exactly what basis, then, do we designate these Christians a social location of thought?

Meeks recognizes that group members do not speak in the texts, Paul does. He argues, however, that from the ideas *Paul* uses we can infer what this group was like. Such inference can of course be a legitimate exercise. But since no model is consistently used, nor any case made for a common base of *previous* social experience among Pauline Christians, nor any carefully studied criteria for group designation provided, it is difficult to know by what criteria some things in the texts count as evidence for a group while other things do not.[27] It is obvious, for example, that many in Paul's audiences did not share his views. Who did? How do we know who (socially) did when those mentioned in the text frequently do not share either Paul's social location or his viewpoint, while those who might have done so are rarely the focus of the texts?

The problem here is that it is almost impossible to construct social locations with the use of inferences drawn from the thought of a single author. There is no doubt that out there somewhere was a significant number of persons who shared Paul's views, and probably his social location as well. At least they must have lived in a social location of sufficient similarity to Paul's that Pauline ideas made sense. Were we to characterize various pre-Christian Roman groups or social processes,

26. Meeks, *Urban Christians*, p. 72.
27. In spite of a strongly worded attempt to eschew the use of social theory (*Urban Christians*, p. 164), Meeks does use theoretical constructs like 'relative deprivation' (p. 172) or 'cognitive dissonance' (p. 173) in seeking to account for the thinking of Pauline communities. Likewise, he uses a feature from sectarian models to place Paul at the transition point from innovation and renewal to internal institution building (pp. 171ff.). The point, however, is that no model is *consistently* used in identifying the Pauline communities as a type of social location.

that is, social locations, and then compare these with a variety of Christian ideas and behavior, we might get a much clearer picture of the social location in which Pauline ideas appeared as the attractive alternative. But when we try to reverse the process, going from the admittedly fragmentary inferences that can be drawn from the work of a single Christian writer back to a social location in which that writer's ideas appealed, the difficulties are almost impossible to surmount. We cannot be surprised that the result is somewhat vague.

It is important to see that what is at issue here is not simply that these Christian groups got together, but: How? Why? What led some, but not all, in that culture to join? What common experience in their *previous* social situation brought this diverse group together in such a way that we can not only designate them a group in the technical sense, but also understand why Pauline Christianity appeared an attractive option among available alternatives? Since their backgrounds would suggest no such commonality, what drew them together?

Meeks offers basically two types of explanation, one theological and the other sociological.[28] Obviously it is the latter in which we are most interested; moreover, it is one which Meeks provides by means of a somewhat eclectic use of social theory. He argues that what drew these Pauline groups together was the profound and winsome character of Christian *communitas* that provided places for the mobile and rootless of the Graeco-Roman cities to belong.[29] A variety of dissatisfactions arising out of 'status inconsistencies', 'cognitive dissonance', and the 'inability to compete successfully in the existing scheme of social transactions' moved people to belong to a group whose myths provided the basis for long-term rearrangement of social relationships.[30] Thus Meeks argues that

---

28. Meeks summarizes his theological understanding of the attraction as follows:

> A group of people who strongly hold a set of beliefs about what is real and valuable, different in some salient respects from beliefs commonly held in the general society, and who also share evocative symbols for those beliefs, naturally find communication with one another easier and more satisfying than communion with those who do not share their way of seeing (*Urban Christians*, p. 91).

A commonly held set of distinctive beliefs thus drew Christians together in a social group that can be distinguished from the wider society or from other associations of the period. More than any other single thing *belief* constituted a cohesive group out of a socially diverse mass—almost as if belief were the social location of belief—an argument that has been traditional for a long time.

29. Meeks, *Urban Christians*, p. 173.

30. All three of these theoretical suggestions raise serious doubts when used as

> Urban society in the early Roman Empire was scarcely less complicated
> than our own, in proportion to the scale of knowledge available to an indi-
> vidual and of demands made upon him. Its complexity—its untidiness to
> the mind—may well have been felt with special acuteness by people who
> were marginal or transient, either physically or socially or both, as so
> many of the identifiable members of the Pauline churches seem to have
> been.[31]

Such comments about the dissatisfactions felt by people who were out
of sorts with the existing scheme of things are, of course, genuinely
sociological, though we cannot help but wonder from which society they
are drawn, ours or that of ancient Rome. The comment above, for
example, appears to be based on the doubtful assumption that marginal-
ity makes one especially sensitive to the over-complexity of life. This
may be true, but sometimes it is the most successful who become acutely
aware of the need to simplify. But then, the point is not whether the
complexity of Roman life worked this way or that, but whether such
attempts to analogize from our society back to that of Rome are
legitimate.

As Talcott Parsons and many others have repeatedly shown, modern
societies are by their very nature highly segmented and differentiated.
Peter Berger demonstrates that this is the result

> of the degree of division of labor brought about by industrial forms of
> production, and from the patterns of settlement, social stratification, and
> communication engendered by industrialism.[32]

It is highly doubtful, therefore, that Roman society was 'scarcely less
complicated than our own'; at least it was not in quite the same way or
for the same people. Appeals to the demands made upon a person in
relation to the 'scale of knowledge available', perhaps unintentionally
patronizing, do little to clarify the issue. Such comments more likely
suggest how readily we project ourselves, our western, industrial, social
selves, onto the pages of history.

This of course is not unlike the old pitfall of ethnocentrism that has

---

the bases for reconstructing *attitudes* in antiquity. Because all three presume to give
insight into the *psychological* state of persons in the respective social locations, and
because such insight is heavily dependent on our knowledge of the reactions of
people in similar positions in the western, industrial world, such judgments are
almost certainly social anachronisms.

31. Meeks, *Urban Christians*, p. 104.
32. P. Berger, *A Rumor of Angels* (Garden City, NY: Doubleday, 1969), p. 43.

plagued the work of anthropologists and historians alike, except that what we are really talking about here might better be called 'socio-centrism': the tendency to see things the other side of the industrial revolution as if that revolution changed nothing in our patterns of social perception.[33] Thus Mary Douglas seeks a 'formula for classifying relations which can be applied equally to the smallest band of hunters and gatherers as to the most industrialized nations'. But, as Peter Steinfels points out,

> the same categories can be applied to societies of such different character, such different absolute size, such different sorts of historical consciousness, only by unduly flattening out one's portrait of advanced societies and by ignoring the historical factors which formed them.[34]

Thus it is all too easy to assume that the social tensions and reactions in antiquity were the same as those of harried Americans, forgetting that the industrial revolution made a difference we simply cannot ignore.[35]

A look at Meeks's work suggests two additional difficulties in group designation. First is the virtual impossibility of inferring social location from the writings of a single author, at least without a sustained attempt to separate the common denominators of *previous* social experience for both the author and friends on the one hand and foes on the other. Secondly, our propensity for sociocentrism, projecting the industrial consciousness onto antiquity, is nowhere more perilous than when working

33. Macro-sociological studies are a neglected but legitimate area of concern for New Testament scholars, if for no other reason than that social anachronisms are so easy to overlook. The enormous literature on the rise of modernity and its characteristic patterns of thought (for example, the study by P. and B. Berger and H. Kellner, *The Homeless Mind* [New York: Random House, 1973]) would much repay our study. So also would social typologies such as those of G. and J. Lenski (*Human Societies* [New York: McGraw–Hill, 1974]) in which they draw the contrasts, both physical and perceptual, between agrarian and industrial societies. Likewise of special interest are studies such as that of H. Perkin, *The Origin of Modern English Society, 1780–1880* (Toronto: University of Toronto Press, 1969), in which he argues that the industrial revolution was a one-way street socially as well as physically and economically.

34. Steinfels, 'Review', p. 51.

35. As W. Herzog pointedly observes, 'As long as one conducts experiments within a paradigm and achieves expected results, one will not question the perceptual field that makes such undertakings possible' ('Interpretation as Discovery and Creation: Sociological Dimensions of Biblical Hermeneutics', *American Baptist Quarterly* 2 [1983], p. 108).

with inferences that are 'fragmentary, random, and often unclear'. Without sufficient data to see patterns fully, we tend to fill in the gaps with social imagination uncritically drawn from the industrial world.[36]

III

We might conclude, therefore, with several observations about what designating a social location of thought properly requires. Doing so will not be easy because while many social theorists have complained about lack of clarity in group designation, few have provided theoretical clues to aid the task. Even Mannheim, who insisted that the criteria of such constructs be (1) *explicit* and (2) verified by *the work of others*, found his own standard difficult to meet.[37]

Nonetheless, we might begin by recognizing what a social location is and what it is not. It *is* what Peter Berger calls a 'plausibility structure', a socially constructed *province of meaning*. It *is not* reducible to the material conditions of life because it is itself a mental construct, a socially produced and maintained picture of the world.

This means that the social base is not the cause of other ideas, but the context in which other ideas are interpreted and understood as realistic possibilities. Few contemporary sociologists of knowledge would assume it is possible to locate the causal origins of particular ideas as if a social location 'accounts for' ideas that emerge in it. Mannheim himself steadfastly maintained that there could be no causal, genetic explanations of meanings, particularly in terms of unmeaning material phenomena.[38] Even Marxists, who routinely assume a correlation between the ideas of a group and that group's social interests, shy away from rigid notions of causality. Social locations are heuristic constructs, not explanatory ones.[39]

36. J. Elliott argues that 'sociological imagination', to use the term of C. Wright Mills, is a necessary skill to be cultivated by those who seek to do sociological exegesis (*Home for the Homeless*, p. 5). While this may be true, it is an imagination informed by the *agrarian* rather than the industrial world that is needed.

37. See the comment of A.P. Simonds, *Karl Mannheim's Sociology of Knowledge* (Oxford: Clarendon Press, 1978), p. 125.

38. Simonds, *Mannheim's Sociology of Knowledge*, p. 118.

39. It is also worth noting here the growing recognition among many sociologists of knowledge that the connection between thought and social location is much weaker than conventional theorists sometimes assumed. Barnes argues persuasively that this connection is 'not an internal, logical one' (*Interests and the Growth of*

To begin to say what social locations *are*, it is necessary to sharpen the way we use the terms 'group' and 'social location', particularly insofar as the former term is commonly used in the non-technical sense. As Abercrombie points out, a generation may be a social location of thought, but it is not a group. It is not an organization or association. It is rather 'a *social category* whose unity is constituted by a *similarity of location* of a number of individuals within a social whole'.[40] Location is thus a *structural* term describing a position in a social system; it is not one designating membership in an organization.

It is obvious, for example, that members of a generation, class, or any other social location may never get to know each other, may have no physical association whatsoever, but nonetheless live, so to speak, at the same social location and hence share similar experience. Thus a generation lives through the same historical period. A class shares the same relation to the means of production. An occupation shares a common experience of work. Common position or *structural* location in a social system is thus the key.

We must also be clear, as Abercrombie points out, that 'the crucial feature of common location is that it limits the range of experience open to an individual'.[41] Certain experience is included while other experience is excluded. Moreover, just as common location in a social structure limits common experience, so also it limits the range of presuppositions, perceptions and plausible alternatives a group is likely to encounter. It is not that certain experiences produce certain beliefs, but that given certain experiences a limited range of beliefs should be plausible options for most of those who share the social location. Even if rejected for other alternatives, a given belief within that range should be understood

---

Knowledge, p. 58). Nothing like simple straight-line connections can be drawn between particular ideas and particular settings simply because we never know enough about either the setting or the individuals who express themselves to draw connections that finely. As Barnes points out, our knowledge does not 'permit beliefs, representations or modes of thought to be assigned to this or that social class, as it were, by inspection. Nor do they lead to any predictions about what a particular class is capable or incapable of embodying in its consciousness' (p. 58). In other words, we must distinguish between 'imputing to a group a common *content* to its members' expressions...and imputing to them a common context of shared meanings' (Simonds, *Mannheim's Sociology of Knowledge*, p. 123).

40. Abercrombie, *Class, Structure and Knowledge*, p. 38.
41. Abercrombie, *Class, Structure and Knowledge*, p. 38.

by those who share the common location. And for our purposes, description of such limited ranges of experience should help us understand the way a set of beliefs were taken by those who adopted them.

What this means first and foremost is that to designate a social location is to describe a position in a social order. It is not to describe those with whom one has a social association. It is a comment on structure, not sociability. Secondly, its clarity will depend on our ability to describe the limits to the range of experience the location implies. With mutually exclusive groups such as males and females, that is relatively easy. With groups such as fourth-century ascetics, the tougher but nonetheless interesting question becomes the limits in the prior range of experience shared by those who chose the different routes of Antony and Athanasius. With Pauline Christians, the problem is far more difficult, however, because we are limited to inferences drawn from a single author, thereby having only minimal access to the typical members of the group or to their prior structural location in the larger social whole.

Finally, designation of a social location should also include identification of the *process* by which the location is constituted. Thus a generation is created by the biological rhythm of life. A class is generated by relationship to the sources of power in economic conflict. If the structural location of fourth-century desert ascetics was generated by particular processes of alienation in ecclesiastical politics, that of their urban counterparts may well have been generated by alienation of a different sort or degree. The important point is that description of such process would help to clarify the limits to a group's range of experience and what it is that makes it unique.

In sum, then, a social location is to be designated by the common structural position occupied by a number of individuals in relation to a larger social whole. Its specification would ideally designate the limited range of experience a position implies (showing how it is unique), together with the process by which that position comes to be occupied.[42] By taking steps of this sort toward clarity on the underlying matter of

---

42. Claims might then be made that members of early Christian groups employed common (or discrepant) conceptual frameworks in beliefs and action. However, such claims will always, as Simonds points out, be both hypothetical and categorical. They are hypothetical because we are never sure our descriptions are accurate or sufficient, yet categorical because some such context of meaning, ours or a more accurate one, *must* be employed if communication is to be possible at all (*Mannheim's Sociology of Knowledge*, pp. 123-24).

social location, drawing correlations between early Christian belief and its social context might become possible indeed.[43]

43. For a recent discussion of the social location of the intended audience of the Gospel of Mark, see R.L. Rohrbaugh, 'The Social Location of the Markan Audience', *Int* 47 (1993), pp. 380-95.

JSNT 27 (1986), pp. 69-88

WHEN TALES TRAVEL: THE INTERPRETATION OF MULTIPLE
APPEARANCES OF A SINGLE SAYING OR STORY
IN TALMUDIC LITERATURE

Jacob Neusner

The Problem

Some sayings and stories pass from one document to the next. They
gain or lose weight as they make the journey. At hand is a substantial
problem, perhaps still more complex than the relationship of books of
the Bible that go over the same matters—for instance, Deuteronomy as
against parts of Genesis through Numbers, or Chronicles as against
Samuel and Kings, not to mention the four Gospels' use of materials in
common. What do the changes indicate and what do they mean?

In another age the problem of parallel versions of what we now think
was a single event (or, more accurately, a single original tale) found an
easy solution. If we have three versions, then we know about three
events. Hence in received Gospels' scholarship comes the famous postulate that in addition to the Sermon on the Mount, Jesus preached a
Sermon on the Plain. In the Hebrew Scriptures, the slightly diverse
versions of the Ten Commandments kept long generations of preachers
gainfully employed. The several versions of creation and of human and
Israelite history supplied by J, E, P, and D challenged the wits of harmonizing exegetes for many centuries. The theory of simultaneous enuncia-
tion of the Ten Commandments in Exodus and in Deuteronomy ('Keep'
and 'Remember' the Sabbath day being stated by a single voice at a
single moment!) kept at bay inappropriate questioning for so long as
people did not give way to doubt. But what began as a serious answer
to a challenge to faith in the literal and linear historicity of the biblical
tale long ago had come to occupy the place of poetry and theology, no

longer that of history. In the rabbinical canon, by contrast, historians even now take several versions of a story to indicate one of three possibilities.

They might say (1) that the sage at hand went around saying the same thing a lot. Thus if the same saying occurs in four passages but in the same sage's name, the sage said it four times ('he often used to say'). If the same saying is placed into the mouths of two different sages, then 'X and Y agreed that...' Or it might be argued (2) that several versions of a saying or story demand integration and harmonization to supply the single reliable and accurate account of what really happened. That is to say, when we can reduce the versions to their 'original' form, we not only account for the (possibly later) revisions—more importantly, we know pretty accurately what had actually been said or done. Or it is argued commonly nowadays (3) that we account for the inclusion of each detail of a saying or story—among a variety of diverse details—by making up a theory on where and how, by whom and for what purpose, a given detail 'might' or 'would' have been added. Let me spell out this third approach to the problem of the thrice-told tale, because it is characteristic of the last century of scholarship and stands as the foundation of much work even now. When we have a long sequence of versions of a single matter, for instance the vision of the chariot described by Ezekiel as that vision was interpreted by Eleazar ben Azariah to Yohanan ben Zakkai, each successive shift and change in the version appearing in the earliest document to contain it will demand, and receive, a manufactured explanation.

The first of these three theories of the meaning and historical significance of the peripatetic saying serves mainly among the yeshiva-primitives and the Israeli Talmudic historians. It hardly demands serious scrutiny. It falls into the class of marvels and wonders, along with 'Keep' and 'Remember' in a single act of speech. Theologians and decisors of law harmonize, drawing on all sources to make one point. Others do not have to do so, and people interested in the formative history to which stories and sayings attest had best not do so. Our work demands studied description, analysis, and interpretation and not a leap of faith.

The second theory is a datum, mostly among the same circles. It hardly contradicts the first but depends on the same fundamentalism.

The third proves popular among the more critical and up-to-date historians of the Jews in late antiquity and of the law and religion, Judaism, in that same period. It is, to say the least, premature, because it rests on infirm foundations. How so? The assumption that each detail testifies to a given historical event or moment, different from other details in the same literary construct, assumes two things. First, the details—it is postulated—represent things that really happened. So the premise reveals that same literalist fundamentalism that allegedly modern historians reject. Secondly, it is assumed that the text at hand from the beginning was preserved exactly as it was written. Any change exhibited by a later version of a saying or story has, therefore, to find its explanation in a later event or a fresh setting. Changes do not just happen, they are *made*, and therefore for reason. The people who make them do so for reasons that the scholar can report (as we shall see, commonly on the basis of no evidence whatsoever). Nothing lacks 'significance' of a historical sort, and everything demands its explanation. No explanation covers everything; each item demands an *ad hoc* interpretation of its own.

So the text is studded with histories, each supplied for its distinct occasion, none proposing to harmonize with or relate to the last or the next. Accordingly, it is theorized, people took a text and rewrote it as new things happened or in new circumstances. They then handed it on to others who did the same.

This literary theory awaits any sort of sustained argumentation, not to mention documentation. But it generates such scholarship as now flourishes on the problem at hand.

In connection with the third theory of how to interpret the shifts and turnings of a single story or saying in its movement across the canon, I take up a current example of 'incremental history' and show how it actually works. The example derives from the newest generation, the work of an autodidact. So I cannot be accused of calling up ghosts or invoking long-repudiated approaches to refute an abandoned theory. What I think becomes clear is that the theory I call 'incremental history' is 'talmudic' in the worst sense. That is, it is *ad hoc*, merely made up, just as the Talmud itself makes up history, to explain several versions of one saying. Indeed, for all its claim to think in fresh and free ways, the newest generation, as represented here, botches the work. In its bungling, the latest Talmudic historians, as exemplified in what follows, display an intellectual incompetence rarely matched in the earlier, in other ways more credulous and more primitive, age of learning.

Incremental History

'*When he was a Student...and When he Grew up...*'
Sages of ancient times recognized that sayings and stories appeared in diverse versions. They too proposed explanations of how a given saying or story could come down in more than a single statement. The principal approach to the question posited that each detail represented a different stage in the history of the story, or of the life of its hero in particular, with one version characteristic of one such stage, and another version attesting to a different and later one. So the successive versions of a saying or story supply a kind of incremental history. Each version tells something about concrete events and real lives (biographies) that earlier versions did not reveal.

The classic Talmudic expression of the incremental theory takes up a passage of the Mishnah in which Rabban Yohanan ben Zakkai is called merely 'Ben Zakkai':

> The precedent is as follows: Ben Zakkai examined a witness as to the character of the stalks of figs [under which an incident now subject to court procedure was alleged to have taken place] (*m. Sanh.* 5.2B).

As we shall now see, at paragraph N in the following Talmudic analysis, exactly the same story is reported, on Tannaite authority. Now Rabban Yohanan ben Zakkai is alleged to have made exactly the same ruling, in exactly the same case. The item is worded in the same way except for the more fitting title. Then, at P–Q, the two versions are readily explained as facts of history. The one of Ben Zakkai was framed when he was a mere disciple. When, later on, he had become a recognized sage, the story was told to take account of that fact. So the theory I call 'incremental history' is simple: *each story related to, because it derives from, historical moments in a linear progression.* The Talmudic passage is as follows:

IX.

A. Who is this Ben Zakkai?
B. If we should propose that it is R. Yohanan ben Zakkai, did he ever sit in a sanhedrin [that tried a murder case]?
C. And has it not been taught on Tannaite authority:
D. The lifetime of R. Yohanan ben Zakkai was a hundred and twenty years. For forty years he engaged in trade, for forty years he studied [Torah], and for forty years he taught.

E. And it has been taught on Tannaite authority: Forty years before the destruction of the Temple the sanhedrin went into exile and conducted its sessions in Hanut.

F. And said R. Isaac bar Abodimi, 'That is to say that the sanhedrin did not judge cases involving penalties'.

G. Do you think it was cases involving penalties? [Such cases were not limited to the sanhedrin but could be tried anywhere in the Land of Israel!]

H. Rather, the sanhedrin did not try capital cases.

I. And we have learned in the Mishnah:

J. *After the destruction of the house of the sanctuary, Rabban Yohanan* b. Zakkai... [*m. Roš Haš.* 4.1]. [So the final forty years encompassed the period after the destruction of the Temple, and Yohanan could not, therefore, have served on a sanhedrin that tried capital cases.]

K. Accordingly, at hand is some other Ben Zakkai [than Yohanan b. Zakkai].

L. That conclusion, moreover, is reasonable, for if you think that it is *Rabban Yohanan* ben Zakkai, would Rabbi [in the Mishnah-passage] have called him merely, 'Ben Zakkai'? [Not very likely.] And lo, it has been taught on Tannaite authority:

N. There is the precedent that Rabban Yohanan ben Zakkai conducted an interrogation about the stalks on the figs [so surely this is the same figure as at *m. Sanh.* 5.2B].

O. But [at the time at which the incident took place, capital cases were tried by the sanhedrin and] he was a disciple in session before his master. He said something and the others found his reasoning persuasive, [41B] so they adopted [the ruling] in his name.

P. When he was studying Torah, therefore, he was called Ben Zakkai, as a disciple in session before his master, but when he [later on] taught, he was called Rabban Yohanan ben Zakkai.

Q. When, therefore, he is referred to as Ben Zakkai, it is on account of his being a beginning [student] and when he is called Rabban Yohanan b. Zakkai, it is on account of his status later on.

The relevance of the Talmudic passage is simple, as I shall now explain.

Modernist scholars have claimed to explain diverse versions of a single saying or story by much the same thesis as we see before us. That is to say, they allege that they know why a given detail is added here, dropped there, changed in the third place, built up and augmented in the fourth, and on and on. Accordingly, the modern, critical scholars accomplish a kind of incremental history. This is the history of what might have actually happened to account for changes in versions of a story, based on a theory of what might have impelled an author to add or revise a given detail. Indeed, practitioners of the incremental approach have not hesitated to declare that they know an entire history for which the text at hand supplied no evidence whatsoever. They then refer to this (entirely undocumented) history in order to explain shifts and changes in versions of a story.

The single best example of the fantasy at hand is supplied by David J. Halperin, *The Merkabah in Rabbinic Literature* (American Oriental Series, 62; New Haven: Yale University Press, 1980). Referring to the Merkavah materials, Halperin posits that prior to the first written versions there was an entire cycle of such stories ('presumably oral'!). He knows that one of these stories had a narrative framework, then lost a miraculous element, then got that miracle reinserted later on. This literary history, claiming to explain shifts and changes in the sequence of stories we saw earlier, derives from not a shred of evidence of any kind. There is *no* version of these stories at all. The author just made it up and wrote it down, then the American Oriental Society printed it. True, as we shall note, Halperin introduces appropriate qualifications and caveats. But he pays little attention to them; they are mainly formalities.

Here is how he states his conclusions (pp. 138-39):

> 1. I postulate the following development for the *merkabah* tradition involving R. Yohanan b. Zakkai: (1) A cycle of *merkabah* stories, presumably oral, recounted the miracles that accompanied the expositions of one or another of R. Yohanan's disciples; the stories of this cycle contained little beside the miracles. (This stage is purely hypothetical, and is not attested by any literary source.) (2) One of these stories, which involved R. Eleazar b. Arakh, was given a narrative framework, which suggested that R. Eleazar exemplified the 'scholar' of M. Hag. 2.1 (*Mek. Rashbi*). (3) The miraculous element was 'censored' from the story of R. Eleazar, possibly by the compiler of the mystical collection (Tosefta). (4) Miraculous details were reinserted, and stories of other disciples added, on the basis of the old *merkabah* stories (PT BT)...
>
> 3. If my hypothesis is correct, the *merkabah* tradition is rooted in a cycle of miraculous legends. Some historical reality may hide behind these legends, but it is nearly inaccessible. Instead of trying to recover it, we should focus on what the legends can teach us about (*maaseh*) *merkabah* and the image of those reported to have been expert in it.

Halperin's exposition of his own theories omits all reference to whatever he holds as a fundamental thesis on the character of the literature and the history of its formation, if he has any. Yet even on the surface, it is clear, he proposes to make up explanations for diverse versions of the

Merkavah-story. Each detail has its day. None is spared the ravages of Halperin's imaginative reconstruction of its individual life-history. Everything means something somewhere—and to Halperin it does not matter where. It follows that the theory of 'incremental history', assigning a particular event or motive or other explanation for each change in a story as it moves from document to document, finds exemplification in Halperin's treatment of the Merkavah-story.

A systematic picture of what Halperin has done and why it is founded on false premises (or on no premises other than an undisciplined imagination) derives from William Scott Green's review of Halperin's book. In his review (*SecCent* 3 [1983], pp. 113-15) Green observes,

> For reasons never specified, Halperin tends to construe each literary unit, each manuscript variant, and each textual version as a discrete historical moment. He then constructs his history by arranging these textual moments into chronological sequence. By adopting this strategy, Halperin forces himself into the grueling exercise of determining the relative dates of decontextualized literary segments. Much is at stake in these demonstrations; the very possibility of Halperin's history depends on their rigor and cogency. Halperin uses a wide range of criteria to date his materials, and he sometimes deploys these inconsistently. That is, he established his chronologies on the basis of the difference among versions of a passage. But the variables he deems decisive are not systematically applied. Rather, they seem to shift from case to case. This sort of unevenness undermines Halperin's demonstrations of chronology and makes at least some of them appear arbitrary. The problems of particular chronologies aside, Halperin's method limits the kind of history of rabbinic, *merkabah* speculation he can write. His catenae of textual events result in schematic accounts that flip and flop, sparse chronicles of unexpected reversals and inversions in which discrete passages undergo marked, sometimes radical shifts of meaning. He argues, for instance, that the Mishnaic rule that the *merkabah* may not be expounded 'by an individual (variant: *to* an individual), unless he is a scholar, understanding on his own' (M. Hag. 2.1) had three distinct meanings before the time of Tosefta's redaction (ca. CE 250). When the passage circulated independently, it allowed the sage, but not the disciple, a list of other biblical passages whose exposition is restricted, 'the effect was to reverse the meaning of the *merkabah* ruling; solitary study of the *merkabah* was no longer the object of the restriction, but a concession granted to certain exceptional individuals' (p. 36). Still later, the meaning of the rule was changed again to make it 'refer to instruction' (p. 36), an alteration reflected in the variant reading. This final meaning is apparent in a story about Yohanan b. Zakkai and Eleazar b. Arakh at t. Hag 2.1, which, ironically, preserves the earliest version of the Mishnaic rule.

This kind of lean and linear history disappoints because it does not account for the changes it describes. Even if Halperin's textual sequences are correct, they leave too much unexplained. For instance, to whom within rabbinism were these changes important? Did the different meanings supersede one another or exist simultaneously? Are these changes literary, or do they reflect deeper theological, religious, and social diversions within rabbinism? Are such changes, particularly the reversal of meaning, accidental or deliberate, the result of misunderstanding or of manipulation? Without some theory of rabbinic culture and society, of textual transmission and tradition, and of literary tendencies, Halperin's textual sequences lead nowhere. They are merely chronologies masquerading as history.

In singling Halperin out, my intent is only to show what people are doing now. I do not want anyone to suppose that I have taken a particularly weak example of an otherwise vital theory. On the contrary, Halperin presents us with as capable an exercise of the incremental-historical theory as is in print. The difficulty is, it seems, he is talking to himself, in the privacy of his study. He clearly is not engaging in reasoned arguments with the generality of interested participants in the inquiry. Only by that theory can I explain how anyone can make up a 'cycle' of Merkavah-stories ('presumably oral'), tell us what was in them, then what was removed from them—and only then relate the whole pre-history of unavailable sources to the actual sources at hand. The theory that details in successive versions of a saying or story bear historical meanings deserves better than it has received to date.

The approach that seeks to account for shifts and changes by reference to the interests of later authors, tradents, and redactors, remains entirely open. Indeed, in due course we may look forward to the rehabilitation of the theory at hand. My criticism, like Green's, is that, so far as Halperin exemplifies the theory, he provides yet another instance of the dreary approach of made-up explanations, never subjected to tests of falsification or validation. That approach, suitable for talmudic exegesis, does not serve for historical and literary work in our day. While both the theory that 'he often used to say...' and the claim that there is an 'original tradition' promise little for the future, another approach demands attention.

A Documentary-Historical Theory

The reader will not find surprising the allegation that the authors of later documents in the canon of Judaism in a fairly consistent way fill holes in stories and sayings from earlier ones. When, therefore, we wish to explain why details are added or dropped, the first appeal will carry us to the matter of rhetoric. We ask whether we are able to explain why a detail makes a first appearance by asking about the relative relationship of the document in which it surfaces to other documents in which it is absent. If we can show that the document bearing the fresh fact comes later in the formation of the canon than the one lacking it, we may appeal first of all to the claim that the later authors' sense of rhetoric, their larger aesthetic theory, precipitated their making up and including that detail. That hypothesis will gain substantial credibility if we can show that, in general, authors of the document at hand did pretty much the same thing with whatever they received.

Yet the theory at hand, which I call the documentary theory, marks the beginning not the ending, of the matter. For aesthetics, including rhetoric, in a system brings to expression the fundamental and generative character of the system as a whole. Aesthetics constitutes a cultural indicator and relates in a contingent way to the culture—in this case, the explanation of why rhetoric takes one form rather than some other simply is to beg the question. Why so? Because in a truly integrated community of culture, such as the canon of Judaism attests for the sages of late antiquity, each detail addressed the whole. Each one in some small way expresses the character of the entire system. The sages' own convictions about the utter harmony of the whole, including the congruity of law to theology, of meal-time to bed-time and of conduct in the toilet to behavior in the synagogue, reenforce the claim at hand. Indeed these commonplace allegations bring it to explicit expression. It must follow that, when we appeal to a rhetorical explanation for the facts at hand and therefore treat the matter as an essentially literary problem, we have only succeeded in restating the question, not resolving it. Aesthetics, including rhetoric, adds up to little more than making something out of interesting arrangements of words into patterns. By itself it constitutes a formalist inquiry into formalism, a quest for trivial explanations of small things.

The fact that later sages rewrote in their own way what earlier sages had handed on to them looms as an enormous presence in the interpretation of the formative age of Judaism. The sages in question surely do not conform to the definition of traditionalism ordinarily imputed to their culture. For while they faithfully handed on what they had received, it never was intact, if in their view it always was unimpaired. This was so because they saw for themselves a role in the process of formation of what would be 'the tradition'. That role proved inventive, therefore creative. It must follow that the facts of rhetorical preference and the configuration of a larger sense of aesthetics in important ways convey definitive traits of the system concerned. But describing and analyzing those traits, interpreting them in context for what they reveal about the larger system—these labors only now begin.

The theory I have called 'incremental history' fails not because it lacks merit, but because it lacks successful exemplars. If we are to move on, the route must carry us not from one detail to the next, but to a height affording a perspective overall. Once we have a theory of how to proceed and a thesis worth testing, then, but only then, we move to the details, from large to small, in proper and proportionate succession. Beginning from the outside and systematically working our way within, we first seek large and definitive traits. These then will tell us what to discern in the small field of an individual story.

The incremental-historical theory then undergoes an appropriately rigorous exercise of falsification, because we must ask whether details conform to the main point. The alternative is that, like Halperin, we make things up as we go along, text by text and detail by detail. But a useful theory will prove its worth if we are able to explain and even predict the course of matters in a consistent and cogent way. The ultimately useless result of Halperin's work, surveyed just now, derives not from the rather private and subjective character of the results, his meditations on this and that. Even though it is easy to dismiss as mere subjectivity Halperin's power of making up version after version of a tradition no one has ever seen, then appealing to hypothetical version A to explain what is lost in imaginary version C, that is not the main point. It is the methodological inconsistency, the made-up character of the whole approach, not merely the manufactured quality of the individual parts, that requires us to dismiss Halperin's work as hopeless. A useful and plausible theory works wholesale, not retail. It cannot come tailor-made but has to come right off the plain pipe-rack, so to speak. Halperin's exemplification of all that can go wrong with the incremental theory therefore should not lead to the dismissal of the theory. What we have to do is consider more thoughtfully how to proceed from the documentary facts, awaiting discovery, to the explanation of the documents' preferences, overall, and then also to details of a given story (such as the Merkavah-one), in proper sequence.

Fifteen years ago I attempted such a program in *Development of a Legend: Studies on the Traditions Concerning Yohanan ben Zakkai* (Leiden: Brill, 1970). What I proposed to do was explain why a story appeared with one set of details in one document, and with a different set of details in another. I used two methods. First, I compared versions of the same story as they appeared in successive texts. Secondly, I asked about the larger tendencies of the framers of the texts, viewed as a whole and one by one. So the two approaches I advocate here to the problem of sorting out and making sense of diverse versions of a saying or a story—documentary, then incremental-historical—find ample illustration in *Development of a Legend*. The main point is that I appealed to the then established facts that one document came from one school among the talmudic sages, another and parallel document from a different school, with its distinctive viewpoint. I took the view that traits (at the time) pretty well known to characterize one school and its documents might also guide me to explain why that same school would tell a story in one way and not in some other. This I did for the entire corpus of sayings and stories concerning Yohanan ben Zakkai.

In context and in intellect the book failed for a host of reasons. In that naive period of my life, I assumed books get read, authors' theories get taken up. I did not know that people could dismiss a book by looking for some minor detail and determining that they did not agree with it (hence: an error), or by saying that the fact was a fact but had already been seen to be a fact before, a claim made without reference to the service the said fact had earlier contributed to some other book (hence: ho-hum). The one serious review the book got recognized its contribution to the study of Yohanan ben Zakkai, but did not take up the larger methodological theory I had tried to define. So much for context. The intellectual failure lay not with the audience but with the author. I never made explicit the methodological experiment I then proposed to carry out. I left matters inarticulate and inchoate. My guilt lay, and it commonly does for me, I admit, in the assumption that things are ineffably obvious. What came to me as self-evident and beyond need for articulation I imagined would prove equally commonplace to everyone else in the world. It has taken me many years to accept the fact that the world is not made up of mind-readers, any more than, in the field in which I work, it is made up of book-readers. It is what it is. If it is to be made better, the work will have to be done one day at a time, and in one book at a time.

Yet these lessons of age, requiring me now to restate in clear and simple terms things I then feared I had said in an all-too-obvious way fifteen years ago, do not lead me to dismiss the project. On the contrary, *Development of a Legend* and the books that carried forward its basic inquiry, *Rabbinic Traditions about the Pharisees before 70* and *Eliezer ben Hyrcanus: The Tradition and the Man*, did invoke the two modes I advocate here for explaining why sayings and stories change as they move. That is to say, I did ask systematically (1) whether the authors of a document made changes in received sayings and stories for reasons characteristic of their document as a whole, that is the documentary theory. And I did ask systematically (2) what we learn about the historical context and viewpoint of the authors of a document that are revealed in received sayings and stories, that is what I call the incremental-history-theory. Let me therefore provide a reprise of how I originally exemplified these two quite distinct approaches to our problem, and then explain what I think is wrong, and remains right, with each of them.

One might ask first about the tendencies of documents' authors. Specifically, will what is established overall allow us to account for shifts and changes in versions of discrete sayings and stories? For this purpose we deal with two collections of scriptural exegeses on the book of Exodus, one attributed to the school of Ishmael, the other to the school of Aqiba. I reproduce both passages, together with my discussion of them, as they originally appeared in *Development of a Legend*. In what follows as a comment, I.i.2 refers to Ishmael's version, I.ii.1 to Aqiba's, of the *Mekhilta*. That is, the former, I.i.2 derives from the *Mekhilta of Ishmael*, the latter, I.ii.1, from the *Mekhilta of Simeon b. Yohai*, who is supposed to have been a disciple of the school of Aqiba. With these facts in hand, the passages will be reasonably accessible.

2(a)   *For if Thou Lift up Thy Sword upon it* (Exod. 20.25). In this connection R. Simon b. Eleazar used to say, 'The altar is made to prolong the years of man and iron is made to shorten the years of man. It is not right for that which shortens life to be lifted up against that which prolongs life.'

(b)   R. Yohanan b. Zakkai says, 'Behold it says: *Thou shalt build... of whole stones* (Deut. 27.6). They are to be stones that establish peace.'

(c)   'Now, by using the method of *qal vehomer*, you reason: The stones for the altar do not see nor hear nor speak. Yet because they serve to establish peace between Israel and their Father in heaven, the Holy One, blessed be he, said, *Thou shalt lift up no iron tool upon them* (*ibid.*, v. 5). How much the more then should he who establishes peace between man and his fellow-man, between husband and wife, between city and city, between nation and nation, between family and family, between government and government, be protected so that no harm should come to him' (*Mekhilta de Rabbi Ishmael*, Bahodesh 11 [ed. and trans. J. Lauterbach, II], p. 290).

On this passage I commented:

I.ii.1, the Aqiban version given presently, substitutes *sons of Torah* for *peacemakers* who escape punishment; it omits the *altar*, and the *sword shortens life* becomes the *sword as a sign of punishment*. The *altar* does not prolong life but *atones* for Israel. I.ii.1 thus shows what the Aqiban party made of this midrash, which was none too palatable to them. The essential element was the exegesis on whole stone/peace. The function of the altar was that of making peace. Therefore peace-makers in this world perform the function of the altar—and more so! This is Yohanan's essential idea; the functions performed by the Temple and its instruments can be replaced by human virtues. So the *qal vehomer* preserved in the Ishmaelean tradition I.i.2 and I.ii.5 is also originally from Yohanan, and the saying of Simeon b. Eleazar in I.i.2 shows an early development of Yohanan's idea in its original spirit; war is bad, peace is good. The Aqibans therefore omitted the exegesis of peace/whole stones; revised the *qal vehomer* to make the essential virtue *not* peace-making but study of the Torah; revised Simeon's saying to make both the sword and the altar symbols of the attributes of the divine nature—judgment and mercy, thus making the sword a good thing too; and attributed all of their revised complex to Yohanan. And they did an amazingly good job—their revised version looks so much like the original that the careless reader would think them nearly identical. It is only when one looks closely that he sees the reversal of the implications.

We proceed to the version of the same saying as presented in what I then thought was the *Mekhilta* to be attributed to the school of Aqiba:

This is what Rabban Yohanan ben Zakkai says, 'What was the reason iron was prohibited more than all [other] metals [for use in building the tabernacle (Exod. 20.25)]? Because the sword is made from it, and the sword is a sign of punishment, but the altar is a sign of atonement. A sign (means) of atonement.'

'And is this not a matter of *qal vehomer*? Stones, which neither see nor hear nor speak—because they bring atonement between Israel and their father in heaven, the Holy One blessed be he said (concerning them) *Thou shalt lift upon them no iron tool* (Deut. 27.5). Sons of Torah, who are an atonement for the world, how much the more so that none of all the harmful forces in the world should ever touch them!' (*Mek. Sby, Yitro* 20.22 [ed. Epstein-Melamed], pp. 157-58, 1.29-31, 1-4).

On this passage I said:

> We have two separate sayings. The first is Yohanan's, that metal is prohibited because the sword is made of metal and is a sign of punishment, while the altar is a sign of atonement. The second saying is the *qal vehomer*, that as stones should not be injured because they bring atonement, so sons of Torah should all the more so be free of injury from harmful forces. The *qal vehomer* has nothing to do with Yohanan's observation, and need not be directly attributed to him, though it occurs in all formulations of this passage. It seems to be a later development.

By way of amplifying the same matter, let me give a further instance of invoking what I then imagined was a trait of Aqiban tradents to explain diverse versions of similarly connected materials:

> Rabban Yohanan ben Zakkai says, 'Behold it says, [*With*] *whole stones* [avanim shelemot] *will you build the altar of the Lord your God* (Deut. 27.5)—Stones which make peace [*shalom*], and behold it is a matter of *qal vehomer*: Stones which do not see and do not hear and do not speak, because they bring peace between Israel and their father in heaven, Scripture says *You shall not lift up iron over them* (Deut. 27.6). A man who brings peace between a man and his wife, between one family and another, between one city and another, between one province and another, between one nation and another—how much the more so that punishment should not come near him!'

I then commented:

> The exegesis is practically identical with I.ii.1. The Scriptures are different. There it is 'why is iron prohibited' and here it concerns the play on words: 'whole stones—stones which make peace'. *Atonement* becomes *peace*, *sons of Torah* become *peacemakers*. The structure is otherwise the same; the thought is the same ('Peace-makers or those who atone for the world should come to no harm'). The details are somewhat different. Yet the differences are not very considerable. I suspect that Yohanan would have said something about the altar/altar-stones in the form of a *qal vehomer*. The context was Deut. 27.5 and 27.6. The play on words concerning the 'whole stones' was dropped in I.ii.1, the stress on 'iron' of all metals was omitted here. Strikingly, the Ishmaelean version, I.i.2, follows I.ii.5, both versions elide the *whole stones* play on words and the *qal vehomer* involving an iron tool. I should thus suppose that I.i.2 = I.ii.5. I.ii.1 differs,

as I said, in omitting 'whole stones' and stressing 'iron'. Both schools preserved an account exhibiting formal parallels (I.i.2 + I.ii.5), but the Aqibans alone preserved the other (I.ii.1), probably because they invented it. Some anterior version was available to both schools, and that anterior version derived from circles close to Yohanan himself. In a period of less than a few decades between Yohanan's death and the formation of the schools of Ishmael and Aqiba, a group of Yohanan's disciples must have put into final form materials which were subsequently made use of by *both* schools. This supposition is likely to be valid if the following conditions are also valid: (1) if both documents actually come from the schools to which they are attributed; (2) if the present form was edited ca. 200, if not somewhat earlier; and most important (3) if they were *not* expanded since that time. Then the story stands in both by AD 200 and was known to teachers in both schools. The common source of the story would have come substantially earlier than the founding of the two schools, ca. 100–120. In that case, as I said, the story is certainly part of the corpus of Yohanan-sayings edited by the time of Yavneh. We may safely go a step further and designate as Yavnean, *all* materials occurring in substantially similar form in materials ascribed to the two schools; as Ishmaelean, materials unique to that school, hence not necessarily later than Yavneh but probably from a circle at Yavneh not known or acceptable to the Aqibans; as Aqiban, materials unique to that school, within the same limitation. It would be tempting to suppose that materials unique to one or the other school were later than materials common to both, but the obvious imponderables prevent it. It is consequential, since we have no documents edited at Yavneh, to recognize that within documents edited later on are materials which probably did come from Yavneh. But it is equally noteworthy that even the materials in the earliest collections have already undergone substantial development. Primitive logia, in which stories or sayings about Yohanan are transcribed close to when they happened or were actually stated, are unavailable. In general, the closest we can come to the man himself is through secondary materials based on Yavnean traditions.

In conclusion I stated these results:

The condemnation of war and reproaches in its aftermath may likewise have been acceptable in the school whose master did not encourage the holy war of Bar Kokhba, but in any event ought to have been quite obnoxious to the one whose master did. Service of the Lord in love would have preserved the prosperity of the people, and the implied condemnation of war is present in the Ishmaelean stories about the Israelite girl.

In all I think it has been proven that no *Tendenz* concerning Yohanan *himself* characterized either school. Both preserved favorable, and more important, authoritative sayings and precedents. His legal role is, if anything, slightly greater among the Aqibans than among the Ishmaeleans, but the data are too sparse for this to matter much. More important: *where the two schools differ in the sorts of stories they preserve about Yohanan, the reason for the difference is certainly found in the interests of the schools themselves, and not in their attitudes to Yohanan.*

As I sadly look back on the exercise at hand, I take comfort that, despite the obvious fundamentalism throughout, I did have the presence of mind to specify the premises. Accordingly, I emphasize that, even then, I stated as a condition that both documents (1) had to come from the schools to which they were attributed and (2) represent matters in a final way as they emerged from those schools at that time. Of course, those conditions were not met and cannot be shown ever to have been met. So the whole in retrospect stands as what I believe to be a good example of method and a bad example of result. But at least I did not make things up as I went along. And the concluding, italicized judgment is one by which I should firmly stand today. Besides paying attention to the definitive traits of a document, we thus ask about how the context of documents explains, and is explained by, alterations in received versions of sayings and stories.

The results just now presented mark the age in which they were composed, just as much as I claim the same for the sources under discussion. The focus of interest—the historical Yohanan ben Zakkai—began with a limited matter. But more importantly, the things taken for granted as facts comprise a long and disheartening list. But even then I asked, what if the *Mekhilta* of Ishmael does not in fact represent the historical Ishmael and his disciples? What if Simeon did not really study with Aqiba, and what if the *Mekhilta* of Simeon is not 'Aqiban'? What if both *Mekhiltas* were made up in medieval times? Then every word I wrote is not wrong but beside the point.

And, of course, I now grasp the obvious fact that the entire exercise at hand in its original formulation rested on premises that I can now call mere fundamentalism. At every point I took for granted that whatever is imputed to a sage really was said about him, with only one exception: Yohanan ben Zakkai. I further assumed that whatever story was told really represented the state of affairs in the time and place to which the story referred, except for the historical setting of Yohanan ben Zakkai himself. On those bases the study rested. But the premises scarcely escape the simple criticism that, at each point, they share those traits of gullibility and credulity that then, as now, I have attempted to overcome.

Asking how we know what Yohanan ben Zakkai really said and did, I failed to inquire into how we know that anything imputed to anyone claiming to know what Yohanan ben Zakkai really said and did also demands answers to exactly the same question. It took me a long time— several more books—to understand that simple fact and also to confront it and draw the consequences dictated by it. Others assuredly recognized the same problem. But I was the only one to try to solve it. And by redefining the foci of inquiry, I did solve it.

The reason that *Development of a Legend* made so little impression in its day, however, is not that it was insufficiently critical. By the standards not only of that day but also of the present age, a decade and a half and many books later, *Development of a Legend* remains too radical in its methods, in its points of fundamental insistence, for the generality of scholars in the field to confront. If they respond to the book at all, it is by pointing out misprints or minor variant readings that do not affect meaning. This means they cannot take up the challenge of the book and all that followed it. Why the avoidance? Because if *Development of a Legend* points to what work must be done, then the sort of scholarly work people now do cannot be done. It is one thing to recognize the utter obsolescence of everything accomplished in the critical study of the history of the Jews and of Judaism in late antiquity, so far as the rabbinic canon constitutes the principal literary source. It is quite another to insist, as I did and do insist, that everything people now propose as a scholarly program rests on the same false premises.

The way lies open to inquiry into the relationship of text to context, of detail to main point of insistence. Results of the inquiry will tell us something about why a given set of ideas became self-evident and remained manifestly 'right' for a very long time. Then we may also find a clue as to why those same ideas, that same system of a world-view and a way of life characteristic of a single social group for a long span of history, lost the trait of self-evidence and became manifestly irrelevant. That is to say, at stake is how to interpret the history of Judaism: its formation and persistence, change and renewal. The first task is to describe, analyze, and interpret the facts in hand. Among these facts, the obvious ones concern how, to the naked eye, a story will change as it is told and retold, a saying will undergo revision when it is repeated.

Let me close by placing into the correct, appropriately large, context the humble facts that have occupied us for so long. Why, specifically, do I regard as indicative the persistence and transformation of sayings and stories? And what do I hope will be indicated? The answer lies in the three basic dimensions by which we take the measure of every document of the canon of Judaism, from the Mishnah through the Bavli.

Every book of the canon stands by itself. Each is *autonomous*.

Except for the Mishnah and Scripture, every book in the canon refers back to some other book. Some of the books relate as a whole to the Mishnah. They serve as exegeses and amplifications of the Mishnah. Others depend upon Scripture. So every book in the canon, except for the Mishnah and Scripture, is not only autonomous but also *connected* to some other book. The autonomy is limited by connection.

And, finally, all of the books together, Scripture and the Mishnah, Tosefta and the Talmuds, Sifra, the two Sifres, Genesis Rabbah, Leviticus Rabbah, and the rest of the compositions, viewed whole, all at once, and in their entirety, constitute the 'one whole Torah of Moses, our rabbi'. That continuity is not merely the *post factum* assertion of the believing community. It also constitutes a fact to be induced from evidence by detailed inquiry into the shared conceptions and values, alleged at the end of the process of the formation of the canon as a whole, to characterize all documents of the canon. Looking backward, I should not be prepared to make an exception in that characterization, even of Scriptures. That is so even though sages, in the manner of their age and all ages before and since, read into Scripture whatever they wished to see there. That qualification should not present an exception to this simple claim: the documents all together do constitute a canon. So they establish a *continuity* from one to the next and among them all.

Two of the three dimensions of the canon—autonomy, connection, continuity—obviously appear to the naked eye: autonomy and connection. A document, by definition, stands alone and autonomous. The Tosefta, the Mishnah, the two Sifres, each will reward examination on its own. The connection of all of the compositions of the canon to either Scripture or the Mishnah comes to vivid expression in the fundamental redactional preferences of each document. The Tosefta is organized in accord with the order of passages of the Mishnah, the two Talmuds with the same structure, and all compilations of scriptural exegeses ('midrashim') follow the order of verses in the book of Scripture they allegedly explain. The variations in degree of explicit dependence, for redactional order and structure, on one or the other of the two base-documents make little difference.

But when we ask whether and how the documents form a continuity from one to the next and among all of them together constitute a canon, where shall we look for relevant data? I see only two sources of facts for the assessment of where and how documents relate as a whole to one another, not only back to a single shared source of structure supplied by Scripture or the Mishnah. One source flows from shared conceptions, symbols, fundamental and everywhere definitive values. The other source derives from shared sayings and stories. The contrast speaks for itself.

The former source—shared symbols—flows at random and aimlessly, much as at floodtide the sea overcomes the shore, and the river its banks. We never know the limits. We form impressions of where the boundaries lie, only to discover, as water recedes and advances, that, short of going out and wading around, we have missed the mark dividing dry shore from ocean or river. But if we wade out in the shifting tide, we may drown. So too if we aimlessly seize upon one ubiquitous value or another and allege that one congeries defines what is shared, uniform, continuous, and another does not, we shall drown in facts. We shall never have a clear criterion for knowing when we are right, and when we are wrong. One need not dismiss as impressionistic the great and valiant efforts of such exemplary scholars as George Foot Moore and Max Kadushin (let alone lesser figures) to recognize the failures they left behind. The field of learning in the nineteenth and twentieth centuries is strewn with the carcasses of abandoned definitions of 'Judaism', including the system of Judaism revealed by the canon concluded in late antiquity.

But there endures that other source of information—shared sayings and stories—on what moves in continuity from one document to another. These constitute the hard facts of the matter. What in fact travels from the Mishnah to the Tosefta to the Yerushalmi to the Bavli, or from a Mekhilta to the Tosefta to the Fathers according to Rabbi Nathan, or hither and yon or here and there? The peripatetic saying and the thrice-told tale—these alone constitute concrete, material proofs of the actualities, of continuity. They define facts of whatever continuity there is among the documents of the canon and so to begin with make possible the claim that autonomous documents relate not in general, in 'values', but very particularly, in verbatim sayings. Then we may see, in the character of detail, that main point that we seek. The shape of the whole, the measure of the dimension of continuity—these to begin with emerge from the simple fact that the same saying or story will be shared among two or more documents of the canon. That synoptic fact validates the claim of continuity, though obviously not exhausting what is meant by the claim. But, in the details of what is like and what is unlike in the travelling tale and the peripatetic saying we see clearly, without distortion, what is common to important components of the canon of Judaism. True, all we have at the moment is detail. But of canonical Judaism we cannot speak just now, except to say that, after all, God really does live in the details.

ADDENDUM

It is correct to say that each document in rabbinic literature is to be described in three relationships: as an autonomous statement on its own, as a writing connected with other writings, and as part of a continuous statement, the oral Torah. It is at the matter of connections of documents that the present article seems to me primitive and essentially retrograde. Looking backward ten years later, I see a major misapprehension in this essay, namely, my erroneous view that shared sayings and stories form a sizable component of the documents that altogether form rabbinic literature in late antiquity. Subsequent research showed me that the continuities comprised by stories and sayings that travel between and among documents in volume and in importance prove inconsequential. In volume such traveling tales do not form a more than negligible portion of a single document, though, as everyone understands, one document may well cite another; for example, the Tosefta cites the Mishnah, and the two Talmuds cite both. How matters look when seen altogether is clear, for I have now completed the documentary description of each of the components of the canon, the final results being spelled out in my *Introduction to Rabbinic Literature* (ABRL; Garden City, NY: Doubleday, 1994). There I spell out why each document has to be described in terms of its own rhetoric, logic and topical (even propositional) program. Where sayings or stories move from one document to another, the changes that characterize the successive versions conform to the requirements of the documents where the versions occur and are predictable.

The relationships between and among documents have to be investigated in two other aspects altogether. First, the documents intersect in certain shared forms. Here too, however, I have found that though some of the same forms occur in more than a single document, the formal program defined by the formers of a given document governs the repertoire of fixed forms that characterize said document; forms have no independent existence, autonomous of documents. This is the firm result of my *The Documentary Form-History of Rabbinic Literature* (to be published in twelve parts and fourteen volumes by Scholars Press in 1997). Secondly, the documents come together because they are deemed to constitute a canon; that is, the oral Torah. Hence the work of systematic theological description ought to show how the several canonical components work together to make a cogent statement. The initial exercise on this problem is my planned *The Theology of the Oral Torah: A Prolegomenon* (Kingston and Montreal: McGill and Queens University Press, forthcoming 1998).

PRACTICE

JSNT 8 (1980), pp. 46-65

REDACTION CRITICISM: JOSEPHUS'S *ANTIQUITIES*
AND THE SYNOPTIC GOSPELS

F. Gerald Downing

Part 1: Josephus

In Josephus's *Antiquities* we can see quite clearly the work of a first-century Hellenistic Jewish redactor. We have his sources (mainly the canonical Scriptures) in a form very close to that which he used, and so can discern the direction and the extent of the changes made. This allows for a useful comparison with the Synoptic Gospels, where the direction (and therefore the kind) of change is still in dispute; and especially with Luke's Gospel, where the stated intentions and the widely agreed 'tendencies' are often identical with those of Josephus.

That the writers of the Synoptic Gospels were redactors is largely accepted. They were neither simply repeating, recording, or working from memory; but neither were they just inventing material. They were using extant traditions, written or oral or both; they were adapting, embellishing, re-ordering, and perhaps also sometimes but not always creating narrative and speech; and it seems possible to detect at least something of the distinctive message that each writer's finished work conveys and was meant to convey. Yet this widely agreed approach produces rather less widely agreed results, at least in part because it is still not agreed as to who among the synoptists used whom: the direction and therefore the character of the redactional process remains undetermined.[1]

---

1.   See, for instance, N. Perrin, *What is Redaction Criticism?* (London: SPCK, 1970) for a convenient bibliography up to that date. On questions that remain in synoptic source-criticism, see, e.g., B. Orchard, 'Are all Gospel Synopses Biased?', *TZ* 34.3 (1978), pp. 149-62.

It may seem therefore doubly worthwhile to investigate the procedures of a contemporary redactor of sources such as Josephus, also writing from a Hellenistic-Jewish milieu; especially when, as will be shown in due course, his stated aims and many of his more obvious tendencies are closely paralleled in Luke among the synoptists. (That Josephus is a 'redactor' in the *Antiquities* is clear to all recent commentators: he recasts, omits, re-orders, adapts, in line with the 'message' which he tells us he intends to convey.) There appears, however, to have been little attempt to relate such studies as have appeared of Josephus's methods, to the issue of redaction in the Synoptic Gospels.[2] This present essay attempts to sketch something of Josephus's manner of working, and its possible bearing on our understanding of Luke in particular, but then also of Mark and Matthew (and John, too). It is also to be hoped that Josephus may appear interesting in his own right.

For his own, earlier, *Jewish War*, Josephus claimed 'not merely to remodel the scheme and arrangements of another's work (but) to use fresh materials, and make the framework of the history his own' (*War* 1.15). At the time he thought it superfluous to do the same for the ancient history of the Jews; but later, persuaded by his 'most excellent Epaphroditos', he undertook to write 'our entire ancient history and political constitution, translated (μεθηρμηνευμένην) from the Hebrew records' (*Ant.* 1.5, Proem; 20.261–62), and became much less complimentary to his 'predecessors' than he had been before.

His sources were the Hebrew Scriptures, to which he refers, and the Septuagint translation, together with the *Universal History* of Herod the Great's courtier, Nicholas of Damascus, the *Letter of Aristeas* (of which we have copies), and part of 1 Maccabees; stylistic sources may have included especially Sophocles and Thucydides. Josephus seems also to have been strongly influenced by Dionysius of Halicarnassus's *Roman Antiquities* (*R.A.*), written a century earlier, but still, it seems, popular. From it he borrowed his title and the division into twenty books, but also much more (*vide infra*). He also inherited, it would seem, an already extensive tradition of rabbinic *midrash*.[3]

---

2.   A useful but limited study on Josephus's procedures, with full bibliography, is H.W. Attridge, *The Interpretation of Biblical History in the Antiquitates Judaicae of Flavius Josephus* (Missoula, MT: Scholars Press, 1976); see further below.

3.   Josephus, *Antiquities, Jewish War and Against Apion* (ed. H.St.J. Thackeray *et al.*; LCL; London: Heinemann, 1927), etc. The editors' notes on rabbinic and classical sources are occasionally referred to in passing; but see also D. Runnals, *Hebrew*

Despite his use of these extra sources, and despite his pride in his own contribution, Josephus insists that there is no discrepancy in the ancient records, and that no Jew would remove or alter a syllable; and also claims that his own work mirrors this accuracy: he will neither add nor omit anything (*Apion* 1.37–42; *Ant.* 1.17, 12.109, 14.1, 20.261). He intends to re-tell with complete accuracy what is already accurately recorded. It should therefore be possible to gauge from Josephus what might 'count as' an accurate reproduction of a sacred text, which interpretation is so clearly legitimate as to need no defence; but also what the limits are that he seems to feel bound to observe, while he conflates, excises, cross-references, and embellishes to make his intended case.

An analysis will be sketched of Josephus's use of two single narratives, *Aristeas* outside the canon, and Joshua–Judges within; of his manner of collecting together scattered legal, teaching and hortatory material (from Deuteronomy, etc.); and of his treatment of parallel accounts (in Samuel–Kings and in Chronicles).

Aristeas is especially interesting, since it is already much more nearly in the style and language that Josephus intends than are the septuagintal texts; and it also provides a comparison with his use of canonical material. There is the further not inconsiderable advantage that his version has already been studied in detail by A. Pelletier, in his *Flavius Josèphe, Adapteur de la Lettre d' Aristée*.[4]

Pelletier makes it clear that Josephus's prime intention is to paraphrase, 'to change whatever he can' (p. 222) if only by inversion. Apart from inventories, and one or two set formulae, Pelletier finds just one (broken) sequence of twelve words, and another of ten, that are identical in both; other than these there are only short phrases or individual words. Even with individual words Josephus will sometimes for

and Greek Sources in the Speeches of Josephus' Jewish War (doctoral dissertation, University of Toronto, 1971); G. Vermes, *Post-Biblical Jewish Studies* (SJLA, 8; Leiden: Brill, 1975). Among studies (of Josephus's methods along with other issues) published more recently, I note T. Rajak, *Josephus* (London: Gerald Duckworth, 1983); P. Bilde, *Flavius Josephus, between Jerusalem and Rome* (JSPSup, 2; Sheffield: JSOT Press, 1988); and many studies by L.H. Feldman (see the bibliography in Bilde, *Flavius Josephus*) and recently Feldman's 'Josephus's Portrait of Manasseh', *JSP* 9 (1991), pp. 3-20; and C. Begg, 'The Gedaliah Episode and its Sequels in Josephus', *JSP* 12 (1994), pp. 21-46. Many more examples of very similar motifs and ideology to those picked out in my study appear in these later ones. For Dionysius see LCL (ed. E. Cary; London: Heinemann, 1937).

    4.   Paris: Cerf, 1962.

(a) substitute synonym (b), only later, on finding (b) in his source, render it by (a) (p. 29). Occasionally technical terms are brought up to date (nearly three centuries divide Josephus from *Aristeas*). And sometimes Pelletier can make a strong case for there being a theological or apologetic motive behind a change or an omission. For instance, in the well-known passage on 'natural religion', it may well be the case that Josephus avoids any suggestion that pagans might find a meaningful *name* for God (as that depends on revelation to Moses) but at the same time is insisting even more strongly that the God they invoke is the God also worshipped by the Jews (pp. 31ff.).

When Josephus omits the whole account of the embassy of Philadelphus to Jerusalem it has been suggested that he had a deficient text. Pelletier argues rather that Josephus is maintaining his concentration on events, in preference to descriptions of countryside and cultus; but it may also be noted that such descriptions have already appeared in his *Jewish War* and his *Antiquities* respectively; and that the reception accorded the embassy is not as respectful as Josephus might expect of his compatriots greeting eminent and friendly foreigners. This section contains in addition a lot of the 'Alexandrian' symbolism which Josephus all but completely eschews, preferring a practical to a speculative Judaism.

Josephus also omits *Aristeas* 37, where anti-Semitic views are expressed; and 293, which might look like a description of an unlawful common meal; he allows only one prostration before the new scrolls, rather than the seven of *Aristeas* 335, which by Josephus's time were held to be appropriate to God alone. He adds a fulsome introduction for Aristeas himself, a flattering appeal to Philadelphus the enlightened ruler, a note on the unaided hard work of the translators, and perhaps an admission that by his time variant copies of the Septuagint were in circulation. He concludes his version of the narrative with 'These, then, were the things done by Ptolemy Philadelphus in appreciation and honour of the Jews' (*Ant.* 12.118), and Pelletier points out that the ensuing paragraphs on Jewish privileges explain the over-riding point of Josephus's inclusion of this lengthy excursus: it provides a precedent for an appeal that the Jews' most recent conquerors (the Flavian emperors) might return the exiles of their day to their ancestral worship and way of life in their fatherland (pp. 32, 206).

Pelletier's list of 'significant' changes takes about seven out of his more than two hundred pages to describe, and amounts in number to about two dozen. Of the remaining changes, quite a few, he is able to show, are 'Atticizing' improvements in vocabulary and syntax. But he urges (I find, convincingly) that mostly they are changes for change's sake.

What follows is not even based on as detailed and minute a study as Pelletier's. However, it is possible to follow other scholars' more piece-meal discussions of Greek style; and a swift glance will show that Josephus seems to have felt as free to change the septuagintal Greek as the non-canonical *Aristeas*, and perhaps even more inclined to. What is offered here is a summary account of changes of content and order in Josephus's use of some of his scriptural sources: first from his version of Joshua–Judges.[5]

a. *Omissions*
These include the following roughly devised classes:

(1) *Discrepancies.* Some material has been left out in an attempt to harmonize, for example, various accounts of what was captured, and what was not (compare Josh. 10.28-42; Judg. 1.8, the complete early capture of Jerusalem; also Judg. 20.27, the Ark's too-early presence in Bethel; with the relevant sections of *Antiquities* 5).

(2) *Duplicates.* Repetition is often avoided: for instance, God's speech at Josh. 1.1b-9 is left out, since it mainly comprises material already included from the end of Deuteronomy. There are no instructions on crossing the Jordan to anticipate the actual event (Joshua 3); nor for the siege of Jericho, nor the second attack on Ai. All but a few details from Judges 5 are excluded from the re-telling of the Deborah–Barak saga (Judges 4).

(3) *Interruptions.* Where possible, the flow of a narrative will be improved by an occasional excision. For example, there is no three-day wait in the hills for the spies (Josh. 2.22); the people do not have to return for stones to erect across the river, they have brought them with them (*Ant.* 5.20, Joshua 4). The account of Phineas's assumption of leadership benefits from the drastic curtailment of Joshua's final speech (Joshua 23–Judges 1). (The 'duplicates' just referred to are of course also 'interruptions' in a sense.)

(4) *Miracle and Magic.* Josephus lived in a sceptical age; and, though for him all is 'providential', he prefers to think of God working through

---

5. R.J.H. Shutt (*Studies in Josephus* [London: SPCK, 1961]) disagrees with Thackeray's (LCL) detection of classical influence.

'nature', rather than by-passing it, through men rather than over-riding them. So the Jordan just becomes shallow, and turns out to have a firm bed (compare Joshua 3). There are no 'magical' gestures with a javelin (Josh. 8.18). As in Joshua 10, there is an unusually long day, but no standstill of the sun. This group of omissions links closely with the next.

(5) *'Inappropriate' Theology.* Josephus is himself convinced of the reality and value of prophecy and of divine communication through dreams, but excludes apparitions if he can avoid them (e.g. Josh. 5.13-15; Judg. 2.1). Gideon's 'angel' becomes a vision of a young man, and Gideon does not need to test his message (*Ant.* 5.213–14).

Other omissions for fairly obvious theological reasons include God's supposed concern for his own reputation (Josh. 7.9); divine determinism (Josh. 11.20; *vide supra* and also the failure to mention any hardening of Pharaoh's heart in *Antiquities* 2); the exhortation to 'love' God (Josh. 22.5, and compare *Antiquities* 4 *passim*, discussed below); and the promise that God's covenant is unbreakable (Judg. 2.1: Josephus may well have supposed it had been broken, *War* 5.413–14, 7.327–28).

(6) *The Apologetically Awkward.* This group also links closely with the two foregoing sections, and it is to be hoped that something of Josephus's theological intentions as a redactor is beginning to emerge. God's exhortation to Joshua may have been left out not just to avoid repetition (see above), but also because such a leader would not need it. And there is no need for the people to 'sanctify' themselves (Joshua 3); Josephus is very sensitive to charges that they had been expelled from Egypt as unclean (*Apion* 1.228–87). Nor do they have to 'renew' the rite of circumcision (Josh. 5.2-9). Past wickednesses of the Israelites no longer appear in the reproaches of *Ant.* 5.106–10. The altar built by the trans-Jordanians is a reminder to themselves, rather than being designed to avert the possible hostility of the majority (*Ant.* 5.112). The homosexual demand of Judg. 19.22 disappears, as do the somewhat discreditable saga of Micah and the Danite cult (Judges 17–18) together with all traces of apostasy from Judges 10. Kings are treated with more respect, often avoiding execution (*Ant.* 5.61, 67). Josephus, who believes (with his model, Dionysius) in 'aristocracy', not tyranny, omits the popular election of Abimelech (*Ant.* 5.234). Nazirite rules do not affect women (*Ant.* 5.270). The heroine Rahab is not a whore (contrast Joshua 2) .

b. *Additions*

Some of the categories are of course simply the contraries of the foregoing.

(1) *Harmony and Continuity*. We have seen that Josephus 'tidies up' the story of the crossing of the Jordan: it would seem to be too obviously important an episode simply to omit. But the elaborate procedure appears to embarrass him, and he has to explain that 'the army was afraid to cross the river, which had a strong current'; it had never been bridged, and could not be in mid-campaign, and there were no boats (*Ant.* 5.16; these are all issues in Dionysius's various references to the Tiber). If a curse is placed on Jericho we must be told at once of its fulfilment (*Ant.* 5.34). Achan's 'burial' is assimilated to the law and to later incidents (*Ant.* 5.44, cf. 124). The Gibeonites' ruse is given an initial explanation (however unnecessary) and confederates who only appear later in Joshua are introduced from the start (*Ant.* 5.49–50). If the Lord tells Joshua not to be afraid (Josh. 11.6) this has to have the somewhat banal 'explanation' that Joshua and the army *were* dismayed, terrified (*Ant.* 5.64, cf. 213–18). If Phineas prophesies 'the will of God' it has to be in answer to the people's eager enquiry (*Ant.* 5.120; Dionysius insists that more than the mere outcome of events must be given by the historian, and the underlying 'causes' that he presents are often of this kind).[6] The harmonization of Josh. 11.21-23 with 13.2, etc., which we have already noted, continues with the insertion of a reference to the strength of the remaining strongholds (*Ant.* 5.71). In case the reader is puzzled by the calling of a second national assembly, he is told in advance that Joshua is too old to travel round, and has ineffective deputies (*Ant.* 5.90). In Judges, upper Jerusalem is left intact for later capture (*Ant.* 5.124).

(2) *Providence and Prophecy*. The crossing of the Jordan is enabled by no 'unnatural' event (as we have already seen), but by a promised and providential 'coincidence' (*Ant.* 5.16, cf. 24). Joshua himself is a prophet (*Ant.* 5.20, cf. 120, 253, 276–85, a frequent addition in Josephus). We are reminded of God's providence again at *Ant.* 5.73, 90–91, and 107 (the goodwill of God their gracious ally; his grace and providence, πρόνοια). Escape from God's authority and vengeance is impossible (*Ant.* 5.109). God's initiative is underlined in the Deborah–Barak story (*Ant.* 5.200–204). Samson's birth is through God's good providence (*Ant.* 5.277), and Samson, for all his pride, ends by admitting that 'all is

6.   Dionysius (ed. Cary), Introduction, pp. xvff., and references.

attributable to God' (*Ant.* 5.302); despite which, and despite being 'under God's providence', he 'needs must (ἔδει)' fall victim (*Ant.* 5.312). Dionysius also hoped to reassert a trust in divine providence.[7]

(3) *Piety and Moral Uplift.* Joshua's angry protest (Josh. 7.7ff.) becomes instead a self-deprecating 'it was from no confidence in ourselves' (*Ant.* 5.38). Achan and others (see above) receive each a decent burial. It is stressed that Joshua is genuinely deceived into allowing the divinely forbidden treaty with the Gibeonites (*Ant.* 5.55, cf. 59). The meeting at Shilo assembles 'with alacrity', and is first reminded how fine and worthy of the Deity who had vouchsafed them were the successes already achieved, and of the excellence of his laws; before getting down to business (*Ant.* 5.73). The trans-Jordanians are reminded, 'it is one God who brought your forefathers and ours into existence...while you remain faithful, God will show himself your faithful ally'. (σύμμαχος, frequent in both *Jewish War* and *Antiquities*, epitomizes a sense of divine grace and human responsibility; it is perhaps borrowed from Dionysius; *Ant.* 5.93–99.)[8] Josephus explains the punitive expedition across the river as being due to zeal for the will of God (βουλ- words are common in his writing); but Phineas must not appear willing to shoot first and ask questions later, so is allowed to concede 'there may have been some pious motive' (*Ant.* 5.102–107). 'Repentance' (μετάνοια), frequently added by Josephus (stressed in Dionysius as well as in native Jewish tradition), is commended at *Ant.* 5.108, 151, 240; and at 302. Shortly before he dies, Joshua, in his shortened speech, reminds the Israelites that it is by piety (εὐσέβεια) alone that they will retain the friendship of God (*Ant.* 5.116; again, compare Dionysius). He receives a glowing obituary: 'intelligent, lucid, brave, daring, a dextrous administrator' (*Ant.* 5.115–18). Samson is similarly commended (for his valour, strength, grandeur, wrath); 'that he let himself be ensnared by a woman must be imputed to human nature which succumbs to sin; but testimony is due to him for surpassing excellence (πάντα τῆς ἀρετῆς) in all the rest' (*Ant.* 5.317). Deborah is asked to pray for God's pity (*Ant.* 5.201), and Jephthah prays for victory (as well as making the rash vow for which Josephus firmly rebukes him; *Ant.* 5.236, 266).

(4) *Apologetics.* Joshua is generous to a fault in rewarding Rahab

7.   *R.A.* 2.68 and *passim.*
8.   Dionysus of Halicarnassus, *R.A.* 6.6.3; cf. Attridge, *Interpretation of Biblical History*, pp. 92ff.; he is wrong (at least of Dionysius) in his denial of a similar stress on 'piety' in Greek historians (*Interpretation of Biblical History*, p. 183).

(*Ant.* 5.30). The trans-Jordanians are reassured that the claims of kinship will not be forgotten (cf. the omission noted above, of any fear that it might be; *Ant.* 5.97). The suggestion in Josh. 22.19 that the land might be unclean is changed to a more tactful query about the distance being possibly 'a hindrance to sober living' (*Ant.* 5.109). To be defeated by words, they are told, is better than to be defeated by war (the whole speech is very reminiscent of those in *Jewish War* made to the rebels by or on behalf of the magnanimous Romans. In the old days, reason would by this stage have prevailed among the Israelites). For reminders of past apostasy (Josh. 22.13-20) are substituted suspicions about the present only (*Ant.* 5.101ff.); the apostasy of Judg. 2.11-23 becomes the decline of an affluent society (*Ant.* 5.132–35, cf. 179ff.). And Deborah rebukes Barak for asking her to lead (it must not appear that female leadership is normal among the Jews; *Ant.* 5.203).

(5) *Interest and Clarity.* Josephus tries to make the bare narrative of Joshua 2 into a more plausible spy-story. The agents are initially taken to be sight-seers, and it is only later that suspicion is aroused and rumour reaches the king, who expresses his intention to torture information from them. Rahab is an inn-keeper (as in the Palestinian Targum), and she makes a much more convincing show of her loyalty to her own monarch. She has in fact been prompted by signs from God to co-operate with the invaders; not just Joshua alone, but the high priest and all the elders ratify the spies' oath to her before any further move is made; and then the operation is carried out with speed (*Ant.* 5.5–15).

When it is a matter of natural phenomena, Josephus is willing to enhance the operation of providence: the hail-storm of Josh. 10.11 includes thunder-claps and thunder-bolts (*Ant.* 5.60; cf. Dionysius *R.A.* 9.55.2). The total slaughter in Joshua 11 is literally 'incredible', so Josephus allows 'a few' to escape (*Ant.* 5.66). Only when Joshua has won the assent of the people to the proposed land-division does he send out 'expert surveyors', who are necessary because of the embarrassing richness of the soil; and the division is by valuation, not arbitrarily by area (*Ant.* 5.76–79; Joshua thus avoids all the agrarian troubles which beset early Rome). Joshua displays the insights of an experienced personnel manager before he allows the trans-Jordanians to depart (*Ant.* 5.94). There are tears and a difficult parting (notes of emotion are a frequent device in Josephus and in Dionysius, to maintain interest, and perhaps in some measure to 'explain' the subsequent action of people so moved, by sorrow, fear, joy and so on; as already noted).

In similar vein, the tale of the Levite's mistress (Judges 19–21) becomes a much more intensely tragic love-story. The Levite ('of the lower ranks') is deeply in love; the woman is beautiful but fails to requite his love (rather than 'plays the harlot'), which coolness only further inflames him, leading to quarrels and her return home to her parents. However, when he follows, they are reconciled; and it is only parental affection that creates the fateful delay. In the assault, the prospective rapists are firmly heterosexual, though otherwise even less concerned with 'righteousness', an they threaten the old man with death. In response he offers only his daughter, and they seize rather than are given, the other woman. We share the full pathos of her broken-hearted death, and of her husband's arrival hoping to console her for her totally innocent defilement (*Ant.* 5.136–49).

In the sequel, the 'rapture' of the daughters of Shiloh, the narrative acquires features drawn from Dionysius's already very similar account of the Sabine incident.[9] Josephus also adds that complaining parents were to be told it was their own fault for being careless; and he explains that the girls were from all the tribes, not two hundred of marriageable age from just one town (*Ant.* 5.170–73).

Details are also added to make the Ehud story more plausible: gifts, a dream, joy (*Ant.* 5.188–93). Gideon is permitted a humorous riposte to the 'young man' who brings God's message to tell him how favoured he is; later it is in a dream (Josephus's preferred vehicle) that God addresses him. The enigmatic device for reducing the numbers in the defence force is rather neatly explained as a choice of those adopting the most cowardly posture. The rout is explained: it was due to the diversity of languages in the Midianite army (*Ant.* 5.213–32).

The Samson saga also allows Josephus his romantic imagination. Manoah's wife is very beautiful (but also prayerful) and the angel appears as a handsome young man (cf. *Ant.* 5.213). The woman's description of her visitor arouses Manoah's jealousy; it is for this reason that she requests a second appearance, to reassure Manoah (*Ant.* 5.276–85).

It is only in this sequence that a veiled allusion to Jewish custom seems

---

9. (Ed. Cary), Introduction, pp. xixff. Dionysius's 'additions' to the sources he often seems to share with Livy are very much akin to Josephus's 'additions' to Scripture. *R.A.* 2.30.5, τῆς ἁρπαγῆς ἐπὶ γάμῳ; *Ant.* 5.172, τῆς ἁρπαγῆς γάμον; the presence of wives as well as of daughters; the males in twos and threes; the end in explicit marriage.

to have been added: Samson not only drinks, but drinks with foreigners (*Ant.* 5.289, 306, 308, 310; cf. 278).

It may thus be seen that the only at all frequent *major* additions by Josephus are speeches, in the section of *Antiquities* under review, but even more elsewhere. Here he has added no story, no major event. And this seems to hold for the whole work (so far as we have Josephus's sources, whereby to check). The one apparent exception, Moses' military campaign in *Antiquities* 2, which gains him his Cushite 'princess', in fact already appears in Artapanus, and would thus have had the warrant of an existing 'source'.[10] Josephus certainly, as we have seen, adds and excises details, and can give a quite new colour and import to 'the same' incident, so that it conveys the impression he wants to create (and avoids any he wishes to eschew). But apart from speeches (as has been noted) he does not create events or incidents, either out of his head or by midrashic exposition (and that despite being aware, as Thackeray and others have shown, of the midrashic tradition). The matter of *sources* (however boldly they are to be re-constituted) is as important to him as it was for instance to Dionysius. As does the latter, Josephus enhances 'romance' for interest, while making the religious, ethical and socio-political points that he intends to convey out of the narrative material to hand.[11]

c. *Re-Arrangement*

(1) *Harmony and Continuity*. Josephus seems, however, to have felt quite free to create a fresh order of events, sometimes for the sake of coherence, sometimes simply to allow the narrative to flow. In particular, as has been already mentioned, if an incident, place or person is to re-appear briefly later, that fact will be noted in advance; if the second reference is brief enough, Josephus will conflate the two accounts and have done with the topic.

Thus Joshua is made to send out his scouts before reviewing the army; and camp has barely been pitched before the scouts return, for their experiences to be given in the form of a report, and the campaign

---

10. *Ant.* 4.269, n. (b): Eusebius, *P.E.* 9.27.432a.

11. See n. 9 above; on the contemporary romantic tradition, see, e.g., M. Braun, *History and Romance in Graeco-Oriental Literature* (Oxford: Basil Blackwell, 1938); B.E. Perry, *The Ancient Romances* (Berkeley: University of California Press, 1967). Dionysius openly admits that he intends to entertain (though he hopes to do more, *R.A.* 1.8.3); for Josephus see, e.g., *Ant.* 14.2ff.

maintains its momentum. The people take stones with them across the Jordan (see above) and so do not need to retrace their steps. Reference to the booty taken in Jericho is postponed till the account of Achan's theft of part of it; the theft is described then, rather than in his later confession (*Ant.* 5.1–33). Details of cultic arrangements are collected from Joshua 8, 18, and 11, 12 and 13, into one section, *Ant.* 5.68–75. The division of land (already referred to) is very much simplified, and follows the same geographical order as that in which the tribes are described as taking possession (*Ant.* 5.128ff.). (The harmonization of the accounts of the captures of the Canaanite cities has already been shown.)

Judges 1.21-22 refers us to Benjamin, Jerusalem, Bethel and Ephraim, and a period of decline. The book ends with stories in which these all figure, at a time when 'there was no king in Israel, and everyone did what was right in his own eyes'. Josephus brings these last sagas forward to the early period of lawlessness: the Levite's woman, the punishment of Benjamin, the brides from Shiloh. The transposition also allows time for Benjamin to return to full strength, to provide Israel's first king, and military support for him (*Ant.* 5.174). The Danite migration is also brought forward, and the migrants do not have to move immediately after providing Israel with a 'judge', Samson. Then there is no break in the line of judges through to Eli, and no interruption of hostilities with the Philistines.

The over-riding impression is one of *simplification*, even more than of rationalization. A clear and coherent story is most likely to appear credible and hold attention, and then allow the intended message to emerge. (We shall in fact be considering re-arrangement again in what follows.)

d. *Assembly*
(1) *Thematic Coherence and Verbal Coincidence*. It is already clear that Josephus takes trouble to unify his material in terms of topic, person, place or event. Similar tendencies emerge in his treatment of legal, teaching and hortatory tradition, where there are already, of course, signs of complex inter-connections in the written sources and versions, and in the subsequent (still oral) tradition of interpretation. Yet here too, despite a willingness to put together illustrations of a theme on the basis of sometimes very flimsy apparent connections, no new material is constructed out of these 'suggestive' coincidences: they provide a cue for the choice of an item to follow, but no more than that.

In *Antiquities* 4, to which we now turn, Josephus promises to give an impression of the 'constitution' (πολιτεία) which Moses left (just as Dionysius is concerned to describe the πολιτεία of Rome). Josephus claims, 'All is here written as (Moses) left it: nothing have we added for the sake of embellishment, nothing which has not been bequeathed by Moses. Our one innovation has been to classify the several subjects' (τὸ κατὰ γένος ἕκαστα τάξαι, *Ant.* 4.197). There is no claim to be inclusive, and we cannot argue much from omissions; Josephus says he intends to present an exhaustive account elsewhere. What he offers in his *Antiquities* is intended to convey the spirit of the legislation (*Ant.* 14.196ff.). Nonetheless, additions and alterations do on occasion occur, if only to existing material.

Josephus chooses as his basis the legislative section of Moses' farewell sermon, Deuteronomy 12 to the end; he conflates that material, and also introduces matter from Leviticus and, in one or two instances, from Exodus.

He begins, as did the Deuteronomist, with the one holy city and temple and altar (but omitting the very negative reference to foreign cult-objects, see below), adding the firm explanation, 'God is one and the Hebrew race is one' (*Ant.* 4.201; cf. *Apion* 2.193).

Then he switches abruptly to the penalty for blasphemy prescribed in Deuteronomy 21 and Leviticus 24; and we can only conjecture the reasons. The penalty may simply emphasize the seriousness of the piety implicit in the introductory section. However, the instructions for the altar have combined elements from Exodus 20 with Deuteronomy 27, in the LXX of which it is forbidden 'to cast a tool against the stones' (...λίθων...οὐκ ἐπιβαλεῖς), and that might have brought Lev. 24.16 to mind; or even Exod. 20.25, the avoidance of sacrilegious exposure while climbing to the altar.

We are returned to Deuteronomy 12 and the three annual festivals, conflated with items from ch. 16, to which is added a Durkheimian comment on religion as a social bond (cf. Dionysius, *R.A.* 2.62.5). Tithes are mentioned, and ch. 14 is referred to, for further detail. Josephus follows tradition and generalizes the permission to sell for ease of transport, though without using the actual phrase 'turn into money' (ἀργύριον). If he then remembered where ἀργύριον is elsewhere mentioned, he would find Deut. 23.19, and v. 18 would tell him of money that must *not* be brought to the altar, to wit, a whore's pay, which is now referred to (*Ant.* 4.206). Next there is perhaps recalled another question of wealth intended, also mistakenly, for cultic purposes. One of the many parallels in Deuteronomy to the start of our ch. 12 comes at 7.25, which warns against coveting silver or gold from (burnt) idols. Josephus takes that as a prohibition against any temple-robbery, and then makes that into a command to respect foreign deities, with the additional basis of Exod. 22.28, respect for the very word 'god' (*Ant.* 4.207; cf. *Apion* 2.237).

Exodus 22.28 also mentions respect for rulers of the people, and is preceded by a note on clothing. The clothing for priestly rulers that both hallows God and precludes any sacrilegious exposure (Exod. 20.26, 28.36-43 may be in mind) is made, according to the Mishnah, of mixed wool and linen, which is therefore forbidden to anyone else (*Ant.* 4.208). One public function for which this clothing is designed is the reading of the law from a raised platform (*Ant.* 4.209ff.). It is a piece of Jewish custom that Josephus feels is very impressive (cf. *Apion* 2.173–81; but also Dionysius, *R.A.* 3.36.4). With this account of the public reading of the law Josephus conflates other passages about learning the law (chs. 6, 11, 30). The first of these chapters includes the passage, 'Hear, O Israel'; and perhaps because the passage is already a part of regular devotions (or because a rule for universal instruction suggests a rule for universal address to God), there follows an injunction to twice-daily prayer. Instruction on thanksgiving is drawn from the same chapters, as are the regulations for the *mezuzah* (*Ant.* 4.212–13).[12]

We have now moved from the centre to the local level, but remain with the theme of divine authority and its human embodiment which (we have already seen) Josephus found very significantly linked at Exod. 22.28, and to which he now reverts. For the actual details of the administration of justice Josephus turns to Deuteronomy 16, but reads it in terms of the practice of his own day.[13] (Cultus and judicial practice are the two strands with which Dionysius chooses to illustrate the pioneering legislation of Numa in Rome: *R.A.* 2.63–76.)

---

12. Philo mentions twice-daily prayer among the Therapeutae, *Vit. Cont.* 27; so, too, at Qumran, 1QS 1.13-15, as noted by G. Vermes, *The Dead Sea Scrolls: Qumran in Perspective* (London: Collins, 1976), p. 176. Vermes also notes a preponderance of Deuteronomy among the Qumran Scriptures, as well as the kind of harmonization we find in Josephus (pp. 201, 207). The allusions that Thackeray and others note in Josephus to recorded rabbinic tradition are numerous in sum, and often significant as indicating that Josephus may not be particularly inventive in matters of substance, if at all. However, there is no sign that the reader was expected to perceive any subtle cross-referencing or implicit allusions.

13. *Ant.* 4.579 n. (c).

It is difficult to find a particular point of origin for the ensuing little homiletic aside, though 'God's strength is justice' might have been suggested by a psalm (Ps. 54.1; Dionysius enlists the gods on the side of justice) or we may note Lev. 19.14b-15, or Deut. 1.15-18.[14] This last passage tells us to refer hard cases back to central authority, which theme constitutes Josephus's next item, elaborated in terms of Deut. 17.8-10 together with contemporary practice; with perhaps Josephus himself adding 'the prophet' (possibly from Deut. 18.15, which speaks of the prophet among the assembled brothers). The treatment of the administration of justice continues with rules for witnesses; the later explicit tradition of excluding women is added (*Ant.* 5.214–19).

Another reader, better acquainted with the rabbinic tradition, might find more or clearer 'connectors'. But the only ones readily discernible are of the kind outlined above. And they have no 'creative' effect at all; at most they help Josephus to decide what to include and what not to, and the order. The few interpretations that he adds are all or almost all evidenced elsewhere, which would strongly suggest that he adds nothing of his own even as interpretation. He certainly keeps his word and produces no new law, however much he might have liked to match some item in Dionysius.

The influence of Dionysius can however perhaps be detected in what Josephus selects for mention, and also in his homiletic asides.[15] 'Aristocracy is best' echoes a frequent theme in the *Roman Antiquities*; 'aristocracy' is also his term for the rule of the Flavians. There is then something of a jump between *Ant.* 4.223–224, and the section 225 on boundary stones. However, rules on boundary stones constitute one of only two themes from Numa's civil legislation that Dionysius chooses to include, and he accords them great importance (*R.A.* 2.74). (The connection with what precedes could just possibly have been made in terms of an epitypically wicked monarch, led astray by a foreign wife, who used lying witness to enable him to misappropriate a neighbour's inheritance. Be that as it may.) The other of Dionysius's themes from Numa concerns contracts privately entered into (*R.A.* 2.75), and a brief reference

14. E.g. *R.A.* 2.62.5; 6.80.4; 8.33.1-4; 11.11.5. And see n. 15 following. Note also Wis. 12.16.

15. Compare *R.A.* 2.18.1-2, the value of common institutions, with *Ant.* 4.203; *R.A.* 3.36.4, an instructed populace, with *Ant.* 4.210; 'natural' duties, *R.A.* 1.5.2, 6.19.4, 8.51, with *Ant.* 4.212; respect for authority, divine and human, *R.A.* 2.6.4, with *Ant.* 4.215.

to such agreements in Exod. 22.7 is also much expanded by Josephus (*Ant.* 4.285–87). Considerable space is devoted to marriage laws; Roman marriage laws are given in some detail by Dionysius, who admires their firmness. At just one point (*Ant.* 4.273) Josephus may have radically altered a law on his own initiative, to allow for the total release of slaves, assimilating Jewish to the more generous Roman practice (e.g. *R.A.* 4.24)—and providing a more telling hint to his imperial readers. But even for such an extension he may have had contemporary precedent.

There is freedom to select, arrange, paraphrase and preach; but there is little if any room for his own interpretation, and probably none for invention. The tradition remains in control. We have no indication that Josephus was following any contemporary catechetical pattern in this compilation. David Daube finds such a pattern in *Apion* 2,[16] but the sequence here is quite different, and may very well have been put together simply for the *Antiquities*, in the kind of way suggested above.

e. *Conflation*
(1) *Harmony and Continuity* (again). With 1 and 2 Chronicles, and 1 and 2 Samuel and 1 Kings (1, 2, and 3 Kingdoms) Josephus was presented with more or less closely parallel accounts of obviously the same events, and may even have realized that one was a redaction of the other. We hereon concentrate on Josephus's approaches to the problems of extensive conflation (*Ant.* 6.368 onwards).

It is immediately clear that where the Chronicler keeps closely to *his* source, maybe changing only a word or a phrase or two, Josephus happily follows. Where it is at all possible he adds together minor divergent items. If the two strands conflict in minor details, he chooses which to follow by the kinds of criteria we have already detected: over-all harmony, piety, moral uplift, apologetic impact, and so on.

For instance, 1 Chron. 10.1-12 gives us almost word-for-word 1 Sam. 31.1-13, and Josephus renders almost every phrase, adding only a note on the valour of Saul and his sons, and a massacre when these heroes fall. However, at 2 Sam. 1.6 he has a second account of Saul's death; and although this may represent a clear deception by the Amalekite, Josephus conflates both versions. He follows 1 Sam. 31.7 where it differs from 1 Chron. 10.7; but uses the more plausible order of 1 Chron. 10.8-9 for what ensues. He returns again to 1 Samuel, save for the

---

16. D. Daube, *The New Testament and Rabbinic Judaism* (London: Athlone Press, 1956), pp. 138ff.

unlikely 'burnt' in v. 12, to which he prefers the Chronicler's 'buried'. 1 Chronicles 10.13 is noted, but a rather different epitaph is written, on the basis of tradition[17] and in the light of Josephus's own soft spot for the 'ventriloquist' of Endor (*Ant.* 5.340).

Where the Chronicler omits a narrative from his source, Josephus is still sure that those events are true and worth relating: thus he includes the death of the Amalekite and the trouble between Joab and Abner; and later the long 'domestic tragedies' of Bathsheba, Tamar, Absolom, Amasa, and so on. He varies the order of his sources much less here than he did in the case of Joshua–Judges (here there is a stronger inherent sequence). Just occasionally he seems to glance across at Chronicles, to check a list of names; or to the LXX of both texts for further variants. When, however, the Chronicler has some additional (but not directly conflicting) material, to wit, David's elaborate preparations for his son to build the Temple, Josephus includes it in the Samuel–Kings narrative that he is here mainly following (*Ant.* 7.335–42); for his tally of builders conflating the basic 1 Chronicles 22 with matter from 2 Chronicles 2 and 1 Kings 3.

When it is a matter of a speech, Josephus appears to feel a lot freer (as has already been noted). The accounts of David's first thoughts about the building of a Temple are very similar in both sources; nonetheless Josephus harmonizes both with the sentiments expressed later in Chronicles, so that God drops all objections to being given a static headquarters, in general approves the plan, and demurs only at David's blood-stained hands; the formal designation of a name for Solomon is also brought forward here. David's reply is also almost identical in both sources; even so, Josephus puts part of what is God's speech in his sources onto the king's lips; and there are other minor conflations (2 Samuel 7; 1 Chronicles 17, 22; *Ant.* 7.90–95). By contrast, there is at least one speech, only in Chronicles (though drawn by its writer from 2 Samuel 7, 1 Kings 2, 5, 8, and perhaps 3 and 6) which Josephus paraphrases almost as it stands (*Ant.* 7.337–42). He shows no sign of any interest in 'unpicking' another's conflation.

If his two sources conflict in a fairly straightforward fashion over

---

17. *Ant.* 5.356, n. (e). For Josephus's procedures, see now the detailed study of T.W. Franxman, *Genesis and the Jewish Antiquities of Flavius Josephus* (Rome: Biblical Institute Press, 1979). He says he found it difficult to characterize Josephus's changes under general headings, pp. 285ff. I would suggest that his analysis broadly supports the foregoing.

some major matter, Josephus follows the older and fuller source. For instance, he does not follow the Chronicler in having David think first of the Ark before starting to build his own palace. And in narrating the transition to Solomon's rule, again Josephus keeps to 1 Kings for the order, only inserting speech-material drawn from the final chapter of 1 Chronicles.

It is only when his sources conflict *in detail* in what is still clearly an attempt to describe the same series of events, that Josephus abandons the attempt to conflate and harmonize. In such cases, of which we have two (the crowning of David with the capture of Jerusalem, and the census–plague–purchase of the Temple site), Josephus seems to 'give up' and decide to write a completely fresh account of his own, taking just some items, almost at random, from both sources. But he refuses on the other hand to follow just one of them; and he certainly shows no sign of attempting first to disentangle them (see below, on the Synoptics).

Josephus begins his version of the first of these two narratives with David acknowledged as king-designate, nominated by Samuel the prophet, and puts a reply on David's lips. He then lists all the tribal forces (to which the Chronicler alludes only much later), and these combine to acknowledge David as king at a single coronation. The capture of the city draws a selection of items from each source; the jibe about cripples (from 2 Samuel) is taken literally. The water-course in the older source provides Joab with the chance to win promotion (1 Chronicles). The double reference to capture (in both) becomes a two-stage operation. Josephus ignores the Chronicler's anticipation of the list of heroes from later in 2 Samuel (*Ant.* 7.53–64).

In the second of his major reconstructions, Josephus accords the initiative for the census to David, rather than to God or to Satan, while inserting a traditional reference back to Exod. 30.12ff. as the reason for God's anger. For a while we seem to be following 2 Samuel (Joab receives instructions on his own, but does take other leaders along with him, and the census lasts nine months and twenty days). He then agrees with the Chronicler to omit Levi and Benjamin, but inserts his own explanation: David repented before the count was complete (his sources each have different ideas as to when David changed his mind). A message from 'the prophets' that turns David to contrition is also Josephus's own contribution. God's message through Gad is in the asymmetric form of 2 Samuel (*Ant.* 7.3.3). Josephus elaborates David's reply, along lines apparently found in later rabbinic tradition. He has Gad report back to God. The plague itself is described in great detail, and the influence of Thucydides may be detected; but also of Dionysius (*R.A.* 10.53.1). A note of time comes from the LXX of 2 Samuel, as does the advance of the plague on Jerusalem (an event only threatened in Chronicles). With his sources then again in open conflict, Josephus makes up his own mind, and has David in sackcloth before he sees the angel in the air (the Chronicler's version). David's self-designation as 'shepherd' appears in some LXX texts, but his 'I ordered it' in 1 Chronicles is omitted. David's contrition is rewarded by an immediate end to the plague (in Josephus's sources, there is a respite, earlier, but in 2 Samuel God does not finally change his mind till after the sacrifice; in 1 Chronicles, he does not rescind the order till then). That Gad is again sent comes from Chronicles, but the remainder of that version is then ignored until David's 'almost prophetic' announcement (which is itself elaborated in terms of the LXX of 2 Samuel). Josephus refers us back to a prior mention of Araunah, and to the sacrifice of Isaac, on this very spot (*Ant.* 7.318–34).

The keynote of Josephus's method is still 'simplicity', and simplicity seems to be a major part of his aim. Where his sources are straight-forward he is happy just to paraphrase; where a single source seems illogical, he tidies it up; and if he has two sources that will not readily combine, he makes up a third account of his own, blithely ignoring large parts of both. But it remains a 'version', quite clearly. There is no major invention, no major allusiveness. And still it remains true that his redaction conveys with clarity the message he announced that his narrative would display (*Ant.* 1.14–15; see below, part 2). The light that Josephus's methods as a redactor may throw on the Synoptic Gospels is the theme of the second part of this essay.

JSNT 9 (1980), pp. 29-48

REDACTION CRITICISM: JOSEPHUS'S *ANTIQUITIES*
AND THE SYNOPTIC GOSPELS

F. Gerald Downing

Part 2: Luke and the Other Two Synoptists

In the first part of this essay Josephus's procedures and apparent aims as
a redactor were briefly analysed: his omissions, additions, re-arrangement, compilation and conflation. Some theological and apologetic motifs
and motives stood out quite clearly; but the over-all impression was of
an attempt to create a harmonious and continuous narrative that would
provide an uncomplicated vehicle for Josephus's intended message. We
now consider the light this may throw on the Synoptic Gospels (where
the question of the sources of redaction is still in dispute) and especially
on Luke's Gospel, where the stated intentions and widely agreed
'tendencies' are often identical with those in Josephus. The argument
will be in line with 'Streeterian' orthodoxy.

It may be unnecessary to point out that Josephus's procedures as
outlined in Part 1 are unmistakably of the kind presupposed in traditional discussions of 'the synoptic problem' over the past fifty or a
hundred years, as represented for example by B.H. Streeter's *The Four
Gospels*; and not at all like the ways of working presupposed in some
recent discussions of the possible influence on our synoptists of a hypothetical 'school' of midrash and lection.[1]

It is still more obvious that even if the account given of Josephus is
broadly correct, that does *not* mean that the synoptists can simply be

---

1.   B.H. Streeter, *The Four Gospels* (London: Macmillan, 1924); cf. M.D.
Goulder, *Midrash and Lection in Matthew* (The Speaker's Lectures in Biblical
Studies 1969–71; London: SPCK, 1974); J. Drury, *Tradition and Design in Luke's
Gospel* (London: Darton, Longman & Todd, 1976).

assumed to have worked in the same manner. It is however worth reminding ourselves again that with Josephus we have an example of redaction from the same period of Hellenistic Judaism, where we possess both the greater part of the 'sources' and the finished product, and that quite undisputably. And although we do not have for instance the common sources of Livy and of Dionysius of Halicarnassus, we have enough evidence to suggest that Josephus's methods were (as he himself asserts) along the lines of accepted convention. We have no clear or undisputed examples of other kinds of hypothetical procedure used to produce a change as considerable as that between, say Mark and Matthew, or Mark with Matthew into Luke. We may note individual specimens of midrash, we may note coincidences with the lectionaries later evidenced; yet, while we must not argue too firmly from silence, we do have to note that we have no obvious examples, in clear stages, of midrash and lection producing the kind of variation that we find among the Synoptics, at the hands of one writer (or even one school) in the time-span required. Midrash and lection afford an hypothesis that can be worked out in coherent (if not always convincing) internal detail; but it is still worth avoiding the multiplication of hypotheses while other explanations are to hand.

It seems possible to show that it is at least very likely that Luke would have followed procedures similar to those discernible in Josephus; and also to show how such procedures can readily 'explain' the divergencies of Luke from and his similarities to Mark and Matthew. Once the greater part of Luke's Gospel material is thus accounted for, there is very little reason to presuppose a very different procedure for producing material in Matthew's Gospel, since the bulk of the substance of it is already accounted for; and Mark can be read in a similar light.

Luke declares his aims and intentions (Lk. 1.1-4; Acts 1.1) in language (words and constructions) that is always similar to and often identical with that used by Josephus discussing his approach to his writing. These come mainly at the beginning and end of the *Jewish War*, at the start of *Antiquities* 1 and of 14, and at the end of 20; at the beginning of *Against Apion*, and especially around 50–55, and at the start of book 2; at the *Life* 357–67, and at the end. The similarities do not seem to have received much attention of late, though they are noted by the commentators of fifty years ago and more, especially, of course, by A. Schlatter.[2]

---

2.   *Das Evangelium des Lukas* (Stuttgart: Calwer, 1931), pp. 23-28. L. Alexander (*The Preface to Luke's Gospel* [SNTSMS, 78; Cambridge: Cambridge University

At this point I note only some of the main features, and one or two examples that Schlatter either ignored or thought not worth mentioning, for which I add references.

Luke is very much briefer than Josephus, and that is the only major contrast. Josephus three times uses a 'forasmuch' construction, to refer to his predecessors (compare also Acts 15.24ff.). Of the words in Lk. 1.1, Josephus *lacks only* ἀνατάξασθαι (but uses συνταξ quite often in these contexts); τῶν πεπληροφορημένων ἐν ἡμῖν (but if it implies prophecy or the will of God fulfilled, one may note, for example, *War* 1.28–29, and if more generally, a 'completed sequence', *Ant.* 1.4, *Apion* 1.47–50, *War* 1.6; and that these events were 'among us' is stressed at *War* 1.1, καθ᾿ ἡμᾶς, 13–15, *Apion* 1.47–57, *Ant.* 1.4, 20.266).

In Lk. 1.2 there is lacking an exact equivalent only to ὑπ-ηρέται in the sense apparently here intended; though Josephus has a very close equivalent phrase at *Apion* 1.55, πολλῶν μὲν αὐτουργὸς πράξεων, πλείστων δ᾿αὐτόπτης (cf. also *Ant.* 1.3; *War* 1.14, 18; *Apion* 1.45, 47). If τοῦ λόγου refers here as it does at Acts 1.1 to 'the narrative' (participants in the story) then there are again parallels in Josephus (*Ant.* 1.7, 17; *Life* 430; *Ant.* 14.2).

A direct parallel is lacking in Lk. 1.3 to ἄνωθεν in this kind of setting, though Josephus uses it in this sense elsewhere, and in talking of his narrative insists as firmly that he starts from the beginning (*Ant.* 1.4, 7; *War* 1.6, 18, etc.). And although καθεξῆς is not used by him Josephus promises τὰ μὲν οὖν ἀκριβῆ...κατὰ τὴν οἰκείαν τάξιν (*Ant.* 1.17; cf. *War* 1.15). Josephus of course addresses his patron in the same way as does Luke, κράτιστε Ἐπαφρόδιτε (*Life* 430; *Apion* 1.l; etc.).

In Lk. 1.4, our closest parallel to ἵνα ἐπιγνῷς in the kind of context in question occurs at *War* 1.6 γνῶναι...ἄκρι-βῶς (cf. *Ant.* 1.3), though Josephus uses ἐπιγνῶναι elsewhere. He uses ἀσφαλεία only more literally; but does on the other hand complain at *War* 1.7 of 'a complete lack of sound (ὑγιές) information'.

And for the first clause of Acts one may compare *Apion* 2.1.

There is again a very similar vocabulary in Dionysius (*R.A.* 1.1-8).

Press, 1993]), argues persuasively that our closest analogies for a preface of this kind at this length are provided in 'middlebrow' technical treatises: nonetheless Luke's declared intentions remain close to those of Josephus, and what follows is not a technical treatise, but a sort of 'biographical historiography'; see F.G. Downing, 'Theophilus' First Reading of Acts', in C.M. Tuckett (ed.), *Luke's Literary Achievement* (JSNTSup, 116; Sheffield: Sheffield Academic Press, 1995), pp. 91-109.

All three writers claim accuracy and comprehensiveness, painstaking research and good order for their own work, in more or less explicit contrast with their predecessors, in the same or very similar words and phrases.

It has been mentioned in Part 1 that Josephus tells us quite clearly that he means the *Antiquities* to convey a message:

> the main lesson to be learnt from this history by any who cares to peruse it is that men who conform to the will of God, and do not venture to transgress laws that have been excellently laid down, prosper in all things beyond belief, and for their reward are offered by God felicity; whereas in proportion as they depart from the strict observance of these laws, things (else) practicable become impracticable, and whatever imaginary good thing they strive to do ends in irretrievable disasters' (*Ant.* 1.14–15).

I have tried to show elsewhere how this message is elaborated in many of the speeches of the *Jewish War* as well as of the *Antiquities*; but also how closely it is paralleled by material in Dionysius, *and by the speeches in Acts*. It would not be fitting even to attempt to summarize that evidence here.[3] We have however seen something of how that message has been expressed in narrative, in Part 1 (with again occasional reference to Dionysius). Similarities with Luke's Gospel narrative will be demonstrated in what follows. Suffice it at this stage to point out that there are characteristics of Luke's work that seem to many readers distinctive when it is compared with Matthew and Mark, and that precisely these are prominent in Josephus (and, as it happens, in Dionysius). I choose deliberately a list from a brief commentary meant for 'popular' consumption. Luke has a concern for all humankind from Adam, and especially in the contemporary Roman world; has an interest in explaining things for outsiders; maintains an emphasis on prayer and piety; gives added space to female characters; highlights joy, sorrow and other emotions, especially in the context of repentance; displays the poor and outcasts in a favourable light (at least 'the worthy' among them);[4] and,

---

3. See F.G. Downing, 'Ethical Pagan Theism and the Speeches in Acts', *NTS* 27 (1980–81), pp. 544-63; also *idem*, 'Common Ground with Paganism in Luke and in Josephus', *NTS* 28 (1982), pp. 546-59; H.W. Attridge (*The Interpretation of Biblical History in the Antiquitates Judaicae of Flavius Josephus* [Missoula, MT: Scholars Press, 1976]), displays a small selection of the narrative tendencies Josephus shares with Dionysius; there are more in narrative, and many more in speeches; and most are also shared by Luke.

4. W. Wilkinson, *Good News in Luke* (London: Fontana, 1974), pp. 12-14.

one might add, from others' observation, has a predilection for travel narrative, and for the strictness of the code of the group being displayed for admiration. And all these are prominent in emphasis and addition in Josephus.

If then Luke does express aims and intentions that are very like those of Josephus (and of others of his age); if (as I note I have argued elsewhere) Luke tries to express his message in terms that may make sense to the same sort of readers as Josephus had in view; and if, as I have just proposed, in the light for example of Josephus's work surveyed in Part 1, Luke uses similar narrative traits to convey his message, and to hold interest and attention, then it seems at least unlikely that he will use a redactional method that is itself much different from that employed by Josephus. What chiefly remains is to review a sizeable section of Luke's Gospel, though briefly, in the light of this very plausible hypothesis, and see how it works. We shall proceed first on the supposition that Luke was using Mark and source 'Q' (still a very widely held view); but we shall also, though more briefly, consider the possibility that Luke instead knew Mark and Matthew; and the further possibility that Mark used Luke and Matthew.

First we need to remember that Josephus's literary dependence very rarely leads to word-for-word resemblance (Pelletier, it will be recalled, found only one twelve- and one ten-word repetition in Josephus's version of *Aristeas*). Josephus can produce a verbally and stylistically very different version of a text, without any help from 'another source'. It is not the divergencies among the synoptists (or even between them and John), in parallel contexts, that are remarkable: it is the extraordinary extent of verbal similarities. The question is, why were they content to copy so much? rather than, why did they bother to change this or that? The procedure is not however mechanical, and there *are* considerable divergencies. But it has to be recognized that the relationship may betoken a much greater respect, one for the other, even than Josephus's for Scripture.

It has to be admitted that even Luke does not attempt to achieve the sort of Greek prose style that Josephus aimed for. But Josephus admits that he was laughed at for his pains (*Apion* 1.53), and a writer such as Luke might have done well to avoid wasting his efforts, and only try to avoid the worst solecisms.

So, if we allow Josephus to guide us (for the sake of the argument) we shall expect to find re-arrangement, paraphrase, the addition or omission of details, the insertion of speeches, and an overall simplification, within the limits demanded by the message that is intended. We shall not expect to find the creation 'out of his head' of any major incident, or even its invention on the basis of hints from Scripture. We would expect our writer to feel the need for some antecedent source, if only in oral tradition. And this expectation would be made all the more firm by our noting how very respectful of each other the synoptists often seem to be (whichever is the direction of the dependence).

If Luke was following redactional conventions similar to those adopted by Josephus, he could have produced from his own pen a great deal of the incidental matter of the infancy narrative ('righteous', 'blameless', 'old', 'fearful', the angelic messages, etc.; compare *Ant.* 2.205–238, Moses' birth and childhood), but not the whole framework of the story. That is not to say that the infancy narrative could not have grown from very small beginnings before reaching Luke; but we would not expect him, if he were following the conventions accepted by Josephus, simply to make it up, even from scriptural meditation, or haggadic legends attached to other figures. But neither would we expect a source shared by Matthew and Luke to have emerged so differently from each: so, they had no common infancy tradition.

Accepting, as announced, the 'Q' hypothesis, we take it that Luke is presented with two accounts of John and of the baptism of Jesus. There is no conflict between them, save for the mis-ascription of Mk 1.2b. Luke does exactly as we would expect from our investigation of Josephus (e, in Part 1); he follows his fuller source, with one or two supplements from the shorter one. Luke gathers discourse material together, and John is given an explicit social message (as he is by Josephus, *Ant.* 15.3.116–19). We are told what people are thinking (as we found Josephus told us (b.1, 3, 5). John speaks again; we are told what will happen to him, and his death will not need to break a later sequence (c.1). There has been no description of his outlandish dress or behaviour to distract us from his admirable message; a much more fitting preparation for his appearance has been given in chs. 1–2. We can then concentrate on Jesus on his own, and he now 'is baptized', and then Luke has him pray (b.3, 5) before the Holy Spirit descends, 'in bodily form' (if Josephus has to admit an apparition, he prefers it to be frankly literal: cf. b.5) (Lk. 3.1-21).

'Son' suggests a genealogy permitting a display of antiquity and of pedigree (important to Dionysius as well as to Josephus, who interrupts his account of Moses in a similar way, *Ant.* 2.229). Josephus can vary his own genealogical lists; even if Luke received one, he might have done his own 'research' to improve it; he is not likely simply to have made it up: which is not, of course, to say that it is 'authentic' (Lk. 3.23-38).

Luke returns to his fuller source for his next incident, the temptation (perhaps exercising his unquestioned freedom to re-order the elements of it), while refusing to allow the main flow to be halted by Mark's wild beasts and angels, but remembering to advise us in advance that the devil is a character due to reappear (Lk. 4.1-13). On the other hand, Jesus is full of Holy Spirit, led by Holy Spirit, returns in the power of Holy Spirit (Lk. 4.1, 14, 18). Josephus, too, is often ready to point up the activity of divine power among his protagonists (*Ant.* 2.265–70; 6.166, etc.).

For narrative, Luke, we take it, now has to depend on Mark. The latter's next pericope has Jesus addressed as a 'man of Nazareth', and Mark will bring him home to Nazareth quite some columns later on. As does Josephus, Luke prefers a tidy geographical sequence (c.1), and finishes with Nazareth now, once for all (chs. 1, 2, 4), using material from Mk 6.1-6. Luke can then include a 'typical' sermon for Jesus (and anticipate the synagogue rejections of Acts), while still resting assured that some such incident of a rejection is in his source (incidents in the lives of Joseph and of Daniel, among others, 'prefigure' events that happen to Josephus) (Lk. 4.14-30).

Luke has combined two brief references to preaching in Mark (1.14-15, and 39), the second of which referred to (plural) synagogues. Luke now needs a second one, which allows him to take Jesus in and out of a second town, Capernaum, in a sequence also happily provided by his source. He adds no other local town names, even to amplify Mark's vague references to Judaean crowds and people from Jerusalem. Mark (2.1) has Jesus return to Capernaum; but Luke (the preferred text) has finished with that town, and moves Jesus straight on to Judaea (Lk. 4.44), despite siting the next pericope on Lake Gennesaret.[5]

An incident from Mark has already mentioned Simon (through his

---

5.   The scant coherence between Luke's narrative and the actual geography of Palestine is made much of by H. Conzelmann, *The Theology of Saint Luke* (London: Faber & Faber, 1960). In the light of Josephus's preference for simplicity, Conzelmann's interpretation of Luke may be over-subtle; so too that of J.C. O'Neill, *The Theology of Acts in its Historical Setting* (London: SPCK, 1970); as well as that of Drury, *Tradition and Design.*

mother-in-law) and he can now be properly introduced in a conflation of Mk 1.16-20 (whose omission earlier precluded any disturbance of the sequence preaching-in-Galilee) with a dramatic fishing-miracle (perhaps a re-positioned resurrection story). It is typical of Luke to provide a lively and fairly detailed prelude to any major character's acceptance of a new role: such a decision needs some 'explanation', which is not afforded by the sudden response of Mk 1.18 and 20. The conflated story also portrays penitence and humility (Lk. 5.1-11). Similar traits are frequent in Josephus (for instance, his introduction to Amram, *Ant.* 2.210ff.; the humble penitence of Samson, *Ant.* 5.301ff.).

Luke then resumes Mark's sequence, with the leper and the paralytic (but the latter is no longer in Capernaum). Jesus' wider travels perhaps allow him to become gradually better known (rather than achieve the oddly sudden notoriety of Mk 3.7-8). The Markan sequence is maintained up to and including the healing of the man with the withered arm, but without the trip to the seaside where nothing in particular happens (Mk 3.7) (Lk. 5.12–6.11).

'Q', we take it, has teaching addressed to disciples, which Luke will insert when he has introduced the leading ones among them (from the next pericope in Mark). But first he will have Jesus pray again (on Mark's convenient mountain); and then the crowds (who have been around for quite a while, as Luke writes the story) can reasonably provide disciples, from among whom the twelve can be chosen (rather different from the arbitrary selection of Mk 3.13). Clearly, the impact of the movement is growing (Lk. 6.12-19).

Someone following Josephus's conventions *could* have started with a collection as long as that in Matthew 5–7, and re-distributed the material into the clusters in which we in fact find the parallels in Luke, but it is not really what we would expect from, for instance the example of Josephus's use of Deuteronomy (d.1), Moses' 'Sermon on the Plain'. There, despite omissions and condensations, we find the basic themes amplified from elsewhere; we do not find part of a discourse used, and the left-overs scattered in all directions. It seems more likely that Luke found the teaching material already in thematic groups, or that he himself put it into such order (we noted Josephus's explanation that this was his procedure, *Ant.* 4.197). There is actually quite a striking resemblance between elements of this first teaching section, and the contents of Josephus's speech for Judah, *Ant.* 2.138–59: divine and human forgiveness, and other beneficence, the avoidance of passing condemnatory judgment, the fatherly concern of God as well as men, the willingness to refuse vengeance and accept wrong. But these are also, in fact, traits admired in Dionysius[6] (Lk. 6.20-49).

It would seem that 'Q' has a story set also in Capernaum, told about a specific and prominent inhabitant; Luke now permits Jesus another visit there. The story (compare Mt. 8.5-13) seems to have been expanded in a way that is characteristic of Luke, but also of Josephus and of Dionysius (b.3). The recipient of the favour has to be 'worthy', and therefore what he has done to deserve it has to be specified.[7] Whether or not the resuscitation in Nain was in Q, it conveniently completes the preparation for Jesus' answer to the Baptist's question, which clearly (in our present hypothesis) was in Q (Luke may not have realized that Nain is geographically incongruous. He is unlikely to have made the story up, but might well have added vv. 12b, 13, 16-17—the kinds of items that Josephus adds) (Lk. 7.1-34).

Reference to eating and drinking in the comment on John perhaps suggests a meal story; and it would be entirely credible for someone following Josephus's redactional procedures to bring forward to this point Mk 14.3-9, thereby also removing an interruption to the Passion narrative. We might well also expect it to be embellished with emotion and (very mild) eroticism, together with a vaguely appropriate parable and a catch-phrase from the tradition (v. 50: Lk. 7.36-50). Josephus adds or elaborates female characters (b.5). In both Josephus and Dionysius people are frequently in tears. Josephus also likes his women to look after their menfolk; such is the role of the bevy Luke next introduces (Lk. 8.1-3).

For the next section in Mark, Luke has a fuller account in Q, one that either includes a thematically more appropriate setting, or for which he feels he can provide one later. He then instead takes up the Markan thread with the discourse on parables (but again avoids the seaside, Mk 4.1). He feels particularly free to re-write the interpretation of the Sower; he postpones Mark's reference to Jesus' family, so that it can reinforce the preceding interpretation: his true family are those who hear and do 'the word of God' (Mk 3.35, 'will'). He omits the remainder of

6.   See the articles cited at n. 3 above; and, e.g., *R.A.* 8.50, but also the whole Coriolanus sequence, 7-8.

7.   Compare Josephus's Petronius, *War* 2.184–203, *Ant.* 18.257–72; contrasting Philo, *De legatione*; Titus's concern for the Temple, *War* 6.241, contrast Severus, *Chron.* 2.30.

Mark 4, having another version of one of the parables in his more important source for teaching (Lk. 8.4-21). In 6.20 to 8.21 Luke has collected a coherent sample of Jesus' public teaching, together with some of the kinds of response offered, interspersed with stories of his healing power. It is coherent and intelligible.

Having shown something of the moral character of Jesus, Luke can now display a few examples of the extent of his power, over the uncanny forces that can make a storm rage, or possess a man, or have power over death and chronic disease. Only now does Luke allow the disciples to share this power (Lk. 9.1; compare Lk. 6.12-19 with Mk 3.15) when the extent of its concentration in Jesus has been manifested (Lk. 5.17; 6.19; 8.46). It also provides a better preparation for the important Beelzebul controversy, which in Mark has taken place after only one specific exorcism.

There is an apparently quite striking contrast with Josephus in this connection. Josephus, we noted (a.4), tends to 'rationalize' miracle, or assume an agnostic stance ('but on these matters let everyone decide according to his fancy', *Ant.* 1.108, drawn in fact from Dionysius, for example, *R.A.* 1.48.1). Luke, as we see here in the stress on a quasi-physical power that can be felt to move (Luke's addition to Mark), seems to be adopting a much more crudely magical viewpoint. But the contrast may be more apparent than real. If Josephus does decide to tell of an event as *miracle*, its miraculous character must be quite unmistakable (for example, the much quoted exorcism at *Ant.* 8.46–49, where the departing demon knocks over a cup of water; but cf. also the appearances to Manoah, b.5, above). And this is not (as has been suggested) a conflict within Josephus: it is another facet of the same rationalizing approach, for only with such circumstantial detail can you hope to impress the incredulous at all.[8] Though Luke displays only one facet of this tendency, it is yet another that he shares with Josephus: both mean to make it clear that (quasi-physical) divine power really is available to members of their group.

In Mark's account the twelve disciples are now sent out (Mk. 6.7-13; Luke anticipated Mk 6.1-6 much earlier). Luke has another mission, in

---

8.   The data in J.M. Hull, *Hellenistic Magic and the Synoptic Tradition* (SBT, 2.28; London: SCM Press, 1974), are relevant, the interpretation, I think, astray; so too, on Josephus, G.W. MacRae, 'Miracle in the Antiquities of Josephus', in C.F.D. Moule (ed.), *Miracles* (London: SCM Press, 1965); better, H.R. Moehring, 'Rationalization of Miracles in...Josephus', *SE* 6 (1973), pp. 376-83.

Q, sufficiently different for him to treat it as a distinct event, rather than conflate the two accounts (though that is what Matthew will do). Luke has prepared for the two missions by making a distinction (Lk. 6.13) between 'disciples' (numerous) and 'apostles' (twelve). He includes people's pertinent questions (from Mk 6.14-15) but has avoided the lengthy interruption of the sequence that stands in Mark (the death of John Baptist: see above on Lk. 3.18-19). Luke 9.9 prepares us for 23.8 (which then prepares us for Acts 4.26-27). Luke sets the feeding at Bethsaida (adapting Mark, who tells us Bethsaida was on the shore opposite, Mk 6.45), and has thus prepared us for Lk. 10.13 (it is worth noting that he does *not* create a story to introduce Chorazin). Yet again Luke dispenses with an 'unnecessary' sea-trip (Lk. 9.1-17)

By now Luke has filled about two-fifths of a fair-sized scroll. He still has a lot of Q to use; and more than half of the remainder of Mark is the Passion story, most of whose elements have a strong internal coherence. Popular questioning in Mark ought not to be left too long unanswered; the intervening material in Mark is very similar to what has just been included. Like Josephus, embarrassed by too-frequent 'doublets' (a.2), Luke simply excises the entire sequence.[9]

As at Lk. 3.21, so too here, Luke has Jesus pray before the next solemn event (9.18-27). At an important point such as this Luke keeps closely to his single source, as we would expect from Josephus's practice. He does, however, add 'daily' to make sure that 'taking up your cross' is interpreted figuratively (v. 23). The transfiguration, however, is extensively re-written, to allow Luke to add some allusions and excise others. Moses and Elijah are treated in a way reminiscent of Josephus's accounts of their 'departures' (*Ant.* 3.75–83, Moses' radiant return from the mountain; *Ant.* 4.323–26; 9.28. At 4.189, Moses calls his forthcoming death an ἔξοδος, cf. Lk. 9.31). The phrase καὶ ἰδοὺ ἄνδρες δύο prepares us for 24.4 and Acts 1.10, as does 'glory' (vv. 30, 32). The omission of Mk 9.9-13 avoids any confusion of John with Elijah (Lk. 9.28-36).

Luke stays with Mark for the next four pericopes, which are largely concerned with discipleship already in Mark's redaction; but then finally abandons Mark's order, to enable the inclusion of much more on this theme (Lk. 9.37-50; 9.51–10.24). At the transition between the two sources he brings the sequence of 'mighty works' to an end with

9.   On sizes of scrolls see, e.g., A.Q. Morton and J. McLeman, *Christianity and the Computer* (London: Hodder & Stoughton, 1964).

9.51-56, perhaps suggested by Elijah, and by Mk 2.17b, which Luke omitted from his list of the twelve. Luke 10.1-16 seems to come from Q, and other material may do. Whether or not that source had a 'rejoicing return' for disciples from their mission, it clearly had a rejoicing on Jesus' part, and an announcement of blessing on those who share his awareness (Lk. 10.21-24). What this enlightened discipleship amounts to is illustrated in what follows: the lawyer's question (brought forward further to simplify the Passion story) with an illustrative parable too long to be likely to have been made up by Luke; an account of Martha and Mary (the latter as attentive as Josephus's Queen of Sheba, *Ant.* 8.165–73); docile Mary leads to an example of Jesus' more intimate teaching, on prayer, followed by the sample prayer (from Q?) and an encouragement to pray importunately (we have seen more than once how Josephus enhanced the piety of his characters, b.3; on importunate prayer see, for example, *Apion* 2.165ff.; *Ant.* 1.228; 3.78; etc.) (Lk. 10.25–11.13).

Luke 11.13 promises holy spirit (power) rather than Matthew's 'good things' ($\dot{\alpha}\gamma\alpha\theta\dot{\alpha}$) (Mt. 7.11). At *Apion* 2.197, Josephus says, 'We should beseech God, not to give us good things ($\tau\dot{\alpha}\gamma\alpha\theta\dot{\alpha}$), for he has given them spontaneously... but for capacity to receive and having received, to keep them.' It would not be stretching things too far to suggest that the Holy Spirit in Luke creates conditions in which people can receive and keep what God wants to give.

Be that as it may, Holy Spirit provides the obvious transition to the Beelzebul controversy, which Luke has found in both his sources. How Luke deals with them we shall consider in a little detail below. From this point onward opposition to Jesus builds up in a consolidated sequence (in contrast with Mark). It may well be, as Christopher Evans suggested some years ago, that in what follows Luke has something of the sequence of Deuteronomy in mind, and that would offer yet another incidental parallel with Josephus, who chooses part of the same work as the basis for his account of the way of life he was seeking to explain and commend. Whether that is so or not, we certainly find here more of the traits we have already noticed that he shares with Josephus.[10] And so it continues.

We have been considering Luke's work in the light of Josephus's, and for the moment supposing that Luke has Mark and Q before him; and to complete this part of the survey we now very briefly examine Luke's

10. C.F. Evans, 'The Central Section of Luke's Gospel', in D.E. Nineham (ed.), *Studies in the Gospels* (Oxford: Basil Blackwell, 1957), pp. 37-53.

Passion narrative, starting at Lk. 19.28. Here it has long been noted that Luke often departs quite considerably from the order and content of Mark (and of Matthew); so much so as to suggest to some that Luke had another Passion 'source'. In what follows an attempt is made to explain these divergencies on the supposition that Luke had only Mark, but was employing, still, the simplifying and harmonizing procedures we discovered in Josephus.

Luke brings Jesus straight into the Temple to cleanse it; there is no double journey, and no distraction with cursed and later withered fig-trees (Mk 11.1-25). The antagonistic questions are not softened by the presence of a sympathetic scribe (Mk 12.28-34, anticipated at Lk. 10.25-28). There is a much briefer section on desolation to come (and it sounds much more like the eye-witness account of Josephus in *War* 6, than does Mark's). There is continuous teaching in the Temple, in advance of 22.53 (Mk 14.49). Judas's plot becomes continuous with the high priests' conspiracy, uninterrupted by the anointing (also anticipated, in Lk. 7.36-50, where it was also 'de-politicized', the anointing transferred from head to feet). The Passover is prepared, and Jesus then and there refuses to eat and drink (rather than explain his abstention later) and the supper goes ahead. (If the shorter text is Luke's, there is some precedent in Josephus's seemingly arbitrary refusal to reproduce in full the decalogue, *Ant.* 3.90, perhaps as a gesture of pious reserve, to match Dionysius's occasional silence on particularly sacred matters of Roman religion, for example, *R.A.* 1.67.4.) At the end, rather than as an interruption, Judas's betrayal is prophesied (vv. 21ff.). This meal being such a crucial turning point, a speech is placed on Jesus' lips, collecting traditional sayings that show how unpretentious are his worldly claims; only then are we prepared for the later appearance of a sword (it perhaps being better to admit and 'explain' rather than conceal the later episode, as though embarrassed by it). There is only one reproach to the sleeping disciples; Judas attempts his kiss without any flash-back to the conspiracy; the significance of the kiss is neatly given in Jesus' question. There is no naked young man, enigmatically disappearing into the night (Mk 14.51-52). Again, where Mark in his redaction may deliberately have divided episodes to maintain dramatic tension, Luke reassembles one: Peter's denial is given without a break. There is only one council meeting, which takes place at the proper time, preceded by quite separate 'horse-play'; the only trial as such is, correctly, before Pilate. The introduction of Herod prepares us for Acts 4.25-27, and could be Luke's invention; but we would not expect quite so bold a move in the light of Josephus's practice. Pilate announces a clear 'not guilty'; Barabbas appears only twice, not three times. The whole procedure, the overall harmonization and simplification, together with other more substantial tendencies, are very much of the kind we found in Josephus's use of his scriptural and non-scriptural sources (Part 1). A writer following the conventions Josephus adhered to could have produced Luke's Passion quite readily on the basis of Mark's Gospel alone.

A writer following Josephus's conventions *could* quite readily have produced Luke's Gospel on the basis of Mark, the supposed source Q (as evidenced from a comparison of Luke and Matthew), and a few other items of oral or written tradition. That does not prove that this is in fact how Luke was produced; but it does, I suggest, show that such a solution is entirely plausible.

We must now ask whether it would have been possible, as easy, maybe even easier, for Luke to have produced his Gospel using Mark and Matthew (as we have Matthew).[11]

It has already been suggested that it would be very uncharacteristic (in terms still, for the sake of the argument, of the conventions found in Josephus's writing) for a sequence as long as Matthew's nativity to be virtually ignored by a writer dealing with the same theme. If he had had Matthew and also material as different as that which we now find in Luke, we would expect conflation by addition, or a 'third' account with bits drawn from both (e.1). Admittedly there are a handful of items such as Davidic descent, virginity, Bethlehem, and divine sonship in common, but no incidents, no phrases; and this from a writer who (on this alternative source-hypothesis) will soon quote almost word-for-word from Matthew (chs. 3–4).

Moving further on in Matthew as an imagined source for Luke, we note chs. 5–7, and other discourses. We would not expect them simply to be left intact by Luke; but we would expect the structure of some to be retained, and perhaps expanded by material from others. Luke 6 barely approaches this relationship with Matthew 5–7. We would not expect what in fact we find here, material omitted from the supposed use in Luke 6 of Matthew 5–7 later redistributed elsewhere. And Matthew's other discourses are followed even less respectfully still.

11. See now F.G. Downing, 'A Paradigm Perplex: Luke, Matthew and Mark', *NTS* 38 (1992), pp. 15-36, responding in particular to M.D. Goulder, *Luke—A New Paradigm* (JSNTSup, 20; Sheffield: JSOT Press, 1989).

But the greatest surprise that awaits us, as we try to pursue the hypothesis that a Luke who accepted conventions similar to those we find in Josephus might have drawn on Matthew and Mark, lies in the *complex and laborious* work which we must suppose him to have undertaken. This laborious complexity would make his procedure very different from that of Josephus; and also, it may be suggested, very difficult to credit. First we must recall how the data in question appear.

There are a number of so-called 'minor agreements of Matthew and Luke against Mark in Markan contexts', and these have long been a minor but real embarrassment to the 'four document' hypothesis (the one we were earlier following, that Luke and Matthew used Q and Mark independently of each other.[12] Surely these 'agreements' suggest either Luke or Matthew knows the other's use of Mark?). The embarrassment that our present hypothesis faces is almost the exact opposite. If Luke knows and uses Matthew (including Matthew's version of Mark), then why are there only *so few* such agreements, and why are they *so minor*? They are enough to worry those who adopt the 'four document' hypothesis; but they are surely too slight to support this one. It is also very rare for any close copying of Mark by Matthew to be copied by Luke; when it does occur it is in the brief 'punch-lines' of pronounce-ment stories, or the short technical climaxes of miracle stories (and Josephus's example would lead us to expect even independent redactors to coincide at such points). It is not that Luke refuses ever to follow Mark closely at any length (he does at, for example, Lk. 4.33-35 // Mk 1.23-25; Lk. 9.48-50 // Mk 9.37-41; Lk. 18.15-27 // Mk. 10.13-27). He follows Matthew's 'additions' to Mark often very closely indeed, almost word-for-word (see below). But where Matthew himself has followed Mark closely, perhaps also almost word-for-word, and thus (on this hypothesis) affords Luke a ready-made conflation, Luke refuses to follow. When Josephus found his two sources in complete or all-but complete agreement, then he paraphrased them almost word-for-word

12. A. Farrer, 'On dispensing with "Q"', in Nineham (ed.), *Studies in the Gospels*; W.R. Farmer, *The Synoptic Problem* (New York: Macmillan, 1964); Goulder, *Midrash and Lection in Matthew*, pp. 4-9, 97. See F.G. Downing, 'Towards the Rehabilitation of "Q"', *NTS* 11 (1965), p. 169. See now in particular F.G. Downing, 'Conpositional Conventions and the Synoptic Problem', *JBL* 107.1 (1988), pp. 69-85; *idem*, 'Word-Processing in the Ancient World: The Social Production and Performance of Q', *JSNT* 64 (1996), pp. 29-48.

(e.1). When Luke as an imagined redactor of Matthew and Mark finds such agreement, he eschews it entirely.

We would have to suppose that rather than accept ready-made conflations, Luke has instead gone to considerable pains to avoid them. Particularly pointed examples are afforded in those passages where Matthew has greatly enlarged an existing Markan sequence (baptism and temptation, the mission of the disciples, the Beelzebul controversy). Here in particular Luke uses often with very little variation the 'non-Markan' elements (see synopses). Where Matthew re-writes Mark (for example, Mt. 3.1-2 // Mk 1.4) Luke further re-writes (and this would not be entirely unexpected: save that it tends to become *less* like Mark, rather than a re-conflation, as in such contexts in Josephus). But where Matthew uses Mark word-for-word (Mt. 3.4-6 // Mk 1.4-6) Luke reproduces not a word. If this refusal to follow Matthew in copying Mark happened just once or twice, we might find a special reason for it (for example, here, Luke not wanting to let John look too like Elijah). But the phenomenon recurs throughout Luke's Gospel. It is not that he refuses every ready-made conflation; it is that (apart from a few 'punchlines' as noted) he refuses *almost* every ready-made conflation; and sometimes goes to great pains to do so.

In most cases where Matthew is either producing a 'version' of Mark, or copying, or inserting quite distinct and self-contained units of tradition, it would not be too difficult for Luke to avoid the passages of 'pure Mark in Matthew'. But in the sequences referred to in the previous paragraph, and especially in the Beelzebul controversy, it would be a very complex procedure indeed. We would have to imagine Luke reading through Matthew and Mark together, and finding our v. 27 of Mark 3 almost identical with our v. 29 of Matthew 12, deciding to re-write completely (Lk. 11.21). On finding doublets in Mt. 12.31-32, Luke would reject v. 31a (= Mk 3.28) in preference for vv. 31b-32a (Matthew's addition), but copy that almost exactly, along with most of the rest of Matthew's 'additions', save for re-casting vv. 22-24a. But where Matthew has largely re-written Mark (albeit without creating substantial disagreement), Luke follows neither, but re-writes in a way that results in still further divergence from Mark. The same phenomena occur in the mission material, and in the synoptic apocalyptic material.

If we try to imagine Luke writing his Gospel with Matthew and Mark before him, we have to imagine him claiming in 1.1-4 the same conventional aims and intentions as Josephus; in his redaction producing often very similar changes to those introduced by Josephus; writing speeches for (it would seem) an audience much the same as the sort Josephus had in mind; but going about the process in almost diametrically opposed ways, and going to considerable pains to be different.

Just taking such pains is itself odd and unexpected. If Luke had wanted to be different from Matthew in his treatment of Mark (though not in treatment of Matthew's additions to Mark) he could easily have paraphrased more. It is possible, as has been said, to find piece-meal reasons for each change of Matthew's close quotation of Mark as it occurs.[13] But it is still strange at the end to find that Luke ends up with 'pure Mark in Matthew' almost totally rejected; revised Mark in Matthew further revised; yet 'new' Matthew accepted, often as it stands. This Luke does not conflate, he disentangles; but neither does he consistently write his own version: items not already conflated he will include almost as they stand. He neither follows the conventions we discerned in Josephus, nor any coherent line of his own. He is far too odd even to begin to be plausible.

A much more likely explanation of what we find at the baptism, temptation, Beelzebul controversy, mission speeches, and apocalypses, and elsewhere in the three synoptics, is that briefly outlined before. Luke has before him Mark, and Q which occasionally overlaps with Mark, and when it does it usually provides a fuller version of the common subject matter. In such passages there are already some fairly close verbal parallels; or else Luke checks between the two sources and introduces a few clear echoes, while primarily following what is at this point the fuller source (just as Josephus does between 2 Samuel / 1 Kings and Chronicles, e.1, above). Luke does not intend often to quote Mark exactly (though he treats the didactic material in Q with greater respect), so there is very little chance of his coinciding with Matthew's occasional exact quotations of Mark, save, as we have allowed, where apothegms and miracles reach their climax. Although Luke uses more of Mark's substance than does Matthew, his versions of Mark will look less like their originals, because, like Josephus if to a less extent, Luke is also a paraphraser. A Luke who effects his redaction in these ways is both self-consistent, and proceeding along lines accepted by his close contemporary, Josephus.

13. E.g. Drury, *Tradition and Design*; cf. C.M. Tuckett, 'The Griesbach Hypothesis in the Nineteenth Century', *JSNT* 3 (1979), pp. 29-60 (this volume pp. 14-43).

Q has the admitted disadvantage of not being available for inspection, and not even being directly documented. It is an imaginary entity, albeit an entirely plausible one.[14] A Luke who could produce his Gospel out of Mark and Matthew is also an imaginary entity, but quite implausible. Documents like the supposed Q have existed; some known to have existed have also disappeared; the genre is not imaginary. But there is no clear evidence available for there ever having existed authors with the kind of redactional procedures adopted by this other imaginary Luke, there is nowhere independent evidence for the production of a document at all like the third Gospel by the procedures presupposed, no evidence to match the clear picture we may draw from Josephus (and the contemporaries on whom he relied). The Luke who made his Gospel out of Mark and Matthew is a fictional entity, the sole exemplar of an equally fictional genre, and we do well to dispense with both.

The remaining hypotheses may be dealt with even more swiftly. The Griesbach hypothesis (that Mark used Matthew and Luke) fails even more signally in its lack of internal coherence; it also entails the use of redactional procedures among the evangelists quite other than those for which we have evidence, and in particular neglects the data that link Luke with these clearly evidenced redactional conventions.

Those who try to resurrect the theory that Mark conflated Matthew and Luke also seize on the 'minor agreements' of Matthew and Luke against Mark in Markan contexts. These 'minor agreements' seem to have an almost mesmeric effect, so that there is an all-but total neglect of the much more significant and weighty 'major agreements of Matthew and Luke against Mark', both in Markan and 'non-Markan' contexts: to

---

14. Cf. C.H. Talbert, *What is a Gospel?* (Philadelphia: Fortress Press, 1977), pp. 116, 122. He rightly points to important structural 'signals' that the Gospels share with other contemporary literature; but for instance in classifying Luke as 'type D biography' ignores the fact that the traits he picks on also appear in Josephus's (and Dionysius's) histories, as do others which he passes over; see the review of the London edition by R.T. France, *JSNT* 3 (1979), pp. 73-76. With my account of these aspects of Luke's procedures as an historian, compare the case made by M. Hengel in *Acts and the History of Earliest Christianity* (trans. J. Bowden; London: SCM Press, 1979), section I; though I would disagree in detail with some of his judgments on Acts—cf. n. 3 above. On genre, see now F.G. Downing, 'A Genre for Q and a Socio-Cultural Context for Q: Comparing Sets of Similarities with Sets of Differences', *JSNT* 55 (1994), pp. 3-26, referring in particular to R.A. Burridge, *What are the Gospels?* (SNTSMS, 70; Cambridge: Cambridge University Press, 1992).

wit, the entire *positive* base for the Q hypothesis, the very many passages where Matthew and Luke have sequences of maybe twenty, fifty,
even a hundred words all but identical in both, and together would seem
to offer any would-be redactor a ready-made conflation; and yet Mark
contains none of these particularly clear instances of 'concurrent testimony to the same gospel tradition'.[15] The near identity of these passages
with each other would make it easy for Mark to excise them; but it is
hard to imagine why he should; and in sequences such as the baptism
and temptation, the Beelzebul controversy, the mission addresses, and
the apocalypses, it is as difficult to imagine how he could, as it was for
Luke. This imagined Mark, intent on conflation, rejects (as too easy?)
every pericope where an all-but total conflation is there ready for him;
and on finding sequences where close parallels are mixed with divergent
and with quite distinct matter goes to great pains to pick out the latter,
sometimes to copy it exactly. Where there is 'concurrent testimony to
the same gospel tradition', he prefers a single testimony. This Mark is
even less credible than that Luke was, and as far from the contemporary
conventions for the use of sources for which we have evidence.

Some though not all of the writers who reject the 'four document
hypothesis' suppose that much or all of the distinctive material in
Matthew, and later in Luke, was produced by a form of 'free association' of ideas, following the free (but not arbitrary) methods of
rabbinic 'midrash' perhaps together with the suggestive collocations in
contemporary lectionaries.[16] Clearly we have examples of midrash from
later rabbinic sources, from Qumran, from Philo and from Josephus, and
from fragments preserved by Eusebius, and from some of the Jewish
apocalypses. We have examples of quite lengthy narratives, emanating
from before and from after the New Testament period (*Aristeas*, Tobit,
Artapanus on Moses, *Joseph and Asenath*), some at least of which may
have been conceived or expanded by midrashic procedures. But none of
these offers any at all precise precedent or analogy for Gospels so
conceived. For the Gospels we would have to suppose a willingness
often to quote almost word-for-word, along with a willingness to invent
out of scriptural hints, along with a quite incredibly painstaking willingness to sort out for rejection occasional examples of precise quotation;

---

15. Possible exceptions only at Mk 2.9-11, 12.36-37b, 13.29-31; compare, in
addition to passages referred to in the text, e.g., Mt. 6.22–7.11; 8.8-11, 19-22; 10.26-
32; 11.4-11, 16-23, etc.

16. See Drury, *Tradition and Design*; Goulder, *Midrash and Lection in Matthew*.

and all this in the portrayal of a supposed recent historical figure. We have no evidence for anyone else adopting so mixed and self-contradictory a method; and I would suggest again that it is so bizarre as to be beyond credence.

The example of Josephus's procedure reinforces the credibility of the four-document hypothesis, especially when we note that Luke makes the same explicit claims, and seems to be responding to very similar stimuli both in his embellishments to narrative and in his construction of speeches. Obviously this does not amount to proof; but it does seem to leave the rival theories without any initial plausibility whatsoever, dependent on the very subjective demonstration of a supposed internal coherence, itself severely in question from the outset.

JSNT 33 (1988), pp. 19-39

THE QUEST OF MARK THE REDACTOR:
WHY HAS IT BEEN PURSUED, AND WHAT HAS IT TAUGHT US?

C. Clifton Black

'New winds are blowing in Marcan research', as Jack Dean Kingsbury observed some years ago.[1] Surely the heartiest gusts have been methodological in character, as fresh literary,[2] rhetorical,[3] sociological,[4] and tradition-critical[5] strategies have been adopted in the interpretation of the

1. J.D. Kingsbury, 'The Gospel of Mark in Current Research', *RelSRev* 5 (1979), p. 106.
2. Among recent major contributions: D. Rhoads and D. Michie, *Mark as Story: An Introduction to the Narrative of a Gospel* (Philadelphia: Fortress Press, 1982); J.D. Kingsbury, *The Christology of Mark's Gospel* (Philadelphia: Fortress Press, 1983); D.O. Via, Jr, *The Ethics of Mark's Gospel—In the Middle of Time* (Philadelphia: Fortress Press, 1985); E.S. Malbon, *Narrative Space and Mythic Meaning in Mark* (San Francisco: Harper & Row, 1986); M.A. Tolbert, *Sowing the Gospel: Mark's World in Literary-Historical Perspective* (Minneapolis: Fortress Press, 1989).
3. Thus B. Standaert, *L'Evangile selon Marc: Composition et genre littéraire* (Brugge: Sint Andreisabdij, 1978); J. Dewey, *Markan Public Debate: Literary Technique, Concentric Structure, and Theology in Mark 2.1–3.6* (SBLDS, 48; Chico, CA: Scholars Press, 1980); C. Clifton Black, 'An Ovation at Olivet: Some Rhetorical Dimensions of Mark 13', in *Persuasive Artistry: Studies in New Testament Rhetoric in Honor of George A. Kennedy* (ed. D.F. Watson; JSNTSup, 50; Sheffield: JSOT Press, 1991), pp. 66-92.
4. V.K. Robbins, *Jesus the Teacher: A Socio-Rhetorical Interpretation of Mark* (Philadelphia: Fortress Press, 1984); H.C. Waetjen, *A Reordering of Power: A Socio-Political Reading of Mark's Gospel* (Minneapolis: Fortress Press, 1989).
5. Note especially R. Riesner, *Jesus als Lehrer: Eine Untersuchung zum Ursprung der Evangelien-Überlieferung* (WUNT, 2.7; Tübingen: Mohr [Paul Siebeck], 1981); W.H. Kelber, *The Oral and the Written Gospel: The Hermeneutics of Speaking and Writing in the Synoptic Tradition, Mark, Paul and Q* (Philadelphia:

Second Gospel. Yet the steady breeze of redaction criticism has persisted for some thirty-odd years and continues to propel Markan scholarship,[6] despite manifold uncertainties surrounding its execution that have long been recognized by cautious investigators.[7] Indeed, given the enormous theoretical and practical problems entailed by the practice of Markan redaction criticism, especially when predicated on the assumption of Markan priority, one wonders why this exegetical approach for so long has held so many interpreters in thrall. This essay is an attempt to address that question: first, by reviewing salient features in the

Fortress Press, 1983); and J.D.M. Derrett, *The Making of Mark: The Scriptural Bases of the Earliest Gospel* (2 vols.; Shipston-on-Stour, Warwickshire: Drinkwater, 1985 [c. 1984]).

6.   Noteworthy specimens include W.R Telford, *The Barren Temple and the Withered Tree: A Redaction-Critical Analysis of the Cursing of the Fig Tree Pericope in Mark's Gospel and its Relation to the Cleansing of the Temple Tradition* (JSNTSup, 1; Sheffield: JSOT Press, 1980); E. Best, *Following Jesus: Discipleship in the Gospel of Mark* (JSNTSup, 4; Sheffield: JSOT Press, 1981); and R. Busemann, *Die Jüngergemeinde nach Markus 10: Eine redaktionsgeschichtliche Untersuchung des 10. Kapitels im Markusevangelium* (BBB, 57; Bonn: Hanstein, 1983); A.Y. Collins, *The Beginning of the Gospel: Probings of Mark in Context* (Minneapolis: Fortress Press, 1992). Though markedly diverging in their presuppositions and practice of the method, almost every major commentary on Mark of the past two decades has been avowedly redaction-critical in orientation: R. Pesch, *Das Markusevangelium* (2 vols.; HTKNT, 2.1-2; Freiburg, Basel, and Vienna: Herder, 1976, 1977); J. Gnilka, *Das Evangelium nach Markus* (2 vols.; EKKNT, 2.1-2; Zürich: Benzinger Verlag; Neukirchen–Vluyn: Neukirchener Verlag, 1978, 1979); W. Schmithals, *Das Evangelium nach Markus* (Ökumensicher Taschenbuch-Kommentar zum Neuen Testament, 2.1-2; Würzburg: Gütersloher Verlagshaus/ Gerd Mohn & Echter Verlag, 1979); C.S. Mann, *Mark: A New Translation with Introduction and Commentary* (AB, 27; Garden City, NY: Doubleday, 1986); M.D. Hooker, *The Gospel according to Saint Mark* (BNTC; London: A. & C. Black, 1991).

7.   Acknowledgments of the difficulty in differentiating tradition from redaction in the Second Gospel are *de rigueur* among Markan redaction critics and are usually invoked by them in qualifying the certitude of their analyses. Two recent studies have responded to this hesitation in contrasting ways: in *Mark as Composer* (New Gospel Studies, 1; Macon, GA: Mercer University Press, 1987), D.B. Peabody has sought to refine the procedure by which putative redactional features in Mark might be identified; in my own study, *The Disciples according to Mark: Markan Redaction in Current Debate* (JSNTSup, 27; Sheffield: JSOT Press, 1989), the methodological quandaries involved in the enterprise have been underscored and presented as unamenable to resolution.

conceptualization of Markan *Redaktionsgeschichte*; secondly, by revisiting the scholarly *Sitz im Leben* in which the method was germinated and nurtured; and thirdly, by identifying both the contributions and the liabilities of redaction-critical analysis, as an aid in our ongoing reappraisal of appropriate methods in the study of Mark.

A Profile of the Redaction-Critical Method

To understand the recent history of Markan exegesis, which has exerted influence on all who currently labor in the field, we might begin by recalling the fundamental concerns voiced by the first self-reflective redaction critics of the Second Gospel. Early on, and in contrast to the form-critical emphasis on the Gospel traditions as products of early Christian communities, redaction critics of Mark[8] emphasized its production by *an individual author*. It is almost impossible to find a *redaktionsgeschichtlich* treatment of Mark and the other Gospels, of either older or more recent vintage, that does not stress this understanding of their literary origins. Thus Willi Marxsen urges that Markan interpreters take into account 'an author personality who pursues a definite goal with his work,...an "individualistic" trait oriented to the particular interest and point of view of the evangelist concerned'.[9] Repeatedly in the secondary literature the claim was made that, in *Redaktionsgeschichte*, 'We are dealing with individual authors not with the "community"',[10] 'evangelists [who] are genuine authors',[11] 'authors in their own right',[12] whose existence 'must at all costs be stressed, even if the extent and delimitation of [each author's] sources, his share in shaping them, his name,

---

8.   Most of the observations on redaction criticism presented in this section would apply, not only to Mark, but to the other Gospels as well.

9.   W. Marxsen, *Mark the Evangelist: Studies on the Redaction History of the Gospel* (trans. J. Boyce, D. Juel, W. Poehlmann with R.A. Harrisville; Nashville: Abingdon Press, 1969), pp. 18, 24. The first German edition of Marxsen's seminal volume appeared in 1956.

10.   R.H. Stein, 'What Is *Redaktionsgeschichte*?', *JBL* 88 (1969), p. 49.

11.   N. Perrin, 'The Evangelist as Author: Reflections on Method in the Study and Interpretation of the Synoptic Gospels and Acts', *BR* 17 (1972), p. 9. Notice also the very title of Perrin's article.

12.   J. Rohde, *Rediscovering the Teaching of the Evangelists* (trans. D.M. Barton; NTL; Philadelphia: Westminster Press, 1968), p. 9. Cf. N. Perrin, *What Is Redaction Criticism?* (Guides to Biblical Scholarship; Philadelphia: Fortress Press, 1970), p. 33.

his home, his fortunes could never be established with complete cer-
tainty'.[13]

Why were redaction critics so insistent on locating the evangelist-
author at the center of exegetical attention? In part, it reflected their
common-sense judgment that only from the redactor's hands have we
directly received the biblical literature; thus Franz Rosenzweig once
suggested that 'R' (referring to the lowly esteemed redactor of the
Hexateuch) should be interpreted as *rabbenu*, 'our master'.[14] In part,
this accent on the author attempted to correct the exaggerated importance conferred by form critics on the *urchristliche Gemeinde* in the
production of the Gospels, a perspective that virtually excluded any
contribution by the individual evangelists.[15] However, the principal
reason for this emphasis on the evangelist as author seems to have been
its association with the idea of the evangelist as *religious thinker* and his
Gospel as the vehicle for *predominantly theological perspectives*. This
connection between authorial and theological intention in the evangelist's
work is expressly wrought by Ernest Best in an early redaction-critical
volume: 'All this means that we must treat Mark seriously as an author.
He has his place in the canon, not because he gives certain historical
facts about the life of Jesus, but because, in the same sense as Paul, he
preaches Christ.'[16]

Alongside regard for the evangelists as genuine authors, this
perception of Mark and the other Gospel writers as theologians might be
considered the most significant redaction-critical concern. Certainly it
has been one of the most frequently voiced: 'the evangelists were not

13. Rohde, *Rediscovering the Teaching of the Evangelists*, p. 18.

14. Cited by G. von Rad, *Genesis: A Commentary* (trans. J.H. Marks; OTL;
Philadelphia: Westminster Press, rev. edn, 1972), pp. 42-43.

15. Thus Marxsen, *pace* Martin Dibelius (*Mark the Evangelist*, p. 20): 'Tradition
is indeed the primary factor which we encounter, but it is the tradition of the
evangelists, that is, the tradition laid down in the Gospels. When we reconstruct their
world (and that means the world of the evangelists) we approach the individual
tradition. Can it then be our first task to proceed to an investigation of the material of
the synoptic tradition, ignoring the evangelists? Is not our primary task twofold—that
of arriving at redaction *and* tradition?'

16. E. Best, *The Temptation and the Passion: The Markan Soteriology*
(SNTSMS, 2; Cambridge: Cambridge University Press, 1965), p. xi. Cf. the subtitle
of E. Haenchen's introductory section in *Der Weg Jesu: Eine Erklärung des
Markus-Evangeliums und der kanonischen Parallen* (Berlin: Töpelmann, 1966),
pp. 32-37: 'Die Evangelisten als Schriftsteller und Theologen'.

merely *Sammler* but individual theologians',[17] 'their redactional work... undertaken to serve a theological conception and particular theological themes'[18] and reflecting 'a distinctive, definable theological outlook as it seeks to relate the story of Jesus in its own manner'.[19] The sort of religious coloration, applied to the narrative of Jesus, that had long been recognized in the Fourth Gospel now was acknowledged as pervasive in the synoptics as well: 'Each Evangelist was a theologian in his own right and possessed a theological purpose for writing his gospel'.[20] From this point of view, redaction-critical exegesis was often depicted as a process of textual threshing, separating the wheat of an evangelist's theology from the chaff of his sources:

> ...having ascertained the evangelist's redaction we seek to find: (1) what unique *theological views* does the evangelist present which are foreign to his sources?...(2) What unusual *theological emphasis or emphases* does the evangelist place upon the sources he received?...(3) What *theological purpose or purposes* does the evangelist have in writing his gospel?[21]

No less than the consideration of the Gospels as individual rather than communal products, this focus on the theology of the evangelists was regarded as a departure from the form-critical approach.[22] If, according to *Formgeschichte*, the evangelist's role was understood as refinishing, dusting off, and rearranging the furniture of the Synoptic tradition, 'from the redaction critical viewpoint,...each evangelist functioned as the architect of his conceptual house of gospel, for which he chose, refurbished, and in part constructed the fitting furniture'.[23]

---

17. Stein, 'What Is *Redaktionsgeschichte*?', p. 47.

18. Rohde, *Rediscovering the Teaching of the Evangelists*, p. 17. Cf. E. Schweizer, 'Die theologische Leistung des Markus', *EvT* 24 (1964), pp. 337-55; *idem*, *The Good News according to Mark* (trans. D.H. Madvig; Atlanta: John Knox, 1970), pp. 380-86.

19. J.H. Hayes and C.R. Holladay, *Biblical Exegesis: A Beginner's Handbook* (Atlanta: John Knox, 1982), p. 99; cf. Haenchen, *Der Weg Jesu*, p. 24.

20. R.H. Stein, 'The Proper Methodology for Ascertaining a Markan Redaction History', *NovT* 13 (1971), p. 181; cf. M.D. Hooker, *The Message of Mark* (London: Epworth Press, 1983), p. 20.

21. Stein, 'What Is *Redaktionsgeschichte*?', p. 54; in the original each of the numbered questions is italicized. Stein further indicates a fourth concern of the method, the *Sitz im Leben* out of which the Gospel emerged; this we shall consider immediately below.

22. Thus Rohde, *Rediscovering the Teaching of the Evangelists*, p. 16.

23. W.H. Kelber, 'Redaction Criticism: On the Nature and Exposition of the

Beyond this slant on the synoptists as authors and theologians, redaction criticism ostensibly emphasized two other aspects of the Gospels, one literary and the other sociological. The literary insight was expressed by different scholars in different ways: some spoke of the significance of the Gospel's narrative framework, overriding its constituent traditions;[24] others expressed a critical concern for larger units of tradition up to and including the entire Gospel.[25] However they put the matter, redaction critics saw themselves as treating *the Gospels as unitary textual artefacts, to be interpreted holistically*: 'By contrast [to tradition and form criticism], redaction criticism emphasizes the wholeness of the Gospels, their literary integrity, and seeks to see not simply the individual parts, but what they were saying when arranged together as a single whole'.[26]

Moreover, redaction critics claimed to contribute an important sociological insight, namely, an understanding of the Gospels in light of *the evangelists' historical context and of the social setting of the communities for which they were writing*. Most scholars concurred with Marxsen's characterization of this component of *Redaktionsgeschichte* as *der dritte Sitz im Leben*: 'If Joachim Jeremias [in his work on the parables] differentiates the "first situation-in-life" located in the unique situation of Jesus' activity, from the "second situation-in-life" mediated by the situation of the primitive church (which form criticism seeks to ascertain), we are dealing here with the *"third* situation-in-life"'.[27]

With allowance for minor modifications and varying shades of emphasis, these three ideas—the evangelist as author and theologian, his Gospel as the immediate product of his and his community's 'setting in life', and that Gospel as a literary entity to be interpreted holistically— have been basic in the formulation of redaction criticism from its inception up to the present day. As such, redaction criticism was conceived to be, not merely another tool to be added to the arsenal of Gospel exegesis, but a comprehensive interpretative approach, equipped to

Gospels', *Perspectives on Religious Studies* 6 (1979), p. 12.

24. Thus Marxsen, *Mark the Evangelist*, p. 23; Rohde, *Rediscovering the Teaching of the Evangelists*, pp. 14, 19.

25. So Perrin, *What Is Redaction Criticism?*, p. 34.

26. Hayes and Holladay, *Biblical Exegesis*, p. 99. Similarly, Haenchen, *Der Weg Jesu*, p. 23; S.S. Smalley, 'Redaction Criticism', in *New Testament Interpretation: Essays on Principles and Methods* (ed. I.H. Marshall; Exeter: Paternoster Press, 1977), pp. 191-92.

27. Marxsen, *Mark the Evangelist*, p. 23.

address the theological, sociological, and literary issues raised by a text. Although comprehensive, the method did not intend, however, to award each of these concerns equal weight; for the center of gravity in redaction criticism, no less than in source and form criticism, remained with the author-theologian.[28] To be sure, practitioners of *Redaktionsgeschichte* believed that the method permitted them to intuit the particulars of the redactor's historical and sociological matrix and to interpret a Gospel as a literary product; *but the point of entry, as well as the confirmation, for both of these investigations resided with the identification of the redactor's theology.* On this point, John Barton's comments regarding Old Testament redaction-criticism are no less accurate as a characterization of Gospel *Redaktionsgeschichte*: 'the original author in some sense is the place where the method comes to rest. Once we have found the meaning or intention of whoever first wrote the text, we have achieved our goal.'[29]

*Redaction Criticism in the Context of Twentieth-Century
Theology and Scholarship*

Inasmuch as redaction critics of the Gospels have been absorbed in the delineation of the evangelists' social and historical setting, it seems not inappropriate to inquire why redaction criticism itself has been pursued with such vigor, and what historical and cultural forces in this century have encouraged that pursuit. The following factors do not constitute a complete explanation; however, no explanation would be complete without mention of these:

1. Initially at least, Markan redaction criticism was a somewhat late-blooming offshoot of the method's application to the other synoptics. The impressive exegetical results of *Redaktionsgeschichte* when applied by Günther Bornkamm and his pupils to Matthew[30] and by Hans

---

28. Thus D.M. Smith: 'The *basic* insight of redaction criticism was that *the evangelists were authors and theologians* painting their own portraits of Jesus and addressing themselves to important theological issues, albeit in the church of the first century' (*Interpreting the Gospels for Preaching* [Philadelphia: Fortress Press, 1980], p. 32, emphasis mine).

29. J. Barton, *Reading the Old Testament: Method in Biblical Study* (Philadelphia: Westminster Press, 1984), p. 202. In context (*ibid.*, p. 201), Barton's remarks apply to source and form criticism as well.

30. G. Bornkamm, G. Barth, and H.J. Held, *Tradition and Interpretation in Matthew* (trans. P. Scott; NTL; Philadelphia: Westminster Press, 1963). The German

Conzelmann to Luke[31] were observed by Markan investigators, and the conclusion was drawn by them, either openly or tacitly, that the method would yield equally impressive results when applied to the Second Gospel.[32] The popularity of redaction criticism was accelerated further by the freedom and rapidity with which Anglo-Saxon and Continental scholarship could be exchanged and translated in the period following World War 2.

2. To say that redaction criticism characterized the *Zeitgeist* of post-war Markan research as did no other interpretative tool is, while true, insufficient to explain why the method so thoroughly captured the imaginations of synoptic scholars to start with. Surely one reason for the ascendance of *Redaktionsgeschichte* was its perceived continuity with previous exegetical methods. In the last section of his form-critical *magnum opus*, Bultmann himself had set the stage for this perception by suggesting that the composition of the Gospels 'involves nothing in principle new, but only completes what was begun in the oral tradition...'[33] Redaction critics ever since have debated among themselves the degree of continuity between their discipline and form criticism;[34] nevertheless, that there was *some* conceptual consonance between them, that *Redaktionsgeschichte* at least grew out of and presupposed the existence of the pre-literary, typical traditions analyzed by the form critics, has never been a serious subject of debate. Similarly, redaction-critical discussion of the evangelists' distinctive literary traits

originals of the essays collected in this volume span the period from 1948 to 1957.

31. H. Conzelmann, *The Theology of St Luke* (trans. G. Buswell; New York: Harper & Row, 1961). The first German edition of this work, under the title *Die Mitte der Zeit*, was published in 1954.

32. For example, see Marxsen, *Mark the Evangelist*, pp. 16 n. 3, 28 n. 38; Perrin, 'Evangelist as Author', p. 9. Like most Markan redaction critics, Marxsen and Perrin assumed the priority of the Second Gospel; thus it was natural for the origination and preliminary development of synoptic *Redaktionsgeschichte* to occur with Gospels other than Mark.

33. R. Bultmann, *The History of the Synoptic Tradition* (trans. J. Marsh; New York: Harper & Row, rev. edn, 1963), p. 321.

34. Contrast E. Best's postulation of the second evangelist's positive respect for, and conservative adaptation of, traditional material ('Mark's Preservation of the Tradition', in *L'Evangile selon Marc: Tradition et rédaction* [ed. M. Sabbe; BETL, 34; Gembloux: Duculot; Leuven: Leuven University Press, 1974], pp. 21-34) with W.H. Kelber's argument for a radical disjunction between oral and literary transmission (*The Oral and the Written Gospels, passim*).

and theological ideas was congenial with, and an extension of, the procedure adopted by such older source critics as Julius Wellhausen[35] and B.H. Streeter.[36] However fruitful or abortive the attempt may be judged, however valuable or valueless the pursuit may be regarded, redaction criticism of Mark and the other Gospels thus promised to shed further light on the oral and literary history of those texts by means of a method based on accepted principles of critical analysis.

3. Perhaps an even more significant reason for redaction criticism's hold upon synoptic scholarship is this: the method has ostensibly offered biblical theologians and preachers constructive theological insights at a time when two important theological movements were disintegrating, much to the chagrin of many adherents of historical criticism. These were the old quest of the historical Jesus and the 'biblical theology movement'.

a. The first of these movements was undergoing its death throes in the early decades of this century, and, in a real sense, a proleptic exercise in *Redaktionsgeschichte* was directly responsible for its demise. In the last half of the nineteenth century, the 'old quest' had been predicated largely on acceptance of 'the Markan hypothesis': the theory that Mark not only was the earliest Gospel and a source employed by Matthew and Luke, but also was the closest chronologically to the original eyewitnesses of Jesus and could therefore be regarded as historically trustworthy for information about the life and ministry of Jesus.[37] Although this position still claims some proponents, its logic was sawn off at the root in the course of William Wrede's explosive and *redaktionsgeschichtlich*-clairvoyant presentation of the secrecy motif in the Gospels:

> It therefore remains true to say that as a whole the Gospel no longer offers
> a historical *view* of the real life of Jesus. Only pale residues of such a view

---

35. J. Wellhausen, *Einleitung in die drei ersten Evangelien* (Berlin: Georg Reimer, 1905).

36. B.H. Streeter, *The Four Gospels: A Study of Origins* (New York: Macmillan, 1925).

37. Though with varying modifications, this theory was most closely associated with C.G. Wilke (*Der Urevangelist: oder, Exegetische kritische Untersuchung über das Verwandtschaftverhältnis der drei ersten Evangelien* [Dresden and Leipzig: G. Fleischer, 1838]) and C.H. Weisse (*Die Evangelienfrage in ihrem gegenwärtigen Stadium* [Leipzig: Breitkopf & Härtel, 1856]).

have passed over into what is a suprahistorical view of faith. In this sense the Gospel of Mark belongs to the history of dogma.[38]

When, some fifty years later, Ernst Käsemann reopened 'The Problem of the Historical Jesus' with the sceptical (and overstated) observation that 'the Gospels offer us primarily the primitive Christian kerygma, and...[historical] criticism can only help us to arrive at corrections and modifications in the kerygma but never at a word or action of the earthly Jesus himself',[39] he was adding in substance nothing new to Wrede's depiction of a historical-critical blind alley, which, if anything, looked by now even darker after form criticism.[40]

In the face of such increasing scepticism about history in the Gospels and the possibility of conventional *Leben-Jesu-Forschung*, Markan redaction critics could and did assume one of two postures. On the one hand, many joined Marxsen in simply bracketing out the bothersome historical questions and devoting themselves exclusively to the discernment of the evangelist's theology: 'With this [redaction-critical] approach, the question as to what really happened is excluded from the outset... [That question] is of interest only to the degree it relates the situation of the primitive community in which the Gospels arose.'[41] Marxsen, in fact, was prepared to grant only minimal credence to the historicity of Mark's Gospel;[42] however, the secret of redaction

38. W. Wrede, *The Messianic Secret* (trans. J.C.G. Greig; Greenwood, SC: Attic Press, 1971 [German original, 1901]), p. 131; see also pp. 115-45. Cf. the similar conclusions of R.H. Lightfoot, *History and Interpretation in the Gospels* (London: Hodder & Stoughton, 1935), pp. 23-24.

39. E. Käsemann, *Essays on New Testament Themes* (trans. W.J. Montague; SBT, 41; London: SCM Press, 1964), pp. 34-35; see also *idem*, 'Blind Alleys in the "Jesus of History" Controversy', in *New Testament Questions of Today* (trans. W.J. Montague; Philadelphia: Fortress Press, 1969), pp. 23-65.

40. Thus, for example, M. Dibelius: 'The first understanding afforded by the standpoint of *Formgeschichte* is that there never was a "purely" historical witness to Jesus' (*From Tradition to Gospel* [trans. B.L. Woolf; New York; Scribner's, n.d.], p. 295). Of course, other form critics maintained a guardedly positive estimation of the historicity of the Gospels' framework and contents: C.H. Dodd, 'The Framework of the Gospel Narrative', *ExpTim* 43 (1932), pp. 396-400; J. Jeremias, *The Parables of Jesus* (trans. S.H. Hooke; New York: Scribner's, 2nd rev. edn, 1972).

41. Marxsen, *Mark the Evangelist*, pp. 23-24. Cf. the similar statement of purpose in Conzelmann, *Theology of St Luke*, p. 9.

42. See Marxsen's *Introduction to the New Testament: An Approach to its Problems* (trans. G. Buswell; Philadelphia: Fortress Press, 1968), pp. 120-45.

criticism's success lay in the fact that one had not to agree with Marxsen's judgment in this matter in order to adopt the method and be repaid with positive exegetical results.

On the other hand, as *Redaktionsgeschichte* increasingly came to carry a certain scholarly cachet, it so fundamentally redefined what the Gospels were that no longer was the riddance of historical questions merely possible or permissible; it now was considered virtually mandatory. As a growing number of scholars came to accept the dictum that 'the gospels must be understood as *kerygma*, and not as biographies of Jesus of Nazareth',[43] the appropriation of the Gospels in a reprise of the old quest of the historical Jesus came to be regarded, not so much as problematic, but as illegitimate:

> The fact is that the very project of redaction criticism methodologically precludes the quest for the historical Jesus... The historical Jesus forms the basis and presupposition of theology. Interestingly, what the gospels give us is not the presupposition, but the theologies.[44]

Although more conservative exegetes found slight consolation in the notion that neither Mark nor any of the evangelists proclaimed the *historical* Jesus,[45] more liberal interpreters tended to regard this as a positive contribution of redaction criticism. It seemed to bridge the enormous temporal and hermeneutical gap between Mark as interpreter of the Jesus-traditions and the twentieth-century theologian as interpreter of the Second Gospel by functionally locating both in the same position: that of elucidator, not of Jesus of Nazareth, but of the early Christian *kerygma* about Jesus. As Eduard Schweizer expressed it,

> [Jesus] can only be proclaimed and to by a believer like Mark... [Although] the historical Jesus is, in the highest possible degree, essential for the faith of the church[,]... this does not mean that we could see anything which would really help us in the historical Jesus, without the

---

43. Rohde, *Rediscovering the Teaching of the Evangelists*, p. 11. Of course, this view had been anticipated by Wrede and, in 1915, by C.W. Votaw (*The Gospels and Contemporary Biographies in the Greco-Roman World* [repr.; Philadelphia: Fortress Press, 1970], esp. pp. 1-5).

44. Kelber, 'Redaction Criticism', pp. 13-14. See also D. Blatherwick, 'The Markan Silhouette?', *NTS* 17 (1970–71), pp. 184-92, esp. p. 192.

45. Naturally, some rejected such a formulation: thus T.W. Manson, *Studies in the Gospels and Epistles* (ed. M. Black; Philadelphia: Westminster Press, 1962), pp. 40-83.

miracle of God's Spirit who, in the word of the witness [i.e., Mark], opens our blind eyes to the 'dimension' in which all these events took place.[46]

In short, redaction criticism responded to the problem of the historical Jesus either by completely ignoring it or by regarding it as of only tangential exegetical or theological consequence, since, on certain *redaktionsgeschichtlich* premises, the Evangelists themselves had responded to the matter in precisely the same way.

b. The waxing of redaction criticism during the middle of this century should be viewed also in the context of the waning of a second scholarly enterprise during the same period: the so-called 'biblical theology movement'.[47] In some respects the *redaktionsgeschichtlich* approach was antagonistic to some of the traits of that movement:[48] thus, given the nonchalance of the method toward matters historical, few proponents of 'revelation in history' found a home among Markan redaction critics, even though some of the earliest *redaktionsgeschichtlich* efforts considered the second evangelist's understanding of history.[49] And redaction criticism did nothing if not stimulate a heightened sensitivity to theological diversity among the Gospels, contrary to the emphasis of biblical theology on the unity of the Bible.

On the other hand, so clearly in sympathy with other aspects of the biblical theology movement was *Redaktionsgeschichte* that it proved to be the successor of the movement, in perspective if not in method. To those weary of the sort of biblical exegesis associated with 'liberal' theology (dry historical analysis, complacent or indifferent to theological concerns), redaction criticism promised, and often delivered, robust interpretations of the evangelists' theologies,[50] based on the established

46. E. Schweizer, 'Mark's Contribution to the Quest of the Historical Jesus', *NTS* 10 (1963–64), pp. 423, 431.

47. The growth and decline of this movement has been carefully chronicled by B.S. Childs, *Biblical Theology in Crisis* (Philadelphia: Westminster Press, 1967), pp. 13-87.

48. For a concise summary and assessment of the characteristics of post-war biblical theology, consult J. Barr, 'Biblical Theology', *IDBSup*, pp. 104-11.

49. J.M. Robinson, *The Problem of History in Mark* (SBT, 21; London: SCM Press, 1957); T.A. Burkill, *Mysterious Revelation: An Examination of the Philosophy of St Mark's Gospel* (Ithaca, NY: Cornell University Press, 1963).

50. Indeed, the very notion that the synoptists displayed such developed and distinctive theological understandings was revolutionary: by contrast, Bultmann had used the synoptics as the source only for 'The Message of Jesus' and 'The Kerygma

exegetical principles of source and form criticism yet readily appropriable by both theologians and churchmen. Indeed, for the church and its ministry of preaching, a concern of vital importance for the biblical theology movement, redaction criticism was regarded as having immediate and positive implications: not only did it provide new exegetical content for preachers; it also offered them new paradigms for understanding the homiletical task. From Willi Marxsen's early, heuristic analogy between the evangelist, his Gospel, and their *Sitz* with a modern preacher, sermon, and congregation[51] it was but a short step to Leander Keck's characterization of biblical preaching as that which not only 'imparts [the Bible's] message-content, but...does so in a manner that repeats the Bible's own way of using normative tradition'—namely, 'in response to particular occasions (usually crisis situation) in the life of communities of faith'.[52]

To summarize: in the mid-twentieth century a number of forces conspired to promote the pursuit of Markan *Redaktionsgeschichte*. Especially significant were the apparent fruitfulness of the method when applied to the other synoptics, its ostensible continuity with previous exegetical procedures, and its perceived theological fecundity during the decline of the biblical theology movement and the old quest of the historical Jesus.

The Contributions and Liabilities of Redaction Criticism

Assets

In retrospect, the *redaktionsgeschichtlich* perspective on Mark and the other Gospels has offered, and continues to offer, some genuinely positive contributions. First, as we have witnessed, redaction criticism was intended to be a comprehensive method, melding concerns for the author, his historical and sociological background, and the literary features displayed by his text. Whether the method was in fact successful in holding together these various interests, particularly by regarding the

---

of the Earliest Church' (*Theology of the New Testament* [trans. K. Grobel; New York: Scribners, 1951], I, pp. 3-62).

    51. Marxsen, *Mark the Evangelist*, p. 24 n. 30.

    52. L.E. Keck, *The Bible in the Pulpit: The Renewal of Biblical Preaching* (Nashville: Abingdon Press, 1978), p. 115. Notice that Keck considers this to be a distinctively *redaktionsgeschichtlich* insight: 'It is precisely at this point that especially redaction criticism becomes fruitful for preaching' (*ibid.*).

author as the methodological fulcrum, is a moot point, and one to be considered presently. For the moment, let this much be underscored: by incorporating the historical, traditional, literary, and theological concerns of its methodological predecessors (especially source and form criticism), *Redaktionsgeschichte virtually 'set the agenda' for the full range of critical inquiry into the Gospels* during the second half of the twentieth century. Obviously, this amounts to no small contribution.

In the second place, *Redaktionsgeschichte* has drawn the attention of biblical scholars to *the evangelists as authors of literary products*. At first blush, such an observation may seem self-evident if not trivial; in fact, it is of utmost significance in light of redaction criticism's methodological precursors and successors. Prior to *Redaktionsgeschichte* the primary critical tasks in the interpretation of the Gospels were the delineation of their literary sources (if any) and the discernment of their literary traditions: that is, source and form criticism. While these approaches were not repudiated with the onset of redaction criticism, the critical perspective did become realigned toward the evangelists as authors and their Gospels as literary wholes. Of course, a shift in interpretative perspective does not necessarily entail a substantive shift in exegetical method or results: many advocates of the so-called 'New Criticism' and other literary-critical strategies retort, with some justification, that redaction criticism remained every bit as 'disintegrating' of the Gospels, oblivious to their narrative wholeness, as were source and form criticism.[53] Nevertheless, without the countervailing stress of *Redaktionsgeschichte* on the synthesis of the Gospels by evangelists who functioned as creative authors, the force of the literary critics' response might have been lost on us. Indeed, without the redaction-critical emphasis on authors and literary products, the current movement toward newer literary-critical approaches might not have been as expeditious.

Thirdly, *Redaktionsgeschichte* has made a persuasive case for *the fundamentally theological character of Mark and of the other Gospels*. To say that various themes are interwoven by the author of Mark in his Gospel is, for the redaction critic, accurate but insufficient: these themes carry theological freight and communicate the evangelist's distinctive *Tendenzen*.

---

53. Among others, see L.M. Frye, 'Literary Criticism and Gospel Criticism', *TTod* 36 (1979), pp. 207-19; A. Stock, *Call to Discipleship: A Literary Study of Mark's Gospel* (Wilmington, DE: Michael Glazier, 1982), pp. 12-15. Also see below, n. 67.

To speak of the evangelists' authorial intentions, and of the Gospels as vehicles of their creators' religious beliefs, has come to be regarded in some quarters as reflective of engagement in exegetical pursuits that are past at best and spurious at worst. (1) Some scholars, for instance, have adopted a position of critical agnosticism: in their view, the notion that the evangelists molded their source materials in accordance with kerygmatic convictions has been merely assumed, not demonstrated. As John Meagher has put it, 'we simply do not know how [the Gospels] were meant to be read'.[54] Doubtless it is possible for redaction critics to exaggerate the extent to which an evangelist like Mark orchestrated his received tradition to the tune of his special concerns; on the other hand, the communication of a distinctive, theological point of view is by no means an improbable assessment of a significant aspect of Mark's intentions (see 1.1; 15.39).[55] Moreover, to discredit from the start the possibility of the evangelists' theological interests is, in itself, a critical overstatement. (2) Among interpreters influenced by 'New Criticism', the recovery of authorial intent, even if possible, is irrelevant if not critically fallacious: for them, the meaning of a text resides in the sense or senses that the words bear or might come to bear, altogether apart from the intention of the author in penning those words. However, it is one thing to suggest, as do William Wimsatt and Monroe Beardsley, 'that the design or intention of the author is neither available nor desirable as a standard for judging the success of a work of literary art';[56] it is quite another thing, and rather doctrinaire, to argue that the meaning intended by an author like Mark evaporated once the ink was dry, or that such meaning is unworthy of critical pursuit, or that a text is only some free-floating sequence of words whose meaning has nothing whatever to do with the author who wrote them.[57] (3) Other scholars insist that Mark's Gospel, like any work of literary art, cannot and

54. J.C. Meagher, *Clumsy Construction in Mark's Gospel: A Critique of Form- and Redaktionsgeschichte* (Toronto Studies in Theology; New York and Toronto: Edwin Mellen, 1979), p. 20.

55. If Meagher is correct (*Clumsy Construction*, p. 22) that Mark's readers were just curious about Jesus, this very well might betoken a theological judgment among that readership that Jesus was an especially apt object of curiosity.

56. W.K. Wimsatt, Jr, and M.C. Beardsley, 'The Intentional Fallacy', *Sewanee Review* 54 (1946), p. 468.

57. For a now classic defence of authorial intention in texts, see E.D. Hirsch, Jr, *Validity in Interpretation* (New Haven: Yale University Press, 1967).

should not be mined for the historical data to which it purportedly refers or to such theological insights as are stressed by redaction critics; the meaning of Mark is utterly non-referential and resides entirely in its own narrative shape.[58] Admittedly, the narrative form of Mark should be respected, not manipulated facilely as a convenient repository for historical or theological data. Still, when Luke prefaces his narrative with the express intention that Theophilus 'may know the truth concerning the things of which [he has] been informed' (1.4), and when John concludes his narrative with the hope 'that you may believe that Jesus is the Christ, the Son of God, and that believing you may have life in his name' (20.30), is not the reader of these works[59] justified in moving beyond the acknowledged character of the Gospels as works of narrative art, following their authors' lead in pursuing legitimately 'ostensive' theological issues?[60]

Notwithstanding these criticisms of their validity, three contributions of *Redaktionsgeschichte* as applied to Mark and to the other Gospels thus seem secure: its emphasis on the evangelists as creative authors in their own right; its recognition of the fundamentally theological character of the evangelists' intentions; and its multiple concerns for the history, tradition, theology, and literary character of the Gospels. To affirm these assets of *Redaktionsgeschichte* is not to deny the many procedural quandaries that have plagued Markan redaction criticism (or, for that

---

58. Thus F. Kermode, *The Genesis of Secrecy: On the Interpretation of Narrative* (Cambridge, MA: Harvard University Press, 1979), pp. 116-23. Cognate arguments are presented by M. Weiss, 'Die Methode der "Total-Interpretation"', *VTSup* 22 (1972), pp. 88-112 and H.W. Frei, *The Eclipse of Biblical Narrative: A Study in Eighteenth and Nineteenth Century Hermeneutics* (New Haven: Yale University Press, 1974), pp. 267-324.

59. The same would apply, *mutatis mutandis*, to Matthew and Mark.

60. Historically, Christian readers have believed that they were so justified: thus Papias (c. 130) asserts, 'I did not rejoice in them who say much, but in them who teach the truth, nor in them who recount the commandments of others, but in them who repeated those given to the faith by the Lord and derived from truth itself' (Eusebius, *H.E.* 3.39.3; trans. K. Lake [LCL]; cf. also Irenaeus's well-known comments on Mark's preservation of the preaching of Peter: Eusebius, *H.E.* 5.8.3). Likewise, throughout the history of biblical exegesis, the assumption has been made that the Gospels are intended to call attention to what they are *about*. For detailed consideration of patristic interpretations of Mark, consult C. Clifton Black, *Mark: Images of an Apostolic Interpreter* (Studies on Personalities of the New Testament; Columbia, SC: University of South Carolina Press, 1994).

matter, *Redaktionsgeschichte* when applied to the other Gospels). At this point, I am not speaking strictly of method or procedure as such. Redaction criticism has always been more than merely a step-by-step recipe for interpreting texts; often its practitioners have not even bothered to articulate such 'steps'.[61] At heart, the term 'redaction criticism' has described a distinctive way of viewing biblical texts, the salient aspects of which were outlined in the first part of this essay. An interpretative approach to the Bible, or to any literature, can present a valid or at least defensible *point of view* on textual interpretation, apart from the success or validity of a particular *method* of interpretation that it may propose. For all of its problems, to which we now must turn, Markan redaction criticism has brought to bear on the text some distinctive perspectives: the importance of the author and his intention, the Gospel as expressive of theological interests, and the need for an exegetical approach incorporating concerns historical, theological, and literary. It is these hermeneutical *Tendenzen* that may prove to be the enduring contribution of redaction criticism of Mark and the other Gospels.

Liabilities

On the other hand, the *redaktionsgeschichtlich* approach is not without its drawbacks. In most cases they are the obverse, or more accurately the overextension, of the very assets we have just observed.

1. For starters, it is one thing to accent the evangelists' authorial intention; it is something else to situate this concern at the center of one's interpretative procedure. As I have suggested, Markan redaction critics were justified in doing the former; the latter, however, has created nothing but problems for practitioners of the method:

a. By placing the author and his intention(s) at the methodological center, redaction criticism of Mark (on the assumption of Markan priority) has sought answers to exegetical questions that are, by definition, unverifiable.[62] Select any redaction-critical study of Mark, or any critical exercise in the refinement of that method's application to the Second

61. Stein's 'The Proper Methodology for Ascertaining a Markan Redaction History' is a conspicuous exception to this general neglect of *redakations-geschichtlich* procedure.

62. The same could be said of the redaction criticism of Matthew, predicated on the Griesbach hypothesis, and of John, on the assumption of its independence from the synoptics.

Gospel, and notice the pattern that emerges: in order to discern the earliest evangelist's redactional (= authorial) activity, every investigator is compelled to engage in often highly speculative conjectures about the history of traditions *behind* the evangelist, assumptions unamenable to empirical analysis yet invariably determinative of that researcher's exegetical or methodological results. Typically, those conclusions scatter in all directions and are impossible to validate, for they are primarily a function of their proponents' divergent perspectival starting-points, and only minimally the result of a controlled method of interpretation.[63] In short, by locating the author at the center of critical attention, Markan redaction criticism has raised fundamental questions that it cannot answer, at least with any reasonable degree of confidence.

   b. Another problem flows directly from the preceding: by concentrating on the author, Markan redaction criticism (again presupposing Markan priority) has been forced to appeal to interpretative clues lying beyond the boundaries of the Gospel itself.[64] The paradox of Markan redaction criticism is that it must traffic in evidence that is not redactional: the key to the enterprise lies in the fragile reconstruction of the shape, development, and utilization of pre-Markan (non-textual) tradition. Since the method demands speculation about hypothetical sources, the *Geschichte* of whose *Redaktion* can be plotted, its practitioners are compelled to devise traditio-historical scenarios of greater or lesser plausibility, extrinsic to the actual content of the Gospel. Periodically, Markan scholars balk at such a dubious procedure and decide to treat the Gospel as a whole, taking it for what it says and refusing to quarry for pre-Markan strata; then, however, they are no longer practicing redaction criticism as it has been customarily defined—nor do they need to do so.

   2. At least intuitively, many Markan redaction critics seem to be aware that their interpretations ultimately cannot be made to turn upon the author and his editorial activity. It is for this reason, I believe, that the focus of so many *redaktionsgeschichtlich* studies of the Second Gospel is not so much on precise redactional discriminations as on particular *themes* that are evident in the text: the mystery of the kingdom of

   63. The substantiation for this claim may be found in my *The Disciples according to Mark*.
   64. More narrowly in connection with Markan Christology, this point has been made by J.D. Kingsbury, 'The "Divine Man" as the Key to Mark's Christology—The End of an Era?', *Int* 35 (1981), pp. 243-57.

God, the disciples' incomprehension, the suffering Son of man, and so forth. Of course, many exegetes have regarded the specification of such themes as an inherently redaction-critical operation;[65] however, this is a point of methodological confusion. Although the identification of the Gospel's themes could be incorporated into a larger redaction-critical paradigm, *such a determination is not an intrinsically redaction-critical criterion but a literary-critical assessment.*

It is equally misleading, I suspect, to follow the redaction-critical path of identifying Mark's thematic concerns as strictly theological in character. Doubtless many motifs in Mark *do* connote special theological interests of the author; yet such themes may also, or in some cases primarily, reflect the historical or social circumstances in Mark's environment or community, or may resonate at a deeper psychological level with the readers of that Gospel.[66] Furthermore, any one or a combination of these referents (the historical, social, theological, or psychological) may be addressed, not only by themes, but also by other literary devices, such as plot, settings, and characters. In any case, themes and other such literary characteristics rightly belong in the center of an interpretation of Mark in a way that 'theology' or 'theological themes' do not, if for no other reason than that the form of the Second Gospel is not that of a self-consciously theological treatise. Mark is first of all a *narrative* and, at least on initial approach, should be treated as such.

3. A third major liability of the redaction-critical approach has been its tendency toward 'methodological imperialism': by attempting to answer questions, not only of theology and *Traditionsgeschichte*, but of literary composition and socio-historical setting as well, redaction criticism has taken on more issues than its critical apparatus was designed to handle. Even more pointedly, it can be argued that the very procedure of *Redak-*

---

65. To select one example among many: E. Schweizer has argued that the methodological starting-point for distinguishing tradition and redaction in Mark should be the delineation of such themes as *Wundercharakter*, teaching, and the suffering Son of man ('Anmerkungen zur Theologie des Markus', in *Neotestamentica et Patristica* [O. Cullmann Festschrift; NovTSup, 6; Leiden: Brill, 1962], pp. 35-46).

66. For an insightful discussion of the subtle interconnections that can exist between an author and his readers in the realm of emotions, values, and belief, consult W.C. Booth, *The Rhetoric of Fiction* (Chicago: University of Chicago Press, 2nd edn, 1983), pp. 89-147.

tionsgeschichte operates at cross-purposes with that method's intention to treat the Gospels as literary wholes:

> Literary criticism seeks to apprehend a text as a whole or as a totality... From Marxsen up to the most recent times, however, redaction critics... have split Mark into tradition (sources) and redaction and have sought to establish chronological-genetic-causal relations between these two strata... As provocative and interesting as these studies often are for historical purposes, the text as a whole, as a narrative, in the form in which it confronts the reader and needs explication, is lost sight of.[67]

Nor has redaction criticism adequately fulfilled its promise to illuminate the historical and sociological *Sitz im Leben* of Mark's Gospel. Thus, while reaping the fruits of *Redaktionsgeschichte* in his own study of the Second Gospel, Howard Clark Kee urges the adoption of more sophisticated tools of social analysis, since 'much of what passes for historical writing about the New Testament is docetic. It fails to take account of the full range of social and cultural factors that shaped the Christian communities and their ideas, their understanding of themselves, and their place in the universe.'[68] Overall, redaction criticism has set forth most of the different kinds of critical questions that can reasonably be posed of the Gospels; it is doubtful, however, that *Redaktionsgeschichte*, or any single methodological approach, is conceptually or practically equipped to answer all of those questions.

Conclusion

Markan redaction criticism is neither a 'sacred cow' nor a 'white elephant'.[69] Born of the marriage of this century's scholarly occupations and theological preoccupations, the *redaktionsgeschichtlich* point of

67. D.O. Via, Jr, *Kerygma and Comedy in the New Testament: A Structuralist Approach to Hermeneutic* (Philadelphia: Fortress Press, 1975), pp. 72-73. Note also the similar criticisms of T.E. Boomershine, 'Mark the Storyteller: A Rhetorical-Critical Investigation of Mark's Passion and Resurrection Narrative' (doctoral dissertation, Union Theological Seminary, New York, 1974), pp. 23, 25, 31, 334-38; and N. Perrin, 'The Interpretation of the Gospel of Mark', *Int* 30 (1976), p. 120.

68. H.C. Kee, *Community of the New Age: Studies in Mark's Gospel* (Philadelphia: Westminster Press, 1977), p. ix. Likewise, L.E. Keck, in 'On the Ethos of Early Christians', *JAAR* 42 (1974), pp. 435-42, upholds the corrective value of an ethological approach to the study of Christian origins.

69. The double metaphor is borrowed from V.P. Furnish, *The Moral Teaching of Paul: Selected Issues* (Nashville: Abingdon Press, 2nd edn rev., 1985), pp. 11-28.

view has schooled us in the appreciation of the second evangelist's literary creativity, the theological cast of his Gospel, and the need for critical breadth in the interpretation of Mark and the other Gospels. Corresponding to these contributions have been certain liabilities of the redaction-critical perspective: its misplacement of the author at the center of textual interpretation, occasioning tendentious and unverifiable exegeses; its overemphasis on the strictly theological quality of the Markan narrative; and its incompetence to answer all of the critical questions that it has raised. The way forward in Markan research lies in the exploration and interrelation of the historical, social, theological, and literary contexts to which *Redaktionsgeschichte* has directed us, and in the clarification and refinement of the critical disciplines germane to those interpretative contexts. In pondering appropriate strategies in the study of Mark, we need not only to move beyond redaction criticism but also, and perhaps more importantly, to move forward in a manner respectful of the lessons it has taught us.

JSNT 45 (1992), pp. 27-57

SOCIO-RHETORICAL CRITICISM AND THE
PARABLE OF THE TENANTS

J.D. [Hester] Amador

Introduction

It is my intention in this article to bring some new interpretative insights
to the parable of the tenants (which is found in Mt. 21.33-46, Mk 12.1-
12, Lk. 20.9-19, and *Gos. Thom.* 65). These insights are the result of the
exploration of a methodology which I call 'socio-rhetorical criticism'. It
is my assumption that a given rhetorical unit brings different interpretative responses depending upon the audience interacting with it, that
is, depending upon a whole set of historical and sociological, as well as
literary, factors.

By and large, modern scholars assume a single rhetorical context/
purpose for the parables: the context of 'kingdom' preaching. The result
is, no matter how insightful and new their interpretations claim to be, the
parables ultimately are viewed as theologically motivated teachings. For
instance, from them we are supposed to learn what God is like, and
about Jesus' vision of the coming (eschatological) realm (Jeremias,
Taylor, Carlston).[1] Or, we gain insight into our existential situation as
humans confronted by the choice of authentic/inauthentic living (Via).[2]
Or, the parables are supposed to reflect how the Church viewed its
place in salvation history (Jülicher, Bultmann, Dodd).[3] Or, we learn how

1.   J. Jeremias, *The Parables of Jesus* (New York: Scribners, 1972): V. Taylor,
The Gospel according to St Mark (London: Macmillan, 1952); C.E. Carlston,
Parables of the Triple Tradition (Philadelphia: Fortress Press, 1975).

2.   D.O. Via, *The Parables* (Philadelphia: Fortress Press, 1967).

3.   A. Jülicher, *Die Gleichnisreden Jesu* (repr.; Darmstadt: Wissenschaftliche
Buchgesellschaft, 1963); R. Bultmann, *Die Geschichte der synoptischen Tradition*

the Gospel authors used the parables for their narrative needs (Drury),[4] and so on. While there exist in these discussions many differing themes and emphases, this is only so within the same assumed theological/ rhetorical framework: the referent of a parable is ultimately not material existence, but divine.

It is my purpose to suggest a different context for interpretation. I suggest that, while religious themes are present, they are but one of many different social factors against or within which the parables interact. It is my assumption that audiences hear different meanings within a given work, and these meanings can find expression and origin within political, economic, sexual-role, sociological, historical, artistic, and many other forums. If we open up the rhetorical possibilities, we find, I think, many levels of interaction and interpretation within the tradition, which the various audiences and speakers/authors brought to the tradition.

With respect to the parable under discussion we see a good deal of interaction, both within the parable structure and in the later interpretations of the parable which eventually entered into the canonical transmissions. Aside from some 'obvious' themes of rich/poor, landed/ landless, perhaps town/country, even questions of law, themes which many others before me have thoroughly explored well beyond my abilities, I wish to bring up a couple of what I see as key points within the traditions which have been entirely overlooked until now. I would like to explore the question of 'inheritance' and its political/economic/ religious implications for the first-century Palestinian audience. Furthermore, I would like to bring out what I see as two *contradictory* responses to the 'original' parable: (1) the theme of reversal, as found in the stone quotation, and (2) the theme of vengeance, as found in the canonical elaboration of the narrative.

The Parable

The Traditions

Mt. 21.33-44	Mk 12.1-11	Lk. 20.9-18
21.33 Hear another parable: There was *a man*, a householder, who *planted*	12.1 And he began to tell them another parable: *A man planted a vineyard*	20.9 And he began to tell the people this parable: *A certain man planted a*

(Göttingen: Vandenhoeck & Ruprecht, 1931); C.H. Dodd, *Parables of the Kingdom* (London: Nisbet, 1946).

4.   J. Drury, *Parables in the Gospels* (New York: Crossroad, 1985).

Mt. 21.33-44 (cont.)	Mk 12.1-11 (cont.)	Lk. 20.9-18 (cont.)
a vineyard and set a fence around it and dug a press in it and built a tower *and let it out to tenant farmers and travelled to a foreign land*. 21.34 And when the *season* of fruit drew near *he sent* his *servants to the tenant farmers* to take his *fruit*. 21.35 And taking his servants, the tenant farmers *beat* one, killed another, and stoned another. 21.36 Again he sent other *servants* more than the first, and they did the same to them. 21.37 And afterwards he sent his son to them, saying '*They will respect my son*'. 21.38 But *the tenant farmers*, seeing the son, said to themselves, '*This is the heir*; come, *let us kill him* and have his inheritance'. 21.39 *And* taking *him they cast him out of the vineyard and killed him.*	and set a fence around it and dug a pit and built a tower *and let it out to tenant farmers and travelled to a foreign land,* 12.2 and he *sent a servant to the tenant farmers at the season* so that he might take from the tenant farmers some of the *fruit* of the vineyard; 12.3 and taking him they *beat* him and sent him away empty handed. 12.4 And again he sent another *servant* to them and him they wounded in the head and humiliated. 12.5 And another he sent and him they killed, and many others, some beating, some killing. 12.6 He still had one beloved son; he sent him to them last, saying '*They will respect my son*'. 12.7 But those tenant farmers said to themselves, '*This is the heir*; come, *let us kill him* and *the inheritance will be ours*'. 12.8 *And* taking *him they killed him and cast him out of the vineyard.*	*vineyard and let it out to tenant farmers and travelled to a foreign land* for a long time. 20.10 And at a *season he sent a servant to the tenant farmers* so that they might give him from the *fruit* of the vineyard. And the tenant farmers sent him away, *beating* him, empty handed. 20.11 And he continued to send another *servant*. And beating and humiliating him they sent him away empty handed. 20.12 And he continued to send a third. And this one also, wounding him, they cast out. 20.13 And the lord of the vineyard said 'What shall I do? I shall send *my* beloved *son*; perhaps *they will respect* this one.' 20.14 But seeing him *the tenant farmers* reasoned among themselves, '*This one is the heir; let us kill him*, so that *the inheritance* will be ours'. 20.15 *And casting him out* outside of the vineyard, *they killed him.*
21.40 *Therefore*, whenever *the lord of the vineyard* comes, *what will he do* to those tenant farmers? 21.41 They say to him, 'He *will* miserably *destroy* those evil ones and will let *the vineyard*	12.9 *Therefore, what will the lord of the vineyard do*? He will come and *destroy* the tenant farmers and give *the vineyard to others.*	*Therefore, what will the lord of the vineyard do* to them? 20.16 He will come and *destroy* these tenant farmers and will give *the vineyard to others*. And hearing they said, 'Let it not be so!'

Mt. 21.33-44 (cont.)	Mk 12.1-11 (cont.)	Lk. 20.9-18 (cont.)
out *to other tenant farmers* who will deliver the fruits to him in their season'.		
21.42 Jesus says to them, 'Did you not read in the Scriptures: *A stone which the builders rejected, This one was made the head of the corner;* This was done before the lord, And it is marvelous in our eyes? 21.43 Therefore, I say to you that the realm of God will be taken away from you and will be given to a nation producing fruits of it.'	12.10 Did you not read this scripture, *'A stone which the builders rejected, This one was made the head of the corner;* 12.11 This was done before the lord, and it is marvelous in our eyes?'	20.17 And he, looking at them, said, 'What, then, is this written thing: *A stone which the builders rejected, This one was made the head of the corner?* 20.18 Everyone falling upon that stone will be broken to pieces; but upon whomever it may fall, it will crush him...'

Gos. Thom. 65 and 66

He said, 'There was a (?) man who owned a vineyard. He leased it to tenant farmers so that they might work it and he might collect the produce from them. He sent his servant so that the tenants might give him the produce of the vineyard. They seized his servant and beat him, all but killing him. The servant went back and told his master. The master said, "Perhaps he [they] did not recognize them [him]". Because the tenants knew that it was he who was the heir to the vineyard, they seized him and killed him. Let him who has ears hear.'

Jesus said, 'Show me the stone which the builders have rejected. That one is the cornerstone.'

The Overview of Traditions

Each parable in the canonical tradition contains at least three different literary units: the Parable, the Question/Answer addressed to the crowd, and the Logion. Each canonical author includes and/or expands upon these various sections according to specific interpretative dimensions he seeks to emphasize. Mark's use of the parable in the greater narrative setting of the Gospel[5] serves to highlight certain allegorical possibilities,

5.   As allegory serving to condense Mark's interpretation of the history of Israel and its (narrative and actual) end, thereby giving a symbolic résumé of the events of

which Mark then elaborates. Among these are the reference to the LXX version of Isa. 5.2 (Mk 12.1), the amplification of the fate of the individual messengers (Mk 12.2-5a) and the summary account of the sending of multitudes of servants (Mk 12.5b). The result is an attempt to put upon Jesus' lips an allegory which serves to prophesy his impending death at the hands of the Jewish authorities, and God's vengeful response to this act by rejecting Israel and turning over the 'vineyard' to others. This allegory is then supplemented by reference to vindication through exaltation: the use of Psalm 118 as proof text of the resurrection serves to change the conclusion of the story from one of revenge to one of triumph.[6]

Matthew intensifies the allegorical direction taken by Mark. He, too, includes the reference to Isa. 5.2 (Mt. 21.33), and the contextual setting of this parable, following the parable of the laborers and of the two sons, makes it 'abundantly clear to the hearer or reader that these three parables are about God's vineyard, Israel, from which he has a right to expect fruit—or abandon it'.[7] He refines, however, the stories concerning the sending of the servants by eliminating Mark's redundancies (Mk 12.2-5a; cf. 12.5b), sending groups of servants twice (Mt. 34.36) in reference to the early and late prophets. Furthermore, by altering the sequence of Mark from 'killing the son, then casting him out of the vineyard' to 'casting him out, then killing him', Matthew may have in mind a reference to the death of Jesus taking place outside of Jerusalem.[8] The interpretation of the parable as allegory is generally the same as that found in Mark; indeed, whereas Mark indicates that the chief priests, the scribes and the elders perceived the parable was told against them, Matthew has Jesus explicitly mention the meaning of the allegory (Mt. 21.43)! Matthew furthers the condemnation by giving to *the chief priests and elders* the response of vengeance on the part of the owner/lord, thereby condemning themselves (Mt. 21.41). Finally, the stone

the Gospel up to that point and a direction along which the following narrative will take: Israel has rejected Jesus (climactically at the Passion), and God's revelation will be turned over to the Gentiles (the proclamation of 'son of God' by the centurion). See Drury, *Parables*, pp. 64-67.

6.   See J.D. Crossan, *In Parables* (San Francisco: Harper & Row, 1985), p. 90, on the function of the stone text as it relates to the developing allegory.

7.   Drury, *Parables*, p. 96.

8.   See Drury, *Parables*, p. 97; Crossan, *In Parables*, p. 89; Carlston, *Triple Tradition*, p. 42; Jülicher, *Gleichnisreden*, p. 394; Jeremias, *Parables*, p. 73.

quotation is given, but this time is offered as the key to interpretation. The chief priests and elders have given the response of vengeance to the question offered by Jesus, and Jesus responds to them by offering this quotation. Since an explicit interpretation is then offered by Jesus concerning both this quotation and the parable, it may be the case that its function is not so much one of referring to the triumphant vindication and restoration of the son (proof text of resurrection), but one which serves to emphasize the theme of reversal: the tenants have been cast out and replaced, the stone quotation speaks of a rejection and the vindication, which Jesus then suggests refers to the future reversal of position with respect to the other nations who will receive the reign of God.

Luke is distinctly less allegorical in his presentation of the parable. It is a very simple story that is given, very similar in style to the tradition behind *Gos. Thom.* 65. There is no theme from Isaiah, and no elaboration on the fate of servants. There is some mention of the owner having gone away 'for a long time', which is distinctly Lukan redaction, but the allegorical significance argued by some does not seem to be overwhelming.[9] Luke agrees with Matthew concerning the death of the son occurring outside the vineyard (Lk. 20.15), but, again, this does not seem overwhelmingly allegorical and may simply be variation in performance. We do need to consider the presence and function of the Question/Answer and the stone quotation; these tend to indicate an interpretation of the parable similar to that of Matthew and Mark, as does the response of the scribes and chief priests (Lk. 21.19). But, in light of the Lukan parable performance, it is possible to see a point in the development of the tradition when the parable is not trying so hard to become an allegorical prophecy of Jesus' death.

What is important for us to keep in mind is that the interpretative context into which this parable is placed by each author, along with the ensuing allegorical elaboration, is not authoritative for our purpose. The variation in performance and meaning can be shown in the case of *Gos. Thom.* 65. Here there is no allusion to Isaiah; only single servants are sent to collect the rents, and this done only twice; there is no elaboration concerning the fate of these servants; no mention of the death of the son 'outside the vineyard'; no Question/ Answer of vengeance on the part of the owner. There is no indication whatsoever of an allegorical meaning to the text. The immediate relationship of the stone quotation of

9.   See Crossan, *In Parables*, p. 87; Drury, *Parables*, p. 157.

Gos. Thom. 66 is significant, in that it serves to show a very early connection of these two sayings in the tradition, but it is clear that the story itself has ended ('Let him who has ears hear') and the process of interpretation has begun only externally. However, unlike some, I do not think this interpretation at this stage of the game is one of allegorization;[10] that will come later. As we shall see below, it is an approving response to the 'shocking story of successful murder'.[11]

The result, upon completion of this survey, is a story which relates the events of a man who plants a vineyard, sends servants to collect the rent who are consistently rebuffed, and then sends his son in the hope that the tenant farmers will respect his claim. These, however, knew the son as heir and seized him and killed him in the hope of claiming the inheritance.

Sometime during the development of this tradition certain interpretative responses were given. The earliest seems to be the attachment of the stone quotation, which is used differently by the different authors. Later comes the interjected rhetorical question concerning the fate of the tenant farmers in the hands of the avenging owner. Later still comes an allegorical twist to the whole story, which seems to have been accepted (if not created) in varying degrees by all three canonical authors. This does not mean, however, that the previous interpretative responses to this parable were created or remembered with only such a view in mind.

My point here is to suggest a methodological shift away from assuming a particular interpretative context given to the parable by the canonical authors. Instead, I am interested in exploring the possibility of multiple interpretative meanings of this parable by immersing it within the socio-historical context about which it speaks: the plight of the Jewish tenant farmer in first-century Palestine. The result is shown to be a story, the differing reactions to which the canonical authors and *Thomas* have recorded. We are here to discern the possible meanings of this text and the varying reactions to them. It is my thesis that we will discover new insight into the meaning of the parable. We will also consider the possibility that the responses to the parable were conflicting (one approving the murderous act of the tenant farmers, the other condemning it), but during the later transmission history they were eventually reconciled by the authors for their particular propaganda purposes.

10. Crossan, *In Parables*, p. 93.
11. Crossan, *In Parables*, p. 96.

The Interpretation

The Vineyard, the Owner and the Tenants

Before we begin to explore the question of 'inheritance', which I believe is the central, generative theme of the parable, it is necessary to set up the socio-economic background of the parable. This background helps us to highlight the important points being made in the story. Furthermore, and perhaps more importantly, it helps us to understand the different reactions to the story as found in the traditions.

Therefore, I begin by indicating that it is my assumption throughout this discussion that within the parable is established a contrast of socio-economic groups through the characters of the landowner and tenant farmers, within the context of a landed estate.

It is useful to recall the territorial situation of Palestine after the return from exile and its effects on the circumstances of the Jewish landholder. There seems to be much evidence that the dominant pattern of land tenure in Palestine remained small, independent family holdings. Most recently scholars have rightly emphasized that this was a stable, centuries-long situation, which even continued through Ptolemaic, Seleucid and Hasmonaean rule.[12] Nevertheless, throughout this time there is evidence of a development towards greater landholdings being concentrated into fewer hands, with such a development found throughout all of Palestine. Under the Ptolemies extensive estates in the eastern Plain of Esdraelon and in the Plain of Beth Shean in Galilee had been held in royal hands,[13] which were passed on from ruling house to ruling house. Under the Seleucid king Antiochus IV there is evidence to indicate that cultivable land in Judaea had not all been held as royal land. Nevertheless, in letters of the later Seleucid kings Demetrius I and II announcing various concessions of taxes and territory to the Maccabaean rulers, the dues remitted bear a close resemblance to those paid by peasants of the royal lands in Egypt, and there are strong reasons for supposing that the toparchies conceded by the same Seleucids to the Maccabees constituted royal property. Jannaeus, after the Maccabaean redistribution of

---

12. R.A. Horsley and J.S. Hanson, *Bandits, Prophets and Messiahs* (New York: Winston, 1985), p. 59; S. Freyne, *Galilee from Alexander the Great to Hadrian* (Notre Dame: University of Notre Dame Press, 1980), pp. 159-60.

13. S. Safrai and M. Stern, *The Jewish People in the First Century* (2 vols.; CRINT, 1.1-2; Philadelphia: Fortress Press, 1974), II, p. 634.

land, attempted to reintroduce the conditions of Hellenistic 'royal lands', and tradition ascribes to him the King's Mountain Country and territories annexed in his campaigns of conquest.[14] Herod had seized the large royal domains of his Hasmonaean rivals[15] and continued on a pattern of land accumulation through confiscation and heavy taxation.[16]

The contribution of these large estates toward the growth of the landless peasantry and tenancy must be noted. It should also be emphasized that tenancy on such royal domains could hardly be described as enviable. While we have little direct evidence concerning the social or economic conditions on these estates, it is significant that three of the foci of revolt after the death of Herod the Great were located on the royal domains of Peraea and Jericho.[17]

In fact, more and more of the best lands in Palestine fell into the hands of the Herodian kings,[18] and the various allocations of these and other lands to 'suitable beneficiaries' occurred so arbitrarily and frequently that one scholar has concluded that 'it is further probable that the Herods regarded the entire countryside, not excluding the city territories, as legally their own to do as they like within given circumstances'.[19]

There are also many examples of private landholders owning large private estates: Eleazer ben Harzum,[20] Flavius Josephus,[21] John of Gischala and Philip son of Jakimus,[22] to name just a few.[23]

Essential for us to note is that the loss of the coastal plain and much of the Transjordan from the Jewish area after the drastic reorganization of Palestine and Syria under Pompey created an acute land shortage in Judaea and, along with the continued growth in large estates, contributed greatly to the increase in the number of landless Jewish peasants.[24] As

14. Safrai and Stern, *Jewish People*, II, pp. 634-35.
15. Safrai and Stern, *Jewish People*, II, p. 657.
16. Freyne, *Galilee*, p. 164.
17. Safrai and Stern, *Jewish People*, II, p. 658.
18. Freyne, *Galilee*, p. 165; Safrai and Stern, *Jewish People*, II, p. 657.
19. Safrai and Stern, *Jewish People*, II, p. 658.
20. J. Jeremias, *Jerusalem at the Time of Jesus* (Philadelphia: Fortress Press, 1969), p. 99.
21. *Life* 422 and 429.
22. C. Rostovtzeff, *Social and Economic History of the Roman Empire* (Oxford: Clarendon Press, 1957), I, p. 270.
23. Safrai and Stern, *Jewish People*, II, pp. 656-57.
24. See also Safrai and Stern, *Jewish People*, I, pp. 95-104, for a discussion of the territorial division of Palestine at the time of Jesus.

one scholar notes, 'This phenomenon may serve as a key to an under-standing of the entire development of the agrarian problem in Judea down to the great rebellion of 70 CE'.[25]

Turning now to the narrative, we must note that it seeks to direct the attention of the audience to the circumstances of the situation of the tenant farmer, and is thereby drawing upon the generally known economic institution of 'sharecropping'. The question addressed by this article is not whether and how much landlessness affected Palestine, but how just such circumstances were interpreted to an audience, and how given audiences reacted to such an interpretation.

Due to the fact of increasing landlessness among the peasantry of Palestine at the time of the performance of this parable, I am assuming that the speaker is referring to a member of one of the ruling or aristocratic classes when he speaks of a human 'despot' (Matthaean tradition from the Greek οἰκοδεσπότης, usually translated as 'a house-holder'), who plants a vineyard, lets it out to tenant farmers (to receive from them the fruit) and then goes into another country.[26] I do not believe it is the intention of the parable to portray the owner as a sympa-thetic figure, but as a central figure to whom a given audience may be made to react. Indeed, as a member of a socially superior class, the reaction by an audience would depend on their own station and social-ization; it is quite likely that a rural peasant audience would not see this figure as one with whom to sympathize at all, but to fear or respect or mistrust.

---

25. Safrai and Stern, *Jewish People*, II, pp. 636-37; see also pp. 656, 660.

26. Safrai and Stern (*Jewish People*, II, p. 657) suggest that 'On the evidence, few smallholders could have afforded slaves, who like the tenants belonged chiefly to the large estates; the crown domains were also worked by the latter category'. However, they go on to note that this parable does not necessarily have to reflect such a situation, since Josephus mentions the fact that many city dwellers owned property outside the city and were not necessarily rich (see Safrai and Stern, *Jewish People*, II, p. 659 n. 4), and since it was typical for the ordinary man to own at least one slave (see Safrai and Stern, *Jewish People*, II, p. 627). I cannot accept their conclusion, as every single tradition we have of this parable suggests that the landowner possessed *many* slaves; that it is unlikely that an 'ordinary' peasant could afford to invest in a vineyard and then go to another country; and, if the parable is less about aristocracy versus peasantry, than town versus country, it is still the case that the city was seen by rural peasants as the location of power and privilege, and all these implications would be understood by the 'original' audience. See Safrai and Stern, *Jewish People*, II, p. 664.

Tenant farmers, on the other hand, are landless peasants who have lost their land to increasing debt. Perhaps a bad harvest, or the burden of secular and religious taxation,[27] or undermining competition from larger estates,[28] coupled with the needs of the peasant to feed his family and livestock, and save enough grain for the next crop, eventually forced him to make loans secured through property. When this was compounded with low productivity, successive bad years, and perhaps even general famine, default ensued, and the peasant was forced to give up his lands.[29] Once this occurred, there was no way for him to retrieve the situation, and he was fortunate if he could survive as tenant on what was once his own land.[30]

27. To provide a thorough explanation of the secular and religious taxation systems present under the Roman rule of Palestine would be far beyond the scope of this paper. However, several factors should be kept in mind: F.C. Grant (*Economic Background of the Gospels* [London: Oxford University Press, 1926], p. 89) suggests that two taxation systems burdened the producer of a definite percentage of the harvest, from 30 per cent to 40 per cent and perhaps even higher. D.E. Oakman ('Jesus and Agrarian Palestine: The Factor of Debt', *SBLSP* 24 [1985], pp. 63-65 [63]) suggests that up to three contending taxation systems were in place, and both landed peasants and tenant farmers were liable (see Freyne, *Galilee*, p. 195). Thus, the Roman government, the old priestly aristocracy and the new Herodian aristocracy each pressed its own demands upon the peasantry without much regard for the other systems (Oakman, 'Jesus and Agrarian Palestine', pp. 63-65; Safrai and Stern, *Jewish People*, I, p. 239, II, pp. 661-62), creating a particularly heavy burden upon the small farmer. (See also Safrai and Stern, *Jewish People*, I, pp. 259-60, for the fiscal situation under the Herods, and II, pp. 661-62; F. Belo, *Materialist Reading of the Gospel of Mark* [Maryknoll, NY: Orbis Books, 1981], pp. 81-82.)

The topic of taxation, both secular and religious, under Roman rule is extensive, but so far not systematically presented. Some of the following references may be helpful. For a survey of the obligations of the Jewish people in Palestine under the religious tithing requirements, see Grant, *Economic Background*, pp. 92-97; Safrai and Stern, *Jewish People*, II, pp. 818-24; see also Horsley's analysis in *Bandits*, pp. 53-55. For a summary of state taxation, see Jeremias, *Jerusalem*, pp. 124-26; Grant, *Economic Background*, pp. 89-91; Freyne, *Galilee*, pp. 187-92. For the method of gathering secular taxes, see E. Schürer, *A History of the Jewish People in the Age of Jesus Christ* (rev. and ed. G. Vermes, F. Millar and M. Black; 3 vols.; Edinburgh: T. & T. Clark, 1979), I, pp. 189-92; Grant, *Economic Background*, p. 101; Safrai and Stern, *Jewish People*, II, pp. 330-33; Belo, *Materialist Reading*, p. 63.

28. See discussion in Safrai and Stern, *Jewish People*, II, p. 662; see also p. 663.

29. Oakman, 'Jesus and Agrarian Palestine', p. 67; Horsley, *Bandits*, p. 58.

30. Freyne, *Galilee*, p. 195. The discussion of debt must be set against an

It is beyond the scope of this paper to provide a thorough review of all the factors contributing to the problem of debt in first-century Palestine. Nevertheless, two key facts must remain in the forefront of the discussion if we are to understand the full possibilities of the parable: a tenant farmer is one who is desperately attempting to protect his means

understanding of the distribution of wealth in agrarian Palestine. In general, the basic flow of goods in a typical agrarian society is through a multi-layered hierarchical structure of society which extends from the smallest rural village units to the central governing center. The direction of the flow is for the most part exclusive, i.e., peasants are coerced into giving a lot more than they ever receive (G. Lenski, *Human Societies* [New York: McGraw–Hill, 1983], pp. 201-202; cf. also *idem*, *Power and Privilege* [New York: McGraw–Hill, 1966], pp. 219-30, esp. p. 228). Certainly there is specific evidence for such a trend in Palestine, and especially from the time of the Ptolemies: agriculture in Palestine was transformed into agrobusiness, controlled and monopolized by the agencies of the foreign domination (Freyne, *Galilee*, p. 171). This development was not changed with the rise of the Hasmonaean and Herodian dynasties (Freyne, *Galilee*, p. 177).

Upon this general background we can begin to assess briefly the factor of debt in Palestine. Oakman ('Jesus and Agrarian Palestine', pp. 63-65) has read the sources and found, *contra* Freyne (*Galilee*, pp. 192-93), indirect evidence for Galilaean debt: concentration of land, population growth, competing tax systems, natural disasters (Schürer, *History*, I, pp. 123, 134, 226) and social unrest (selectively Schürer, *History*, I, pp. 109-262. Oakman ('Jesus and Agrarian Palestine', p. 67) summarizes the situation:

> The overall result of escalating debt, whether its nature was private or fiscal, was the growth of tenancy and the landless class. Conversely, more and more land came under the possession of fewer and fewer landowners. Of both phenomena in first-century Palestine there are numerous indications.

(A general view of growth of tenancy in this period is given by Rostovtzeff, *Social and Economic History of the Roman Empire*, pp. 99, 292, 344.)

What must have been maddening to the tenant farmer as a victim of debt is the fact that there existed a long biblical tradition which attempted to guard against the socio-economic effects of debt. This tradition was based on an ideal social order of equality under YHWH, an equality which was to ensure access to the land.

> Prescription or problems related to debt are mentioned in all of the major divisions: legislative (Exod. 22.25-27; Lev. 25; Deut. 25; 23.19-20), prophetic (Isa. 5.8; Hab. 2.6), historical (1 Sam. 22.2; 2 Kgs 4.1; Neh. 5.1-5), and wisdom writings (Prov. 22.7). The tradition uniformly opposes usury and the permanent transfer of real property (Exod. 22.25; Lev. 25.13; Deut. 25.2) (Oakman, 'Jesus and Agrarian Palestine', p. 60).

Such strong testimony in the tradition, I suggest, would have to reflect a great social impact.

of livelihood, in contrast to the figure of the owner. The connection to the land experienced by the Israelite peasant holds far deeper significance than purely financial considerations,[31] and it would take an act of total desperation for the farmer to give up his ancestral plot, which is his connection to the past.[32] A tenant farmer, then, is one step away from losing all connection to the land, as the only other means of support would be to work as a day laborer, a slave or a beggar.[33]

Secondly, the tenant farmer is in no better financial position than he was before he lost his land. Primarily, these liabilities continued to consist of taxes and tithes,[34] and now any surplus goods would have to be split with a landowner. This would leave him in a state of perpetual debt, perhaps even to the point where, after all was said and done, he simply did not have enough left to live on and would be forced off the land altogether.

Heir

With these factors kept in mind, I would like to turn first to the character of the heir. Up to this point, one could say that the story has progressed along relatively predictable lines. A time for harvesting has come, causing the landowner to send his representatives to collect a portion of the produce from the tenant farmers. The tenant farmers, however, dispute the claim for the produce, and the slaves are beaten and sent back empty-handed. In considering the seriousness of the situation, the landowner sends his son. It is particularly the legal dimension to the presence of this figure in the story upon which many commentators choose to focus.

The motivation on the part of a landowner to send a son has a sound Jewish legal foundation in first-century Palestine, so that 'respect' takes

31. Freyne, *Galilee*, p. 170; see below under the heading *Heir*.

32. Freyne, *Galilee*, pp. 159, 195; Safrai and Stern, *Jewish People,* II, p. 664. It is also important to keep in mind that the basis of determining class distinction, especially in a rural setting such as Palestine, was land ownership; see Freyne, *Galilee*, pp. 155, 170.

33. See Jeremias, *Jerusalem*, pp. 109-19, for a summary of the plight of these figures in first-century Palestine.

34. Safrai and Stern, *Jewish People*, II, p. 660. The tenant farmer remained liable to the tithe; compare *Bikk.* 1.2 with *Bikk.* 1.11, *t. Dem.* 6.1 (56) and *Dem.* 6.1. Freyne (*Galilee*, pp. 183, 281-87) indicates that Galilaeans especially respected the payment of the tithe. Freyne (*Galilee*, p. 195) states that both landed peasant and tenant farmer continued to pay secular taxes out of the produce of their lands.

on certain litigational implications to the Jewish audience. When someone who had been wronged wished to make recourse, he had to make a
formal protest in front of witnesses, warning the defendant that legal
action would be brought against him.[35] This protest, however, could not
be made by servants, nor could they adjure witnesses.[36] At that time it
was also not possible to deal through an agent; the plaintiff would have
to have transferred his right to the representative.[37] If the parable were
reality, the owner would have no choice but to transfer at least a portion
of the ownership over to the son to make him a legal claimant; thus, his
presence would indicate to the tenants that legal action was being taken
up against them.

Of course, it should be kept in mind that this would have been one of
the last alternatives left to the owner. He would have been at a distinct
disadvantage if he sought legal assistance from the local authorities,
assuming he lived at a distance from the vineyard. Derrett[38] points out
that 'one of the most curious features of the Jewish law was its tender-
ness to robbers'. On the one hand, it is evident in our sources that

> the plaintiff could not easily succeed in action for recovery of possession,
> since actual possession is in favour of the defendant (*t. B. Qam.* 27b).
> Only in exceptional cases was the defendant asked to prove his title (*m. B.
> Bat.* 3.3; *t. B. Bat.* 2.6).[39]

As Snodgrass[40] is careful to point out, the administration of justice often
sought the way of least resistance, and for the local authorities the
maintenance of peace would have been more important than legal aid
for an outsider. On the other hand, the most that the thief might have to
do is return the property if he made no improvement upon it. Furthermore, under the Jewish legal concept of *ye'uš*,[41] if an owner of a piece of

---

35. K. Snodgrass, *The Parable of the Wicked Tenants* (WUNT, 27; Tübingen:
Mohr [Paul Siebeck], 1983), p. 37; J.D.M. Derrett, *Law in the New Testament*
(London: Darton, Longman & Todd, 1970), p. 302; cf. *b. B. Bat.* 38a, 39.

36. Snodgrass, *Parable*, p. 37; Derrett, *Law*, p. 302; cf. *Šeb.* 4.12.

37. Snodgrass, *Parable*, p. 37; Derrett, *Law*, p. 303; cf. *b. Bek.* 70a.

38. *Law*, p. 304.

39. Safrai and Stern, *Jewish People*, II, p. 523.

40. *Parable*, p. 37.

41. Although only extended to movables, it is likely that this limitation is a later
development, and hence at the time of the parable an owner could be forced into a
position in which it is claimed that he had mentally abandoned his land; cf. Derrett,
Law, p. 304.

property could be said to have abandoned it, the thief maintains both the title and any improvements, having only to make restitution based on the value of the property at the time of misappropriation.

Certain legal concepts present in first-century Palestine also give foundation to the motivation of tenants to kill the son and heir. There are a number of laws, perhaps implicitly assumed in the 'background' of the parable, which govern the claim of the proselyte and ownerless lands.[42] Jeremias[43] suggests that perhaps the tenants assumed that the presence of the son implied the death of the father, and thus to kill the son was to render the property ownerless, which they could then claim as their own. Another scenario is suggested by Derrett,[44] who takes us through a labyrinth of legislation that would allow the tenants, who have enjoyed the produce of the land for three years without payment to the owner, to claim ownership themselves by the fourth year's harvest. The death of the son would prevent any legal action by securing the fourth harvest, which would prove interest in the property on the part of the owner. Snodgrass[45] counters by saying that *usucaptio libertatis* is explicitly denied to tenants in the Mishnah[46] and they thereby had no legal foundation for the attempt. Nevertheless, the fact that the discussion is so extensive proves the popularity of such attempts.

I do not find these discussions very helpful for several reasons.

1. They seem uncertain in light of the difficulty encountered when attempting to date the rabbinical material that is the basis for scholarly exploration.
2. It seems reasonable to assume that peasants and tenant farmers were not such experts in rabbinic law. The audience would probably not have thought of the actions of the tenants in the difficult and extremely complex legal terms that modern scholars seem capable of elaborating.

42. Snodgrass, *Parable*, p. 38 and n. 28: *B. Bat.* 3.3; *b. B. Bat.* 53a-55a; *b. Giṭ.* 39a; and *b. Giṭ.* 61a.

43. *Parables*, p. 76.

44. *Law*, pp. 300-301. See p. 300 n. 4: *B. Bat.* 3.1; *b. B. Bat.* 28a, 35b, 38a; Maimonides 13.4.18, 6; 11.1.18; 14.2.21, 7. See also p. 301 and nn. 1-4, and p. 302 and n. 1, and p. 303.

45. *Parable*, p. 38. See also 'usucaptio' and 'usucaptio libertatis', 'usucaptio servitutis' in A. Berger, *Encyclopedic Dictionary of Roman Law* (Philadelphia: American Philosophical Society, 1953), XLIII.2, pp. 752-53.

46. See Snodgrass, *Parable*, p. 38 n. 30: *B. Bat.* 3.2-3; Maimonides 13.4.13.

3. The concentration upon the legal basis of the sending of the son simply does not help us to understand the parable.

The very simple question to be asked is, 'Why did the landowner send the *son*? He could have gone himself and the legal contextuality of the parable would not have been altered.' What is at stake here is not so much a discussion of the legality of these acts, but of the interaction between the key figures as representatives of certain groups, and the resulting understanding of 'inheritance' and 'heir' arising from their interaction.

Here, I think, lie the central generative themes of the parable-as-story, themes which no scholar has yet explored: (1) the relationship of *land* to the concept of 'owner', (2) the question of *inheritance* and who is the heir to the land, set against the background of (3) the *indebtedness* of tenant farmers as mentioned above, and *their dedication to ancestral ways and land*. The parable has carefully woven a story concerning land, produce and the relationship which two key groups have to these and to each other. The speaker has introduced the figure of the son specifically to bring to mind the concept of *inheritance* explicitly within the context of these varying relationships, and indeed mentions it in such a way as to be used as a 'catchword'. It is up to us, now, to try to explore the historical implications upon which such a story is based. We will begin with a discussion of the relationship of land to the people of Israel in the mind of the first-century peasant and tenant farmer, then we will turn to the relationship of land to the concept of inheritance.

Primarily, it must be remembered that the basis of the relationship to the land among the people of Israel was seen to be God's ownership/possession of the land.[47] Aside from viewing the land as sacred and precious to YHWH, it is the promise of the inheritance of the land given by God to Israel which is important for our understanding. Because the land is YHWH's to give, his promise to Israel that it is theirs to inherit must be fulfilled. Such a promise 'was so reinterpreted from age to age that it became a living power in the life of the people of Israel'. It was, in fact, 'a formative, dynamic, seminal force in the history of Israel. The

47. For a thorough discussion, see W.D. Davies, *Gospel and the Land* (Berkeley: University of California Press, 1974), pp. 27-31. See also Belo, *Materialist Reading*, p. 50.

legend of the promise entered so deeply into the experience of the Jews that it acquired its own reality.'[48]

κληρονομία (Mt. 21.38; Mk 12.7; Lk. 20.14), which in the LXX translates *nachalah* 145 times out of 163, should be translated as 'inheritance', and means:

> (a) something which is given, normally by testament; (b) something that continues to remain in possession, inalienable property; (c) something which is a family possession, a patrimony; (d) something which may be conveyed by adoption to persons originally outside the family; that is to say, the family line is renewed, in case of the failure of the line to continue, in order that the thing possessed might remain in the family.[49]

This concept shows a diverse and important development in the history of Israel.

In the Old Testament it is intimately related to the promises which God made to Abraham concerning the land of Canaan (Gen. 12, 15, 17): it is because of these promises that he led them out of Egypt (Exod. 13.5, 11; Deut. 1.8; 6.10) and would not let them be destroyed in the wilderness (Exod. 33.1; Num. 14.15, 23; 32.11).[50] While Abraham never possessed the land, he was made legal owner of it, according to the authors of the Old Testament, when God showed it to him and promised it to him, and thus it became the inheritance also of Isaac, Jacob and their descendants.[51] The authors of Numbers and Joshua naturally speak of the inheritance in terms of families and tribes, as the land was divided by lot once it came into the possession of the Israelites. By the time of the writing of Deuteronomy, the Psalms and the Prophets, however, the concept of the inheritance of the land has less to do with the patrimony of distinct lands than of the collective land. The writers of these books, primarily influenced by the rise of the monarchy, the splitting off of the Northern Kingdom, and the Exile, looked back again to the promise to Abraham: 'The whole Land of the Abrahamic Promise is the [inheritance] of all of Israel'.[52]

In the inter-testamental literature, certain changes in the concept of

48. Both quotations are from Davies, *Gospel and the Land*, p. 18; see pp. 15-24 for a survey of the promise of the land in the hexateuch.

49. J.D. Hester, *Paul's Concept of Inheritance* (*SJT* Occasional Paper, 14; Edinburgh: Oliver & Boyd, 1968), p. vii.

50. Hester, *Inheritance*, p. 22.

51. Gen. 13.14; 15.17; 17.8. Cf. Hester, *Inheritance*, p. 24.

52. Hester, *Inheritance*, p. 25.

inheritance had been introduced. While for the most part they stuck to the Old Testament view of inheritance, in light of the fact that after the Exile the Israelites (primarily the ruling class, as the peasants were not taken into exile) simply could never satisfactorily resettle themselves and could never claim full possession of the land, at least two new developments arose: (a) 'The Law was described as the inheritance of the people of Israel for at least two reasons. First, because of its increasing importance in post-exilic theology, it developed the qualities of an inheritance... Secondly, it was through the present observance of the Law that the future possession of the Land was guaranteed. The Law was the key to the Inheritance.'[53] (b) A more widespread development was 'the placing of the full possession of the Land in the Eschaton. This can be explained as a natural development from the failure of the tribes to fully possess the Land. With the disaster of the destruction of the Northern Kingdom, and with the defeat and exile of the Southern Kingdom, earthly fulfillment was assigned to the spiritual realm of the Coming Aeon.'[54] Thus, the land continues to hold its place of importance in the concept of inheritance, and its importance throughout the political and religious development of Israel is almost mythical in proportion.

It is my view that when an Israelite farmer's livelihood depended so deeply upon the produce from the land, he continued to emphasize the holiness and intimacy of that relationship. I base this assertion upon both sociological and historical data.

Sociologically, in agrarian societies, rural peasants 'are bearers of the culture's "Little Tradition", that is, a simplified and often outdated expression of the norms and ideas embodied by the city elites'.[55] For the first-century Israelite, rural peasant farming was performed out of duty to ancestral ways and tradition. The older value system of folk tradition which resided in the villages remained for the most part intact, reinforced through seasonal and/or annual religious festivals.[56] Thus, it would be precisely within the Israelite peasantry where we would find

53. Hester, *Inheritance*, p. 31.
54. Hester, *Inheritance*, p. 33.
55. B.J. Malina, *New Testament World: Insights from Cultural Anthropology* (Atlanta: John Knox, 1981), p. 74. The difference in the views of the elite classes and peasant villagers is quite large, the rural peasant being several times removed from the expression of ideals, norms and values of the governing classes.
56. Freyne, *Galilee*, p. 196.

the last vestiges of a conservative and intimate relationship with the land.

Historically, many examples can be offered that display the immediacy of this relationship in the lives of the Israelite peasantry. First, we have the evidence of banditry as a concrete social form of pre-political rebellion, which in Israel arose among the Jewish peasantry *as a result of chronic indebtedness and ensuing loss of land*.[57] This thesis is supported by the historical circumstances of the rise of the bandit Ezechias. His struggle on the Phoenician border against the village areas of Tyre was simply one part of a long conflict arising from an acute shortage of cultivable land at a time when the tracts at the disposal of the Jewish population were drastically curtailed.[58] The same circumstances brought about the rise of the power of John of Gischala immediately prior to and during the Great Revolt. His band was recruited from among those peasants who had suffered under the extension of Tyrian lands on the Galilaean eastern borders.[59] One should also note that the debt archives were burned in Jerusalem,[60] and that Jewish banditry concentrated its raids exclusively upon the elite classes of Palestinian society.[61] What this would tend to indicate is that for the peasantry the loss of the land, and the situation of debt, were quite serious matters.

Furthermore, we must consider the socio-religious aspects of the traditions concerning the relationship between the land and the people of Israel. Ideally, as God's possession, the gift of the land to the people as inheritance insured inalienable access to and possession of the land for all of Israel.[62] One simply needs to consider the laws of the year of jubilee in Leviticus 25, in which

57. Safrai and Stern, *Jewish People*, II, p. 691; Horsley, *Bandits*, pp. 48-63.

58. Safrai and Stern, *Jewish People*, II, p. 638.

59. Josephus, *War* 2.587; 4.84.

60. Josephus, *War* 2.427.

61. Horsley, *Bandits*, pp. 69-76. Note that such movements were quite universal among the peasantry around this time (and even today): 'The abolition of debt was frequently encountered as a revolutionary slogan of the disenfranchised, usually accompanied by a demand for the redistribution of land' (Oakman, 'Jesus and Agrarian Palestine', p. 59; see Rostovtzeff, *Social and Economic History of the Roman Empire*, chapter 1).

62. For additional proof, consider Davies's assessment of the Maccabaean, 'Zealot' and Bar Kochba revolts: while the literature does not mention an appeal to the land, he correctly finds an assumed loyalty to the land as the primary axiom for the rebels; Davies, *Gospel and the Land*, pp. 90-104.

provision is made for the return of all land to its original owners or their descendants. The tribal allotment was inalienable property. It could not be sold in perpetuity because it belonged to the Lord (25.23). Only possessions bought from a stranger could be kept and bequeathed to a man's heirs (25.45-46).[63]

While historically it is uncertain that the jubilee laws were enforced, they were nevertheless an ideal intimately related to the concept of extension, which provided the basis for the tithing laws and the care of the poor of the community.[64] In other words, while many scholars remain skeptical, we must view the jubilee laws as rules integral to the community's greater ethical structures, and which could not therefore be easily ignored, overlooked or forgotten. The jubilee laws were but one section of many rules which were concerned with the distribution of the wealth brought forth from the land.

Additionally, it is important to consider the fact that the rabbis remembered (or created) the tradition concerning the *prozbul*, ascribed to Hillel. I believe this should be viewed as further evidence of the depth of respect the community felt for its laws governing the distribution of its wealth and debt: the religious leaders felt compelled to create a justification for the abrogation of those certain laws which attempted to free the Israelite from debt.

Finally, as indicated above, there still existed in the period encompassing the Maccabaean and Bar Kochba revolts a concept of the inalienability of the land as the motivating factor for the rebellion of the people. This would indicate that while nationalism and the search for the fulfillment of the promise of the inheritance of the land were important

---

63. Hester, *Inheritance*, pp. 4-5. One should also consider the story of Naboth and Ahaz, found in 1 Kgs 21.1-4; the story of the daughters of Zelophad in Num. 27.1-7, 36.1-12; laws forbidding interest, prohibiting the alienation of property, and protecting any necessity of life in Deut. 23.19 and Exod. 23.26; and the Deuteronomic admonition not to change the ancient landmarks in Deut. 19.14 (written after the landmarks had long since been forgotten! Hester, *Inheritance*, p. 26). While the emphasis concerning the specific tribal allotments had to be changed in the postexilic period, and thus we find in Sir. 42.3 that a man should not be ashamed of the division of his inheritance, this emphasis was made out of the seriousness with which the inalienability of and direct access to the land continued to be operative factors in the lives of the people of Israel. See Safrai and Stern, *Jewish People*, II, pp. 794, 896.

64. See Belo, *Materialist Reading*, p. 44.

to the Israelite peasant, the concept of the inalienability of the land took on basic economic expectations.

Therefore, the parable should be viewed as referring to a long social and religious tradition concerning the relationship of the land as YHWH's to the people of Israel as *inheritance*, especially among the peasantry. Thus, the presence of the son and the question concerning inheritance are not incidental to the parable. When the speaker introduces the idea of 'inheritance' in the figure of the son, he is referring to a specific and definite concept ('catchword') of the relationship of YHWH to his people, and its manifestation in the relationship between the people and the land. By juxtaposing two extreme classes of Palestinian society in one scene (a rare occurrence itself) under the rubric of this theme, the speaker is causing the listener to consider the varying relationships to the land shown by the characters. In light of the discussion above, where I established the fact that tenant farmers are landless peasants with indirect access to the land, that is, they have lost their inheritance to the land-owner, the central question of the parable is, 'Whose land is it really?'

The answer comes forcefully in the death of the 'legal' heir: it is the proper inheritance of the tenant farmers, the landless Israelite peasants. At this point, then, it was the purpose of the parable to pose the question to the audience: 'What do you think of such a situation, of such an answer to this situation?' The effect of such a question is pronounced. It leaves the listeners with a powerful ending that they must consider seriously.

Thus, it is my claim that, set against the background of debt and continued monetary liability, the death of the son simply could have been interpreted/interpolated as an act of desperation on the part of the tenants to secure their right to subsistence from the land.[65] This right was threatened by the presence of the son, which would be understood by the audience as a legal attempt by the owner to secure his access to the produce of the land. Furthermore, by sending the son rather than the owner, the speaker is referring to (by means of a 'catchword') the significant concept of 'inheritance', bringing to the fore the question of

65. This is a very different assumption from that offered by a majority of scholars, who have simply imposed their own anachronistic and socially irrelevant judgments concerning the actions of the tenants as purely, universally, and 'obviously' 'greedy'. See, for example, the incredibly imperialistic (!) discussion of Via (*Parables*, pp. 135-37) and note the almost universal title of the parable among scholars: The *Wicked* Tenants!

the concept of 'ownership' of and access to the land. Finally, the speaker has emphasized the question of the relationship to the land by bringing these two extreme classes into unnaturally close and exaggerated relation to one another: on the one hand, the 'inheritance' of the 'heir' of the elite landowner class; on the other, the tenants' assertion that they themselves are, in fact, the rightful heirs. These are views of two differing classes with respect to the land, two opposing views exposed for consideration by the presence of the son as a literary mechanism in the parable.

Logion?

I am changing the order of the material as handed down to us in the canonical accounts because of what I consider to be a more important rhetorical point to be made at this time. The differences in the form and purpose of the rhetorical question of vengeance and the logion suggest that these are distinct from the parable proper. Some have suggested that they are later additions to the parable,[66] which serve to elucidate the allegorical meaning of the parable:

> The vineyard is clearly Israel, the tenants are Israel's rulers and leaders, the owner of the vineyard is God, the messengers are the prophets, the son is Christ, the punishment of the husbandmen symbolizes the ruin of Israel, the 'other people' (Mt. 21.43) are the Gentile Church.[67]

It is my thesis, however, that they show a relationship to one another which no one has yet explored: the rhetorical Question/Answer of vengeance and the logion contradict each other. As we shall immediately explore, I suggest that the logion indicates a very early interpretation which the rhetorical question amended. Based upon this, we shall explore the implications of the logion first, and then turn to the question of the role of vengeance of the owner at the end of this presentation.

It was Taylor who first introduced the possibility that the use of the stone quotation in the apologetics of the early Church arose from Jesus' own use:

> On the whole it is more probable that the interest of primitive Christianity in the thought of Christ as the λίθος rejected by men, but made by God the cornerstone of a new Temple, is based upon the memory that He used Psa cxviii.22f. in a devastating attack upon the Jewish hierarchy.[68]

66. Jeremias, *Parables*, p. 74.
67. Jeremias, *Parables*, p. 70.
68. Taylor, *St Mark*, pp. 476-77. Such a proposal would not survive the criterion

If Taylor is correct, then possibilities are wide open for reinterpreting the tradition history of the stone proof texts and the function of this particular text in the development of this parable's tradition. Now, I do not agree with Taylor that Jesus necessarily used this text against the Jewish hierarchy per se. I suggest more simply that this text may have been used as reinforcement of a *theme of reversal* (which is found so often in certain traditions within the Gospel materials, e.g. Mt. 19.30 // Mk 10.31 // Lk. 13.30 // *Gos. Thom.* 4 // *P. Oxy.* 654.4; Mt. 20.16 // Mk 10.44; Mt. 23.11; Lk. 22.26; Mk 9.33; Lk. 9.48; etc.) which was independent from, and perhaps prior to its use as proof-text for the resurrection.

The connection of this stone quotation to the parable, therefore, could have been early, certainly earlier than the allegorical interpretation of the canonical Gospel authors. Furthermore, its connection was with respect to an emphasis which the communities saw in both parable and logion regarding 'reversal'. Consider *Gospel of Thomas* and Luke, both of which view some sort of connection between the two, but which also do not view the parable allegorically. This would also explain how the later allegorical development of the parable came about, that is, if the stone quotation emphasized 'reversal', then the later use of the verse among the early churches (focusing the referent of reversal upon Jesus) would explain all the elaboration we find in Mark and Matthew. Furthermore, the referent which brings these two traditions (i.e. the parable and the quotation) together would not then have been the 'son' at all: the tradition in *Gospel of Thomas* shows the independence of the tradition of the quotation from the rhetorical Question/Answer; there is nothing in the parable story itself that suggests a reversal of positions with respect to the son.[69] The only possible referent of this Scripture emphasizing reversal is not in the vengeance of the death of the son, but with the new position of the tenant farmers.

---

of dissimilarity. However, while I view this as an important method of discerning later from earlier tradition, I consider it one among many different possible means of discrimination.

69. Contra Crossan, *In Parables*, p. 93, where he suggests that the logion shows an early stage of the 'allegorization process involv[ing an] *external* juxtaposition of an allusion to the triumph of Jesus to the murder story' (emphasis his). It certainly may be the case that the stone quotation later became proof text for the early Church, but as I state above, it may also be the case that the emphasis on reversal herein has in mind a different referent.

It is not the point of this argument to suggest that any contrary development in the tradition could not take place. It is certain that within particular communities the Easter experience became the interpretative paradigm for viewing the life of Jesus. Nevertheless, it is possible to construct a social setting for a given parable, based upon its own characters, settings and plot, and elaborated with given facts of social, political and historical relevance, which need not refer to the Easter event. Once this is done, we are in a position to reconstruct the history of interpretation on the basis that a given story changes meaning as contexts change through time/space. In our case, we have a parable that refers to the significant concept of 'inheritance'. The tradition remembers an early and independent connection of this parable with a quotation that emphasizes reversal. An 'original', that is pre-Easter, setting would suggest that the referent of reversal would be the tenant farmers. The one interpretation maintained by a certain community would suggest an exalted position on the part of the tenant farmers, much like the reversal of position often found in other traditions ('last will be first', etc.). Once another community's traditions have taken over, and then a final compilation, redaction and creativity on the part of an author have taken place, a certain amount of manipulation has entered into the performance. As Jeremias, Dodd, Crossan and Scott have argued, the eventual interpretation we find in the canonical Gospels is both late and even (according to Crossan) contrary to the 'intended' allegorical meaning of the canonical tradition. Once we admit that such may be the case, we are left having to struggle with recreating a new context and meaning.

This is what I am proposing here, even to an unexplored extreme. With the parable ending at the death of the son, we must ask who exactly is it that was once rejected, but now, according to the storyline, is exalted? What if communities circulating these two traditions together did not see 'reversal' in the story of the son, but in the tenants who were now the 'head of the corner'? This is a fascinating possibility, one which points to a plurality of interpretations arising from the confrontation experienced by the various members of the audience upon hearing this parable. While the traditional interpretation saw in the landlord a sympathetic protagonist facing 'evil' attempts of his tenants, this need not have been the only reaction: another early tradition might have seen in the figures of the tenants a powerful example of justice.[70]

Vengeance?

We now turn to the section of the parable that was skipped over above. It is found in the canonical accounts but not in *Gospel of Thomas*, and appends to the end of the parable proper the question concerning the reaction of the owner to the death of his son.

For the most part (there are notable exceptions) modern scholarship assumes that this development within the structure is a later elaboration, each author giving his various reasons. The most interesting reason, one offered by Crossan, assumes a narrative incompatibility: the answer given by the canonical Gospel authors with respect to the action of the vineyard owner simply does not fit the story, seeing it as arising out of

> the actualities of the Gentile mission rather than…the possibilities of agrarian experience. The vineyard is taken from Israel and given to the Gentiles. Indeed, the whole idea of this punitive expedition by the master is very improbable against the rest of the story. If such power had always been available to him, the pathetic hope for respect becomes somewhat ludicrous.[71]

Nevertheless, just such a response not only is probable but would be acceptable to and expected by the audience. Two points should be noted: first, as Lenski has pointed out, in general, acts of violence directed against members of the elite and their agents

> are always taken very seriously. The severity of the punishments undoubtedly reflects a recognition of the existence of widespread, latent hostility toward the holders of power and the realization that anything less

---

70. In all of this I do not intend to communicate the assumption that I believe the quotation and the parable to have been composed as an original unit. Rather, I am suggesting that they circulated perhaps 'independently', but also within certain traditions inseparably, and were connected through the theme of reversal. I am also not suggesting that it is necessarily the case that the quotation was intended as an interpretation of the parable per se, but rather the early communities saw in them both an emphasis of 'reversal', and that the referent of the reversal in the parable was not, in their eyes, the son (as the resurrected Jesus), but the tenants who met with unexpected 'success'. The parable itself does not necessarily indicate such an interpretation, but the interpretation would reflect the community's position with respect to the action presented in the parable.

71. Crossan, *In Parables*, p. 90.

than prompt and severe punishment may encourage more widespread violence.[72]

Secondly, within the specific context of first-century Palestine, such a response by the owner may also be understood as a response out of honor. The scenario may best be described in this way: the owner's response to the implicit claims made by the tenant farmers was/is simply dictated by legal complications or disadvantages. While the violent acts against his slaves may have been pushing the limit of acceptability, severe and violent retaliation by the owner would simply not yet be necessary.[73] To put it another way, violent action only became strictly necessary under the honor system at that point when the son was killed. Up to that point in the parable, the honor of the landowner was not challenged; it was simply impudence on the part of the tenants. Death of one's kin, on the other hand, is a dishonor so extreme that no revocation is possible, and would *require* a response not short of vengeance on the part of the owner.[74] Thus, the response on the part of the landowner to the murder of his son is quite in keeping with the *possibilities* of the time and the parable, and several members of the audience (even a predominantly peasant audience) would have accepted just such a response as plausible.

I am not necessarily arguing for the authenticity of this part of the parable. It is distinct from the parable form, functions to generate a specific interpretation of the parable, much like Lk. 10.36-37 once the

---

72. Lenski, *Power and Privilege*, p. 86.

73. According to the social patterns of the honor contest, only equals can play. Malina (*New Testament World*, p. 36) states:

> Only an equal can actually challenge another in such a way that all perceive the interaction as a challenge. Only an equal—who must be recognized as such—can impugn a person's honor or affront another. The reason for this is that the rules of the honor contest require that challengers stand on equal social terms. Thus an inferior on the ladder of social standing, power, and sexual status does not have enough honor to resent the affront of a superior. On the other side, a superior's honor is simply not committed, not engaged, by an inferior's affront, although the superior has the power to punish impudence.

74. Malina, *New Testament World*, p. 40; see p. 41: this sort of first-degree dishonor must be done within a natural grouping; outsiders are not sacred, and therefore homicide committed against them is not sacrilegious. But before we leap to any possibilites regarding the alien status of the landowner, it must be kept in mind that the relations between wealthy landowners and resident tenants constituted a natural grouping.

parable of the Good Samaritan is complete, and appears nowhere in the *Gospel of Thomas* tradition. Furthermore, Scott's insight, set against the cultural background we have established above, helps us to understand why it is not likely to be original to the parable: normally, Jesus does not answer the questions provoked by his parables. Rather, this question and its answer can be seen as 'a normal response by a reader—a reader/performer expects a master to punish'.[75] Once it is clear that the parable ends with the death of the son, then its storyline serves to provoke a response by the listener, who is surprised by the sudden, unexpected 'incompletion' of the narrative situation. The question and its answer which have survived in the pre-canonical and canonical traditions are simply one culturally correct response that would indicate a particular reaction to the scenario presented. In fact it betrays, I would argue, a pro-elite position on the part of the traditions, or at least a defensive response by someone to the question of land distribution and violent action against the landowning classes. It is not, however, the only possible response.

The question which now poses itself by the presence of the response of the owner in the tradition is, 'What kind of person, in light of all the evidence of debt, is implied by the owner?' He seems to deny the accessibility of the land to the tenants, and undermines the socio-religious view of 'inheritance' of the land as the right of all of Israel. He is, in fact, undermining the very essence of inheritance and the possession of the land by those to whom it had been guaranteed by God. Would this not be in direct contradiction to the conception of YHWH and his promise of the land if this figure were intended to portray God? Given the location of the parable in a time when questions of right to land abound, it is not likely that the parable was intended to say this at all, but rather simply intended to get its audience to start asking how it viewed its relationship to the land, its view therefore of the promise YHWH made to Israel; what it would do if it were faced with the desperation of losing access to the land.

Since the earliest traditions of the parable did not end with vengeance, the parable does not bring about closure, but allows the audience to ask questions. The answer to such questions by the audience, and the questions themselves, would reveal to the audience how it interpreted the parable.

75. B.B. Scott, 'Essaying the Rock', *Forum* 2.1 (March, 1986), pp. 22-23.

Summary and Conclusions

The story of the parable is about a landowner who plants a vineyard and leases it out to tenants. When slaves are sent to collect the rent from the harvest, the tenants beat them in an attempt to secure the produce. In response, the landowner sends the son, with the implication that legal proceedings are being brought against them. Recognizing this, they see in the son the potential for securing their subsistence through taking over the property, and they therefore kill the son. The generative theme of the parable is the relation of tenant farmers to the land in light of the promises of YHWH to the people of Israel, a theme introduced through the character of the son as 'heir'. The limited situation must be seen against the background of debt and the tenant farmers' precarious position in securing subsistence for their family. The parable displays a system of relations and attitudes among the various characters which are historically accurate, poses a problem as a potential insight into the social situation, and leaves it in the hands of the audience to judge its portrayal. At the end of the story it is the tenants who have become the authentic heirs of the promise of the possession of the land given by YHWH to Israel. The parable portrays a concrete act of revolt, and asks the audience, who may have been tenant farmers or landless peasants, how they feel and what they think about it. Ultimately, it asks the audience whether it accepts the understanding of the inheritance to Israel (represented by the tenant farmers), and causes them to reflect upon their own experience in relation to the land/inheritance. It is in fact a theme in direct contradiction to the experience of the audience, and this 'reversal' of expectation was accepted by some who then attached the stone quotation to the parable. To these the restoration of the 'head of the corner' was the restoration of the tenants as the 'true Israel'.

It seems that the traditioning process has not accepted the parable's 'revolutionary' interpretation, but rather paints the owner in sympathetic shades, eventually leading to an allegorical equation of the owner to God with appropriate expansions attempting to fit the parable into a salvation-historical perspective. The development could be explained as follows. The 'revolutionary' interpretation of the parable could have been remembered by certain members of the Jesus movement, up to the point of Jesus' death. At this time, a reformation of the original vision of the movement took place. With respect to this parable in particular, the movement reinterpreted the parable as a prophecy of Jesus regarding his coming death; the stone quotation had also become a proof text for the resurrection and exaltation of Jesus. The characters of the owner and the son, who may have already been interpreted in some traditioning communities as protagonists of the story, now represent YHWH and Jesus. The tenants are no longer the referent of the theme of reversal (exaltation), but through the stone quotation the son now becomes the referent. Finally, new tenants are introduced in the appended Question/Answer, who have now become, through the vindication of the death of the son by the owner YHWH, the 'true Israel'. That is, what has happened is that in some trajectories of the tradition, certain early Church communities have come to accept Paul's new thesis of the Church as the 'true Israel' and the parable is now made to fit this Christian theology. The parable has been reinterpreted against a context foreign to its original one, and the result is an interpretation different from that first intended and understood. And it has been this interpretation and this context that scholars continue to reinforce.

Nevertheless, what I have been exploring in this article is a possible means by which such later developments or interpretations can be avoided when discussing a given parable. Through a sociological approach to the historical context of the Jesus movement, and by proposing that the intention of this parable was to expose systems of group and class relations within the Jewish communities of first-century Palestine with respect to the theme of 'land' and 'inheritance', I found a new teaching at its heart. It only now remains to be seen whether such an approach can be generalized and used to explore and explain other parables successfully. It would view the images, characters, structures and themes of the parables (the parables' narrative dynamics) against the background of appropriate and applicable social systems of first-century Palestine. One possible goal could be to shed new light on the ministry of Jesus, or on the movements fostered by Jesus. Another could be to explore the development of the interpretation of a given parable found in specific, or among various, traditions. If its application is at all successful, many new possibilities are open for discussion, and relief may be found for those hoping for a new theme in the monotony of parable scholarship.

JSNT 40 (1990), pp. 97-113

RHETORICAL IDENTIFICATION IN PAUL'S
AUTOBIOGRAPHICAL NARRATIVE:
GALATIANS 1.13–2.14

Paul E. Koptak

While most studies of Paul's autobiography in Galatians 1.13–2.14 acknowledge the importance of Paul's relationship with the Christians of Galatia, little attention has been given to the language Paul uses to describe relationships within the autobiographical narrative itself. This study will examine the relationships that Paul portrays and creates with the Jerusalem apostles, his opponents, and the Galatians as a means to depict symbolically the issues at stake in Galatia. The literary-rhetorical method of Kenneth Burke will be employed to this end, with special focus on Burke's idea of identification.

Introduction

Until very recently, most studies of Galatians have followed the suggestion of Martin Luther that Paul's autobiographical remarks in Galatians 1 and 2 were 'boasting and glorying' that followed out of his divine calling. Paul defended himself in order to defend the gospel.[1]

H.D. Betz took this tradition[2] one step further when he compared

---

1. Martin Luther, *A Commentary on St Paul's Epistle to the Galatians* (repr.; Westwood, NJ: Fleming Revell, 1953), pp. 33, 87.

2. John Calvin, *The Epistles of Paul the Apostle to the Galatians, Ephesians, Philippians and Colossians* (trans. T.H.C. Parker; London: Oliver & Boyd, 1965), pp. 4-5. See also J.B. Lightfoot, *Saint Paul's Epistle to the Galatians* (New York and London: Macmillan, 1905), pp. 64, 71; E.D. Burton, *A Critical and Exegetical Commentary on the Epistle to the Galatians* (New York: Scribners, 1920), p. lxxii; F.F. Bruce, 'Further Thoughts on Paul's Autobiography', in *Jesus und Paulus: Festschrift für Werner Georg Kümmel zum 70. Geburtstag* (ed. E.E. Ellis and

Paul's letter with the rhetorical handbooks of the time and concluded that the whole of Galatians took the form of an apologetic letter.[3] Betz's commentary has not failed to attract criticism.[4] New methods of rhetorical and literary study have challenged the apologetic model and have suggested alternative understandings. Three examples follow.

George Kennedy has argued that the presence of a hortatory section (5.1–6.10) indicates that Galatians as a whole functions as deliberative rhetoric (that which deals with future courses of action) and not as the forensic rhetoric of *apologia*.[5] Kennedy understands the narrative of 1.13–2.14 to be proof of Paul's statement of the *proem* (1.6-10) that there is no other gospel; it is therefore not part of an apology. Kennedy also does not use the term autobiography for this narrative. It is rather a proof, a building block of Paul's argument.

Another rhetorical approach was taken by George Lyons, who found parallels between Galatians and Graeco-Roman autobiographies (Cicero, Isocrates, and Demosthenes).[6] Lyons claims that Paul's comments should

E. Grässer; Göttingen: Vandenhoeck & Ruprecht, 1975), p. 22; A. Oepke, *Der Brief des Paulus an die Galater* (THKNT, 9, Berlin: Evangelische Verlagsanstalt, 1973), pp. 29, 53-54; J.P. Sampley, 'Before God I Do Not Lie (Gal. 1.20): Paul's Self Defense in the Light of Roman Legal Praxis', *NTS* 23 (1977), pp. 477-82.

3.   H.D. Betz, *Galatians: A Commentary on Paul's Letter to the Churches in Galatia* (Philadelphia: Fortress Press, 1979), pp. 14-15. Betz designates Gal. 1.12–2.14 as the *narratio*, a statement of the facts that serves as the basis for later argument (pp. 58-62).

4.   R.Y.K. Fung, in his *The Epistle to the Galatians* (NICNT; Grand Rapids: Eerdmans, 1988), pp. 28-32, surveys the reviews that are critical of Betz's approach and concludes that '*apologia* is *not* the most appropriate category to apply to the letter as a whole'. However, against Fung's assertion that no examples of apologetic letters exist (quoting Meeks and Russel, p. 30), see K. Berger, 'Hellenistische Gattungen im Neuen Testament', in *ANRW* (Berlin: de Gruyter, 1984), II.25, pp. 1272-74. Berger upholds Betz's decision and also cites Plato's *Seventh Letter* as an example that merged the forms of letter, autobiography, and apologetic speech.

5.   G.A. Kennedy, *New Testament Interpretation through Rhetorical Criticism* (Chapel Hill: University of North Carolina Press, 1984), pp. 146-48. See Aristotle, *Rhet.* 1.3.1358b, 1-20, for the distinction between three types of rhetoric: forensic, political, and ceremonial.

6.   G. Lyons, *Pauline Autobiography: Toward a New Understanding* (SBLDS, 73; Atlanta: Scholars Press, 1985), p. 135. These autobiographies all recount the subject's ἀναστροφή (conduct), πράξεις (deeds), λόγοι (words), and make a σύγκρισις (comparison) of the subject's character with that of another.

be explained as an effort to demonstrate his *ēthos* (character) to his readers.[7]

Beverly Roberts Gaventa presented a third challenge to the apologetic model. Gaventa concluded that Paul's reference to the 'revelation of Jesus Christ' in 1.15-17 is central to the text and places its focus on the manner in which Paul received his gospel.[8] She thus argues that Galatians 1 and 2 cannot be confined to the category of apology. Further, Galatians is closer in form and purpose to the letters of Seneca and Pliny than to the autobiographical narratives cited by Lyons and the advice of Quintilian cited by Betz. Seneca and Pliny wrote with the purposes of moral exhortation and instruction in view. In a similar manner, Paul used his narrative to offer himself as a paradigm of the power of the gospel (Gal. 4.12).[9]

These new studies give some additional attention to Paul's orientation toward the Galatian audience and thus follow the advice of the classical writers.[10] Emphases on Pauline exhortation, *ēthos*, and example do turn the focus of study toward Paul's relation to the Galatians and away from Paul's answer to the charges of his opponents.[11]

Yet these studies also cast Paul as an individual communicator who addresses his audience by means of a letter. Comparisons with classical examples and prescriptions only strengthen the emphasis on Paul's references to himself and overlook the statements he makes about others.[12]

7.   Lyons, *Pauline Autobiography*, pp. 102-104, 61. See also the similar comments by D.E. Aune, *The New Testament in its Literary Environment* (Philadelphia: Westminster Press, 1987), pp. 189-90. Aristotle distinguished the ethical, logical, and emotional modes of persuasion (*Rhet.* 1.2.1356a, 1377b-1378).

8.   B.R. Gaventa, *From Darkness to Light: Aspects of Conversion in the New Testament* (Philadelphia: Fortress Press, 1986), p. 28.

9.   B.R. Gaventa, 'Galatians 1 and 2: Autobiography as Paradigm', *NovT* 26 (1986), p. 326.

10.   W.R. Roberts held that the focus of the entire second book of Aristotle's *Rhetoric* was on the audience (*Greek Rhetoric and Literary Criticism* [New York: Longmans, Green, 1928] p. 50). See also Cicero, *De Oratore* (trans. J.S. Watson; Carbondale: Southern Illinois University Press, 1970), p. 51; 'That no man can, by speaking, excite the passions of his audience, or calm them when excited…unless (he is) one who has gained a thorough insight into the nature of all things, and the dispositions and motives of mankind…'

11.   See Lyons's critique of the 'mirror method' reconstruction of the opponent's charges, *Pauline Autobiography*, pp. 96-104.

12.   Studies on Graeco-Roman biography and autobiography often single out a focus on the individual as the constituting feature of the genre. 'Biography, Greek',

To date, no study has paid particular attention to Paul's depiction of his relationships *within* the autobiographical narrative as a means to enhance further his relationship with the Galatians and to urge them away from circumcision.[13]

In addition, no study has examined the narrative as a dramatization of the issues confronting the Galatians. Above all else, the autobiography is a story with a distinct rhetorical component. As Paul tells his story, he draws a number of symbolic parallels between his own past and the present situation at Galatia. In particular, Paul means to point out the exact parallel between those persons who opposed him by attempting to compromise the gospel and those who were putting pressure on the Galatians to be circumcised. By drawing clear lines between those who stood against him and those who stood with him, Paul intends to show the Galatians the results that their choice will bring. As he draws a narrative portrait of his past relationships, he at the same time invites them to affirm their present relationship with him by resisting circumcision. In order to study these relationships, a summary of Kenneth Burke's rhetorical-literary concept of identification will be outlined below.

Kenneth Burke and Identification

Kenneth Burke began his career as a poet, a writer of fiction, and a literary critic. In the course of his thinking about literature, he noted that imbedded within all literary form was a rhetorical component. In time, he expanded his idea of rhetoric to embrace all of human communication: 'Wherever there is persuasion, there is rhetoric. And wherever there is "meaning" there is "persuasion".'[14]

---

and 'Biography, Roman', in *OCD* (Oxford: Clarendon Press, 1949), p. 136; 'Biographie', in *Der Kleine Pauly-Lexicon der Antike* (ed. K. Ziegler and W. Sontheimer; Stuttgart: Alfred Druckenmuller, 1964), pp. 902-903; G. Misch, *A History of Autobiography in Antiquity* (London: Routledge & Kegan Paul, 1950), pp. vii, 69; D.R. Stuart, *Epochs of Greek and Roman Biography* (Berkeley: University of California Press, 1928), p. 39. This approach has been criticized by A. Momigliano, *The Development of Greek Biography* (Cambridge, MA: Harvard University Press, 1971), pp. 11-18.

13. Although Betz does note Paul's use of the friendship motif to enhance his relationship with the Galatians in Gal. 4.12-20, he does not treat Paul's depiction of relationships in Gal. 1–2 (*Galatians*, pp. 220-37).

14. K. Burke, *A Rhetoric of Motives* (Berkeley: University of California Press, 1969), p. 172.

A central idea in Burke's approach to rhetoric is the principle of identification, which may be understood as the attempt to overcome human division through the establishment of some common ground. His description of human division often makes use of biblical terminology, as for example, his 'problem of Babel':

> The theologian's concerns with Eden and the 'fall' come close to the heart of the rhetorical problem. For, behind the theology, there is the perception of generic divisiveness which, being common to all men, is a universal fact about them, prior to any divisiveness caused by social classes. Here is the basis of rhetoric.[15]

Traditional approaches to rhetoric have described the attempt to overcome division as 'persuasion'.[16] In this view, a communicator seeks to persuade an audience by winning it over to a given position so that the situation becomes, in effect, a contest of opinions and wills. Through identification, however, a communicator seeks to elicit consensus and cooperation by demonstrating what Burke calls a 'consubstantiality' between communicator and audience. The depiction of consubstantiality points out where persons 'stand together' (from the etymology of the word) and shows how they share a similar concern or interest.[17]

Although Burke himself has said that the difference between persuasion and identification distinguishes traditional rhetoric from the 'New Rhetoric',[18] he adds that in his mind, the two are not in conflict:

> As for the relation between 'identification' and 'persuasion': we might well keep it in mind that a speaker persuades an audience by the use of stylistic identifications; his act of persuasion may be for the purpose of causing the audience to identify itself with the speaker's interests; and the speaker draws on identification of interests to establish rapport between himself and his audience. So, there is no chance of our keeping apart the meanings of persuasion, identification ('consubstantiality') and communication...[19]

---

15. Burke, *Rhetoric of Motives*, p. 146.

16. Aristotle gave this idea its clearest expression when he defined rhetoric as the 'faculty of observing in any given case the available means of persuasion' (*Rhet.* 1.2.1355b, 25).

17. Burke, *Rhetoric of Motives*, p. 62; *idem, A Grammar of Motives* (New York: Prentice–Hall, 1945), p. 57.

18. K. Burke, 'Rhetoric Old and New', *The Journal of Education* 5 (1951), p. 203.

19. Burke, *Rhetoric of Motives*, p. 46

Identification is a two way process. As the communicator establishes rapport by identifying with the audience's concerns, the audience begins to identify with those of the communicator. The sharing of opinion in one area works as a fulcrum to move opinion in another.[20]

A Burkean approach to the study of Paul's autobiographical narrative seeks to discover both the ways in which Paul sought to identify with the Galatians and the ways in which he asked them, directly and indirectly, to identify with him and his message. One also watches for evidence of Paul's attempts to highlight relationships that are based upon a common understanding of the circumcision-free gospel. By depicting these relationships, Paul creates a consubstantiality (a standing together) that he asks his hearers, the Galatians, to join by rejecting circumcision. Similarly, Paul also creates relational distance between himself and those who do not share that common understanding of the gospel. As the Galatians hear Paul tell his story of his past relationships, they are forced to decide whether they will stand with Paul and his understanding of the gospel, or with those who are urging them to be circumcised. What Paul makes clear to them is that they cannot have it both ways. In addition, the narrative also shows that Paul is really concerned for their welfare, while those urging circumcision are not.

Identification in Galatians 1.13–2.14

Galatians 1.1-12
Burke recommends that the analysis of any written work should begin with the 'principle of the concordance'.[21] The critic builds an index of significant terms: terms that recur in changing contexts, terms that occur at significant points in the narrative, terms that seem heavy with symbolic meaning. One also looks for oppositions, beginnings and endings of sections and subsections, and indications of hierarchies.[22]

One of Paul's most significant terms and oppositions occurs three times prior to his narration of his past life that begins in 1.13. After the opening introduction of his name and title 'apostle' in 1.1, he states that

20. Burke, *Rhetoric of Motives*, p. 56.
21. K. Burke, 'Fact, Inference, and Proof in the Analysis of Literary Symbolism', in *Symbols and Values: An Initial Study* (Thirteenth Symposium of the Conference on Science, Philosophy, and Religion; New York: Harper & Brothers, 1954), p. 283.
22. Burke, 'Fact, Inference, and Proof', pp. 299-306.

his apostleship is not from or through any human agency (ἄνθρωπος). Rather, its source is Christ and God.

The same opposition between human terms and Christ/God terms occurs in vv. 10 and 11-12. In the questions and answer of v. 10, Paul seeks to win God over, not humans (ἄρτι γὰρ ἀνθρώπους πείθω ἢ τὸν θεόν;) and wants to please (ἀρέσκειν) Christ, not humans (ἀνθρώποις). The use of ἔτι ('still') in v. 10 suggests that Paul here refers to a human-pleasing desire that was part of his own past.[23] In vv. 11-12 Paul asserts that his gospel (like his apostleship in v. 1) is not a human gospel nor was it taught to him by any human (ἄνθρωπος). Rather it came by a revelation from Christ.

Here then, a pattern of opposition appears three times in the course of the first dozen verses of the epistle. The opposition of the divine and human terms and the orientations they represent structures Paul's thoughts about his apostleship, his motives, and his message.[24]

In addition, this opposition also gives shape to Paul's narrative, particularly as it aids him in his depiction of his relationships. Paul stands (identifies) with those who identify with the divine principle and stands against those who do not, claiming that they have embraced a human principle. The repetition of ἄνθρωπος (seven times in vv. 1-12, four of them plural) highlights the contrast.[25] In other words, Paul has introduced his narrative by stating simply and plainly, 'I did not receive my apostleship or my gospel from any human source, and I do not want to

23. Gaventa, 'Galatians 1 and 2', p. 314.

24. Gaventa has noted a similar antithesis between 'Christ–new creation' and 'the cosmos', based upon Paul's crucifixion to the world in 6.14. This antithesis subsumes a number of minor antitheses which appear throughout the letter (Christ–law, cross–circumcision) (*idem*, 'The Singularity of the Gospel: A Reading of Galatians', in *SBLSP* 1988 [ed. D.J. Lull; Atlanta: Scholars Press, 1988], p. 24). However, the sevenfold repetition of ἄνθρωπος indicates that a primary antithesis exists between Christ on the one hand, and human motives and sources on the other.

25. Lyons (*Pauline Autobiography*, pp. 152-56) appreciates the twofold function of the human–divine contrast; Paul asserts both the divinely revealed character of the gospel and his own intention to remain loyal to it. However, Lyons believes that Paul's chief purpose was to show that his message was revealed and possessed divine authority, even while Lyons holds that Paul's report of the Antioch incident was meant to show 'how easy it was to set aside the grace of God and pervert the gospel' (p. 163). This study argues that the matter of human allegiance to the revealed gospel is equally prominent with Paul's assertion of its divine origin, and that the former follows from the latter.

please any humans. I received my apostleship and gospel from God and Christ and God and Christ are the ones I want to please.' Every action and motive that follows is measured against Paul's basic statement, and Paul relates to every person as friend or foe for that same reason.

Galatians 1.13-24

The structure of opposition continues throughout Paul's retelling of his past life in Judaism. He states that he advanced beyond his contemporaries and was zealous for his father's traditions (1.14), thus describing his experience of Judaism in human, not divine terms. The divine motive enters in when God chooses to reveal his Son and Paul's mission (vv. 15-16). Paul adds that he did not consult human authorities (flesh and blood, apostles) about this, but went away to Arabia.

The above summary suggests that a large part of the motivation that Paul reveals in his narrative up to this point centers in his repudiation of his former way of life.[26] The opposition between his old life and the new is patterned after the opposition between human and divine authority seen in vv. 1-12. There Paul defined his new life as a striving for God's pleasure over that of other men. Here he contrasts God's revelation of his Son with the traditions of his fathers.

As for the apostles, he neither competed with them nor inquired[27] of them (as compared with his relations within Judaism), but rather ignored them. His move away from the apostles to Arabia, therefore, signified his break from a bondage to human tradition and authority. The con trast between Paul's old and new relationships is clear. Whereas Paul described his former life in Judaism as focused on human relationships with his contemporaries and predecessors, his depiction of his new life is so centered on his relation to God that he as yet has no relationship to the other apostles.

Paul then goes on to report that he did finally visit the apostles Cephas and James after three years (1.18). The only indication of his purpose for the visit is given in the verb ἱστορέω, which carries the

---

26. J. Becker, *Die Brief an die Galater* (NTD, Neues Göttinger Bibelwerk, 8; Göttingen: Vandenhoeck & Ruprecht, 1976), pp. 14-15. Becker maintains that the contrast between Paul's old and new life is the point of narrative, and thus places the 'not from men, but from God' idea in the foreground.

27. 'Inquire' may be understood in the sense of 'submit for judgment' (J. Behm, 'ἀνατίθημι', *TDNT*, I, pp. 353-54).

sense of 'visit to inquire of or get information from'.[28] Paul stresses the brevity of the visit and the fact that he met with only two of the apostles. After his visit he returned to Gentile territory (1.21, Syria and Cilicia; in 1.17 he goes to Arabia and Damascus). Paul seems determined to emphasize that he was a stranger to Judea, for he adds that even the churches did not know him by sight (1.22).

Yet even while Paul establishes this physical distance between himself and the apostles and churches, he declares a common purpose; the churches hear that Paul now preaches the faith he tried to destroy. Even while many miles separate him from the churches of Judea, he has become one with them through a common faith in the gospel. Paul has established a relationship, a consubstantiality, with Christians throughout Judea. Their praise of God on his account (1.24) indicates that Paul has become a success in his new vocation of pleasing God.

The climax of the first portion of Paul's narrative does establish that he did not receive his gospel from a human source, but it does not imply that Paul worked apart from the Jerusalem authorities because he was a rebel or did not agree with them. In fact no reason is given for the departure to Arabia apart from the ongoing opposition of the divine and human motives. In reaction to his prior life, it seems he did not wish to be taught by humans any longer. The churches hear the report (perhaps through Cephas and James) that Paul preached the faith that he once persecuted among the Gentiles, the same faith that the apostles preach.

The chapter ends in a scene of harmony, the division between the old Paul and the Church having been overcome through God's revelation of Christ to the persecutor. The source of division between Paul and the Church (Christ and the gospel) has now become the source of a consubstantiality. Although Paul states that he has never met the people of these churches, he has used the principle of identification to build a relationship with them within the narrative. Paul has done much the same with the Jerusalem apostles. He shows that he is one in purpose with the apostles, although he is separate from (but not independent of) them. They are joined in allegiance to the purpose of God, whom Paul is anxious to please (1.10). It is Christ, however, whom he serves, not the apostles.

Issues of circumcision and the inclusion of the Gentiles have not yet surfaced in the narrative; therefore, the Galatians are not yet drawn into

28. BAGD, p. 383.

the story. As they hear this portion, they may simply observe the contrast between Paul's old and new life and notice the harmony created by a common commitment to the faith (1.23). Most of all, they would see the contrast, drawn by Paul, between a commitment to the human traditions of Judaism and faith in the divinely revealed gospel.

Galatians 2.1-10

Paul established that his mission to the Gentiles was greeted with favor in the first section of the narrative (1.1-24). In the second section (2.1-10) Paul adds that the gospel he preached to the Gentiles was circumcision-free. He reports that he went to Jerusalem and met with the apostles, but he laid out before them the message he brought with him; this was not a time for them to instruct him. The mention of revelation in 2.2, whatever else its purpose, clarifies that Paul's ultimate allegiance is to God, not the Jerusalem apostles. Yet Paul also states that he needed to lay out his gospel before the apostles for evaluation in order to forestall some problem, which he believed might cause his work to be in vain, or without lasting effect.[29]

Here within the narrative Paul has defined his relationship with the Jerusalem apostles as a relationship between equals, not that of a subordinate to superiors.[30] The meeting was intended to secure a common understanding of the gospel as circumcision-free. Therefore Paul is not seeking to invoke apostolic authority by appealing to Jerusalem; he has already established that he speaks with apostolic authority himself. Rather, Paul intends to show that the Jerusalem apostles stood with him in his understanding of the circumcision-free gospel and with God who revealed it to him.

Paul notes two major results of the meeting: Titus was not compelled to be circumcised and Paul's mission to the Gentiles was received warmly. Although the sentences of 2.2-5 appear to be incomplete and do not follow grammatical convention, the use of διά with the accusative in v. 4 suggests that the false brothers were behind the push to circumcise

29. J.D.G. Dunn, 'The Relationship between Paul and Jerusalem according to Galatians 1 and 2', *NTS* 28 (1982), p. 468: 'what he sought was not so much their approval (without which his gospel would have no validity) as their recognition of his gospel's validity (without which his gospel would lose its effectiveness)'.

30. Dunn, 'Relationship between Paul and Jerusalem', pp. 466-68. Dunn argues that contemporary uses of ἀνατίθημι do not indicate a distinction in status between Paul and the apostles.

the Gentile Christian. Paul's response was firm; Titus was not compelled
(2.3) and Paul and his companions did not submit for a moment (2.5)
because he saw that the false brothers wanted to bring them into
bondage.

The use of the term 'bring into bondage' or 'enslave' (καταδουλόω)
also appears in 2 Cor. 11.20 in the context of false teachers. Here in the
immediate context of Galatians 2, the term is set in contrast with 'freedom in Christ'. In the larger context of the epistle, it is also set in contrast
with Paul's servant-bondage to Christ (δοῦλος) in 1.10. If the οἷς οὐδέ
is accepted as the original reading,[31] Paul here claims that he did not submit to those who would enslave them. Paul uses the first person plural in
2.4 to indicate that enslavement of the Gentiles would mean enslavement
to the principle of bondage for the Jewish Christians as well.

With this assertion Paul has set up another opposition between human
and divine authority. Paul knew that he could only submit to one authority. If he submitted to the false brothers he would betray his loyalty
to Christ and compromise freedom in Christ. The false brothers stand in
relation to Paul as did his old life; they are both rejected as 'still pleasing
humans' (1.10). No consubstantiality exists, therefore Paul stands against
them rather than with them.

When Paul speaks of preserving the gospel for the Galatians in v. 5,
he stands against the false brothers for the sake of the Galatians. In other
words, the struggle at the Jerusalem meeting not only resisted the
enslavement of Paul and his company, but, by extension, the enslavement of the Galatian believers as well. However, the Galatians are not
enjoying their freedom, but are fighting the same battle with those who
are urging them to undergo circumcision. The advocates of circumcision
are like the false brothers who opposed Paul, and they too will bring the
Galatians under bondage to human authority. Paul, on the other hand,
represents a commitment to God's authority as revealed in the circumcision-free gospel.

The scene, as Paul depicts it, shows the two principles and parties in
conflict in parallel situations. The same issue is at stake now in Galatia as
it was then in Jerusalem. The Galatians cannot have it both ways; they
must choose to identify with one principle or the other. If the Galatians
stand with Paul they will stand with one who has fought for their freedom as well as the truth of the gospel (2.5). If they choose to undergo

31. Betz, *Galatians*, p. 91.

circumcision they will not only be trying to please humans; they will be enslaved to them.

The Galatians are also encouraged to identify with Titus, who, with Paul's help, responded to the circumcision-free gospel of Christ instead of the human desires of the false brothers. Like Titus, the Galatians have been affirmed as believers without the requirement of circumcision, and have avoided the enslavement of those who would require it. Finally, to identify with Titus, Paul, and the apostles is to identify with Christ who revealed the circumcision-free message that resists the threat of bondage. These are relationships of freedom.

When Paul turns again to the apostles (those reputed to be something), he states that their evaluation of his message suggested no revisions or additions (2.6). The major implication of Paul's statement is that there is a basic relationship of equality between himself and the Jerusalem apostles in the sight of God.[32] This is given explicit statement in 2.7-8; both Paul and Peter have been entrusted with the gospel. This recognition of grace led the 'pillars' to offer the right hand of fellowship so that the missions to the circumcised and to the uncircumcised are given equal standing. There is no submission to human authority, nor is there any of the competition that characterized Paul's former life (1.14). Rather, those who have been entrusted with the truth of the gospel submit together as equals under the authority of the one who entrusted it to them (2.7) and gave Paul grace (2.9). The apostles have joined Paul in a common desire to please God rather than any human authority (1.10).

Paul's second section of the narrative, like the first, ends in harmony. For the second time a source of division has been dealt with through a realization of the grace of God that was at work in Paul (2.8-9; compare with 1.24). Once again divine action has brought about a consubstantiality as it is perceived by the Church. The narrative does not establish Paul's independence from Jerusalem, but rather a relationship of cooperative interdependence based on the truth of the gospel that embraces Jew and Greek The circumcision-free gospel that Paul brought to Jerusalem now stands in consubstantial unity with the gospel preached

---

32. The similarities of 'God shows no partiality' (2.6, πρόσωπον [ὁ] θεὸς ἀνθρώπου οὐ λαμβάνει) with 1 Sam. 16.7, 1 Esd. 4.39, Sir. 4.22, 27 and Lk. 20.21 suggest that Paul is using an idiom to state that God does not judge by appearances, or, in this case, titles and offices. Cf. D.M. Hay, 'Paul's Indifference to Authority', *JBL* 88 (1969), pp. 36-44.

by the Jerusalem apostles; therefore Paul's relationship with the apostles is also one of consubstantial unity.

In addition, the Galatians are welcomed with Paul in the narrative through his identification with the Gentiles. As Paul is granted the right hand of fellowship, the Gentiles he represents are welcomed into the fellowship of believers as Gentiles, not converts to Judaism. They will be treated as equals with the Jewish Christians and, like Paul's friend Titus, they will not be required to be circumcised. They can trust that in heeding Paul's apostolic authority, they are also in accord with the authority of the Jerusalem apostles.

In opposition to this decision stand the false brothers who do not have apostolic authority based on the truth of the gospel, and would not grant equality to the Gentile believers. Instead, they would require circumcision, a status of bondage to their will Paul has used his narrative thus far to force the Galatians to see the consequences of a decision to submit to circumcision by identifying the false brothers of 2.4 with those who are urging circumcision upon the Galatians. To choose their position over that of Paul, Titus, and the other apostles would be equal to pleasing humans and, worse yet, a relationship of bondage.

Galatians 2.11-14
The final portion of Paul's narrative does introduce division between himself and the apostles. As the climax of the narrative it demonstrates how the consubstantial principles of unity and equality are betrayed when one chooses to base one's actions on the desire to please humans rather than God. It is not, as James Hester argues, a digression from the narrative that brings the reader back to the conflict that might have gotten lost in the irenic settlement of 2.9-10.[33] The conflict is a negative frustration following what has up to this point been a positive illustration of unity in the circumcision-free gospel. As relations break down between Cephas, Paul, and the Gentile Christians at Antioch, the Galatians are given another picture of what lies before them should they choose to undergo circumcision.

Whatever the number and purpose of the party sent from James, its presence led Cephas to abandon the example of inclusion he had set by

---

33. J.D. Hester, 'The Rhetorical Structure of Galatians 1.11–2.14', *JBL* 103 (1984), pp. 231-32. Hester, following Betz's outline of Galatians, suggests that 2.11-14 is structurally and functionally separate from 1.15–2.10 and makes the *narratio* shorter, thus better meeting the criterion of brevity.

eating with the Gentiles. Paul interpreted his action according to the same opposition between the divine and human will that he has set up throughout the narrative. He states that Cephas withdrew because he feared the circumcised (περιτομῆς, 2.12; compare with 2.7 and 2.9) and was not walking straight according to the truth of the gospel (compare with 2.5). In fearing the circumcised (περιτομῆς), Peter was seeking to please these men rather than God. As a result, his relationship with the Gentiles was broken.

Again, the revealed circumcision-free gospel is set in opposition to human authority. The choice of the human will over the divine suddenly brings division where there was once unity. In Paul's interpretation of the events, there is only unity in the gospel, which is both revealed and circumcision-free. Once that gospel is compromised, there will be no place for Gentiles and, by implication, the Galatians in the church unless they also circumcise.

Should the Galatians choose to enter the fellowship through what Paul calls the human principle of circumcision, there will be no equality either. In confronting Peter, he charged him with compelling the Gentiles to Judaize (live like a Jew, be circumcised). To Paul, Peter was doing the same as the false brothers tried to do in Jerusalem (the word for compel, ἀναγκάζω, is used in both 2.14 and 2.3).[34] Therefore, if the Galatians choose circumcision, they will no longer be servants of Christ; they will be servants of a human authority, namely those who require circumcision. They will be living as Paul did in his former life, trying to please humans instead of God.

Only here has Paul placed real relational distance between himself and the apostles in his retelling of the story, for only here has any apostle (Peter and perhaps James)[35] chosen a human principle. If the Galatians had any concerns about Paul's relationship to the Jerusalem church, he has shown them that the apostles, Paul included, had been in harmony and equality until the revealed, circumcision-free gospel ceased to be the basis for fellowship.

For this reason the narrative portrait of Paul's relationship with the apostles is not simply meant to show that Paul was not taught by them;

34. Betz, *Galatians*, p. 112.
35. Paul does not make explicit whether the arrival of the party signified a change in James's policy regarding circumcision. In any case, Paul's argument depends on the priority of the Jerusalem meeting and considers any departure from its conclusion to be an aberration.

it is also meant to model the unity that is only possible in the fear of God and the revelation of Christ in the gospel. The incident at Antioch shows that any other principle of fellowship, based on subservience to human authority and distinctions, ultimately brings division.[36]

In contrast to his opposition to Peter, Paul continued his relationship of identification with the Gentiles in the Antioch incident by standing alone with them when all the Jewish Christians had withdrawn. As the Galatians heard this, they were still in a relationship of identification with Paul and the Gentiles that began back at the meeting with the Jerusalem apostles (2.1-10). Once again, they see Paul fighting for the right of the Gentiles (including the Galatians) to be included in the fellowship without the requirement of circumcision. Paul has shown them that the decision whether or not to be circumcised is not only a matter of freedom but is also a matter of community. The community of Christ and his circumcision-free gospel is inclusive and egalitarian; the community of circumcision is no community at all.[37]

The Galatians must therefore choose, not only whether to be circumcised, but whether or not they will continue to identify with Paul who has identified with them. Will they choose to continue a relationship of identification with Paul, begun when they first believed and continued in Paul's narrative? Or, will they choose to please humans rather than God and withdraw themselves from Paul as Peter withdrew from them? Having placed the choice before them, Paul says, 'Brethren, I beseech you, become as I am, for I also have become as you are' (4.12).

Summary and Conclusion

The antithesis between pleasing God and pleasing humans in Gal. 1.10 and the corresponding antithesis between the gospel of Christ and that of humans in 1.11-12 are dramatized by Paul in his autobiographical narrative. While he demonstrates that his message was not taught to him by the Jerusalem apostles, this is not the sole purpose of his narrative. A Burkean approach has shown that Paul also depicts a community

36. J.D.G. Dunn ('The Incident at Antioch [Gal 2.11-18]', *JSNT* 18 [1983], p. 36) argues that the Antioch incident caused Paul to see the incompatibility of a system that called Gentiles 'sinners' (Gal. 2.15) with the gospel of Christ.

37. T.D. Gordon ('The Problem at Galatia', *Int* 41 [1987], pp. 37-40) argues that Paul replaces the exclusive identity symbol of Torah with an inclusive symbol of faith in Christ.

created by a common response to the gospel. The community remains intact as long as its members seek to please God on the basis of the revealed, circumcision-free gospel rather than seeking to please other humans. The community also is inclusive and egalitarian when the same principle is kept, since the gospel itself becomes the sole ground for consubstantiality. Circumcision, which Paul identifies as a desire to please human authority, divides.[38]

A Burkean approach also shows how the narrative forces the Galatians to decide with whom they will stand on this issue. If the Galatians wish to be in relationship with the larger Church and the Jerusalem apostles, they must identify with Paul, for all the apostles are of the same fellowship in the gospel, the Antioch incident notwithstanding. The circumcision-free gospel and apostolic authority both come from God, not from any human standing. Therefore, in order for the Galatians to please God, they must continue in a relationship of identification with Paul and the other apostles (as portrayed in 2.1-10), and not enter a new relationship with those who tell them to be circumcised. To choose circumcision is to please human authority; indeed, it is to become enslaved to it.

Finally, a Burkean approach demonstrates that Paul also uses the principle of identification to enhance his relationship with the Galatians. He depicts himself as a defender of their interests, fighting for their freedom and their right to enter the fellowship without any requirement but faith in Christ. He brings the Gentiles into fellowship with the Jewish church and he alone stands with them when all other Jewish Christians withdraw. He has been an advocate for the Galatians and all Gentiles in the past; certainly his present stormings and pleadings have their interests at heart now.

No one model can appreciate the richness of Paul's autobiographical narrative. The model proposed here, based upon Kenneth Burke's literary-rhetorical method, is offered to show that Paul not only sought to strengthen his relationship with the Galatians through his autobiographical narrative, but that he used the depictions of relationships within the narrative to create a rhetorical community that the Galatians were

---

38. C.B. Cousar (*Galatians* [Atlanta: John Knox, 1982], p. 28) has stated that Paul's first purpose in the autobiography was to assert that his gospel was from no human source, and his second purpose was to state clearly that the unity of the Church was based on one gospel of grace. This study asserts that the former purpose serves the latter.

forced either to join or to reject. Thus to reject circumcision was to identify with the community of Paul and the Christ who sent him.

JSNT 47 (1992), pp. 49-74

THESSALONICA AND CORINTH: SOCIAL CONTRASTS
IN PAULINE CHRISTIANITY

John M.G. Barclay

According to the book of Acts, Paul founded five churches during his
first mission to Europe: Acts 16–18 records successful evangelism in
Philippi, Thessalonica, Beroea, Athens and Corinth. For most of the
details of this narrative we have no external check on Luke's account,
but in the case of three of these churches—Philippi, Thessalonica and
Corinth—we have first-hand historical evidence in the form of Paul's
letters; and these provide enough incidental information about the
founding of the relevant churches to enable us to question or confirm
some parts of the narrative in Acts. In particular, 1 Thessalonians confirms the information given by Luke that Paul arrived in Thessalonica
from Philippi, that he was forced to leave the city much earlier than he
would have liked, and that he headed south and visited Athens. There is
thus sufficient correspondence between Acts and 1 Thessalonians to
make it highly likely that when Paul wrote to the Thessalonians a mat
ter of weeks (or, at most, a few months) after his departure from
Thessalonica he was already engaged in his mission in Corinth.[1]

We can be reasonably confident, then, that there was only a small
interval between the birth of the church in Thessalonica and the establishment by the same evangelist of a Christian community in Corinth.
And yet these sibling communities developed remarkably different interpretations of the Christian faith. Any careful reading of Paul's letters to

1. See E. Best, *The First and Second Epistle to the Thessalonians* (London: A.
& C. Black, 1972), pp. 7-13. Despite their differences in the absolute chronology of
Paul's life, G. Lüdemann (*Paul: Apostle to the Gentiles: Studies in Chronology*
[London: SCM Press, 1984]) and R. Jewett (*Dating Paul's Life* [London: SCM
Press, 1979]) agree in placing the writing of 1 Thessalonians at this juncture of
Paul's mission.

these churches reveals that they had very different characteristics; and any thoughtful analysis of these differences shows how they diverged not just in superficial matters but in their whole perception of the faith they had learned from Paul. The aim of this essay is to explore these divergences in Pauline Christianity and to inquire into their causes. The exploration will highlight one factor in particular which has so far received too little attention, namely the social relations between Christians and non-Christians. Without claiming that this is the sole significant factor, I will advance the hypothesis that the presence or absence of conflict in social interaction with outsiders had an important influence on the development of these two churches and on their perception of their Christian identity. In the interests of space, and because they provide our earliest evidence, I will focus almost entirely on the letters known as 1 Thessalonians and 1 Corinthians; but, as the conclusion will indicate, the subsequent letter(s) would not modify but merely confirm our findings here.

The Thessalonian Church: Apocalyptic Hope and Social Conflict[2]

Paul's Apocalyptic Message and its Reception

We are fortunate to be able to reconstruct with some confidence Paul's gospel message as he preached it in Thessalonica. In 1 Thessalonians Paul refers so many times to the terms of his preaching, and reminds his converts so often of the traditions he had given them, that we can paint a quite detailed picture of his missionary proclamation and his basic instruction of the young church in that city. In its outline and in its central focus that picture is unmistakably apocalyptic. The Thessalonians were told about Jesus, God's Son, how he had died ('for us', 5.10) and been raised (4.14). Most especially, the converts were given instruction about the παρουσία of Jesus, which they were eagerly to await (1.10). The Lord Jesus would suddenly appear with his ἅγιοι (3.13), like a thief in the night (5.1-11), and it was their responsibility always to be ready for his arrival. It is clear that Paul had led his converts to believe that they would live to see the Lord's παρουσία. This is one reason for the shock in the church when some of their number died (4.13-18): it appeared that the deceased had missed the moment which they were all waiting for.

The Thessalonians were also taught to expect that God's wrath would break out on the rest of humanity; although those 'others' imagined that

---

2. I have examined the Thessalonian situation in more detail in 'Conflict in Thessalonica', *CBQ* 55 (1993), pp. 512-30.

there was 'peace and security', they would soon be overtaken by a sudden and inescapable destruction (5.2-3). Paul's converts, however, would be rescued from such a fate (1.10; 5.9). They had come to know the true and living God in turning from 'idols' (1.9); and, as beneficiaries of his love and his election (1.4), they had been called into his kingdom and glory (2.12). For the present, as Paul warned them, they would experience troubles (προελέγομεν ὑμῖν ὅτι μέλλομεν θλίβεσθαι, 3.4); they should expect their Christian lives to be characterized by suffering. Through it all they should ensure that their behaviour remained holy (4.1-3) and their hearts blameless (3.13): the moment of their vindication was near.

The atmosphere created by this message is heavy with apocalyptic excitement. The standard dualisms of Jewish apocalyptic—between heaven and earth, the present and the future, the elect and the lost—are all present here and given sharp focus through the death and resurrection of Jesus.[3] In this gospel, Christian faith is firmly located within an apocalyptic framework and takes its significance from that special time-frame within which it operates. Moreover, there is every reason to believe that the Thessalonian Christians have been decisively moulded by this structure of belief. Paul is well informed about his converts in Thessalonica following the recent visit by Timothy, but he gives no hint that they have dissented in any significant way from the terms of the gospel which he first preached and now reiterates. The tone of 1 Thessalonians is that of positive reinforcement, not rebuke or correction. The Thessalonians are, in Paul's view, excessively grieved about the deaths of some of their number; but that is because their expectation of the παρουσία is so highly charged that they had not reckoned with the possibility that death might intervene. Paul does not consider that they have given up hope for the παρουσία, only that they have given up hope for their brothers or sisters who had died. Hence the stress in 1 Thess. 4.13-18 is not on the fact that the παρουσία will soon come (he takes for granted that 'we who are alive will be left until his coming', 4.15, 17), but on the hope that the dead in Christ have not been abandoned (4.15-16). This

---

3. There are, of course, many definitions of apocalyptic theology, which also had many variations within Judaism. I follow here the working definition of W. Meeks, 'The Social Functions of Apocalyptic Language in Pauline Christianity', in D. Hellholm (ed.), *Apocalypticism in the Mediterranean World and the Near East* (Tübingen: Mohr [Paul Siebeck], 1983), pp. 687-705, in an essay whose observations on 1 Thessalonians are particularly pertinent.

surely indicates that, when Paul addressed the question of 'times and seasons' in 5.1-11, he was led to do so not by a waning of interest in the παρουσία in the Thessalonian church, but precisely by their restless impatience as they daily awaited the signs of the outpouring of God's wrath on unbelievers and their own rescue by the heavenly saviour, Jesus.[4]

Social Conflict in Thessalonica

If the symbolic world of the Thessalonian church is decidedly apocalyptic, its social context is dominated by conflict. Paul's references to his initial proclamation of the gospel in Thessalonica make clear that his efforts were attended by controversy:

> although we had already suffered (προπαθόντες) and been abused (ὑβρισθέντες) at Philippi, as you know, we had courage in our God to declare to you the gospel of God in the face of great opposition (ἐν πολλῷ ἀγῶνι) (1 Thess. 2.2).

The parallel with Philippi suggests vigorous, possibly physical, opposition—and to this extent Paul's remark supports the account in Acts 17. Indeed, that Paul was the target of at least slanderous attacks from non-believers in Thessalonica is the most likely explanation of the painstaking personal defence he mounts in 2.3-12.

But it was not just Paul who came under attack in Thessalonica. It is clear that his converts also have experienced considerable hostility: 'You became imitators of us and of the Lord, having received the word in circumstances of considerable affliction (δεξάμενοι τὸν λόγον ἐν θλίψει πολλῇ) together with joy in the Holy Spirit' (1.6). Moreover, this θλῖψις has continued to affect their lives as Christians. Paul refers to the things they have suffered at the hands of their fellow-countrymen (2.14) and it is evident that he sent Timothy back to Thessalonica out of his deep concern lest they be shaken by such afflictions (3.3). His warning that they were to suffer θλῖψις (3.4) appears to have been entirely accurate.

---

4. R. Jewett (*The Thessalonian Correspondence* [Philadelphia: Fortress Press, 1986], pp. 96-100) incorrectly takes 5.1-11 to indicate that the Thessalonians were no longer interested in future events since 'their intense experience of realized eschatology...sustained an unwillingness to live with the uncertainty of a future eschatology' (p. 97). He has been unduly influenced by the similar conclusions of W. Lütgert (*Die Vollkommenen im Philipperbrief und die Enthusiasten in Thessalonich* [Gütersloh: Bertelsmann, 1909], pp. 55-81).

Although punctuated by these general references to θλῖψις, Paul's letter gives no hint of the forms it took or its causes. θλῖψις can mean merely mental distress (3.7), but the parallel in 1.6 between the Thessalonians' experience and that of Paul and Jesus suggests that at least vigorous social harassment is in view. Elsewhere I have explored the most likely causes of this harassment—in the offensive abandonment by the Thessalonians of traditional religious practices as they turned from 'idols' to 'the true and living God'.[5] The arrogant refusal of Christians to take part in, or to consider as valid, the worship of any God but their own was the cause of deep resentment in the Graeco-Roman world and is probably the root cause of the Thessalonians' troubles. As Acts, 1 Peter and later Christian apologists show, mockery, slander and ostracism were among the many forms of harassment typically employed against such deviant, and threatening, behaviour.

It is clear, then, that the relations between Christians and non-Christians in Thessalonica were severely strained. Although the deaths of some of the converts cannot be directly attributed to such θλῖψις (Paul would hardly have missed an opportunity to celebrate the deceased as martyrs), it would certainly be easy for non-Christians to mock those whose faith in a 'saviour' appeared so ineffective. That more than one death occurred so soon after the founding of the church would surely appear more than just coincidental: it is not difficult to imagine hostile comments about the gods' punishment of the impious! There are also signs that the conflict could be heightened by the Thessalonian Christians themselves. Paul has to instruct them not to return evil for evil (5.15) and in 4.11-12 urges them to live quietly, to mind their own affairs and to behave in a seemly fashion towards outsiders. We should probably perceive behind such remarks the dangers of aggressive evangelism which ridicules 'idols' and calls attention repeatedly to the sudden destruction about to fall on all who do not believe in Jesus.[6] Paul knows that the church is already in enough trouble without attracting more through such a public confrontation of outsiders.

---

5. Barclay, 'Conflict in Thessalonica'.

6. See E. von Dobschütz, *Die Thessalonicher-Briefe* (Göttingen: Vandenhoeck & Ruprecht, 1909), pp. 180-82, although his suggestion of political involvement is unnecessary and unconvincing. Cf. Best, *Thessalonians*, p. 175, and W. Marxsen, *Der erste Brief an die Thessalonicher* (Zürich: Theologischer Verlag, 1979), pp. 25-26, 62.

The Correlation of Apocalyptic and Social Alienation

Thus far I have merely set out side by side the apocalyptic structures of the Thessalonians' beliefs and the social alienation which they have experienced. But it is obvious that there is some correlation here between beliefs and experience which merits investigation.

The symbolic world of apocalyptic is, as we have seen, structured by dualisms; it posits, in particular, a strong distinction between the circle of believers and all the rest of humanity. The Thessalonians were encouraged by Paul to think of all non-believers as 'outsiders' (οἱ ἔξω, 4.12) and to lump them all together in the category of 'the rest' (οἱ λοιποί, 4.13; 5.6). Moreover, such people are described in consistently derogatory terms: they do not know God (4.5); they are 'children of darkness' who merely sleep and get drunk (5.7); and they have no hope (4.13). Although from any 'normal' social perspective Paul is an 'outsider' to Thessalonica, and believers elsewhere in Macedonia, in Achaea and in Judaea are foreigners to the Thessalonian converts compared to their fellow Thessalonians, Paul redraws the social map in order to bind his converts to such comparatively remote people and to loosen their ties to their συμφυλέται nearer to hand (1.7; 2.14-15; 4.10).

Such a dualistic perspective does not rule out the possibility of further conversions; those who have recently been 'children of darkness' themselves might well want to rescue others before it is too late. But it does establish clear boundaries which mark outsiders as alien unless and until they come 'inside'. In some circumstances this fundamental sense of alienation might be mollified or even overruled, where, for instance, close affective bonds tie individuals together across these boundaries. Even apocalyptic symbols can be variously interpreted, according to the interests and circumstances of those who are influenced by them. But where such symbols take a powerful hold in circumstances of social conflict, it is obvious how experience and symbolic world can reinforce each other.

Thus, on the one hand, the Thessalonians' apocalyptic perspective will encourage them to embrace social alienation as normal; indeed, it will sustain their social dislocation by discouraging them from any significant attempt to reduce the conflicts they experience. They will be comforted by the knowledge that their sufferings are only to be expected (they are part of the apocalyptic agenda) and by the assurance that they cannot last for long. The apocalyptic language they have adopted reinforces the social dualism they find operating in practice and injects a strong dose of hostility into their attitudes towards others. All those outside the circle of believers are viewed as actual or potential aggressors. The whole of life is a battle-field and the universe as a whole is caught up in a massive power struggle. Frustration and difficulty is the work of Satan (2.18). The consolation is that those who are responsible for the present troubles will soon themselves be caught up in that sudden destruction due to fall on all objects of God's anger. Thus, every instance of social harassment can be given its 'proper' explanation in this symbolic world structured by oppositions, contrasts and conflicts.

On the other hand, every experience of conflict serves to validate the apocalyptic symbols which the Thessalonian Christians have adopted and to give such symbols vivid and visible meaning. The more they are ridiculed or ostracized, the more clearly is defined the distinction between believers and non-believers, insiders and outsiders; and thus the more obviously correct is the apocalyptic divide between those destined for salvation and those destined for wrath. The more opposition they encounter, the more obviously their opponents are darkened in their understanding, captured by the power of evil forces and justly deserving of the judgment they will shortly face.

Here, then, apocalyptic symbols and social dislocation maintain and reinforce each other. This is, in fact, a classic example of the dialectic between symbolic worlds and social processes in which the symbols suggest a certain interpretation of social events and that construction of events is embraced as confirmation of the 'reality' one believes in. There is no suggestion of determinism intended here: neither their apocalyptic beliefs nor their experiences of harassment determine the development of the Thessalonian church in any simple way.[7] But the coherence of belief and experience in the highly-charged atmosphere of a fledgling community accounts for the special intensity which marked this church and enabled it to survive in a hostile environment.

It will be observed that the focus of this investigation has been on the *social interaction* of the Thessalonian Christians with outsiders rather

---

7.   For a critical discussion of correlations between symbolic and social structures, see B. Holmberg, *Sociology and the New Testament* (Minneapolis: Fortress Press, 1990), pp. 118-44. He rightly emphasizes that the quest for such correlations must begin from good factual information about social data and must be continually reminded of 'how complex and subtle such relationships typically are' (p. 142). His distinction, drawn from Lampe, between genetic and supportive causality (the latter referring to those factors which enable the continuation of a certain phenomenon) is particularly suggestive for this essay.

than their *social status*. These two issues are, to an extent, inseparable: status depends, in part at least, on the value which others place on one's goods and achievements. But I have deliberately departed here from the concentration on the question of status which characterizes most socio-logical studies of Pauline Christianity in general and the Thessalonian church in particular. In this case we know almost nothing about the social status of the Thessalonian converts,[8] and there is a particular danger of subscribing to the false assumption that an apocalyptic ideol-ogy is necessarily founded on, or fostered by, particular economic conditions.[9] For the present investigation we do not need to know about the social origins of Paul's converts or the reasons for their adoption of Christianity. It is only important to observe how their experience as Christians matches and reinforces the apocalyptic symbols which they learned from Paul.

The Corinthian Church: Spiritual Knowledge and Social Harmony

We may turn now to examine the church in Corinth, founded so soon after that in Thessalonica. In this case it is harder to be confident about the terms in which Paul preached the gospel when he arrived in Corinth. 1 Corinthians is so intensively focused on developments in the church since its foundation that Paul's pristine preaching and church instruction is no longer in the foreground.[10] In the case of Corinth then, I will begin the other way round, investigating first the social interaction of the church with Corinthian society, then outlining the dominant understand-ing of Christian faith among the Corinthians, before exploring what part

---

8.   Jewett (*Thessalonian Correspondence*, pp. 118-23) argues from 1 Thess. 2.9-12, 4.11 and 2 Thess. 3.6-12 that the Christians were mostly manual workers, and from 2 Cor. 8.2-4 that they suffered extreme poverty. But this is hardly a reliable basis for a social profile of the congregation. 2 Cor. 8 is heavily influenced by rhetor-ical considerations and it is possible that Paul's injunctions show no more than that *he* assumes that work means work with one's hands.

9.   For the theoretical problems here, see R.L. Rohrbaugh, '"Social Location of Thought" as a Heuristic Concept in New Testament Study', *JSNT* 30 (1987), pp. 103-19 (reprinted in this volume, pp. 122-38).

10.   J.C. Hurd, *The Origin of I Corinthians* (London: SPCK, 1965), is a coura-geous attempt to excavate through 1 Corinthians to the earliest level of Paul's dealings with the Corinthians; but it is generally acknowledged that his case becomes less convincing the further he goes.

social factors may have played in the Corinthians' interpretation of Paul's gospel.

Social Harmony in Corinth

One of the most significant, but least noticed, features of Corinthian church life is the absence of conflict in the relationship between Christians and 'outsiders'. In contrast to the Thessalonian church, the believers in Corinth appear neither to feel hostility towards, nor to experience hostility from, non-Christians. In writing to the Corinthians, Paul certainly refers to the rejection and harassment which *he himself* experiences. He fought with 'wild beasts' in Ephesus, and claims to be in peril every day (1 Cor. 15.30-32); he is hungry and thirsty, ill-clad, homeless and abused, a public spectacle, like a convict sentenced to die in the arena (4.9-13). But precisely in this passage, where he gives his own catalogue of suffering, Paul notes (with some bitterness) the painless experience of the Corinthians: 'We are fools for Christ's sake, but you are wise in Christ. We are weak but you are strong. You are held in honour, but we in disrepute' (4.10). In the light of Paul's usage of similar terms in 1.26-28, we might be inclined to think that he is referring here only to the minority of Corinthians with relatively high social status. But the ironic rebuke is directed at the whole church and may reflect a consciousness among the Corinthians that, whatever their social origins, their status had been enhanced by their adoption of Christianity.[11] It is particularly significant that Paul refers to them as ἔνδοξοι (in contrast to the apostles who are ἄτιμοι) since the context shows that these terms concern their public reputation. Clearly, whatever individual exceptions there may be, Paul does not regard social alienation as the characteristic state of the Corinthian church.[12]

11. The terms in 4.10 do not, then, refer to the original social status of Paul's converts (*pace* G. Theissen, *The Social Setting of Pauline Christianity* [Edinburgh: T. & T. Clark, 1982], pp. 72-73). But neither is it necessary to interpret them as indicating only the Corinthians' spiritual illusions (so G.D. Fee, *The First Epistle to the Corinthians* [Grand Rapids: Eerdmans, 1987], pp. 176-77, and W. Schrage, *Der erste Brief an die Korinther* [EKKNT, 7.1; Zürich: Benzinger Verlag; Neukirchen–Vluyn: Neukirchener Verlag, 1991], p. 343). Paul's ironic contrast between the Corinthians and the apostles depends on the fact that the Corinthians have good grounds for considering themselves 'wise, strong and honoured', just as Paul has grounds for describing himself as the opposite.

12. While there are many opponents in Ephesus (ἀντικείμενοι πολλοί, 16.9) there is no hint of any such opposition in Corinth. The illness and death referred to in

In fact there are plenty of signs suggesting the social acceptability of the Corinthian Christians. That some of them (presumably the wealthier) take their disputes to the civic law-courts (6.1-6) signals their confidence in the legal system; they do not anticipate that believers will receive prejudicial treatment at the hands of non-Christians. Corinthian Christians are invited to meals in the houses of non-believers (10.27) and, conversely, non-believing friends or neighbours might well drop in to the house where the Christian meeting is taking place (14.24-25). Most significant, however, is the fact that some of the leaders of the Corinthian church (whose example others are likely to follow) are to be found as participants in parties and feasts in the dining rooms of the temples (8.10). As Theissen has shown, these people must be not only of some social status, but also sufficiently integrated into Corinthian society to be strongly disinclined to raise any objections on the grounds of religious scruple;[13] it was important for them to retain the social contacts which such temple-dinners provided. Of the individuals named in 1 Corinthians, leaders like Gaius and Stephanas might well have acquired their wealth through that trading and 'dealing with the world' which Paul lists as the occupation of some Corinthian Christians (7.30-31); and, of course, Erastus, as the οἰκονόμος τῆς πόλεως (Rom. 16.23), whether or not he subsequently became aedile, must have sought some tolerable *modus vivendi* with his non-Christian associates at work.[14]

It is clear that Paul is somewhat uneasy about the degree of integration which the Corinthian Christians enjoy. To be sure, contacts with 'outsiders' are to be expected, and indeed welcomed, as opportunities for witness (9.19-23; 10.32-33; 7.16?). Paul is concerned that his converts should be able to buy freely in the meat-market and share non-cultic meals with unbelievers (10.25-27). He is careful to show that those married to non-Christians are not thereby polluted (7.12-16) and he

---

11.30 is divine punishment, and the suffering of individual members in 12.26 is non-specific; there is no indication in either case of the agency of hostile parties. In 7.26 Paul refers in general terms to the 'present distress' (ἐνεστῶσα ἀνάγκη); this may refer to eschatological woes (cf. 7.28-29; Lk. 21.23) or to difficult physical conditions in general (cf. 2 Cor. 6.4; 12.10); there is nothing to indicate an experience of persecution.

13. Theissen, *Social Setting*, pp. 121-43.

14. Theissen, *Social Setting*, pp. 69-119. At 7.18 Paul appears to counter the desire of some of the Jewish converts to cover up the marks of circumcision. This indicates a concern to avoid dishonour, but it appears that opprobrium would attach to them not as Christians but as Jews!

recognizes as a general principle that complete separation from the world is impossible (5.9-10). Nonetheless, he has a much more sectarian and separatist expectation of the social standing of the church than the Corinthians. He attacks their recourse to the law-courts not just for pragmatic reasons but on ideological grounds: it is absurd for Christians to submit to the judgment of the ἄδικοι and ἄπιστοι whom they will soon themselves judge, along with the rest of 'the world' (6.1-3).[15] In fact, 'this world' and 'the present age' are spoken of in consistently derogatory terms throughout the letter, for they, together with their rulers, are doomed to imminent destruction (1.18–2.8; 3.18-20; 7.31). In the Corinthians' easy dealings with the world Paul detects a failure to comprehend the counter-cultural impact of the message of the cross (1.18–2.5); the wisdom of the world to which they are so attracted is, he insists, a dangerous enemy of the gospel. Such a consistent stress on the church's distinction from the world would hardly have been necessary in Thessalonica! But in Corinth such things needed to be said, and with heavy emphasis. The Corinthians must be warned against the corrupting influence of 'bad company' (15.33). As the holy temple (3.16), they are a distinct body of 'saints', washed and purified through their baptism (6.11). Their dealings with the world must be controlled by the ὡς μή principle which recognizes its imminent collapse (7.29-31).

In fact there is good evidence to suggest that the Corinthian Christians were quite conscious of their difference from Paul on this matter. Paul's remarks about his earlier letter (5.9-13) indicate that the relationship between believers and non-believers had already been a contentious issue between them. It is possible that the strange outburst in 2 Cor. 6.14–7.1 is a fragment of that earlier letter, with its clarion call to separate from unbelievers.[16] But even if it is not, and if, as Paul now claims (5.10), his

15. What concerns Paul is not just the embarrassment caused by the public display of dirty linen, nor the corruption endemic in Corinthian civil courts (so B. Winter, 'Civil Litigation in Secular Corinth and the Church: The Forensic Background to 1 Corinthians 6.1-8', *NTS* 37 [1991], pp. 559-72). It is the fact that the Corinthian judges are 'unbelievers' and representatives of the 'world' which makes them inappropriate adjudicators of the affairs of believers. If, as appears likely, Paul refers to them as οἱ ἐξουθενημένοι ἐν τῇ ἐκκλησίᾳ (6.4), the apocalyptic venom is unmistakable.

16. See the discussion by V.P. Furnish, *II Corinthians* (AB, 32A; Garden City, NY: Doubleday, 1984), pp. 375-83. If, as most concede, this passage does not belong in its present context, it is much more likely that it has been interpolated from another part of Paul's correspondence with Corinth than from some other Pauline (or

earlier letter urged only separation from wayward Christians, that would still represent an attempt to establish boundaries quite different from those the Corinthians are willing to accept. While allowing a degree of social contact with 'outsiders', Paul still paints the starkest contrast between the Church and the world. He understands the Church as a community whose rules govern all departments of life and he expects the members to find in it their primary and dominant relationships: their ties to their fellow ἀδελφοί and ἀδελφαί are to be more significant that any others.[17] The Corinthians, however, seem to understand the social standing of the Church quite differently. They see no reason to view the world through Paul's dark apocalyptic spectacles and are no doubt happy to enjoy friendly relations with their families and acquaintances.[18] Their reluctance to excommunicate even such a flagrant moral offender as the man discussed in ch. 5 may suggest that they do not see the Church as a moral arbiter at all; they may have considered that it had no claim on their lives outside the worship gatherings. The behaviour of the wealthier members at the Lord's Supper and the legal disputes between members are eloquent testimony to the lack of close affective ties within the Church; and it is clear, from their continued participation in temple-dinners, that those who are socially well-placed set much more store on the opinions of their non-Christian friends than on the feelings of their 'weaker' Christian ἀδελφοί. Paul's vision is of a church community, where members are open to the world but nonetheless forever conscious of the difference between 'insiders' and 'outsiders', and where the intense relationships among members of the family make belonging to the Church the core of their existence. The Corinthian Christians apparently do not see themselves in this light; and their different self-perception is surely not unconnected to the harmony they enjoy in their relationships with non-Christians.[19]

non-Pauline) source. The usual objection against the identification with the 'earlier letter' is that it urges separation from unbelievers; but this is precisely how the Corinthians have understood it, and Paul's claim in 1 Cor. 5.10 that he meant otherwise is supported by a suspiciously ambiguous πάντως.

17. Hence the rule on excommunication in 5.1-13; it is assumed that contact with a 'brother' will corrupt the church in a way that contact with 'outsiders' will not.

18. N. Walter rightly notes the oddity for Gentiles of the notion that religion could be the cause of suffering, in 'Christusglaube und heidnische Religiosität in paulinischen Gemeinden', *NTS* 25 (1979), pp. 422-42.

19. On 'boundaries' in general, see W.A. Meeks, *The First Urban Christians* (New Haven: Yale University Press, 1983), pp. 84-110; cf. M.Y. MacDonald, *The*

The Corinthian Interpretation of Christian Faith

The title of this section is of course over-simplistic. There is no single interpretation of the Christian faith operative in the Corinthian church, but many different perspectives existing alongside or in competition with one another. There are libertines and ascetics, rich and poor, weak and strong—not to mention the four parties whose slogans Paul ridicules in 1 Corinthians 1–4. In contrast to the Thessalonian church, where no major differences of opinion are detectable, the Corinthian church contains a complex tangle of varying interests and opinions.

Yet it is still possible to talk of a dominant ethos in the Corinthian church, a consistent theological pattern which is the recognizable target of Paul's critical comments in most sections of the letter.[20] Judging from Paul's citations of the Corinthian letter in ch. 8, the leading Christians in Corinth are proud of their knowledge (γνῶσις); and this, it seems, is what Paul has in view in his discussion of wisdom (σοφία) in 1.18–3.23.[21] In his concern to disparage 'the wisdom of the world' and to relativize knowledge (1.18-2.5; 3.18-23; 13.8-12), Paul does not clearly describe what content the Corinthians gave to it; but we know that it concerns the understanding of mysteries (13.1-2) and it seems to include some conviction of the oneness of God and the insignificance (or non-existence) of εἴδωλα (8.4-6).

What is sufficiently clear is that the special insight the Corinthians enjoyed was a product of their much vaunted possession of the Spirit. We can legitimately deduce from Paul's ironical remarks in 2.6–3.3 that these Corinthians considered themselves πνευματικοί and τέλειοι in a

Pauline Churches (Cambridge: Cambridge University Press, 1988), pp. 32-45. However, in both cases their description of the boundary-rules of 'Pauline Christians' are generalizations over-dependent on statements made by Paul himself, while MacDonald adopts uncritically Wilson's model of a 'conversionist sect'. The different views and different circumstances of Paul's churches are not adequately explored.

20. The problems in reconstructing Corinthian theology are fully laid out by Schrage, *Der erste Brief an die Korinther*, pp. 39-47; but he rightly does not despair of the task altogether.

21. It is possible that Paul deliberately changes the terminology in this passage. While he can only be positive about the possession of γνῶσις, apart from the danger of arrogance (1.5; 8.1-3; 1 Thess. 4.5; Gal. 4.8-9), it is easier to rubbish an attachment to σοφία, whose connotations are more ambiguous. 'The wisdom of the world' can denote mere sophistry and 'the wisdom of words' mere rhetorical ingenuity; it would have been a lot harder to build pejorative associations into a discussion of 'knowledge'.

way which set them apart from the ordinary mass of ψυχικοί.[22] When Paul claims that he too possesses the Spirit of God (7.40), we can be sure that we are picking up echoes of Corinthian claims; indeed Paul directly describes them as ζηλωταὶ πνευμάτων (14.12; cf. 14.1, 37). They had first drunk deeply of the Spirit at baptism (12.13) and they continued to be nourished at the Lord's Supper with the πνευματικὸν βρῶμα and πνευματικὸν πόμα (10.3-4). It was in such gatherings for worship that their possession of the Spirit was vividly displayed—first of all in glossolalia (polemically relegated to the end of the list by Paul), but also in prophecy and inspired speech of every kind. 1 Corinthians 11–14 provides a fascinating glimpse of the electric atmosphere of such gatherings; the sparks of the Spirit, in the shape of prophecy, tongues and knowledge (13.8), flew indiscriminately between male and female πνευματικοί (11.4-5).

The confidence provided by this surge of spiritual energy is evident in the slogan of authorization, πάντα ἔξεστιν. The primary context for its use seems to have been in matters of food (6.12-13; 10.23), and, in particular, the consumption of meat imbued with cultic associations. How far this principle of ἐξουσία was extended, it is difficult to know: perhaps as far as the conscious rejection of sexual taboos (5.1-2). The 'knowledge' provided by the Spirit was evidently a versatile commodity; it also provided a sense of immunity and of indifference to apostolic warnings.

Some features of Corinthian practice and belief are not so easily explained. It is unclear, for instance, what motivated the sexual asceticism which prompted a major section of the Corinthians' letter to Paul. Sexual abstinence, in varying degrees, was advocated for so many reasons in early Christianity that the pursuit of parallels could lead us in many different directions.[23] Perhaps the most plausible explanation is the one most closely tied to the Corinthians' passion for πνευματικά. Both in Judaism and in Graeco-Roman religion it was recognized that receptivity to the divine was greatly improved where there was no interference from sexual activity. Perhaps, like Philo's Moses, the πνευματικοί

22. It is generally recognized that Paul here polemically reuses Corinthian vocabulary (cf. 15.44-46); such terms are not used similarly in other letters. See B.A. Pearson, *The Pneumatikos–Psychikos Terminology in 1 Corinthians* (SBLDS, 12; Missoula, MT: SBL, 1973).

23. See especially P. Brown, *The Body and Society: Men, Women and Sexual Renunciation in Early Christianity* (London: Faber & Faber, 1989).

in Corinth wished to hold themselves 'continually in readiness to receive prophetic oracles' and to that end 'disdained sexual intercourse'.[24] Even Paul considers prayer a good reason to abstain from sex (7.5) and it is not unreasonable to surmise that the women who aimed to keep themselves holy in body and spirit (7.34) were those who most desired to act as channels of the Holy Spirit in their prayer and prophecy (11.5).[25]

It is also not entirely clear why some of the Corinthians said there was no resurrection of the dead (15.12). Paul uses such a variety of counter-arguments in ch. 15 that it is not easy to identify his target, and it remains possible that he partially misrepresents or misunderstands the Corinthian position.[26] However, if the extensive argument about σῶμα in 15.35-58 is not wholly irrelevant, it would appear that it was the notion of bodily resurrection in particular (rather than continuance beyond death in general) which the Corinthians could not accept. And this again can best be explained in the light of the Corinthians' fascination with πνευματικά. The human person was generally regarded, according to their cultural koine, as a hierarchical dualism of soul and body; few could imagine, or wish for, a bodily existence beyond death. But the gift of the πνεῦμα, with the extraordinary and special powers which it brought, would serve to sharpen this dualism and to throw the body further into the shade of inferiority. In their ecstatic experiences they rose high above the tawdry concerns of the body—indeed, even above the realm of the mind (14.19); in moments of ecstasy it was unclear whether they remained within the body at all.[27] From this perspective the body would obviously seem a hindrance one could well do without (6.13); the notion of a bodily resurrection would be particularly unpalatable to such πνευματικοί.

It has become the scholarly fashion to refer to Corinthian theology as

24. *Vit. Mos.* 2.68–69; see Brown, *Body and Society*, pp. 65-82, and, for Judaism, G. Vermes, *Jesus the Jew* (London: SCM Press, 1973), pp. 99-102. Compare the decades of celibacy practised by Anna (Lk. 2.36-37) which established her credentials as a reliable prophetess.

25. M.Y. MacDonald, 'Women Holy in Body and Spirit: The Social Setting of 1 Corinthians 7', *NTS* 36 (1990), pp. 161-81.

26. The continuing debate on such matters is most recently reviewed in A.J.M. Wedderburn, *Baptism and Resurrection* (WUNT, 44; Tübingen: Mohr [Paul Siebeck], 1987), pp. 6-37.

27. Cf. Paul's uncertainty in his competitive account in 2 Cor. 12.1-10. On the possible understandings of ecstasy in the Graeco-Roman world, see Wedderburn, *Baptism and Resurrection*, pp. 249-68.

an example of 'realized' or 'over-realized' eschatology. While some dispute continues about the relevance of 2 Tim. 2.18 (those who claim 'the resurrection is past already'), it is widely held, on the basis of 4.8 and Paul's continual references to the future, that the Corinthians considered themselves to have arrived already in the sphere of heavenly glory. But it is important to be aware how Paul's perspective on the Corinthian church tends to control our description of them. *In Paul's view* the freedom, knowledge and spiritual ecstasy enjoyed by the Corinthians constituted a falsely claimed pre-emption of eschatological glory: 'Already you are filled! Already you have become rich! Without us you have come into your kingdom!', he sarcastically remarks (4.8). But did the *Corinthians* see their experience as related to an eschatological time-frame like this? Did they consider that they had already entered the future, or did they simply not operate with Paul's typical contrasts between present and future? Paul downplays present Christian knowledge as partial and imperfect (13.8-12) because he holds an apocalyptic world-view in which the future will be radically new and glorious in contrast to the present (15.42-44): 'if for this life only we have hoped in Christ, we are of all people most to be pitied' (15.19). But the Corinthians apparently see nothing pitiable about the present, because their non-apocalyptic perspective anticipates no radical disjunctions in the future. Their Spirit-filled lives are not an early experience of the future; they simply consider themselves to have reached the heights of human potential. If Paul had read Philo's descriptions of the soul's ascent above the concerns of the world to the pure vision of reality or of the wise man's ecstatic and joyous contemplation of divine truths, 'borne aloft into the heights with a soul possessed by some God-sent inspiration', he would no doubt have scribbled in the margin, 'Already you are filled!'[28] It would be misleading to describe Philo's theology as '(over-) realized eschatology'; his theological framework is simply non-eschatological. Perhaps this is also true of the Corinthian Christians.[29]

28. *Spec. Leg.* 3.1–2; cf. *Op. Mund.* 70–71; *Deus Imm.* 148–51; *Gig.* 31, 53, 60–61; *Somn.* 2.234-36.

29. This parallel with Philo is not meant to suggest that Corinthian theology is derived from 'Hellenistic Judaism', as has been argued by Pearson (*The Pneumatikos–Psychikos Terminology*) and by R.A. Horsley (in a number of articles, including 'Pneumatikos vs. Psychikos: Distinctions of Spiritual Status among the Corinthians', *HTR* 69 [1976], pp. 269-88, and '"How Can Some of You Say that there Is No Resurrection of the Dead?": Spiritual Elitism in Corinth', *NovT* 20

Unlike the Thessalonians, the Corinthians did not regard their Christian experience as an eager anticipation of a glory ready to be revealed at the coming of Christ. Rather, their initiation in baptism and their receipt of the Spirit had signified the grant of a superior insight into divine truths. The regular infusion of the Spirit in the Lord's Supper gave them privileged access to knowledge, and the display of spiritual powers in worship confirmed the superior status which they had attained. They did not daily look up to heaven to await the coming of the Son who would rescue them from the wrath to come, nor did they eagerly search for signs of their impending vindication. Their Christian enlightenment, through the agency of the divine Spirit, was their salvation, and their prophetic, glossolalic and miraculous powers were the proof of its effectiveness.[30]

[1978], pp. 203-31). Their (and other similar) attempts to pinpoint the 'background' to the Corinthians' theology in 'analogies' and 'parallels' from Philo and Wisdom of Solomon are problematic on several counts.

a. They fail to explain what is different and new in Corinth, in particular the heavy emphasis on πνεῦμα (and its associated adjective πνευματικός). In their concern to deny that the Corinthians have adopted a 'gnostic' package of terms and ideas, they have simply substituted a package from 'Hellenistic Judaism'. The extent to which the Corinthians may be forging new language under the influence of Christian teaching and their experience of the Spirit is not explored.

b. Their thesis puts some weight on the role of Apollos as the mediator of such 'Hellenistic Jewish wisdom speculation'. But one can hardly imagine Paul urging Apollos to return to Corinth (1 Cor. 16.12) if he was responsible for an interpretation of Christianity which so greatly threatened Paul's gospel. In any case, many of the Jewish features of this theology (the oneness of God and nothingness of 'idols', the emphasis on πνεῦμα and its connection with knowledge) could have been as easily derived from Paul and from the LXX as from Apollos!

c. Many of the purported parallels from Philo are from passages where Philo strives to interpret the biblical text in terms drawn from Stoic or Platonic philosophy. It is quite possible that the Corinthians, without any Philonic influence, were engaged in a similar process, combining their Hellenistic theological culture with Jewish terms and traditions taught by Paul. They were forging a form of Judaized Hellenism, parallel to (in the strict sense, not dependent on) Philo's Hellenized Judaism. This would account for the fact that Paul associates their 'wisdom' with the interests of Greeks, not Jews (1.22).

30. I have resisted referring to this interpretation of Christianity as 'gnostic'. New Testament interpreters this century (notably W. Schmithals, *Gnosticism in Corinth* [Nashville: Abingdon Press, 1971 (1956)] and U. Wilckens, *Weisheit und Torheit* [Tübingen: Mohr [Paul Siebeck], 1959]) have so muddied the waters with their loose combination of sources that this term is still liable to mislead (even if one adopts the

Factors Influencing the Corinthian Interpretation of Faith
We come now to the most difficult stage of this investigation. In the case
of the Thessalonian church we saw an obvious correlation between their
apocalyptic understanding of Christianity and the social alienation which
they experienced from the very beginning. I have now set out the evidence for the notable absence of hostility in the Corinthians' social
relations and have sketched in outline their interpretation of Christian
faith, with its distinctive emphasis on Spirit and knowledge. The question
thus arises: can we posit in this case, too, some correlation between the
structure of their symbolic world and the character of their social
experience?

We must consider first what other factors might have been at work in
shaping the Corinthian hermeneutics.

a. By the time Paul writes 1 Corinthians, there have been other
Christian teachers active in Corinth and some would attribute the particular ethos in Corinth to such figures. Attention has focused especially on
Apollos, whose name continually recurs through 1 Corinthians 1–4.[31]
Now, it would be rash to deny that Apollos may have had some influence in this connection, but he can hardly bear the sole, or even the
chief, responsibility for the theological stance of the Corinthians. In
1 Corinthians Paul nowhere suggests (as he does to the Galatians) that
his converts started off running well, but have been misled by subsequent instruction. The burden of the blame lies on the Corinthians themselves, not on Apollos. As far as we know, in the first formative period
of the church's life it was Paul alone who had the dominant influence,
and there is no clear indication that the Corinthian church has undergone a radical shift since Paul left the scene.

---

distinction between *gnosis* and Gnosticism). There are in fact some important similarities between Corinthian theology and that which became popular in educated
'gnostic' circles in later generations, some of whom found parts of the Corinthian
letters extremely congenial. But if 1 Cor. 8.4-6 reflects Corinthian views at all, it is
incompatible with that radical pessimism about the material world which is one of
the hallmarks of Gnosticism.

31. See, e.g., C.K. Barrett, 'Christianity at Corinth', in *Essays on Paul* (London:
SPCK, 1982), pp. 1-27; cf. the views of Pearson and Horsley discussed above in
n. 29. The reference to the Cephas party in 1.12 has led some to posit the influence of
conservative (Palestinian) Jewish voices; so, most recently, M.D. Goulder, 'σοφία in
Corinthians', *NTS* 37 (1991), pp. 516-34. His thesis founders on the distinction he is
forced to create between the advocates of σοφία in 1 Cor. 1–4 and of γνῶσις in
1 Cor. 8–10.

b. That leads us to ask whether Paul himself preached the gospel in Corinth in different terms from those he had used in Thessalonica. Did he abandon apocalyptic language on his way south from Macedonia? We are hampered here by our lack of information about the way Paul first preached in Corinth. Apart from the creed in 15.3-5, the tradition about the Lord's Supper (11.23-26) and his exaggerated claim that he knew nothing among them except Christ crucified (2.1-2), we have no direct evidence to go on.[32] However, I think there are strong reasons to doubt that there was any significant change in Paul's message between Thessalonica and Corinth. When he writes 1 Corinthians Paul has just as much an apocalyptic understanding of the gospel (6.1-3; 7.25-31; 15.20-28) and just as sectarian a view of the church (see above) as in his initial preaching and subsequent letter to the Thessalonians. It is unlikely that Paul has done a double about-turn, first abandoning apocalyptic then taking it up again. Moreover, it is highly probable that Paul wrote 1 Thessalonians precisely while he was on his initial visit to Corinth. The apostle could be all things to all people, but it is doubtful that even he could present such an apocalyptic face in his letter to one church but effectively veil it in his preaching to another!

In fact, one can well imagine how the apocalyptic emphases in Paul's preaching could give rise to a concentration on knowledge as the focus of salvation. An essential element in many forms of apocalyptic thought, including Paul's, is the announcement of secret truths to a select coterie. In Paul's ministry this elite group is defined by initiation through baptism and by receipt of the divine Spirit. It was natural for the Corinthians to conclude that they had been given access in the Spirit to mysteries hidden from others. In other words, the *mode* of revelation was the all-important fact for the Corinthians (not least because it was re-enacted in miraculous ways at each gathering); the *content* of the message could be

32. Hurd's reconstruction of Paul's original preaching in Corinth (*The Origin of I Corinthians*) is subject to criticism on a number of counts. It posits the unlikely influence of the 'Apostolic Decree' on Paul in causing him to undergo a fundamental volte-face in his theology (only to revert towards its original form in 1 Corinthians!). He follows Knox in abandoning the chronology of Acts and thus creates a crucial interval between the mission to Corinth and the composition of 1 Thessalonians. This reordered Pauline chronology has rightly failed to gain wide support. Despite this, I am in general agreement with Hurd's thesis that the Corinthians' theology arises from Paul's own preaching; but instead of Hurd's suggestion of radical changes in Paul's thought, it is only necessary to imagine a particular socially- and culturally-related Corinthian hermeneutic.

either ignored or reinterpreted. The possibility of variant interpretations of similar language can be well illustrated from 1 Cor. 2.6-16. Here Paul probably adopts a number of the Corinthians' terms, which emphasized their sense of privilege in the knowledge and communication of 'deep truths'. Paul is able to rework this language, and to fill it with apocalyptic content, by stressing the eschatological nature of the truths revealed (2.7, 9). One can imagine, then, a reverse process in which an apocalyptic message is interpreted by the Corinthians in non-apocalyptic terms: the eschatological message could be lost under the impact of its revelatory medium.

c. It seems, then, that the Corinthians' style of faith is not entirely the responsibility of Paul nor wholly the result of later Christian instruction. We need to investigate also the responsibility of the Corinthian Christians themselves. The fact that most were of Gentile origin (12.2) is not a sufficient explanation: so were the Thessalonian believers. Would we come closer to an answer if we focused on their social status? G. Theissen's well-known social investigations of the Corinthian church have certainly demonstrated the importance of the few leading members of relatively high social status; and one would be inclined to think that higher social standing and greater exposure to Hellenistic education might play a significant role in the interpretation of the Christian faith. Those deeply enmeshed in the social networks of Corinthian life at a higher level would certainly have a lot to lose if they adopted too sectarian a mentality; and their Hellenistic training would give them an established mental framework within which to understand Paul's message.

The social status of the dominant minority in the Corinthian church is certainly a factor of some significance. But it would be a mistake to build everything on this foundation alone. In discussing Thessalonica I suggested that there was no necessary correlation between economic deprivation and an apocalyptic world-view; similarly, in Corinth, wealth and its associated social status are not necessarily wedded to a non-apocalyptic and non-sectarian perspective. It is possible for those of high status to undergo major social dislocation and significant resocialization, under the influence of a newly adopted ideology or as a result of social denigration by others. Thus, we cannot rule out the possibility that some of the 'weak' in Corinth—those who had scruples about eating food offered to idols—could have been among the wealthier members of the church; indeed, if they were present at the same dinner parties as the strong (10.27-30) we would have to assume that they were of the same social class.[33] Their unease about such food was, in that case, the product of a strong theological conviction about the dangers of 'idols' which overrode their social convenience. But even if such social dislocation is not self-imposed, it can be imposed by others. The Corinthians' retention of their social status was only possible so long as others did not reject them as 'impious' or 'atheist'. In other words, continuing social interaction with 'outsiders' is at least as significant in determining the Corinthian outlook as initial social status.

When the Corinthian church was founded it did not, apparently, suffer the social ostracism experienced by its sister church in Thessalonica. It is possible that this was because the leading converts deliberately played down the potential offensiveness of their faith, and this may be not unconnected to their social status. But it is intriguing to note that even Paul did not run into trouble in Corinth the way that he did in Thessalonica. Although he lists his woes in 1 Cor. 4.9-13 and 15.30-32, he does not locate any of them in Corinth itself. Indeed, it is striking that the account in Acts 18 has him staying in Corinth more or less peacefully for 18 months. The narrator seems to have felt the need to give some explanation of this unusual phenomenon; he records a specific vision of the Lord which reassures Paul: 'I am with you and no-one shall attack you to harm you; for I have many people in this city' (Acts 18.10). The only opposition comes from some Jews, and their attempt to arraign Paul before Gallio is abortive (Acts 18.6, 12-17). Even after this incident Paul is under no compulsion to leave the city.

The correlation between the harmony of the Corinthians' social context and their particular theology is evident at a number of levels.

a. In the first place, the Corinthian focus on knowledge and possession of the Spirit creates a distinction from the mass of ordinary people, but a *distinction without a sense of hostility*. As πνευματικοί, they are certainly of a superior status, but the rest, the ψυχικοί, are not thereby classed as evil or threatening, merely inferior and unprivileged. The Corinthian symbolic world is structured by contrasts, to be sure, but not such contrasts as represent struggle or conflict. There is no 'present evil

33. It is crucial to Theissen's argument (*Social Setting*, pp. 121-43) that the 'weak' are socially inferior and that the informant in 10.28 is not a Christian. However, see the contrary opinion on 10.28 in C.K. Barrett, *A Commentary on the First Epistle to the Corinthians* (London: A. & C. Black, 2nd edn, 1971), pp. 239-40; cf. earlier, J. Weiss, *Der erste Korintherbrief* (Göttingen: Vandenhoeck & Ruprecht, 1910), pp. 264-65.

age' to be redeemed from, no cosmic warfare against Satan and his powers, no destructive wrath due to fall on all non-believers. That apocalyptic and tension-laden perspective is not characteristic of the Corinthians; their own symbolic world gives them a sufficient sense of superiority to make their conversion worthwhile, without fostering a sense of hostility towards (or the expectation of hostility from) non-Christians.

b. Secondly, Corinthian theology correlates well with the practice of *differentiation without exclusivity*. The infusion of the divine πνεῦμα at baptism, and its dramatic presence in their midst in worship, were clearly prized features of their Christian existence. They presumably felt that this was in some respects a deeper or richer experience of divine power than they had known before in Graeco-Roman religion (12.2). Yet this did not necessarily annul the claims of others—prophets, poets, seers and philosophers—to similar experiences of ecstasy or inspiration.[34] Their knowledge of the 'oneness' of God was not unlike the monotheistic convictions of those educated in Hellenistic theology. Since others did not define their Christian convictions as alien, there was no reason why they could not accept a kind of theological pluralism, which distinguished their views without discounting all others. This is a theology which both reflects and fosters harmonious relationships.

c. Finally, their religious ethos permits an *involvement in the church which does not entail significant social and moral realignment*. It is important to note the limited context in which the identity of the πνευματικός is displayed: in the worship meetings of the church where the practice of knowledgeable speech, tongues and prophecy fulfils the initiate's calling. Outside these semi-private gatherings in the house of Gaius, the Corinthian Christians might consider their faith of only limited significance. If the church's ecstatic celebrations were the peak of its experience, they could also become its sole focus of interest. Beyond that socially (and temporally) confined context, the πνευματικοί had authority to behave as they wished. They were not bound by a moral tradition which tied them to a distinctive communal lifestyle; indeed, the authority of each individual πνευματικός could not be challenged (2.14). If behaviour is, then, not a matter of ethics but of 'consciousness' and self-understanding, the Christian is not committed in advance to any group norms which might have awkward social implications.[35] The

34. See Wedderburn, *Baptism and Resurrection*, pp. 249-68.
35. On the individualism of the Corinthians, expressed through their term

Church is not a cohesive community but a club, whose meetings provide important moments of spiritual insight and exaltation, but do not have global implications of moral or social change. The Corinthians could gladly participate in this Church as one segment of their lives.[36] But the segment, however important, is not the whole and not the centre. Their perception of their church and of the significance of their faith could correlate well with a life-style which remained fully integrated in Corinthian society.

Once again, then, we have an example of the mutual reinforcement of social experience and theological perspective, which this time involves a major realignment of Paul's apocalyptic symbols. When the first Corinthians became Christians, they did not experience hostility, nor was their apostle hounded out of town. And the more firmly the church got established in conditions of social harmony, the more implausible the apocalyptic content of Paul's message became, with its strong implications of social dislocation. In the face of continuing close and friendly relations with 'significant others' it was hard to sustain an atmosphere of beleaguered hostility. And the more the Corinthians understood their faith as a special endowment of knowledge and a special acquisition of spiritual skills, the less they would expect or embrace hostility: any intimations of conflict would be resolved or minimized. To posit this is not to succumb to some sociological determinism, but simply to note the complex interplay between beliefs and social experience. We must remember how successful the Corinthian church appears to have been, both in its numerical strength and in the intensity of its spiritual experience. The apocalyptic notes in Paul's theology which harmonized so well with the Thessalonians' experience simply failed to resonate with

συνείδησις, see R.A. Horsley, 'Consciousness and Freedom among the Corinthians: 1 Corinthians 8–10', *CBQ* 40 (1978), pp. 574-89. He rightly suggests that 'for the Corinthians...the eating of idol-meat and other matters were issues only in an internal personal sense, for one's own individual consciousness, and not in a truly ethical, i.e. relational, sense' (p. 589).

36. This could help explain how the Church survived despite its many divisions. The Christians' maintenance of social interests and contacts outside the Church prevented them from involving themselves with the internal disputes of the Church with such intensity as is typical in more sectarian groups. Those whose participation is more segmental are likely to put less investment into getting their own way in the Church; see L.A. Coser, *The Functions of Social Conflict* (London: Routledge & Kegan Paul, 1956), p. 153.

the Corinthians. It is possible that some of them would have felt distinctly uncomfortable in the Thessalonian church and would not indeed have joined, or remained members of, the church in Corinth if it had developed the same ethos as its Thessalonian sibling.

Conclusion

This study of the divergent development of these two Pauline churches has shown how misleading it is to generalize about 'Pauline Christians'. It is ironic that it was the church in Corinth which diverged most from Paul's own point of view although he apparently spent much more time there than in Thessalonica! That may be a salutary lesson to us, as it was to Paul, that he had less control than he imagined over the ways his converts interpreted their own conversion.

If we were to follow the development of these churches beyond the point of the writing of 1 Thessalonians and 1 Corinthians, the picture would be enlarged but not substantially altered. If 2 Thessalonians is inauthentic, we can pursue our quest of the Thessalonian church no further. But if, as I am inclined to think, it was written by Paul in close succession to his first letter, it shows a church still undergoing fierce persecution (2 Thess. 1.4-9).[37] There are also signs that the apocalyptic atmosphere in the church has reached a feverish level; there are some who think that 'the day of the Lord' has already arrived (2.2), perhaps interpreting some local or national disaster as the start of that 'sudden destruction' which Paul had prophesied for unbelievers. Paul is sufficiently concerned about this to write another letter, this time with a more frigid and authoritarian tone intended to counter a serious imbalance in the church. Paul's apocalyptic chickens had come home to roost!

The development of the Corinthian church can be more confidently traced, through 2 Corinthians and, much later, *1 Clement*. In 2 Corinthians there is every indication that the church continues to thrive and that its emphasis on spiritual knowledge and power has been reinforced by the authority of 'super-apostles' (11.5) whose 'signs and wonders' create much more impression than Paul's. If there is talk here of the Corinthians suffering θλῖψις (1.6-7; 7.8-13), this appears to be caused not by 'outsiders' but by an internal trauma in the church; indeed, if this is

---

37. I have given a tentative reconstruction of the *Sitz im Leben* of 2 Thessalonians in 'Conflict in Thessalonica'.

connected with Paul's 'sorrowful visit', it is Paul himself who has brought about the only Corinthian θλῖψις![38] There are still ironic contrasts in this letter between Paul's weakness and his converts' strength (13.9; cf. 4.12), and 12.21 suggests that serious moral problems remain. If such matters no longer take the foreground in this letter compared to the first, that is because Paul now realizes that he cannot issue correction at all until he can re-establish his authority over the Corinthian church. But his emphasis on the suffering and weakness of this lifestyle (4.7-15; 6.3-10; 11.23-33) suggests that they still declined to accept his counter-cultural vision of the gospel; and the trouble he takes attempting to squeeze money out of them (chs. 8–9) indicates that they still failed to appreciate the significance of their bonds with other Christians. *1 Clement* is perhaps too distant chronologically to be of much value, but it may be significant that the author speaks of troubles in Rome but not in Corinth; the church he writes to is not persecuted but torn apart by an internal power struggle over the leadership of the congregation.

It appears, then, that the contrast we have perceived between 1 Thessalonians and 1 Corinthians reveals a genuine divergence of striking proportions in Paul's churches. I have highlighted here one factor which contributes to the explanation of this divergence, the social context of the churches and particularly their social interaction with outsiders. But it should be clear that this only makes sense alongside other factors and that social causes here are not intended to provide total, simple or direct explanations of theological beliefs. Nonetheless the correlation of beliefs with social realities is important and the question of interaction with outsiders is one that has been unduly neglected in sociological studies of early Christianity.[39] After a period of intensive study of the social status of Paul's converts, it is high time to explore further the question of social interaction—and to take care in so doing

---

38. A suggestion I owe to Mr Leslie Milton, a research student in my Faculty.

39. A. Schreiber (*Die Gemeinde in Korinth* [Münster: Aschendorff, 1977], p. 105) cites Mucchielli's comment that 'die Geschichte der Beziehungen einer Gruppe mit anderen Gruppen ihrer Umwelt beeinflusst Meinungen, Beratungen, Gefühle und Tätigkeiten der Gruppenmitglieder'. It is a pity that Schreiber's own work, which focuses on the group dynamics of the Corinthian church, does not address these issues in any detail.

not to subscribe to the false assumption that all Paul's churches were of the same stamp.[40]

40. Scholarship on Thessalonica and Corinth since the first publication of this article expands but largely confirms the portrait painted here. See, e.g., K.P. Donfried and I.H. Marshall, *The Ideology of the Shorter Pauline Letters* (Cambridge: Cambridge University Press, 1993); A.D. Clarke, *Secular and Christian Leadership in Corinth: A Socio-Historical and Exegetical Study of 1 Corinthians 1–6* (AGJU, 18; Leiden: Brill, 1993); D.B. Martin, *The Corinthian Body* (New Haven and London: Yale University Press, 1995); D.G. Horrell, *The Social Ethos of the Corinthian Correspondence* (Edinburgh: T. & T. Clark, 1996).

JSNT 45 (1992), pp. 105-20

THE PASTORAL EPISTLES AND THE ETHICS OF READING

Frances M. Young

The enquiry undertaken in this paper was stimulated by George Steiner's book, *Real Presences*, subtitled, *Is There Anything* in *What we Say?*[1] The context of his essay is the present intellectual scene in the humanities: the breakdown of that romantic/historical approach to literature and the arts which may be summed up in the phrase 'thinking the author's thoughts after him'; the advent of the New Criticism, then of structuralism; the development of deconstruction and theories of reader reception. The resultant fascination with critical theory means that it is not just the intention of the author, or even the possibility of 'dialogue' with the author, that has been lost, but the very possibility of meaning and communication.

Yet, says Steiner, 'no serious writer, composer, painter has ever doubted...that his work bears on good and evil... A message is being sent: to a purpose.' 'But the problem I wish to clarify', he continues, 'is a more particular one, often unobserved. It is not so much the morality or amorality of the work of meaning and of art. It is that of *the ethics of its reception*.' The presence of the 'other' impinging upon us requires our respect and attention or, as Steiner puts it, a certain tact, welcome, civility, courtesy. The etiquette of courtesy 'organizes' our meetings with the 'other'. So, he suggests, an initial act of trust underlies all language, aesthetics, history, politics... Our response is a moral act for which we are responsible. In the case of great works of art, 'it is on our capacities for welcome or refusal, for response or imperception, that their own necessities of echo and of presence largely depend'.[2]

So my basic question is: How are we to receive or read in an ethically

1. London: Faber & Faber, 1989.
2. Steiner, *Real Presences*, pp. 145-48.

responsible way texts we have learned to believe are pseudonymous? Has the scholarly consensus and what has been called the hermeneutic of suspicion destroyed the possibility of welcoming the Pastorals with courtesy, of beginning without distrust? I will eventually turn to the specific case, but first let us explore this ethics of reception a little further.

Steiner's approach was anticipated in the work of the American literary scholar, Wayne Booth. His important book, *The Company we Keep*,[3] was twenty years in formation. To begin with doubt is to destroy the datum, he suggests,[4] and he contrasts 'analyzing texts' with 'reading stories', reclaiming the traditional notion that actually we read for the sake of personal improvement—we expect to be changed by what we read, as people have been since classical times. In every age readers have been taken over by what they read, until recently, literary theory encouraged us to believe that we should keep a critical distance. Booth treats friendship as the principal metaphor of reading. The burden of his book is a rehabilitation of ethical criticism.

Among theologians, the writer who has tackled the ethics of reading is Werner Jeanrond.[5] After exploring the hermeneutics of Hans Gadamer and Paul Ricoeur, and the reading theories of Wolfgang Iser and Stanley Fish, he states, 'No reading is ethically neutral, since every reading represents an answer to a textual claim, an answer which may be responsible or irresponsible'.[6] He sees the reading of a text as 'a dynamic process which remains in principle open-ended', for the reader does more than decipher signs printed on paper: reading always involves the projection of a new image of reality to which both the text and the reader contribute.[7] 'The reader enables the text to influence his/her situation', yet not uncritically. Criticism, or assessment, is what allows the text to speak in the best possible manner and 'for this purpose, to orient the individual reader and the reading community in relation to self-criticism and criticism of content'.[8]

The point that responsible reading involves criticism, not just in the

---

3.   Berkeley: University of California Press, 1988.
4.   Booth, *The Company we Keep*, p. 32.
5.   *Text and Interpretation as Categories of Theological Thinking* (trans. T.J. Wilson; Dublin: Gill & Macmillan, 1988).
6.   Jeanrond, *Text and Interpretation*, p. 128.
7.   Jeanrond, *Text and Interpretation*, p. 104.
8.   Jeanrond, *Text and Interpretation*, p. 113.

sense of articulating and analysing response so as to increase reading competence, but also in the sense of judgment/assessment, Wayne Booth emphasizes too. We discriminate between our friends, after all. Respect for the 'other' involves the articulation of difference. 'Courtesy' towards the text does not require capitulation. Indeed, readers have responsibilities not only to the text (or—Booth does not hesitate to suggest—the author), but also to themselves:

> I serve myself best, as reader, when I both honor an author's offering for what it is, in its full 'otherness' from me, and take an active critical stance against what seem to me its errors or excesses.[9]

(Perhaps we should note that throughout his discussion of the ethics of reading, Booth has difficult questions such as pornography and censorship in the back of his mind: he is not just concerned with classics.)

It seems that respect for the 'other' and respect for the 'self' are involved in responsible reading, and this means the articulation of 'difference'. It is time we turned to the Pastoral Epistles with these perspectives informing our reading, and it would seem that the articulation of differences might be a good place to start.

As soon as we begin to read, we note that the stated reader is Timothy or Titus. 'I' or 'we' are apparently not implied by the text. So to put the question in the simplest and most direct way possible: can we read responsibly a text which belongs to another's private correspondence? Further reading of these texts soon legitimates our involvement, however. The content of these letters is clearly not meant to be private. The subject matter concerns the proper public ordering of a community, and therefore these documents were from the beginning public documents and meant to be so.

So, to identify the implied readership, as distinct from the stated readership, is to envisage a Christian community somewhere, sometime (the texts might offer clues, but they are not explicit) in the first (or possibly second) century. 'We', the present readers, are not part of that community. Can we responsibly read texts if we are not the implied readership? Clearly we can and do, but the distinction between the implied reader and the actual reader should enable us to grasp the importance of what Jeanrond has called 'reading genres'.[10] In the case of a modern novel, the implied reader is likely to be much closer to the

---

9. Booth, *The Company we Keep*, p. 135.
10. Jeanrond, *Text and Interpretation*, p. 117.

actual reader than in the case before us—although identity will never be exact: for example, the implied reader might be one who can spot the allusions to Shakespeare or the Beatles, and the actual reader might lack the knowledge or experience to be capable of doing so. The closeness of identity, however, usually ensures that the implied function of reading the novel is approximately the same for text and reader, and so there is but one 'reading mode' implied. For a biblical text, however, Jeanrond can point to several 'reading genres' that relate to the function of reading such a text, or the use to which the text is being put:

> When, for example, a letter of St Paul is sent by post to a community, it is in the first place the function of communication which stands in the foreground. If, on the other hand, one reads out the same text at a liturgical service, what stands in the foreground is the religious teaching character. The same text can again be studied as a document of its time, its documentary function is accentuated in this case.[11]

On this analysis, then, it would seem that, until recently, biblical criticism had become wedded to the 'documentary' reading mode: hence, in reaction, the welcome given to the new 'literary' methods.

But when Jowett in *Essays and Reviews*[12] controversially argued that the Bible should be read like any other literature, he did not envisage such a narrowing historical or documentary outcome. Espousing the kind of philological and historical reading then current in standard classical education—the Bible was to be read like Sophocles and Plato—did not rule out appropriation by the reader, since the 'romantic' view that one could and should 'think an author's thoughts after him' was firmly entrenched. So, to learn the language of the author and enter into the author's mind was the route to grasping meaning. For Jowett this was the answer to the false multiplication of senses and to spurious and divisive doctrinal readings, and he was confident that this historical principle would validate the sublimity of Scripture and release its transcendent quality, recognizing that there are depths which to the author may be 'but half revealed'.[13]

One hundred and thirty or so years later we have become disillusioned, not just because of the breakdown of the romantic reading, but also because there has been no agreement about the 'original meaning',

11. Jeanrond, *Text and Interpretation,* p. 117.

12. B. Jowett, 'On the Interpretation of Scripture', in *Essays and Reviews* (London: Longman, Green, Longmans and Roberts, 1860), pp. 330-433.

13. Jowett, 'On the Interpretation of Scripture', p. 380.

any more than there was about the proper doctrinal reading. Further-more, the practice of historical reading has both highlighted the prob-lems of identifying the 'original author' of many biblical texts and caused scholars to adopt the documentary reading mode, increasingly attempting to reconstruct the original situation and context rather than reading the text as addressed to readers who were expected to respond.

To return to the Pastorals, what is the appropriate 'reading mode' for 'us', readers here and now who are not identical to the implied readers in the texts?

Clearly, reading them as historical documents is an important possi-bility, and recent attempts at sociological study of the Pauline commu-nities and their institutionalization do exactly that, as have earlier studies concerned with the church order, setting, authorship, identity of the implied opposition and so forth. But such reading tends to analyse and exploit texts rather than read and assimilate them: the dynamic balance of an ethical reading as outlined earlier is missing.

Another of Jeanrond's possibilities presents itself, namely to read them as liturgical/canonical texts within a reading community claiming a certain continuity with the original reading community. This possibility, while undoubtedly legitimate, falls, I suggest, into a somewhat special category, and inspection of the current lectionary of the joint liturgical group proves that such reading is successful largely because it is selec-tive of passages which are acceptable to the current reading commu-nity—in other words such reading is rarely capable of a responsible reading of whole texts. To explore a canonical reading would take another paper, but I will return to the liturgical reading now and again as we proceed.

The third possibility is to respond to the text imaginatively as it asks to be read. That is, to read it as a communication to implied readers, taking seriously what the implied author wishes to communicate, so being open to the courteous and sympathetic reception of the 'other', while being free to retain a certain critical distance. In this way there is a dialectic between the response of the implied readers and our actual response, and both critical assessment and responsible appropriation become genuine possibilities.

It is this third possibility which seems to me to constitute an 'ethical reading', since it respects what Wayne Booth calls the ethos of the text, while allowing readers to recognize their 'double' identity and their consequent responsibilities to themselves as well as to the author/text. It is not exactly any of Jeanrond's reading genres, but, so far from reading genres constituting a hierarchy, as he suggests,[14] I think in practice I shall show that an ethical reading of this kind requires an appropriate interaction between the different reading genres he isolates.

So far then we have been focusing on the first area of 'difference' which needs to be articulated and clarified, namely the implied and actual readership. There is a sense in which the reading strategy proposed by attending to this necessitates something similar to Ricoeur's method of 'entering the world of the text', and that introduces the second major area of 'difference' that needs to be articulated. The text implies a whole 'world' of assumptions and cultural norms which present readers share only partially or not at all. (That, of course, is common to all acts of reading in the sense that the implied author of a text inhabits or creates a 'metaphoric' or 'symbolic world' of meaning which is likely not to have the same identical boundaries as the reader's symbolic world.)

In the case of the Pastorals, that 'other world' is not exactly like the world of fictional narrative. An extreme example of such an imaginative world would be *Watership Down*, which invites the reader to accompany the implied author into a very strange, and largely self-contained, world of the imagination in which remarkably realistic rabbits behave remarkably like human beings in human societies. To enter the 'world' of the Pastorals is not like that. Yet it is to enter a fictional world in two senses: the sense in which all our 'worlds' are sociolinguistic interpretative constructs, and in the sense that the responsible reader has to reconstruct in the imagination a situation that is not existent. To do so responsibly requires the interaction of the text-content, which evokes its world, with other accumulated data from the historical world from which the text comes. The success of the operation will depend to a considerable extent on the knowledge and imaginative capacity of the interpreter, a competence which can be constantly improved by learning and practice. Thus, reading as historical document is part of reading responsibly (as I said, the reading modes need to inform one another!).

Four areas of 'difference' between the world of the Pastorals and our world can be usefully articulated, although to do justice to any of them lies outside the scope of this paper. Yet the articulation of these 'differences' may be precisely what creates the potential for sympathetic

14. Jeanrond, *Text and Interpretation*, p. 117.

engagement, imaginative identity and sensitive criticism, so it must be attempted, however sketchily.

The first area I wish to highlight is the difference in the reading process. For most people today reading is a private activity, but it seems that in the ancient world, even though one might read privately in a study, that process was usually rehearsal for public recitation. Reading was a performance of dramatic quality; writing was only a way of recording the voice, the spoken word. Even a letter was treated as a way of making an absent person present.

All texts from the ancient world were meant to be persuasive documents, and authors were concerned about getting the best reception— they were audience-oriented. So, texts were rhetorical pieces addressed to an audience, intended to move that audience and effect a result. An ethical reading that respects the 'otherness' of these texts requires that we listen to what they have to say, allow ourselves to identify with the implied audience and be open to persuasion rather than be critically distanced. So, here the reading mode comes close to what Jeanrond calls the liturgical reading genre. Yet audiences in most contexts reserve the right to disagree—even heckle—and insofar as we are not actually the implied readership, we may need to oscillate between sympathy and distance. So, the character of the reading-process to which these texts belonged reinforces two points already made: these texts are public documents, and an ethical reading requires both criticism and respect.

Secondly, these texts both imply and seek to foster certain kinds of social relationships within the 'hearing' community, and between that community and the outside world. Unless we take seriously the historical enterprise to uncover that context, we cannot enter into an informed relationship with the text. Recent work highlights the nature of the Graeco-Roman household and the analogy between the organization of the early Church and such a household. This is reflected clearly in the duty-codes of these texts, essentially household-codes adapted to church use, with a strong emphasis on a good church overseer having to have the same qualities as the head of a household. We can understand the concern of a marginalized group to avoid contention and disruption of the basic social unit, and the need to be accepted as respectable by the neighbours. There may be both defensive and missionary motives at work in the attempt to order the community as the household of God. All these points have been discussed in the scholarly literature and would repay closer investigation if there were space here.[15]

What has been overlooked in these discussions is, I suggest, the influence of synagogues, which were also often adapted households. It is a common observation that new religious movements ape older styles of organization: the New Age movement has produced bishops! The history of the synagogue is itself somewhat problematic, but it must have pre-dated the arrival of the Church, and in some sense provided a model. It is perhaps no surprise to find that women have acceptable, although well-defined, roles in a society conceived as a household (however patriarchally structured from our perspective), whereas synagogue influence might encourage the view that the praying quorum consists only of adult males, each of whom is a *bar mitzvah*. And the vexed question of the relationship between the often (but, I suggest, erroneously) identified ἐπίσκοπος in the singular and the plural πρεσβύτεροι may well be illuminated by analogy with the *chazan ha-knesset* who organized the meeting for prayer and the senior members of the community who represented the Jewish community in the civic life of the locality and generally exercised leadership.

However, leaving further pursuit of these questions to other occasions, the point of raising them here is simply to signal the impossibility of too straightforward an application to the actual readers here and now of the advice given in these texts to their implied readership. The implied readers belonged to a different social world.

The third area of difference relates to this, in that the sociology of knowledge has alerted us to the social dimension of all understanding and belief. However, it is important to specify the unarticulated or implied beliefs and assumptions 'incarnated' in the sociolinguistic community to which both implied author and implied readers belonged. Some of these, like belief in God, some of us may share. The reading community may claim to have a certain continuity with the original community that received these texts. Yet there may well be subtle differences in the resonances even of those ideas or beliefs we think we

---

15. Recent relevant studies include: R.E. Brown, *The Churches the Apostles Left Behind* (New York: Paulist Press, 1984); M.Y. MacDonald, *The Pauline Churches: A Socio-Historical Study of Institutionalisation in the Pauline and Deutero-Pauline Writings* (Cambridge: Cambridge University Press, 1988); P.H. Towner, *The Goal of our Instruction: The Structure of Theology and Ethics in the Pastoral Epistles* (JSNTSup, 34; Sheffield: JSOT Press, 1989); D.C. Verner, *The Household of God: The Social World of the Pastoral Epistles* (SBLDS, 71; Chico, CA: SBL, 1983).

share, and there will be some hard, if not impossible, texts for present readers (e.g. 1 Tim. 2.11-15).

This leads us into the fourth distinguishable area of difference, namely the articulated beliefs, ideas, norms, standards, advice, warnings and the like, which constitute the content of the text, and which an ethical reading requires us to hear sympathetically, but perhaps not adopt uncritically.

The further we get into this process of articulating differences in order to enter the world of the text, the more we have to recognize that just as important as the reading genre is the text genre. Taking the text-type of the documents under discussion at face value, we have letters. The stated author of these letters is Paul, who addresses the stated reader, Timothy or Titus. The different, implied readership has already been noted: these are in some sense public community documents, not private letters. What about the implied author?

The mere fact of these texts being letters implies Paul's absence, and the written text becomes a way of evoking his presence. How long or how distant has Paul's absence been? Timothy and Titus are recognized as those who bear his mantle and his authority, and they in turn give authority to the ἐπίσκοπος, the deacons and the presbyters, whose functions and character form a principal concern in the body of the letters. The letters would appear to be indirectly addressed to communities in order to confirm the authoritative position of their leaders as inheritors of the tradition and authority of Paul. So, the text-type slips from the surface genre of personal letter, to the implied genre of manual of instruction. Furthermore, the need for this manual seems to relate to an implied, specific crisis, a situation in which that tradition is under threat from teachers of 'gnosis falsely so-called'. The manual aims at establishing an enduring order for the preservation of this authoritative tradition in the face of such threats.

Thus, an ethical reading requires the placing of these texts in a plausible narrative, the implied narrative of events that caused these texts to be authored. Only as the reader is drawn into such an implied narrative can a truly sympathetic reading occur.

What I have indicated so far strongly suggests that such an implied narrative involves the absence of the stated author, and a crisis in a community which looks to the stated author as probably founder, certainly hero, undoubtedly authority. The texts are rooted in a social situation. An ethical reading demands that that situation be taken with the utmost seriousness. But does it demand Pauline authorship? Could it not be that here too is an important area of 'difference' to be articulated?

In the modern world, pseudonymity easily gets associated with deception (although we accept quite willingly the notion of a 'pen name'). But suppose the fear of admitting that Paul was not the actual author of these texts is a modern 'culture-specific', linked with our excessive individualism and worship of creative originality.

The ancient world was far more interested in tradition than novelty, which was one of the problems faced by the promulgators of this 'new superstition', Christianity. Ancient wisdom was valued rather than creative genius, and the great work of art was far greater than its often anonymous creator. There are enough analogies from that culture to make it entirely plausible that an anonymous disciple or anonymous disciples took on the persona of Paul in order to preserve what they believed to be the genuine Pauline tradition in a situation in which it was under threat. In fact we have several examples of exactly that among the apocryphal literature: for example, the third epistle to the Corinthians in the *Acts of Paul*, and the *Epistle to the Laodiceans*. The implied narrative and the implied readership seem to demand an implied author other than the stated author, and a truly ethical reading, which takes seriously the ethos of the text, requires us to recognize that, if we are to respect the text's true 'otherness'.

The problem for us is the consequent loss of respect for these texts in the eyes of modern readers, who are immediately made suspicious if the possibility of pseudonymity is proposed. So, quite apart from the fundamentalist reaction, in much modern scholarship the Pastorals have become a sad fall-away from the great theology of Paul, and merely provide examples of the loss of a charismatic dynamic in the process of institutionalization, rather than seeming texts worth reading for their inspirational qualities. An ethical reading should perhaps redress that insult.

Let us then agree that an ethical reading, which respects the claim of these texts, requires us to recognize that they fit into an implied narrative in which (1) the surface text-type is not its implied text-type, the letter-form having become 'classic' for early Christian communication, doubly convenient in this case because it makes a figure of the past still accessible; (2) the readership implied is not the stated recipients; and (3) the implied author is not the stated author. What then is the rhetoric of these texts? How are we, the present readers, to respond to them?

The rhetorical dynamic of texts is based in the interaction between speaker, hearer and subject matter, and each of these poles was subject to analysis in the ancient rhetorical textbooks which were used in schools to train effective public speakers. Methods of argument related to each pole. The so-called 'logical' arguments related to the subject matter (*logos*) and were intended to convince of its truth and rightness. The so-called 'ethical' arguments were designed to create an atmosphere of trust in the speaker, to substantiate a claim to be listened to on the basis of the speaker's *ethos*, his character, habits and so forth.[16] The so-called 'pathetic' arguments were intended to move the hearer, to stimulate *pathos*, such as sympathy with a defendant in court so as to acquit, or enthusiasm for taking a corporate decision like declaring war. The response of the hearer was an essential part of the intention: rhetoric was called the art of persuasion, and assent to the speaker's viewpoint was its aim.

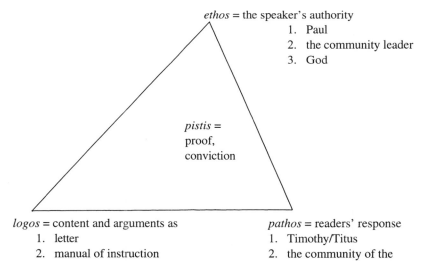

ethos = the speaker's authority
1. Paul
2. the community leader
3. God

pistis = proof, conviction

logos = content and arguments as
1. letter
2. manual of instruction
3. Scripture

pathos = readers' response
1. Timothy/Titus
2. the community of the second or first century CE
3. the Church universal

To analyse the rhetorical dynamics of the Pastorals presupposes, therefore, the whole of our previous discussion, and is conveniently set out in the diagram above, in which each pole has three possible 'levels',

16. Here the term 'ethical' is being used in a technical sense within rhetorical convention, not as previously in discussing 'ethical reading', where normal English usage suggests the sense.

roughly similar to Jeanrond's three reading genres, all of which may interact with one another, while some oscillation between levels one and two is apparent in the text itself. The time has come to do some reading, in other words to consider some passages in the light of all this.

Titus 3.4-8a

The 'saying you can trust' formula seems to alert the implied readers to reliable bits of tradition, and what we have here is itself somewhat formulaic—a summary of the essential gospel. It is a popular expression of Paul's doctrine of grace, although not expressed in his characteristic language. It is linked with the 'bath of re-birth', an un-Pauline phrase, somewhat like the language of contemporary mystery religions but clearly referring to baptism and having entirely Christian associations if you consider other streams of New Testament tradition (e.g. the dialogue with Nicodemus in John 3).

The rhetoric works at levels two and three; it is a bit artificial at level one, but is clearly the way the complicated Paul was simplified for general consumption. That should command respect. A Christian reader easily identifies with the text and, in a mission situation, others might be persuadable.

1 Timothy 6.11-16

This reads as direct address to a church leader, which can work rhetorically at all three levels. Christ is the example put before the leader by the one who gives the charge. It is easy to imagine Paul saying this to Timothy, with the same words applying also at levels two and three, although, as women take leadership positions in churches, the third level becomes increasingly problematic unless broadened to include women alongside the 'man of God'.

Yet the idea of Christ's testimony before Pilate is closer to martyr exhortations in the wider Church than anything we find in authentic Pauline literature; and the final doxology clearly comes from liturgical traditions used in the implied community and is not characteristically Pauline.

What should be noted, however, is that an ethical reading of the text demands that we allow ourselves to imagine what it would mean for a church leader to be persuaded by this rhetoric and to live that way, rather than focusing solely on the difficulties of Pauline authorship.

What is noticeable is that most of the passages actually used in the current lectionaries fall into these categories: they work at levels two and three, while fitting more or less easily into the 'fictional' surface text-type, with its stated author and reader.

But let us now consider passages which exploit the character of the 'speaker' or stated author, therefore challenging the suggestion that the surface-presentation of the text has fictional elements. These are the 'ethical' arguments in the rhetorical sense of the term, establishing the character and authority of the persuader.

1 Timothy 1.12-17

Here is a Paul we recognize, testifying to his call to apostleship and hinting that his converts should imitate him—or is it? There is a subtle and interesting shift. Paul has become the typical Gentile 'sinner', his sin exemplified in his past persecution of the Church, a theme deeply important to the narrator of Acts but not to the authentic Paul of the epistles. Paul is set before us as the converted sinner, exemplifying the sure tradition ('the saying you may trust') that Christ Jesus came into the world to save sinners. Yes, the theme of God's grace and patience is Pauline, but here is the great theme of Paul's theology couched in popular slogan, not Pauline argument, simply to be accepted and not fought for with passion.

So how are we to account for the first person testimony? In the apocryphal work known as the *Acts of Peter*, Peter is presented as preacher, and in first person testimony he sets himself forth similarly as the great sinner who denied Christ and was forgiven. As time passes, both Peter and Paul become idealized model Christians, who embody the gospel (cf. v. 16, 'that I might be typical'), and whose personal testimony is imaginatively set before the Church as a pattern, in a way that would subsequently become typical of evangelical preaching.

Large sections of 2 Timothy seem to be of this character, but one further example must suffice.

Titus 3.3

Here Paul is depicted as identifying himself with the situation of the implied readers who have been converted in ways he has not. He was a

Pharisee of the Pharisees, blameless according to the law (Phil. 3.5-6), not one lost in folly and disobedience, a slave to passions and pleasures and so on.

What we find in the Pastorals, then, is the portrait of a model figure, who is clearly the authoritative leader with the charisma to persuade the implied readers. It is not an entirely false picture, but it is idealized, and its rhetorical function is to authorize the authors, together with the network of church leaders who inherit Paul's mantle.

But not just to authorize: rather, to persuade others to follow the hard path of suffering and persecution Paul once took for the sake of the gospel. Much of the text is implicitly about change, conversion, transformation, a new way of life into which the implied readers have been taken up, and which they are to preserve by following the advice given in the letters. The rhetoric of these texts requires us to attend to their persuasive voice, not just to exploit them as historical documents, and that is what an ethical reading would seek to do.

The rhetoric of these epistles may enable us, then, to respond positively to their persuasive message and to respect their claim to attention. However, if we turn to passages that do not appear in the lectionaries, the 'otherness' of their differences might well demand a process of ethical or ideological criticism in the 'judgment' sense, rather than whole-hearted response. Surely the perspective of those household codes turned church codes enjoins culture-specific duties on church members and church leaders. They are, after all, illuminated by other ancient texts characterizing, for example, the good general. Surely they belong to level two only. Let us consider an example.

1 Timothy 3.2-7

In such a passage the content will certainly appear differently depending upon reading mode. Managing a household is a different thing in the case of the modern nuclear family from the kind of social unit the implied author and readers knew, an extended kinship network, with servants and slaves, tenants and workers, and clients—a large sub-set of the city or state. Nor is it likely that a recent convert would get rapid preferment in our post-Christian world.

And yet, do we not in fact have here an important set of qualities, many of which are not simply culture-bound? The ways in which a bishop may develop an upright and inoffensive character or lifestyle may in practice be somewhat different in different communities at different points in history, yet the language is 'translatable', even if it loses some dimensions in a 'foreign' sociolinguistic setting.

Furthermore, the interaction of conventional and specifically Christian standards, which may be observed by an informed reading at level two, may provide interesting analogies for the development of analogous codes of practice in the Christianity of a different social world, thus enabling a creative reading at level three which may go beyond the text, but remain within its spirit.

In conclusion, I suggest that an ethical reading of the Pastoral Epistles is possible, even if we accept their pseudonymity. Such a reading will involve both respect for texts that have in fact mediated the Pauline tradition to the later Church, and responsible assessment of their content from the present readers' perspective, as distinct from that of the implied readers. So this ethical reading will attend to the following questions:

1. To what extent is the claim of these texts that they pass on the authoritative tradition of Paul valid? In what ways is that tradition appropriately developed further for a new situation?

2. In what ways do these texts confirm or challenge communities/churches which now claim to be in the same tradition? What is acceptable straightforwardly as advice? What needs rethinking in a different socio-cultural milieu? How is the ethos of these texts to affect the ethos of these communities? What inspires to radical reform?

In other words, a responsible reading must involve attention both to past meaning and future potential. And maybe then the suspicion or neglect with which these little letters have been treated will be superseded by a recognition of their power to transform, to communicate Paul's gospel in simple summary slogans, to motivate mission, to confirm Christian identity and even, with some critical adaptation, to structure positively relationships within the Church.[17]

17. See now F.M. Young, 'Allegory and the Ethics of Reading', in F. Watson (ed.), *The Open Text: New Directions for Biblical Studies?* (London: SCM Press, 1993), pp. 103-20.

NEW TESTAMENT

THE BIBLICAL SEMINAR

JOURNAL FOR THE STUDY OF THE NEW TESTAMENT
SUPPLEMENT SERIES